to Dorothy & Roman

Your Friend
Monte Holm
7/27/2000

MW01040171

Once A Hobo . . .

The Autobiography of Monte Holm

By Monte Holm and Dennis L. Clay

Proctor Publications, LLC • Ann Arbor • Michigan • USA

Proctor Publications, LLC
P.O. Box 2498
Ann Arbor, Michigan 48106
800-343-3034
Printed in the United States of America

Publisher's Cataloging in Publication
(Provided by Quality Books, Inc.)

Holm, Monte
    Once a hobo-- : the autobiography of Monte Holm /
by Monte Holm and Dennis L. Clay. -- 1st ed.
    p. cm.
    LCCN: 99-74413
    ISBN: 1-882792-76-9

    1. Holm, Monte. 2. Tramps--United States--
Biography. 3. Children of clergy--Washington
(State)--Biography.   I. Clay, Dennis L.
II. Title.

HV4505.H65 1999   305.5'68'092
                    QBI99-737

The characters, issues and circumstances described in
this book are based on the recollections of Monte Holm.

Dedication

To my wife, Ruth Gulbrandson Holm,
for putting up with this old hobo for more than 60 years!

Foreword

The beauty behind survival of the fittest is that sometimes it produces a Monte Holm.

And the beauty in a life story told straight forward, unencumbered by rationalizations or embellishments, is that sometimes it becomes a story we feel in our hearts. It becomes a sort of seamless screenplay that puts us behind the camera as a lifetime unfolds within the larger story of history. It becomes a book such as *Once A Hobo ...*

Monte's story is the Depression seen through the rough frame of an open boxcar door and beneath the starry expanse of the night sky over Montana sheep country. It starts small and simple and warm, and then is somehow spliced onto a larger, chilling documentary of a nation plunged into despair. It's as though someone, without artistic training, pointed a camera at those years and unintentionally caught not only the essence of the *Grapes of Wrath*, but those little windows into the human spirit.

Nothing about this book promised a great read; there is no guile or shell game arrangement of words or plot. But you become caught up in a boy's story that opens into, and rolls across more than half this country at a time when it was convulsing with economic and social chaos. Not a whole lot of us then wanted to admit that this land is your land ... and we were more likely to tell the Monte Holms knocking at our back doors, so long, it's been good to know yuh.

There are caveman-style murders in hobo jungles. And there are moments of humor, such as when boys in a small Montana town coax a cowboy's horse into contributing to the contents of that man's whiskey bottle. And Monte's story is peopled with a sorry army of bums, "Bo's" as they called themselves, working to just stay alive, chopping wood, shoveling snow, and stealing the occasional chicken.

And in all this grittiness, the reader can believe that a young boy grown too soon into a young man, can be seeking a purpose to his life. And in all the despair, the reader can feel that basic goodness and yes, love, is what makes a difference. There are scenes involving his mother, his Lutheran pastor father, and his step-mother in this screenplay of a book that touch you deep inside. And you know they are written from deep inside this man. And there are scenes of indifference, selfishness, and outright cruelty that would justify revenge in any other man's book. But he wrote the book, and it seems that strong negative feelings are the weight Monte Holm had to jettison to stay afloat, not only as a hobo, but in all his 80-something years.

Seldom do you read something so simple and straight-forward that reaches so deep and so far ... into you as well as the writer. We are jaded in our information age lifestyles to the point where even our emotions are write-protected. But not against something like *Once A Hobo ...* There's something in this book by Monte Holm and Dennis Clay, something that comes out of Monte Holm himself, that makes you want to believe in the basic goodness of people.

Jon Hahn
Columnist, <u>Seattle Post-Intelligencer</u>
Seattle, WA,

September, 1999

Introduction

Having lived a full life, I would not like to pass on without leaving something about my life for future generations. I fully understand my wife, daughter, and grandsons might be the only ones interested in reading this book, but a person never knows; there might be others.

Many people my age will recall the tough times of the Depression and some will even remember whole families going hungry because food was sometimes scarce. But there are a few who, like me, had no home to go back to and these are the ones who relive their time riding the rails whenever they see a train or hear a train whistle.

Spending time on the range and being responsible for a herd of sheep can still be experienced today, but I will bet the job is just as lonely as it was when I was a sheepherder.

Anyone who says that they have experienced the same things written here are my brothers and sisters of the road. To everyone else, let this serve as a textbook about what life was like for those on the range herding sheep and those on the road, riding the rails.

Yes, everyone who lives a full life has a story to tell, and I believe they should tell it. This is my chance.

Acknowledgments

Many friends and family members have helped with this book. To them we are grateful. Deserving special thanks is a specific group of individuals who have read, corrected, joined discussions about, provided information for, and validated facts.

With us from the beginning, and sticking with us through the arduous, yet rewarding, process were Kevin Courtney, Ruth Sawyer, and Brad Chandler. Joining them were Hazel Proctor and Kathy Wilde from Proctor Publications. These five people formed our foundation and helped us stay on the straight and narrow path required for this project.

Later we needed more help and, without hesitation, our efforts were rewarded as more friends helped with facts and general guidance. It's impossible to name everyone, but a few include Ross Crab, Patricia (Patty) Nelson Leonard, Cheryl Elkins, Regan Bonato, Diane Smith, Mel Hurd, Jon Hahn, Doug Clark, Ed Spalding III, Gary Mason, and Lynn McIntyre.

Thank you seems to be such a small term at this point, but it is truly from the heart.

Monte and Dennis

Photographer - Covers by Joel Goplin

The Artists - Five local artists were invited to submit sketches for use in *Once A Hobo* ... The sketches are superb and add immensely to the telling of the story. The artists' sketches appear throughout the chapters of this work and are generally not identified as to which artist completed each specific drawing. Some sketches include the talents of more than one artist.

Carolann Swartz - Carolann is a long-time resident of Moses Lake. She received her formal education at the University of Washington in Seattle, the Pratt Institute in New York and Eastern Washington University in Cheney, Washington. She received a Bachelor of Arts from EWU. Carolann has taught numerous art classes for the Moses Lake School District and for the Moses Lake Art Center, also known as the MAC. She has dabbled in many art mediums, but in recent years her interest has centered around water colors.

Harlan Beagley - Harlan started sketching when he was 4 years old. He graduated from Pacific Northwest College of Art and was a professional artist for 10 years in Las Vegas before moving to Moses Lake. He currently works as the advertising director for the Columbia Basin Herald. Harlan conducts several cartoon classes each year for the MAC.

Patricia Engel Jensen - Patty is a native of Moses Lake and a graphic artist by trade. This is the second book Patty has helped illustrate. Besides sketches, Patty is known for her paintings. She has sold many pieces of her artwork and has been invited to participate in many art shows throughout the Northwest, including several one-woman shows.

Darrel Jensen - Darrel is Patty's 14-year-old son and an honor roll student. His favorite art subjects are cars and people, and he is currently developing his air brush skills.

Rebecca Jensen - Rebecca is Patty's 16-year-old daughter. She is an honor roll student. Her art embraces a multitude of subjects including, but not limited to, tigers, people and sunsets. She is developing her skills in the new techniques of colored pencil.

WARNING

Hopping a freight train today is different than it was during the Depression. The risk of injury or death is extremely high.

Be smart!
Do not ride the rails or attempt to ride the rails.

Monte

Table of Contents

Once A Hobo . . .

1

The Clarkston Years

My earliest memories are of family life centered around the Lutheran Church in Clarkston, Washington. The Reverend N. J. Holm was a nice man. He was patient and kind. He was my father.

Just like it is today, a minister and his wife, no matter what religious denomination, form a team that cares for the members of its congregation. The Reverend and Mrs. Holm were a good team.

Every man, woman and child in the world was a soul to be saved, and my parents did their part. Although my mother and father didn't stand on the street corner and pull prospective converts into the church, they were available when an individual expressed an interest in seeing the light and joining the congregation. After that was accomplished, the person's relationship with God needed to be nurtured so that the saved soul would not stray too far from the teachings of the Lord. The flock was my parents' responsibility. My mother and father attended to their flock with loving care during the happy times and the sad times of life.

Every Sunday my father would preach a sermon, and many people would attend the services to hear what he had to say. Preaching was serious business to my father. I learned to be quiet, sit still and listen along with the rest of my family and the congregation. Although I didn't understand all of what he was trying to get the congregation to understand, the basic teachings did sink in; that hard work would be rewarded, to tell the truth and to be kind to others.

While Sunday school and the one-hour church service was a serious time, Sunday afternoons and evenings were times when the congregation would relax and have fun. It was a chance for the adults to visit and for my friends

1

and me to play. Sometimes we would go on a picnic or visit a church member's house, and always the ladies served an afternoon meal with enough food to fill the bellies of all the people there.

Other happy times included weddings, when people would make a special effort to assemble on days other than the Sabbath. Once again there would be laughing and playing and I would eat and eat, and I felt good.

Sad times were also part of life for the flock of a Lutheran preacher. Some of the gatherings were somber occasions, like when the congregation would say good-bye to a member of the flock. These were sad events, with the relatives of the departed crying.

My father preached at these sorrowful services and, even as a child, I marveled at his ability to maintain his professionalism and composure when so many people were mournful and brokenhearted. My mother was extraordinary in her role as a preacher's wife during these sad affairs. She assisted my father in consoling the grieving family and was just as strong as he, although I did see a tear roll down her cheek more than once.

I learned that funerals were more serious than sermons, and although food was abundant after the services, it was not a time to play or be happy.

My parents spent a lot of energy on their flock, but they devoted a lot of time to their children as well. They started our training early, so we would know how to act at church services, weddings and funerals.

We all had chores to do; usually in the morning and again in the evening. This provided a perfect opportunity for my mother and father to teach their children about doing a good job and completing a job once started.

Our family had a vegetable garden, and part of our chores was to tend it during the growing season. Here my brothers, sisters and I learned to plant and grow food for the table. Some of the

vegetables were eaten fresh on the day they were harvested, but most were processed for eating the rest of the year, when fresh vegetables were not available from the garden. Home freezers had not been invented, so the only method available to preserve the vegetables was canning, although we did dry some fruits, like apricots.

I remember learning to pick string beans without damaging the plant, so it would produce more beans. When all the bean plants were producing a couple of bushels of beans a week, our family would preserve the excess. Canning season was a busy time in the kitchen. The younger members of the family, of which I was one, helped with removing the strings, washing and snapping, which was done outside the house.

We were required to stay outside as my mother and older sisters boiled water and cleaned the jars inside the house, filled the jars with beans, then boiled them in a bath canner. It was quite a production for the entire family, and green beans were just one item we canned. Other vegetables included beets, tomatoes, carrots, turnips and peas. Our family also canned fruit (peaches, apricots, cherries, prunes and applesauce) that was given to us.

Tending the garden and canning what we raised were just some of the work we did to feed our family.

Other chores included feeding and milking our cow. It was a twice-a-day chore. We also had about 50 chickens in the coop. From an early age, we were taught how to take care of our livestock. It didn't matter that all we had was one cow and a few chickens; they needed care and it was our responsibility to provide that care. From those animals, we obtained butter, milk, eggs and lots of fried chicken.

In those days we even canned a lot of meat. Members of the congregation would give us the hindquarter of a cow or part of a pig from time to time. Our family would eat some of the meat fresh, but canning was required to preserve the rest.

The meat was cut into small chunks, cooked,

placed in quart jars and canned in a water bath.

Our family would sit at the table together for meals and the training continued there. Before we were allowed to eat, we would join hands and my father would thank the Lord for His generosity and for looking after our family and his congregation.

As we ate, we were taught to respect our mother and father and other adults, and to sit still and be quiet when another person is talking. When further discipline was needed, my father would have a private talk with one of us to explain what was expected of that child in the future.

There was love in the Lutheran parsonage and it was felt by every child who lived there. I remember the caring hands and soothing voice of my mother as she cared for one of us after we scraped an elbow or a knee.

When it was time for bed, and after our bedtime prayers, my mother and father would tuck us in and they would tell us they loved us and give each of us a hug. The warm glow of love was throughout our house. My dreams would be about laughing, playing with my friends and a table covered with good food that I could eat and eat, and I felt good and was happy.

I didn't know it at the time, but my early training as a preacher's son paid dividends that probably saved my life more than once when things got tough later on.

2

The Move

My younger years in Clarkston, Washington, were full of love and fun. I was not wanting for any basic necessity. We, my family and I, had a roof over our heads and a pattern to our lives that included helping people. At least once each month, and many times more often, we would have one or more guests eat at our table. Now and then the people would spend the night.

Preachers and their families were common guests, but there were also members of the congregation and everyday people moving from one part of the country to another. If there were children, it was a chance for my brothers and sisters and me to play with some new kids during the time they spent at our house.

Sometimes listening to the people talk was fun and other times there was a tone to their voice and a mannerism about them that made them different and strange. As a child, I was able to recognize the contrast. My father was kind and giving, but also firm. He watched over us to make sure anyone invited to our house behaved themselves or they weren't invited back.

One day I discovered two marks on a post not far from our house. One was a "+" and the other was a small circle inside a larger circle. My mother explained that the marks were made by men who didn't have food to eat or a place to live.

"Monrad, those marks mean this is a friendly house where these men can expect a handout of food," my mother told me.

I understood completely. Our house was a friendly place and we were helping people almost every day in one way or another.

A few days later there was a soft knock on the back door. I opened it and before me stood a dirty man in shabby clothes. In those days, we didn't have all the deodorants available that there are now, but still you could tell when a person would take care of themselves by taking a bath at least once a week.

"Hi there, boy," the man said.

My mother was by my side in a flash.

"Mornin' ma'am, do you have some food to spare?" he asked.

"Here you go," my mother said, handing him a quarter loaf of bread, a few oatmeal cookies and three eggs. "God bless you," she added before she closed the door.

My mother was nice, but not as friendly as she usually was to strangers, and this caused a little confusion on my part.

"That man smelled worse than we do when we shovel out the chicken coop," I said.

"Some people don't take care of themselves

4

and they don't care what they do to others," she said. "That man was lazy, Monrad, and good for nothing, but in the eyes of the Lord ...."

"But mother, doesn't the Lord want us to work for our food?" I asked.

"Yes, Monrad," she said. "Do you remember the man who split wood for us last week? He first asked if there was any work and when he finished splitting that pile of wood, I gave him some food."

This little lesson made me more aware of my surroundings. Even though my family gave away a lot of food and helped many people in other ways, we were better off than some families in Clarkston.

I began to notice every person and family we helped. There were those who asked for food at the back door without mentioning work and others who would ask to work knowing when they finished working, they would be rewarded with food. It became a game with me; trying to guess if this man or that would first ask for food or work. Even at that young age, I became quite good at correctly guessing the outcome. I also learned that life was good for me and my family and we were happy, but other people weren't so fortunate.

I didn't know it then, but my father had come into a little money about this time. My grandparents lived on a farm in Minnesota and, when they died, my father inherited their land and money.

My father used the money to help with his work – preaching the word of the Lord – and he bought a 1917 Mitchell. This allowed us to attend church meetings in nearby towns as a family. It was great fun to ride in that car, all seven of us packed in like sardines.

One evening, after we finished eating supper and were seated at the dinner table, my father made an announcement.

"The Lord has called to me," he said.

A statement like that didn't mean much to me at first. After all, my father traveled quite a bit to preach in this town or that one, where there wasn't a regular preacher or the regular preacher wasn't available.

"We're going to move to Montana and start a church there for the Lord," he said.

"What do you mean?" I asked.

"We're going to take everything we own to Montana and live in a different house," he said. "It will be a great adventure, Monrad."

Oh, I was excited. We were going on an adventure. I couldn't wait and was ready to go right then. And it wasn't long, just a few short weeks, before my family said good-bye to Clarkston and headed for Montana. The household furniture was sent by rail; my father rented a boxcar for that purpose.

The seven of us made the trip in the Mitchell. It was packed. My father tied five extra tires on the back of the car, and we brought along three large trunks of clothing. Expanding side rails were fixed to the running boards, which allowed that area to be packed with suitcases and boxes full of canned vegetables and fruit.

My father drove the car and my mother sat in the passenger seat. My brothers and sisters and I would sit in different spots. Sometimes we sat in front between our parents and other times in the back.

Finally, we were off on a great adventure. I remember my mother looking back at Clarkston for one last look before the town was out of sight.

The trip took us seven days and it was an adventure in every way. The roads were terrible. There were ruts and rocks to contend with, and we were jostled around quite a bit.

I swear on a stack of Bibles, we had a flat tire every 10 miles. My father had to be the most patient man I ever knew to fix all those tires without a word of discontent. When a tire would blow, he would stop and shut off the motor. My family would pile out of the Mitchell and watch him fix the flat, which was no simple chore.

First he would loosen the lug nuts, jack up the car, remove the tire from the vehicle, take it

5

off the rim and take out the inner tube. I remember there was always great interest in finding out where the hole was, and the ring of children watching would close in to help my father find it. When it was detected, the area around the hole was scuffed up a bit with sandpaper and a patch placed over the area. A device called a vulcanizer was clamped over the patch to hold it to the tube. A small amount of gasoline was poured into a basin in the vulcanizer and set on fire. The heat generated from the fire would weld the patch to the tire. After the device cooled, it was removed and the tire was reassembled.

The 1917 Mitchell was the first automobile to have an air compressor attached to the engine and an air hose long enough to reach each tire. This made my father happy because he didn't have to use a hand pump. Instead, he simply attached a hose to the compressor, started the engine and pumped the tire full of air. Then, we would jump in the car and head down the road for another 10 miles.

We traveled to Montana by way of Spokane, Washington, where the church headquarters, or Synod, was located for the Pacific Northwest. Then we headed east through Idaho and into Big Sky Country. My mother and father had it planned so we could stop every night at a different Lutheran minister's house, just like those traveling people would stop at our house in Clarkston to have a meal and spend the night. With so many kids and no rest areas then, like there are now, it was quite a trip. We ate our noon meal beside the road like a picnic, saw deer, elk and even a bear during our trip. It was a real adventure, just like my father said it would be.

At last we neared our destination, the town of Rapelje. As we topped the hill and the town came into view, my mother turned to my father and said, "Oh no, not this place."

There was not a tree in sight and dust was blowing down the dry, sun parched main street. It was no doubt the saddest place my mother had ever seen. She was born in Norway and had lived in the western part of Washington State before moving to Clarkston, so she could not imagine living where there was not a forest in view. But, there she was, in Rapelje with the husband and family she loved, determined to make the best of what life had to offer.

3

A Machine from the Sky Visits Rapelje

Windy afternoons in Montana are as common and predictable as cows wanting to be milked twice a day. On one windy day in the fall of 1922, my brothers, our friends and I were playing tag beside the church when we heard a noise.

We were accustomed to the puttering sounds of automobiles and trucks. Also familiar were the sounds of a locomotive letting off steam and the squeal of the brakes as it began slowing to a stop, for Rapelje was the end of the line. The chug, chug, chug of the powerful train engine beginning its pull with a full load heading out of the small town was also a common sound. This sound was different.

Today I would describe it as a drone, but back then the sound was new. I looked to the tracks with the other kids, but the train was still taking on a load of grain. The engine was not making any sound and emitting only a barely-visible steam vapor.

The strange sound did not come from that train, the only one within 200 miles. I looked to the left and right, up and down the road, but no vehicle was in sight.

The whine of an engine was growing louder and louder, and finally the direction was clear. It was coming from behind the church. The church windows began to shake and, for a moment, a fear of the building falling apart came over me. Suddenly the source of the sound was visible. My head snapped back as my eyes instantly went from looking at church windows to the sky above.

I stood there, staring straight up, mouth open, eyes large as dinner plates, as a machine in the air, just roof high, passed over the church, over me and headed down the main street of the town. It then turned to the left, c i r c l e d t h e town once a n d landed in a wheat field behind the Molt house, about 1/2 mile from the church and our house.

"Let's go," one of the kids yelled.

He might not have been so inclined to do that, but the rest of the town was running towards the machine and, as young boys do, we followed the crowd.

I remember my father near me at one point and I asked him, "What is it, father?"

"It's an airplane, Monrad," he said.

The word held no meaning to me. I had never heard it before, but once a person can associate a word with an object, it stays with him forever.

"Look at the airplane, Monrad," my father said with genuine joy in his voice, while using hand movements that he commonly used while preaching his Sunday sermons. I watched as a man stepped down from the machine that had been introduced as an airplane to me by my father.

As I mentioned before, the wind blows most afternoons in Montana, and this was no exception. On the ground, the airplane wobbled from side to side and seemed to be fighting the fact that it was on the ground. The man from the airplane asked for rope and someone brought some. Each wing was tied to a fence post and the machine settled down to a gentle rock, moving from side to side, as the wind continued to blow as it does every day in Rapelje.

I later learned that the man, the one who operated the airplane, was called a pilot and, in those days, pilots would fly from town to town and take people up for an airplane ride for a fee. It was called barnstorming.

With the wind blowing so hard that day, going up again was not practical. The pilot, obviously disappointed, visited with the townspeople for an hour or so. My father invited the man to join us for supper and to spend the night.

We walked from the airplane to our house by the church, with most of the townspeople walking with us. My father and the pilot were side by side, but they walked so fast, I had to run to keep up with the back side of the crowd. There was a festive air about the man and the airplane. It was a fun afternoon in the town of Rapelje, Montana. Once the crowd was near our house, the pilot once again visited with the people and slowly people began to drift away.

It's hard for me to describe my feelings that day. This pilot, the man from the air, was like having Neil Armstrong, the first man to walk on the moon, or the President of the United States, visit your house and spend the night. I was in total awe of this man from the sky.

My father and the man visited for a long time before supper was ready and I, along with my brothers and sisters, sat nearby and listened to every word they said. Although I could not understand most of what they were saying, it was evident the pilot enjoyed this new freedom of flying.

My mother joined in the festive mood of having a special visitor as she prepared supper with the help of my older sisters. The place settings were laid out, the food was brought to the table and we sat down. As was customary when we had visitors, which was quite often in a preacher's house, mother gave up her place at the end of the table opposite my father and sat next to him. The visitor, the pilot this night, was given the seat of honor.

We kids didn't have an assigned seating arrangement and there was usually a scramble for the seats next to a visitor, depending upon who that visitor was. This evening, I planned ahead and was at the table before anyone else. The man from the sky had my attention, and I wanted to watch him up close and listen to him talk. I sat in the first chair to his left.

My father bowed his head to say grace and everyone at the table held hands. My sister, to my left, grabbed my left hand and the visitor opened his left hand to me. I reached out to him with my right hand, expecting a different kind of feel than just a mere human hand, but it felt the same. During grace, I didn't bow my head completely and close my eyes as I usually did. I couldn't take my eyes off my hand in his, this man from the sky.

"Eat your supper, Monrad," my mother said once during the meal.

I looked at my plate and realized that listening to this visitor held more interest for me than food, which was unusual for me. I did manage to eat, but when this man would speak, I would watch the way his mouth moved or the way he cut his meat. He wasn't loud and boisterous, but rather humble and soft spoken. Supper went fast. It doesn't take long to eat at the table of a large family.

After supper, Father and the visitor talked some more. I tried to stay awake and listen to it all, but sleep overtook me. My mother helped me to my feet and, with me half asleep, walked me to my bed.

I'm not sure which bed the pilot slept in, but I'm sure we kids were made to sleep two or three to a bed, which was the custom at our house when visitors spent the night.

We were up early the next morning. The visitor drank a cup of coffee and ate breakfast, but declined an invitation to stay another night, saying he had to get back to Billings. We, my entire family, walked him to the airplane. I jostled for position with my brothers in order to walk beside the visitor and it worked for part of the way. I bumped into his leg once and was embarrassed, but this man from the sky simply reached down and placed his arm around my shoulders to reassure me that everything was all right.

The airplane was still there, tied down in the wheat field behind the Molt house. After taking the ropes off and turning the airplane away from the fence, the pilot thanked my parents, waved to us kids and climbed into his flying machine.

The sound of the engine up close was loud. The wind from the propeller was like a very windy day in Rapelje. With dust flying, the machine started to roll across the field, gaining speed as it went and then, suddenly, it was in the air. I stood and watched as it grew smaller and smaller in the sky, then disappeared.

Five years later, word reached the small town of Rapelje about a pilot flying the Atlantic Ocean for the first time. The next scheduled freight to arrive in town had with it a copy of the current Billings newspaper. My father gathered the family together at the kitchen table and showed us the paper, and the picture of the man who made the historic flight. It was the same man from the sky who had sat next to me at the supper table that night five years before.

"Left stranded and almost penniless after the breakup of a barnstorming tour ... Charles A. Lindbergh, who, a few years later, was to acquire world fame as the "Lone Eagle" of aviation, spent three months in Billings in the summer and fall of 1922... During the time he was (in Billings), the plane gave exhibitions at Red Lodge, Cody, Winnett, Roundup, Rapelje, and a number of other places..."

Billings Gazette, August 2, 1931

4

A Sad Day

My mother was a strong person. She had to be. After all, she had seven children and they required lots of care. Like other women of those times, my mother cooked the meals for the family, maintained a clean house and canned vegetables and fruits so we could eat during the winter months. Besides all that work, my mother was expected to have the sensitivity of a preacher's wife.

While it is true that my father was an ordained Lutheran minister, my mother also had a calling and I'm sure it was to be there for my father and to assist in his ministry. My mother was the right person for the job. I don't remember a time when she was not available for those who needed her assistance. On any given day, those in need might include one of her own children or a neighbor's child with a skinned elbow, an adolescent girl that needed a shoulder to cry on or the elderly widow who was facing life without her husband. My mother had the unique ability to advise and guide her own children and adults alike without making either feel out of place. She would be there for other people with problems, but I don't remember one time when she needed assistance.

My mother was pregnant three times after I was born. I was too young to recall much about what was happening when my brother Norman was born. When she was pregnant with my brother Paul, I remember her getting big like all pregnant women do and, when the time was at hand, two women came to the house and a baby was born.

The last time she was pregnant, I was more aware of how her actions were restricted as her condition advanced. She wasn't able to lift as much as usual and I noticed that my older sisters pitched in and helped around the house more. Still, my mother was caring and loving. She and my father would tuck us in each night and there were hugs for everyone. My mother was still available to any person who needed her assistance including my brothers and sisters and the entire membership of the church.

One day, my mother said she didn't feel

well. There were times when any member of our family might be sick, but this was different. Staying in bed was unusual for my mother. After all, she was young, in her 30s. I had always known her to be active, cooking meals and taking care of her children, which included the entire Lutheran congregation.

A day or two later, my father sent for the druggist, who was the closest thing we had to a doctor in town in Rapelje. He told my father that he should get my mother to Billings, and the closest medical doctor, right away.

I remember when my mother left the house that day. She walked to the Mitchell and sat in the front seat. Then she talked to each one of her children individually. She told each of us she would be back soon and that she loved us. My mother then gave each of her children a hug.

My father placed two suitcases in the back seat of the Mitchell, then climbed into the driver's seat and drove off. I watched my mother and the car until they were out of sight.

In those days, communications weren't the same as they are now. My older sisters cooked and took care of the younger children, but we had no word of what the situation was with our mother in Billings. My father stayed with my mother because, naturally, he was concerned about her, but also it was not easy to travel the muddy, rutted roads.

Two days after my mother and father left Rapelje for Billings, my father returned. My friend Basil Minnie and I were sitting on a fence near the house talking when I noticed the Mitchell coming down the road. I wasn't overly concerned when I first noticed that my father was alone because my sisters told me that mothers and newborn babies sometimes stay in the hospital for two weeks after the birth. The Mitchell stopped close to us and my father got out. I ran to him expecting to hear about a new brother or sister. Instead, he approached me with a sad face and put his arm around me.

"Monrad, your mother has gone to Heaven," he said.

My heart skipped a beat and I couldn't catch my breath for a moment. I couldn't speak and I just stood there.

My father and I walked together to the house, with his hand still on my shoulder, and the rest of his children gathered around as soon as we entered the front door. He told them the sad news and everyone started crying.

I remember him telling us that we had a new baby sister, but that was all but lost by the fact that our mother was gone.

That sequence of events is as fresh in my mind as if it had happened yesterday and so is the funeral.

My mother's funeral was held four days af-

ter my father returned from Billings. It started at 11 a.m. and my family walked together from the parsonage to the church next door. I noticed the church was full of people from my father's congregation and the town of Rapelje. We walked to the front of the church and sat in the front row. My mother lay in her casket just three feet in front of us.

There were three other Lutheran preachers, friends of my father, at the service. They wanted to participate, to be with him and help him in his time of grief. My father spoke first, then the others. They preached over my mother for at least two hours. I sat and watched my mother the entire time. I was numb with sadness.

When the service was completed, all of the people filed passed the coffin. When there was just our family left, we gathered around my mother and held hands as my father prayed. I didn't close my eyes, but instead kept looking at my mother. When the prayer was over, I watched as the coffin lid was put in place and secured with nails.

The coffin was carried to a horse-drawn hearse, and the family, along with a good many other townspeople, walked behind it to the cemetery. It was a two-mile walk, which was a long walk for a family with young children.

Another service was held at the cemetery with more prayers, then my mother was lowered into her grave using three ropes slung under the casket.

We returned to the house where there was lots of food to eat and people talking and children playing. I was numb with an empty feeling that I still feel to this day when I think of that fine woman, my mother.

5

My Aunt

It was common in the old days to adopt out members of a family after one of the parents passed away. I don't know of a family that liked the idea, but it was a necessary fact of life back then.

My father traveled to many outlying towns in his work as a Lutheran minister. He would make a circuit to visit different churches, which required that he spend at least one night, but more often several, away from home. That meant he wouldn't be home all the time to see to the upbringing of his children.

If my father would have been a blacksmith or a butcher, I'm sure the eight of us would have remained together as a family, with my two older sisters watching over us when my father was away. However, no matter how well intentioned my older sisters were, watching after the rest of us during my father's overnight absences was not a good idea.

Gertrude Ann was about two months old when she was adopted out to the Reverend and Mrs. A. A. Holbeck. My father sent my younger brother Paul and me to live with my mother's sister, who lived about 10 miles from Rapelje with her husband, Mr. Munson. They were newlyweds.

My Aunt Avilda was 27 years old and Mr. Munson was somewhat older. They were married, went on a two-week honeymoon, then they returned to the place Mr. Munson had home-steaded. They found out, upon their return, that my mother died the day they were married.

Communications being what they were in those days, there was no way they could have known of my mother's death or even that she was near death on the day of their wedding. Nor was there a way to get in touch with them on their honeymoon.

My mother's death was a shock to my aunt. She was crushed because, not only did her sister die on the day of her wedding, but also because she was not with our family to grieve.

I'm sure Paul and I were not a welcome addition to the household. After all, Mr. Munson had just married a beautiful young woman, and all of a sudden, there were two young boys taking much of his wife's time. To be fair, Mr. Munson had never been married, and now that I look back at that time as an adult, I'm sure he just didn't have the social skills required of a father. Many times he would bark orders about tasks to be completed, not realizing that, as a young boy, I didn't have the knowledge or skills to complete some of the assignments like a grown man would. Still, I did the best I could.

My aunt, on the other hand, was as loving and caring as my mother. She realized my mother's death had a devastating affect on me and that her new husband had a lot to learn about raising two boys. She watched over my brother and me like we were her own children and seemed to relish the role of surrogate mother.

I loved my aunt. She seemed to sense when I was thinking about my mother. When those melancholy moods overcame me, my aunt would spend time talking to me about the loss we shared. We both knew she could never replace my mother, but she and I became as close as an aunt and nephew could after the loss of a loved one.

The Munson homestead was far enough out of town, about 10 miles, that visits with the rest of the family were difficult. But we did get together every couple of weeks or so when Mr. Munson went to town for supplies.

Those visits were fun, but strained. The rest of the family missed our mother as much as I did, and each time we were together the good memories swelled in each of us as well as the memory of our loss.

My brother and I had been staying with my aunt and her husband for a few months when I noticed familiar signs in my aunt's behavior. After all, my mother had exhibited the same behavior and weight gain a few times, and each time a new brother or sister joined the family. It was apparent to me that my aunt was with child.

When the pregnancy was in the advanced stages, my aunt stayed in bed more and more each day.

Before he headed to work in the fields one day, Mr. Munson told me, "Monrad, your aunt is sick and if she gets sicker, you come out in the field and get me."

The instructions seemed simple, but it was a big assignment for a little guy. I would go to my aunt's bedroom, walk to her bedside and talk to her. Then she would ask me to check on Paul and I would leave the bedroom to be with my brother. I played with my brother and made sure his diaper was clean and dry, then I would check on my aunt again. If my aunt was asleep, I would not talk to her, because I knew rest was important to a lady in her condition.

In the early afternoon, my aunt told me that she loved me and that I was doing a good job looking after my brother.

"I love you too, Aunt Avilda," I told her and left the room to look after Paul.

I went back into the bedroom an hour later. My aunt was turning black and blue and she wouldn't open her eyes or talk, even if I yelled her name.

I knew something was terribly wrong with my aunt, but I was stuck and didn't know what to do. I couldn't leave my brother alone in the house and I didn't know which field Mr. Munson was working that day. In my mind, there was no choice for me but to stay with Paul.

At sundown, Mr. Munson came home. I ran across the yard to him when I saw him nearing the house.

"Aunt Avilda is real sick," I told him.

He bawled me out for not coming for him, as we hurried to the house. He told me to stay put in the kitchen, then he went into the bedroom.

He returned in a couple minutes. He walked towards me and stopped in front of me. He grabbed me firmly by the shoulders and looked me in the eye.

"You let your aunt die, Monrad," he said sternly.

Mr. Munson released me, then left the house and headed for the barn. He didn't have a car or a telephone, so he saddled a horse and left Paul and me at the homestead while he rode to town for help.

I was so scared. It was only about nine months before that my mother had died, and now I was facing death again. After Mr. Munson rode away, I peeked into my aunt's bedroom. The outline of her body was apparent, but I couldn't see her face. I stepped into the room and walked to the point where she had smiled at me just a couple of hours before. Mr. Munson had pulled a blanket over my aunt's head, so I couldn't see her face.

It's spooky to be in a room with someone who is dead, but who was a loving and caring person just hours before. I don't know what possessed me to go into the room, but there I was, and I didn't want my aunt to be dead. Then I heard a noise and I was scared. I caught my breath, turned and ran out of the room. I grabbed Paul and headed out the front door. I was shaking and shivering, yet I wasn't cold. I walked directly to the clothesline pole, sat Paul at the base and climbed it.

I sat on the crossbar and looked down to see my brother sitting there, below, looking up at me. Paul, as young as he was, seemed to understand that things weren't normal. He was content to busy himself with the dirt and the pebbles that were within his reach. His baby chatter let me know that he was all right and not in need of

anything.

I relaxed a little then, not worried about the brother below me, and tilted my head back to look up. I noticed the stars, there were lots of them, and I thought about my mother. Oh, I missed her so. Then I thought about my aunt, and I missed her, too. I felt sad and so alone, but somehow the darkness and the stars seemed to wrap around me and I felt better, not completely content, but not as sad and alone as I did before.

An hour or so later, someone arrived at the house in a buckboard. I don't remember who it was, but they took Paul and me back to Rapelje and delivered us to my father's house. Paul was fed, changed and put to bed for the night. I was exhausted, but remember talking with my sisters as I ate at the table. I don't remember what we talked about, but I was numb from fatigue.

Sleep must have overcome me as soon as I finished. The next thing I remember was waking up the next morning.

There was another funeral, similar to the one for my mother. I walked behind the hearse again, all the way to the cemetery. We laid my aunt to rest beside my mother. I watched as my aunt was lowered into the ground just like my mother.

Shortly after the funeral, Paul was adopted out to the Rev. O. K. Davidson, but I was allowed to stay at home with my sisters and the rest of my family.

6

Summer Jobs

It was expected during the summer months that the boys in the family would go to work on nearby farms. I went out to work for the Dallmans when I was 7 years old. These were good people and they treated me well. I liked them. The family consisted of Mr. and Mrs. Dallman, their daughter and teenage sons, Bill and Carl Jr.

The days were full of hard work, as running a ranch required, but the Dallmans accepted the hard work and enjoyed life, too. Mrs. Dallman was a good cook and her daughter helped her in the kitchen. Sometimes when a meal was being cooked, I would sneak into the kitchen and take a sample of whatever was within reach. Mrs. Dallman surely knew what I was doing, but she never let on. I'm sure Carl Jr. and Bill did the same when they were growing up, so their mother knew what to expect when another boy was visiting. No matter what was cooked, there was lots of it and it was delicious.

The Dallman house was small by today's standards. Some may describe it as a large shack. The small size of the dining room aided with the family entertainment. Each evening, after the supper dishes were cleared, a fiddle and a harmonica were brought out of the closet. The three men would tilt back, resting their chair backs against the wall, place their heads on the wall and play song after song until it was time to go to bed. I felt good during my stay with the Dallmans. They made me feel like I was part of their family. I worked hard and put in long hours, but a person doesn't mind doing that when he is treated fairly.

One of my jobs was to drive a team of horses during harvest. The horses were smarter than me and they knew what to do, which was a good thing because I certainly didn't know much about driving horses at the age of seven.

I also herded sheep. One day, when I was taking my flock to their daily feeding grounds, the train arrived on the scene; on schedule, as usual. I wasn't ordinarily bothered by the train going to and from Rapelje. In fact, I rather enjoyed watching the iron machine glide over the rails, and the whistle was music to my ears.

This day, however, I was troubled because the flock of Dallman sheep that I was responsible for, and that numbered around 600, was straddling the tracks. The engineer, seeing the problem from afar, brought the train to a graceful stop. The train crew disembarked and herded the sheep off the tracks. I was embarrassed, yes, but thankful that the animals under my care were not injured.

In town a few days later, I strolled into the general store to see what was new in the way of candies. As I was bent over a glass jar filled with red and white sweets, I heard a familiar voice. It was the section boss from the train that had to stop for my flock.

"Yeah, Sam, if that sheepherder lets those sheep back on the track again stoppin' the outbound, I'm goin' to shoot 'em," he said.

"The sheep or the herder?" Sam asked.

"The herder of course," the section boss said. "Ain't those sheeps fault."

I stayed low, acting like each piece of hard candy needed close examination. Then I announced that the third piece from the right side of the jar would do me just fine, while not lettin' on one bit that I knew what they were talking about.

I left the store figuring the good Lord had saved me from certain death by not letting that

section boss know it was me who was herding those sheep.

The next day I started my flock out early, so we would be sure to cross the tracks before the outbound was due passed our point of crossing. The sheep had a different idea. They picked that day to get on the track and travel outbound, in the same direction the train would be heading. What puzzled me was that those sheep seemed to enjoy walking between the rails. It was as if they had found a new playground and they weren't going to give it up for anything.

I ran to the head ewe and pushed her off the track, then grabbed another and moved her out of the way. It was no use. They would head back to the track as soon as they were pushed off. The sound of the whistle made my head jerk towards Rapelje. The outbound was on its way.

I tried and tried to get those sheep off the tracks and the train got closer and closer. When I could make out the engineer leaning out of the cab shaking his fist in my direction, I figured it was time to make myself scarce. Not wanting to let that section boss live up to his promise to shoot me, I found a culvert and crawled inside. Rattlesnakes, known to frequent dark areas like culverts, were the least of my worries as I scrambled to the middle and sat there.

The train crew made lots of noise as they forced my sheep from the tracks. Finally I heard the train start forward, gaining speed little by little. The engineer blew the whistle as the train passed over my hiding spot and the section boss fired a couple shots into the air. I stayed put until I couldn't hear the train anymore.

Whenever I saw the section boss after that,

I would run and hide. Looking back, I don't think he would have really shot me, but as a kid I took him very seriously.

Not all of the people I worked for during the summers were as good to me as the Dallmans. One summer, my brother Gary and I worked on a farm a few miles out of Rapelje. This farmer and his wife had lots of cattle for us to take care of and many other animals, too. They had no children and they treated us like hired hands who were grown men, not growing boys who were learning about life. These people were no doubt the worst people I ever worked for. I've never minded working hard. In fact, I expected to work hard, as everyone did in those days, but I also expected good food and lots of it. This couple never fed us enough and they worked us longer and harder than they should have. A grown man would have quit and found a better job, but Gary and I were stuck. We had to do the work for our room and board, meager as it was.

Working summer jobs during that early part of my life taught me a lifelong lesson. There are basically two types of employers: those who take advantage of their employees will find that their workers do only what is required and usually resent their bosses. On the other hand, workers don't mind working hard, will generally give more of themselves and do a better job if the employer treats them with respect and in an honest manner.

7

The Streets of Rapelje

Rapelje, Montana, was a western town. It still is. In the early 1920s when I lived there, Rapelje was like the western towns you see in cowboy movies. There was a general store where people would purchase, or put on account, everything from flour and coffee to guns and cloth.

The blacksmith shop was located near the livery stable. Both of these businesses were vital to the community because horses were as much a part of life then as vehicles are now.

Rapelje also had a train depot, a school, two churches, a bank, a saloon, a hotel with restaurant, a jail and a barber shop. Most of these businesses were located on the main street, for Rapelje was basically a one-street town. It was your typical western town with real cowboys, sheepherders and a sheriff.

A regular pastime of us kids was to visit the general store and look at the hard candy in glass containers, even if we didn't have money to buy any. One day I had finished looking at the candy and was walking out the front door of the store when I heard a horse far off to my right. The horse was traveling into town at top speed with a cowboy in the saddle spurring it along. It was strange for someone to run a horse through town. Usually wagons traveled slowly, with the horses at a walk, or maybe a trot, as they neared the outskirts when they were headed out of town.

I looked to my left and saw another cowboy, also on a horse and headed into town at top speed. They were about 100 yards apart when I recognized the man to my right as Mr. Maxey. Bang!

My head snapped to the left, and I saw smoke from the cowboy's pistol. Mr. Maxey drew his gun and aimed.

Bang!

I dove behind a barrel near the store front and watched as both cowboys exchanged fire.

Bang! from the left.

Bang! from the right.

Bang! from the left.

The horses were just 30 yards apart now, still traveling at full speed.

I could now see both cowboys without turning my head. I watched Mr. Maxey aim and fire again.

Bang! The cowboy flipped off the back of his horse as if hit square in the chest by a 16-pound sledge hammer. His body turned a complete somersault, and he landed flat on his back just 10 yards from me.

Mr. Maxey reined in his horse to a fast stop, dismounted in a flash and walked to the fallen man with his gun at the ready. The man on the ground didn't move. He was dead before he left his horse.

Suddenly the town was alive as people ran into the street and gathered around the body. I was there first and stood near Mr. Maxey. His gun was cocked and still smoking.

I looked at the man on the ground. Blood was flowing from a hole in the man's chest and staining his shirt. It was the first time I had seen a man killed. I looked up at Mr. Maxey, and he looked down at me. He uncocked his pistol and put it in his holster.

"You all right, Perry?" the sheriff asked when he arrived.

"Yeah, Sheriff."

And that was it. There was no further investigation and no arrest because this was just an argument between two cowboys, and it was settled the way cowboys in those days settled arguments.

Also during the 1920s it was against the law for people to drink alcoholic beverages; even cowboys in Montana. It was called Prohibition. But, they would still visit the saloon to play poker and visit with each other and any women who might be there. This was a chance for the cowboys to socialize after a lonely week on the range chasing cattle.

Though it was illegal for saloons to sell whiskey, most cowboys had a bottle stashed in the saddlebags on their horses, which were tied to the hitching rail in front of the saloon. It wasn't uncommon to see a cowboy walk out of the saloon, take a swig from a bottle hidden in the saddlebag, then return to the saloon.

One day there were four of us in the 8-to 12 year-old range with not much to do. We were walking toward the general store to look at the candy, when a cowboy came out of the saloon and took a long pull from a near full bottle.

"Say, I've got an idea," my brother Oscar said when the cowboy was back in the saloon.

One stood watch as the other three gathered around the saddlebag. Oscar took out the bottle of whiskey, and I poured half of the bottle on the ground near the water trough. Next we filled the half-empty bottle with horse urine. This is an easy task if the cooperating horse has been standing at the hitching rail for a long time. The bottle was returned to the saddlebag.

The four of us then hid behind some barrels across the street. It wasn't long before another cowboy came out of the saloon and went to the saddlebag. He retrieved the whiskey bottle, pulled the cork and took a big drink. As soon as the rancid-tasting liquid hit his mouth, he was spitting it out. He ran to the water trough and washed his mouth out. Then he went into the saloon yelling. The first cowboy and several others came out with the second cowboy, who was still yelling. He thought the first cowboy had pulled the trick on him.

The first cowboy was mad, too, because his bottle of whiskey was ruined. Both had pistols strapped to their hips, and for a minute I thought they were going to have a shoot-out right then and there. Another cowboy brought out a good bottle of whiskey; they all had a drink, and that seemed to settle things down a bit. Then they went back to the saloon.

I was sure glad. I would have felt bad if a cowboy had been killed because of the prank we had pulled.

Yep, you never knew what you were going to see on the street of Rapelje.

8

My Father's New Wife

One summer day when I was eight years old, my father sold the 1917 Mitchell. The car had been a big part of my life and I hated to see it leave the family. After all, the image of my mother sitting in the front seat of that vehicle during our move from Clarkston to Rapelje was still fresh in my mind. In fact, the last time I saw my mother alive, that's where she was; seated in the front seat of the Mitchell.

I associated the car with good times, fun times and my mother. Perhaps it held similar images for my father, and that's why a change was necessary. In its place, the family now owned a Model T Ford.

It was common for my father to be gone for several days at a time because of his job duties as a Lutheran minister, and when he returned from those trips he would always have some horehound candy for me. On one occasion, after my father had been gone for several days, I saw him coming down the road and stop at the house. I ran to the house from the field where I had been playing with my friends, excited about getting some candy.

My father got out of his side of the Model T, then he walked around and helped a woman out of the other side.

"Who's that?" I asked one of my older sisters.

"That's Father's new wife," she said.

"Now line up," my father said. "I've got someone for you to meet."

So all my brothers and sisters and I stood side by side as this new woman in our lives stopped in front of each of us.

"And this is Monrad," my father said when the woman was standing in front of me.

I held my hand out, just like my other brothers and sisters had done, and smiled. My father's new wife took my hand in her right hand and turned it over, then back. Next she used her left hand to bend my fingers back the way they don't normally go. It hurt, and I yelled.

"Your hands are not clean," she said, giving me a dirty look.

Of course I had dirty hands! When kids play in the dirt their hands get dirty. If I would have met this woman just before we sat down to the

21

dinner table, my hands would have been clean, because my mother taught me to clean up before sitting down at the table. My mother also knew kids needed time to play, and getting dirty was a part of playing.

My father's new wife apparently didn't know this facet of child raising. Evidently she thought young boys and girls should be prim and proper and clean all the time. I was living proof that just the opposite was true of boys at the age of eight. I took an immediate dislike to my father's new wife, and it was apparent that she didn't like me much either.

I'm not saying that I was a saint and never got into trouble. But this woman did not treat me in a fair and honorable manner. Today, people would say we had a personality conflict, but, back then, she was in charge, and I was a troublemaker from her perspective.

My father's new wife was nothing but mean in my eyes. Her wrath wasn't always aimed in my direction. My brothers and sisters weren't treated well by this woman either.

During my life I've seen other people who had a mean streak like that woman did. I've even had a chance to talk to a few of them, and when the subject of growing up is discussed, none of these people had a happy childhood. Maybe that was the problem with my father's new wife. Maybe she just didn't know how to act around young children because of the way she was raised. Perhaps she wasn't allowed to have fun when she was a kid and she was going to use the skills she was taught to raise the children under her care in the same way. No matter what the reason, the result, from my view, was suffering, agony and misery.

The Holm family settled down to what I'm sure my father hoped would be a normal family life style. My father continued to do the best he could as a preacher to support a wife and several children. His new wife utilized her child-raising skills, crude and undeveloped though they were, to make the Holm household a home in her eyes.

I continued to act like the 8-year-old kid that I was, while learning how to avoid my father's new wife as much as possible. Life was easier for me if I was not seen or heard.

If asked today about the pain this woman put me through, I would say it was worth all the anguish and sorrow, but for only one reason. In my eyes, the only good thing to come out of the marriage between my father and this woman was my sister, Ruth.

9

My First Venture Into the Junk Business

I experienced my first dealings in the junk business at an early age. There was an old junkman who came to our town about once a month in a wagon pulled by an old horse. Everyone knew that he was looking for junk, mainly brass or copper, but that he would take other things that people didn't want.

My friends and I

old bachelor homesteader who lived about three miles east of town. The joy of his life was a 1923 Maxwell road car. He probably saved his meager earnings for many years to buy the car, and his pride was apparent.

Everyone knew when this homesteader was in town because he would honk the horn often, and people would look his way, just as he wanted them to do. I have to admit, that Maxwell was a fine-looking car. The homesteader and the Maxwell were seemingly inseparable,

would acquire any brass or copper items we could get our hands on and would hide it, so no one else was aware of it. When we presented our stash to the junkman, he would give us each a couple of pennies, or maybe a nickel if we had a bunch of good junk. We would then head to the general store and buy candy.

Most of the time we picked up junk items nobody else wanted, but there was a time when the goods were just too tempting. There was an

so my friends and I knew we were witnessing an unusual event when we saw him arrive at the train station riding in the car of another rancher.

"Thanks for the ride," he said as he pulled his suitcase out of the back seat.

There was always a lot of activity at the station when a train was about to depart Rapelje. All that activity in our little town might not seem like much when compared to a larger town or city, but, for young boys, the train station was where the action was. We were seated on one of the benches near the station door when the homesteader walked by a few minutes before the scheduled departure of the Billings-bound train.

"Where's the Maxwell?" the station master asked as the man was buying his ticket.

"Left her at the ranch," the man said, offering no other explanation.

He told the station master that he would be back in five days, picked up his suitcase and boarded the train. Three minutes later, the outbound started to roll, and my friends and I watched until the caboose was out of sight, as was our usual practice.

"When's that old junkman due back in town?" one of my friends asked.

"Day after tomorrow," I answered.

The next morning, we were on the road to the homesteader's ranch, just after we watched the morning train pull out of the station, of course. We didn't consider the three-mile hike to be unreasonable because walking was our usual means of travel back then.

The ranch was deserted, and the Maxwell was parked inside the barn. We found a hammer and the five of us spent the next hour busting all the brass and other items off of that beautiful car. We carried our loot, including the carburetor and radiator, to our secret hiding spot and covered it with brush.

The next day, the five of us watched as the rest of the townspeople traded with the junkman, then we ran alongside his wagon, as we always did, when he headed out of town.

"We've got extra stuff for ya today," one of my friends said after a bit.

"Ya do?" he asked. "Where's it at?"

"A bit more out of town, hidden," I said.

"You boys better get on this here wagon, so we can get there faster," he said.

We sold the junkman all of the stuff we broke off that Maxwell, and he was pleased to get it.

"I don't wanna know where you boys got this stuff," he said. "And I can't pay ya as much as I normally would for it because I might get into trouble for takin' it. All I can give ya is 50 cents each."

My friends and I thought we were rather smart businessmen as we watched the junkman head down the road at a faster pace than I thought that old horse could travel. The five of us celebrated our business success by heading straight for the general store. We each bought 50 cents worth of hard candy — a fact that was not overlooked by the store owner — then we went to the train station. There we sat on our regular bench and ate every piece of that candy.

A few days later, the homesteader returned to Rapelje. We watched as he headed out of town, on foot, with his suitcase in his hand. We also watched as he walked back into town three hours later. He looked mad and headed straight for the sheriff's office.

The sheriff investigated the incident over the course of an hour or so. A stop at the general store was a major part of the investigation. That's when the five of us decided it was time to go to our respective homes. But it wasn't hard for the sheriff to determine who had spent more money than usual during the past few days. The five of us conspirators were rounded up and confronted. We confessed.

Three of my friends

yelled so loud that their screams could be heard all over Rapelje as they were whipped with a leather strap. My father didn't spank me, but his talk was just as painful. I let my father down and it was painful when he told me so, because I loved my father. I made a vow to him and to myself to procure future junk in an honest manner. My father's new wife was just plain mad at me, and it showed.

Furthermore, our little group of five was reduced to three because the parents of two wouldn't let them play with us anymore. I thought that was rather narrow-minded of them. After all, we didn't get into trouble all the time.

I don't know how the homesteader was compensated for the damage we caused to the Maxwell. I don't ever remember seeing him drive another automobile into town. I do know it wasn't long after the infamous car bashing event that the old homesteader died. The three of us were discussing our options one morning when the old homesteader was again mentioned.

"I wonder where that old guy hid his pistol?" one of my friends asked.

We knew he owned a revolver because we had seen it strapped on his hip from time to time.

"It has to be in his house," another friend said.

"I guess it's not like stealin' it from him, because he has no use for it now," I said.

So we walked to the homesteader's ranch again. I stood watch and the other two went into the house and found the gun. It was hidden in the attic of the house, which was accessible by lifting a trap door.

We left the ranch and headed back to town. Halfway there, we stopped and admired the pistol for a few minutes; then we didn't know what to do with it. We couldn't buy any ammunition for it and we couldn't wear it in town. The pistol was a prize that caused more of a problem to keep than it was worth to us.

There seemed to be only one reasonable solution to our predicament: We buried the gun in a secret spot and never talked about it again.

10

Tough Times in Rapelje

As the children of a Lutheran minister, we didn't want for food or clothing. In fact, our family, although not rich by any means, was a little more financially secure than most people in the town because of the money my father inherited from his parents. My father, being a wise man, put his extra money in The First National Bank of Rapelje, where he thought it would be safe.

Then the economy of Rapelje and the rest of Montana soured over a period of several years. Wheat farmers began to experience tough times. Wheat prices bottomed out at 50 cents a bushel or less, and some crops were wiped out or damaged by hail storms. Some of the wheat farmers felt they needed more land to make a living, so they bought up other homesteads. However, the high mortgage rates and low wheat prices, coupled with the lack of working capital in the bank because they had invested much of their money in land, were a deadly combination for many.

Some of them divided their time and money between cattle and wheat, but there were problems with cattle, too. Grass and hay were in short supply and the winters were long and cold with deep snows. The Rapelje freight trains shipped out whole herds to the yards in Omaha and Chicago to prevent their starving.

The troubles of the farmers and ranchers trickled down to the town of Rapelje. The saloon, general store, restaurant and hotel also suffered when people had less money to pay their bills. Financial pressures affect different people in different ways, and my father, the Lutheran minister, helped a lot of people understand that it wasn't their fault if a crop failed because of a hail storm or if deep snows made it impossible to reach a group of cattle and they starved. Some ranchers stuck it out, but many were forced to leave their homesteads and Rapelje.

The situation deteriorated until one day word spread through town that the bank was broke. My friends and I ran to that part of town and found most of the other townspeople there. I saw my father standing in a line that came out of the door of the wooden building that housed the bank and snaked several yards down the street. He looked sad and worried. The only other time I saw him look this way was when my mother died.

"What's happening, Father?" I asked.

"Oh, Monrad," he said, "this is not a good day."

"But Father, what does it mean?"

"It means the bank doesn't have any money," a man in front of my father said.

A woman behind my father started crying.

"What will I do?" the woman said. "It's all the money I have."

"Let's string up the bank president," another man said.

"Now listen," my father said. "The Lord will see us all through this hard time. We don't even know how bad it is. Let's not do something we'll regret. This is a time for prayer, and if you can't find it in your heart to pray, I'll be praying for you."

The reasoning seemed to soothe the crowd and they didn't say much after that. The woman continued to cry, and my father bowed his head to pray quietly. I looked at the faces of all the people in the line trying to find a glimmer of hope, but found none. All I saw were the sad faces of beaten men and women.

Shortly after the bank failure, the town suffered a fire. On the night of September 20, 1925, the Lynne Hotel caught fire. Rumor had it that the fire was not accidental. Some said a gasoline can was found at the rear of the building, and others reported that the owner was seen coming out of the hotel at about three in the morning tying his tie. This was unusual, since his hotel was on fire.

A bucket brigade was formed, and there was a futile effort to fight the blaze. The valiant effort was useless, and one third of the businesses on the hotel side of the street burned until there was no more wood to burn.

Placing sheet metal in front of the businesses on the opposite side of the street was the only successful attempt to keep the fire from spreading. The hotel owner left town a couple of days later. I heard he had a sizable amount of insurance on the hotel, so he was happy.

Some of the people rebuilt their stores, but more moved away. The economy of Rapelje was suffering already due to low wheat prices and cattle problems, so when entire families moved, the loss was an additional near-fatal blow to the community.

My father continued to tend to his flock, and he was sad to see the town dwindle in size. There were times, especially during the harsh Montana winters, when the only members of his congregation to sit in the church pews and hear his sermon were his immediate family. I admired him for conducting church services through the lean times, just as he did when Rapelje was booming and the church would be overflowing with congregation members.

I'm sure my father's ability to help people see the positive side of situations, even though times were tough, helped save marriages, helped neighbors settle disputes in a civil manner and prevented suicides. This was a time when I believe my father's character and constitution were being tested by a higher authority, and he passed the series of tests thrown at him.

It turned out that my father had about $500 in the bank when it failed, which was a lot of money back then. A couple of years later, he and the rest of the investors received a settlement from the bank that amounted to about five percent of their money.

The church congregation grew so small in Rapelje and the surrounding areas that it was not possible to keep a full-time minister in the town. Our family moved again; this time to Wilmot, South Dakota.

It was a different kind of move because we didn't have the big Mitchell, but the smaller Model T. The family was smaller, too, as two of my younger siblings had been adopted out and my two older sisters stayed in Montana. The newest member of the family, my half-sister Ruth, was in her mother's arms as we loaded up the Ford and headed for South Dakota.

I turned and looked at Rapelje through the back window when we were at the edge of town. I could see the house my father built and the church that held so many family memories. I looked back again, about a mile down the road. I could see the cemetery where we had left my mother and my aunt and I felt sad.

11

Kicked Out

I never really cared much for Wilmot. I'm sure it was because of my relationship with my stepmother, which continued to deteriorate with each passing day. The only solace was the closeness I felt for my brothers and my baby sister Ruth.

In order to pay my way in the family, and to stay away from trouble at home, I would work on nearby farms. It was hard work, and the pay was little for a young boy. I'm sure the amount of work I was required to accomplish on the farms would be called abuse by today's standards, but back then it was a way of life. A favorite saying was that hard work builds character and never hurt anyone. People believed in and lived by those words, and I wasn't complaining, but I did expect to be paid when the job was completed.

One summer, I worked on a farm for three months. When the summer's work was complete, the farmer asked if I wanted an old bicycle he had instead of cash. I thought it was a grand idea and accepted. I had never owned a bicycle before and only learned to ride one when a friend taught me the year before. A bicycle would be a great improvement on my only other mode of transportation, which was by foot.

I rode that bicycle home to Wilmot, which was a distance of about 10 miles. It was mine. I earned it. My pride was evident as I showed it to a couple of friends I saw in town. But my fun with the bike was short lived. When I arrived at the house, my stepmother came out.

"Where did you get the bicycle?" she asked.

"It's my summer's pay," I said. "Isn't it great?"

"You can't have it," she said without further explanation, and she took it from me.

For the first time, I contemplated leaving home. I might not have followed through with the idea, but another boy I knew, who was three years older than me, was experiencing some similar thoughts. We each had a dollar in our pockets when we started walking out of Wilmot.

Not far out of town, a man driving an old truck stopped and picked us up. We shared space in the cargo area of the open truck with five other men. Traveling in the truck let us get away from Wilmot in a hurry, and we were grateful for the ride. My friend started to sit down when the .22 caliber pistol that he had tucked into the waist band of his pants slid down his pants leg and came out near his shoe. The revolver made a thud as it hit the truck bed.

The other men gave us some curious looks as my friend picked it up and again placed it in his pants. One man walked over and sat down next to me. He started asking questions, about my age and where I was from. Another started asking my friend questions, and I saw him look at the pistol. It was obvious to me that these men did not have our best interests at heart. Just then the truck was nearing a road intersection.

"Driver! Driver, this is where we get off!" I yelled, and the truck slowed to a stop.

"What did ya do that for?" my friend asked as the truck pulled away from us.

"Those men wanted your pistol," I said.

"Oh," he said.

We were about 100 miles south of Wilmot by the afternoon of our second day away from home. My friend couldn't find his dollar; I suspected that the men on the truck took it, so we spent part of mine for some food in the next town.

"I sure do miss my mother," my friend said when he finished eating.

I knew right then and there that we would be

heading back to Wilmot. The powerful feeling of one who is homesick is hard to just push aside, but I tried to talk him out of going back.

"Let's see what's around the next bend," I told him.

"But I want to go home, Monrad," he said. "My mother will be baking bread, and it tastes so good."

I remembered my mother baking bread in Clarkston and Rapelje. It was delicious when it was fresh from the oven and covered with butter or jam. Suddenly, I, too, was consumed by a deep and overpowering homesickness. Not for my father's family in Wilmot, but for my mother whom we buried in Rapelje and for the fun we had there.

Although my family life was not good, I realized that my friend may have been able to salvage some good memories from his.

"OK," I said. "Let's go back."

We turned around right there

and headed north. At dusk we were at a crossroads that had a general store and a gas station. They were closed, but we were looking for a place to get out of the wind for the night, so we tried the doors of both. They were locked. Then I saw the outhouse. It was not much warmer inside it, but at least the wind could not touch us.

My friend pulled out some matches and I ripped a few pages out of the nearby Sears catalog. A little fire, we thought, would warm us during the night. As the flame of the fire would die down, I would pull another page or two from the catalog and place them on the fire. After a few minutes, the ashes from the burned catalog pages were glowing and the fire seemed to be burning on its own.

It was then that we realized the wood on the outhouse floor was on fire. At first that was fine with us because we didn't have to find more fuel to put on the fire. Plus, the little house was warming up to a comfortable temperature.

"Slow it down so it will last all night," my friend said.

"Yeah, I guess we better just keep a small fire going," I said.

I tried to stop the fire from growing, but couldn't. The flames got bigger and started one side of the outhouse on fire.

"Let's get out of here," I said. We ran outside and up the road, stopping to watch at a respectable distance. It was quite a sight. The funny thing was that even though there were a couple of houses nearby, no one seemed to notice the fire. But I'm sure they missed that building because it was so important to people in those days.

It took us two more days to get home. My friend got a whipping. My father was upset with me, but he would never hit me. He couldn't understand why I was causing so much trouble. I didn't tell him the real problem was between his new wife and me. I did promise to try harder and not cause so many problems. My stepmother didn't say anything to me while my father was home, but, from her glare, I knew she was mad. I dreaded the times when my father would be out of town and she would have control over me.

I was home another year before the conflict between my stepmother and I came to a head. I was a troublemaker in her eyes even if I did good things. No matter what I did, it was the wrong thing to do. But in all fairness, I have to admit that the title of troublemaker was worn well by me. As long as I was getting into trouble anyway, I had some fun and didn't always do what I was told by my stepmother.

My father was away on business one day when she confronted me about something I did. I owned up to the deed and expected the usual punishment, but she surprised me.

"I just can't put up with you anymore," she said. "You're going to have to leave."

I was 13 when I stepped out of my father's house for the last time.

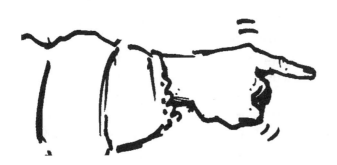

12

On the Road

A feeling of sorrow and sadness was deep within me when I stepped out of my father's house that day. Although my father would always consider me a member of his family, I was no longer a member of my father's household; the household controlled by a stepmother who didn't want me around. I didn't belong there. I was on my own.

With two dollars in my pocket and just the clothes on my back, I closed the door behind me and took a deep breath. I was sad, yes, but there was a tingling of excitement in the air, too. Now I would control my own destiny. My destination would be where I wanted to go, and I would do what I wanted to do. My first thoughts at the time were innocent, and I was naive to think that life was so simple. However, what was a 13-year-old kid to think when he was told he was no longer welcome at the house where his father and stepmother lived?

There was no going back, so I elected to think positive, that everything was going to be fine. My first destination was Billings, Montana, as my stepmother had suggested, where I would find Ann Sheppard, my oldest sister. Getting to

Billings would be easy. I would simply hop a freight.

I stepped off the porch and walked a few steps. I stopped, turned and looked for a few moments at the house representing my childhood. I thought of my mother, buried in Rapelje, and my father, away on church business, who would think that his son had simply run away again. The sorrow and sadness returned, this time with an intense lonely feeling. I felt tears forming, but I shook them off.

"There's no going back," I thought to myself. "Must get to Billings."

I turned and ran for the tracks.

I hopped the next freight out of town. It was headed to Milbank, South Dakota. I was alone in an empty boxcar listening to the clickety-clack, clickety-clack of train wheels on rails. I liked the rhythm. It made me feel welcome.

From Milbank I caught a west-bound train, a Milwaukee Railroad freight. This time I shared a boxcar with a few other hobos. This didn't concern me because they seemed friendly and willing to talk. Being lonely and coming from an upbringing that taught kindness and love, I felt comfortable with these friendly men. My new friends, along with the cadence of the wheels and track, gave me a cozy and snug feeling that made sleep come easy.

Aberdeen, South Dakota, is the first division on the railroad going west. The freight arrived early in the morning, and I awoke when the train slowed, my stomach growling. I was hungry; famished. Any young boy can confirm the need for a constant supply of food just because he is growing and needs the nutrition. However, the constant vibration of the railroad boxcar has a way of making anybody, no matter what their age, very hungry.

I asked the other hobos if there was a place to eat nearby. One directed me to a small cafe near the railroad yard, which catered to railroad crews and hobos with cheap but wholesome food. I found it and went inside.

The place held two other customers and a policeman. The stew was 10 cents, so I ate a bowl full, along with all the bread that came with it. I ate in a hurry because the freight was due to pull out in a few minutes. I sopped up the last bit of liquid in the bowl with the crust of the bread, popped it in my mouth and sat back. The food was good and my belly was full. But I couldn't sit and enjoy the good feeling because my train would leave without me if I didn't hurry.

I walked up to the owner, who also served as cook, waiter and cashier, to pay for the meal, but I couldn't find my two dollars. I rummaged through all my pockets, but there was nothing. I caught my breath as I thought about the friendly hobos on the freight.

"I had two dollars yesterday," I told the cook. "Someone must have taken it when I was sleepin'."

"You bums are all alike," he said.

"Can I do dishes to pay for my food?" I asked.

The owner looked at the policeman and pointed at me. I knew what was going to happen, so I took off running with the cop right behind me. My freedom was precious to me, and my father always said I could run like a deer. I proved it that morning. That policeman never caught me, but he ran me far enough that I was hungry again. I ran away from my freight, but circled around in time to catch it. Again my nose was pointed west.

I never went back to that little cafe, and I came through Aberdeen, South Dakota, many times after that. I was always afraid the owner would recognize me and send a cop after me again.

I was chased many times during my days on the road, by cops and railroad bulls, but the pursued has a great advantage over the pursuer because he has much more at stake – his freedom.

33

13

Providing the Meat

When I'm asked what I remember most about my years on the road as a hobo, the first thing that comes to mind is hunger. Of course, I was just a young boy, and, by nature, growing boys are always hungry. Besides, these were the depression years and food was in short supply for everyone in the United States, not just me. During that time, life boiled down for many to the simple matter of finding the next meal, and I was no exception.

As the freight I was on headed west out of Aberdeen, South Dakota, I noticed five other men in the boxcar with me. I studied them carefully, but could not recognize any of them as the ones who were with me when the freight arrived. These men were friendly, too, but my recent experience made me more cautious of the people around me.

The effect of having a full belly had worn off during my run from the cop and I was hungry again. I settled back against the side of the boxcar, fending off sleep for a long time. When I realized that all I had to my name were the clothes on my back, I relaxed, and the steady clickety-clack of the wheels on the rails lulled me to sleep.

At the next stop, I hopped off the boxcar with the rest of the hobos and just stood there as the others walked away. They were heading away from town and I could see no reason to go that way. One of the hobos looked back and waved to me.

"Come on," he said. "We're goin' to the

jungle."

A hobo jungle is a place where hobos congregate. They could be described as little campgrounds, but they weren't as elaborate as what people think of campgrounds today.

The ideal spot for a hobo jungle was close to a railroad yard and near a river or creek because running water was necessary for cooking. Water also allowed a hobo to wash himself and what clothing he had, if he was a clean person.

We arrived at the local jungle a few minutes later.

"Hi, Joe," one of our group called out.

"How ya doin', Sam?" Joe answered. "I thought you was goin' down south where there was some work."

"I been south, ain't no work there," Sam said. "Just lots of 'bos lookin'-."

"Who's the kid?"

"This here's ..., say what is yer name, kid?" Sam asked.

"I'm Monrad Holm, but my friends call me Mooney."

"Nice to meet ya, Mooney," Joe said.

And there were handshakes all around and I met everyone there, just like after one of my father's church services.

In all, there were about 25 men in this hobo jungle. Some were in their twenties and some were elderly, but most were in their middle years. I was the only young boy.

Someone brought out a five-gallon can. With the top cut out, as this one was, they made good cooking pots.

"I'll get some water and we'll make a stew," Old Clarence said. He walked to the creek and filled the pot about half full. He was by far the oldest of the group and the others listened to what he said.

"Now, we need some carrots and onions, spuds, and whatever else you can find," Old Clarence said.

It was obvious he was in charge of cooking and it sounded like he knew what to do with the

vegetables once he got them.

"Now, if we only had a few chickens ...," Old Clarence said, glancing up from his position on one knee near the fire.

"I know where there's a chicken coop," One-Eyed Bill said.

"You do?" Old Clarence asked.

"Yeah, 'bout half-a-mile north, near the big willow."

"OK, here's what we'll do," Old Clarence said. "Some of ya pay a visit to a garden or two and, ah, two of ya get some chickens. Now, who is the fastest of us here?"

The old man looked around the group of men and the men looked at each other, but, in the end, all eyes settled on me.

"Mooney, you're the youngest of us and the fastest, for sure," Old Clarence said. "You should get the chickens, if n' you have a mind to help out a bunch of old hobos, that is. How about it boys? Is Mooney our man?"

They all thought that was a good idea, so, after dark, while five men went after vegetables, I started for the chicken coop with One-Eyed Bill showing me the way.

I know it's not right to take what doesn't belong to you, but hunger changes a person's viewpoint about what's right and what's not. I was mighty hungry and besides, my upbringing taught me to help people in need. This group of hobos was certainly in need of a bunch of chickens right then.

"There's the place," One-Eyed Bill said pointing to a small shack. "Grab as many as ya can."

I stepped into the chicken coop without making a sound. The chickens were sound asleep and didn't know I was there. I grabbed two chicken necks in my right hand, another two in my left and started for the door. Those chickens didn't like it much that they couldn't breathe with my hands around their necks. They started flapping their wings and making such a racket that the other chickens were having a hard time sleeping, too.

If a person were able to sneak into a room where 50 chickens were asleep, you'd think that person would be able to glide right out of there without much trouble, even if the other 46 chickens were now wide awake. After all, I wasn't doing anything to them.

It just isn't that simple. The four chickens held tightly in my two hands were trying to fly in four different directions. I had a hard time making my two arms go in the direction I wanted them to go. At the same time, the other chickens thought harm was coming their way and they wanted the whole world to know about it. I headed for the door, but only found a wall. It was hard to tell where the door was with all the dust and feathers flying around my head. I turned left and found another wall.

"Who's out there?" came a voice from the direction of the house. "Edith, get me my shotgun."

I turned left again and found the door handle. I stepped out of the coop and was running at top speed in five steps.

"Stop! Stop or I'll shoot!"

Boom!

I dropped the two chickens that were in my left hand and increased my speed another notch, a feat I didn't know I was capable of achieving. Then I shifted one of the chickens to my left hand for better balance.

Boom!

My speed increased again.

I flew by One-Eyed Bill and didn't slow down.

"Mooney, you can stop now," he yelled. "You're out of range."

I slowed, but didn't stop until I reached the jungle. The other hobos treated me like a hero as

I trotted up to Old Clarence.

"Good goin', Mooney," he said as he reached out and took a chicken in each hand. "Uh, you can let go now, boy."

He pulled.

"Let go!" he shouted.

I released my grip on the chicken necks.

"Look here," Old Clarence said. "Mooney squeezed 'em so hard he's killed 'em for us."

The other hobos laughed and slapped me on the back, and I felt proud of myself for bringing food to the table of my friends in need.

The chickens were cleaned and placed in the pot with boiling water. The vegetables were added and we all sat around watching our food cook. The smell of the stew, along with my hunger pains, about drove me nuts.

"I got the chickens, so I'll be the first in the pot," I thought.

An hour later, Old Clarence declared the stew done and I stepped forward for my share.

"Now, Mooney," he said. "Didn't your folks teach you to respect your elders?"

I said that they did and waited while the others took a share. When it was my turn, all that was left was a little broth.

I swallowed every drop, of which there were only a few, and I was still hungry. But, the lessons learned that night were invaluable to me for the rest of my hobo days and beyond. They turned out to be the best lessons I have ever been taught: that I was going to have to take care of myself because no one else was going to do so, and not to steal because it is a horrible feeling to be shot at.

This hobo business was not as romantic and fun as some of the stories I had read about life on the road.

I was back on the west-bound freight when it pulled out of the station. The next stop was Miles City, Montana. There I had to switch to the Northern Pacific Railroad, a couple miles away. I went to the hobo jungle and found over 100 men in it. All of them were hungry.

I sat down on a rock which was about twenty feet from an old hobo cooking a hot cake made of flour and water. Another hobo, a big man, walked up to him and watched him for a few moments.

"I want your hot cake," he said.

Hobos are usually a friendly and sharing lot, but when there isn't enough to share, a hobo will say so.

"This is all I have, and I'm hungry," the old man said.

The big man stepped away for a moment, then he reached for a rock. He raised the rock high and brought it down on the old hobo's head. The sound was sickening. The old man didn't know what hit him. He died instantly.

The big hobo grabbed the hot cake and began eating it as he ran away.

Other hobos looked in the direction of the dead man, grabbed their things and high-tailed it out of that jungle. The cops would pick up the first hobo they found and charge him with the crime when the murder was discovered, and no one wanted to be put in jail for something they didn't do.

I had been a hobo for less than a week and already had a lifetime of experiences. But I was to find out soon that it was just the beginning.

14

Destination Yakima

My oldest sister, Ann, welcomed me to her home in Billings. It was a bit crowded with Ann, her husband, their baby and me living under the same roof of a small house that should have housed only two people. But the bond of love that Ann and I shared in our earlier years was still strong. There was no question in her mind or mine that her home was also mine.

I felt so comfortable living with Ann and Cecil that I was able to finish the school year in Billings. I had the feeling that Ann liked having me around, too. It was like having a bit of our old family back again.

After school was out, it was time to find work for the summer, like I had done for the seven years before. However, the jobs were scarce in Billings. I visited the hobo jungle and heard that there were jobs in the orchards around Yakima, Washington.

"After finishin' the summer's work in the orchard, youse can stays on 'n' pick them same apples youse helped grow all summer," one hobo told me and three others.

"That's for me," I said.

"Me, too."

"And me."

"Let's catch the westbound."

"What time's it leave?" I asked.

"3:30."

"I'll be back," I said. "I have to say some good-byes."

It was tough to tell Ann good-bye. She didn't want me to go.

"I'll worry about you alone on the road, Monrad."

"Ann, I love you, but I have to work during the summer," I told her. "I can't just sit around and do nothing."

"You've never been one for doing nothing, Monrad. I love you, too, and you know you're always welcome in my home."

She gave me a hug and kissed me on the cheek. I hugged her back, then turned and headed out the door.

I met up with the other hobos an hour later, and we were westbound out of Billings at 3:30.

The freight stopped at a division along the way and the group I had been traveling with headed for the jungle. There was no food for us there; so some headed for town. I knew from past experience that I would be better off to look for food on my own.

I knew there were housewives that were generous and would give a hobo food in exchange for work, just like my mother had done for the hobos that visited our house when we were in Clarkston. I knew what signs to look for. A plus sign meant the people in the house were alright, and would share food. One circle inside another meant they were great people and would go out of their way to help those in need.

On my first attempt to beg for food, I got

38

within 30 feet of the front door and lost my nerve. I guess I was not quite hungry enough. I approached a second house, but, again, the results were the same. It took five more approaches and failures before my hunger pains pushed me past my bashfulness. I stood on the backdoor step, my hat in my hand, and knocked on the door. A few moments later, the door was opened and before me stood a young woman.

"Well, you're just a young boy," she said. "Can I help you?"

"Ma'am, would you have any work I could do for something to eat?"

"Follow me."

She took me to the woodshed, and gave me an ax and showed me a pile of wood to be split.

It was common for every house to have a wood pile because the cooking and heating were accomplished with wood-burning stoves. During the times when hobos were common in our great country, there were two wood piles. One pile contained the easy-to-split wood, and the other held the wood that was full of knots and therefore hard to split. Hobos looking for food were always directed to the second pile.

Hard work was not foreign to me, so I began making smaller wood chunks out of larger ones. With all those knots, sometimes it took me 20 swings of the ax to bust apart one piece of wood.

After an hour of using the ax, the young woman ap-

peared.

"My, my, you've done well for a young boy. Are you hungry?"

That was no doubt the most stupid question she could have asked me, but I answered quickly, with no sarcasm.

"Yes, ma'am."

"Well, you just sit right there on the porch, and I'll bring you something to eat."

I did as she said and, in about five minutes, she handed me a ham sandwich. It was a good sandwich, but it sure didn't fill me up. I thanked the woman for her generosity, then walked back to the train station. I never liked going to houses to ask for work in exchange for food, but it was one of the primary ways a hobo got food. When I analyze that part of hobo life, I guess it was a contractual agreement, but the hobo was always on the lower end of the deal.

One freight had already left the station by the time I got there with most of the group I had been traveling with. I waited another four hours for the next train and was again headed west, feeling the clickety-clack, clickety-clack of the rails through my body as I sat in a boxcar.

The train pulled into Ritzville, Washington, for a short stop. The need for food was so powerful that I felt I would die if my belly didn't get something to cure the hunger pains.

I looked out the front of the depot and saw a creamery across the street. I walked there and opened the door. The man inside was cleaning the machinery after a day of processing.

"Sir, I'm awful hungry and I don't have time to help you, as I usually would if I had the time, but the train I'm ridin' won't be here long, so I can't help you as I usually would, because I'm heading for Yakima to help in the orchards and with the harvest this fall and ..."

"Whoa, slow down there," the man said. "I've got some food for you."

The man gave me all the food he had with him, which consisted of a few bread rolls. I started to eat them when he stopped me.

"Here take these with you, put them in your shirt," he said. "But you need more than bread. You go down to the Womack Cafe and tell Charlie to give you a full meal, and put it on my tab."

I thanked him and ran to the cafe. Charlie fed me good. I was sopping up the last of the juice on my plate with a slice of bread when the train's whistle sounded. I waved to Charlie as I left the cafe.

The train was moving when I arrived at the track. I spotted my boxcar and grabbed the ladder at the front of the car. A short hop put my feet on the ladder. The weather was pleasant, so I rode on top of the car during the trip to Pasco. I was the only person on top, as I had hoped. If there had been others, I would have been expected to share the bread I had in my shirt, which I surely would have done. But I needed that food to nourish my body, so I could maintain my strength. I was thankful to be alone in that instance.

Pasco, Washington, is a railroad division. When the train slowed to a stop, I crawled to the ladder and climbed down. There to meet me was the railroad bull. I later learned his name was Pasco Bill.

"What are you doin' in my yard?" he yelled not wanting an answer.

Then I heard a loud "crack." It sounded like a rifle shot, but I knew the sound came from a bull whip because I felt the air from the tip of the whip near my right ear. I felt air from the second swing of the whip, too, but I was young and could run fast, so he didn't touch me.

Rumors circulated through hobo jungles in the Pacific Northwest about Pasco Bill and his ruthlessness when dealing with hobos. Having a bull make life worse for hobos was simply sadistic.

When the freight leaving Pasco for Yakima started to roll, I jumped from the bushes where I had been hiding and ran for a flatcar. I know Pasco Bill was very much alive when I left Pasco, because he had been hiding in some bushes near me. He snapped his whip at me two more times and although he did not touch my skin, the tip of his whip made a hole in my shirt. I hopped aboard the train with the words of Pasco Bill following me.

"And don't come back," he yelled.

About 20 other hobos were on board with me, headed in the same direction to find the same kind of work.

We were on a flat car; a car that has no walls.

The weather was nice, and I visited with the other men and relaxed again. I was sure glad to be out of Pasco.

During the trip, I was sitting with my feet over the edge of the car with other men alongside of me to my left and right. It was a common way to sit when the weather was nice. The scenery was nice too, and there was nothing else to do but visit and enjoy the view. As the train passed by a shale rock cliff that had a beauty of its own, a rock vibrated loose and fell on the flat car. It hit the old hobo sitting just an arm's length to my right. The rock fell on his head, killing him, then bounced off the train to the other side. There was nothing the rest of us could do until the train stopped in Yakima. Then we told a railroad worker about the incident, and that was the last I ever heard about it.

In Yakima, I was excited about getting a job in an orchard and helping with the harvest in the fall. The trouble was every other hobo west of the Mississippi had gotten word that there was work in Yakima. A park on Front Street was full of hobos sleeping on the lawn, and that is where I slept, too.

I tried to get work in Yakima for about 10 days, but there were just too many hobos. I did not work one day, and it was hard to get food. There was a mission down on skid road and after listening to the services for an hour, each hobo would get a bowl of soup that helped to keep us alive.

Most of the hobos would sleep during the preaching, but before you could get your soup, you would have to attend the services. I listened to the preaching and thought about my father and mother and the way things used to be.

After about 10 days, I decided to leave. It was evident that the people of Yakima did not want a hobo to stay in their town very long.

"In the early 1930s, my family moved to Issaquah, Washington, while my father, Jack Kastle, was starting a creamery in Ritzville, Washington. To get the creamery started, my father would drive to Ritzville, a journey of over 200 miles, on Monday mornings with a load of salmon and other seafood, which he would sell in towns along the way.

"He would return home to Issaquah on Friday evening. One Friday, as the family gathered at the table for supper, he told us about a young boy who was riding the rails. This boy begged some food from my father and my father bought him a meal at the Womack Cafe, located near the creamery. This had to be Monte. The fact that a young boy was riding the rails affected my father deeply because he also was a hobo when he was young."

Bobbie Campbell, daughter of Jack Kastle

15

Hobo Pirates

Sitting in the hobo jungle in Yakima, I was faced with the question of which way to go to find work. I could head west to the Washington coast, south to Oregon, or east to Idaho and Montana. The talk around the jungle was that there was no work anywhere, so it didn't matter which way a person headed. The 10 days spent in Yakima taught me that being in a medium-size city was not good when hundreds of men were looking for work. The thought of trying to look for work in a large city like Seattle or Portland, competing with all the other hobos that were surely there, did not appeal to me.

I came from the east, so I decided to head back that way. I figured there would be less people in that direction and maybe that would mean a chance at a job.

I climbed aboard a boxcar that was headed toward the rising sun. There were two other hobos already in the car.

"Where ya headed?" one asked.

"Spokane and then Montana," I answered. "How about you?"

"Pasco," one said.

"Missoula," said the other.

"Watch out for Pasco Bill," I said. "He's one mean bull. He put this here hole in my shirt with a lick of his whip."

"That's why I'm going to Pasco, to pay old Pasco Bill a visit. He hurt my brother real bad and I've heard he's hurt lots of others. I'm aimin'

to make sure that bull don't get no older."

I didn't pursue that line of questioning any more, but settled into a corner of the car. Not all of the people who worked for the railroad hated, or were mean to, hobos. In fact, many of them watched out for those who had to ride the rails. Perhaps they had a son or brother or other relative in the same situation I was in. Whatever the reason, I'm grateful. I'm sure I wouldn't have survived those early years on the road if it hadn't been for them. One such person was a brakeman in Yakima.

Just before the train started rolling, he stopped by the open door of our boxcar.

"As far as I'm concerned you're welcome to ride any train I'm workin' on," he said. "But I want to warn you about hijackers on this stretch between here and Pasco. They figure some hobos might have money from workin' and robbin' them is an easy way to get that money."

"We can fight 'em off," one of the hobos said.

"Don't even try. If they get into the car, do what they say or they'll throw ya off the car. We've found many bodies along the tracks on the way to Pasco. What you want to do is secure this door closed from the inside and be real quiet. The hijackers will tie a rope to the top of the car and swing down over the side and try to open the door. Good luck fellas."

The brakeman gave us a wave and continued down the tracks.

"Let's close this door," I said as the brakeman walked away. "And no one say a word during the ride, no matter what."

The three of us worked to secure the door. As the train started to pull out of the yard, the three of us settled down into separate corners of the car. I sat there looking out of one of the few cracks in the car wall. I watched the light from the setting sun fade as the clickety-clack, clickety-clack of train wheels on track lulled me to sleep.

I awoke to the sounds of three men walking on the roof of the boxcar and sounds of ropes being tied to iron supports on the roof.

"There's at least two in here," came a voice from above. "I saw em' climb in."

"Ready?" another voice asked.

"Let's go," said the third.

I could hear the hijackers start over the side. The

ropes gave them the assist they needed to go from the roof to the side of the boxcar. Then there were a few places to set a foot and get a hand hold.

"Ugh!, I can't get the door open."

"Let me help ya."

"It's stuck."

Then one pounded on the door.

Bam! Bam! Bam!

My heart was pounding too and I was afraid.

"We know you're in there," he said. "Open this door!"

"Open up right now, or we'll get you when we stop in Pasco," one of the others said.

"Oh, let's just get to the next car. I know there's eight men and a woman in there."

"A woman?"

"Yeah, let's go."

I heard them work their way back to the roof. It was dangerous for these train pirates to be on the outside of a moving boxcar. But I found myself torn between what I wished for those men and the teachings of my parents to be a nice person – I wished those men would fall and be killed, so they wouldn't hurt anyone else.

I relaxed a little and felt as secure as a hobo can be on a moving train with hijackers about. I fell asleep and dreamed of my mother. I felt warm, like I was in her arms, and she talked to me softly, telling me I was fine. She was looking out for me as best she could and the Lord was watching over me too. My mother told me to do what must be done, to avoid the men that would do me harm, and that I shouldn't worry when my thoughts about those kind of men were bad. I snuggled deeper into her arms and felt the warmth of her presence.

"Mother, I love yo ..."

A scream jolted me from sleep.

"What was that?" I asked.

"Keep your voice down," came a whisper from another corner. "Someone just got thrown off the car ahead of us."

Then another scream rent the night.

The three of us crawled to the door of the car and tried to look out.

Four more men were tossed from the car. We

heard their screams, but could see nothing. Some of the screams continued after the hobos hit the ground, so we knew those men at least survived the fall. But some of the screams stopped abruptly, leading us to believe the man was killed, either by hitting a tree or suffering a broken neck.

All was quiet for a few minutes, then we heard another scream. This was the scream of a woman, and she wasn't being thrown off the train.

"They're takin' her," someone in my car said. I didn't know what that meant, but I did know it wasn't good.

There wasn't another sound for the rest of our trip to Pasco, except the clickety-clack, clickety-clack of train wheels on railroad track.

Finally the freight began to slow to a stop. At rest in the Pasco yard, we waited a few minutes before opening the door to our car.

The brakeman was there to greet us.

"You guys OK?" he asked.

"Yeah, they tried to get in, but we fixed it so they couldn't."

"Good thing, about 50 others were robbed during the trip and some were thrown off."

"We heard some, but there wasn't anything we could do," I said as an apology.

I turned to my fellow travelers, "Good luck, you guys and remember to be on the lookout for Pasco Bill."

"Yeah, that's who I'm looking for. Pasco Bill I'm lookin' for you!" the one with revenge on his mind yelled.

I took off running in the direction of the next scheduled freight to Spokane. I didn't want to come close to the tip of Bill's whip again. I ran past two cars and passed several hobos along the way. Then I passed a hobo who was hunched over and sobbing. I stopped and took a closer look. It was the woman. My heart felt for her and I wanted to put my arms around her for comfort, but I knew it was not right to console another hobo in that manner.

"You all right ma'am?" I asked.

"Yeah, I'm all right," she said. "I'd like to kill those guys ..."

"I understand," I said. "My father is a preacher and – well, I am sure he would tell you that the Lord will watch over you."

The words seemed hollow after I had said them, but it was the only thing I could think to do.

I turned and ran again. The trip from Yakima to Pasco had been filled with turmoil and, along with the ever present hunger pains, I felt emotionally drained.

16

Dreaming of a Full Belly

The hobo jungle in Pasco was crowded. There must have been 125 people camping on a two-mile stretch of the Columbia River, which was about a mile from the train yard. Plus, there was a constant stream of hobos walking between the jungle and the yard. Half of the people were headed for Yakima to find one of the many jobs that were rumored to be waiting for them.

The other half were returning from Yakima. They knew that the rumors were just another pipe dream that caused unemployed and hungry men and women to travel hundreds of danger-filled miles with the hope of finding work.

I reached the river and headed downstream.

"Hey Mooney, over here."

I couldn't see who it was at first, but as I drew near, One-Eyed Bill welcomed me with a handshake.

"How ya doin' boy?"

The only good thing about there being so many hobos in the Pasco area was the possibility of finding a familiar face and the possibility of sharing a bit of food. I was lucky to find one right away.

"I'm all right Bill, just hungry like always."

"I'll share with ya, Mooney," he said. "Take a dip of this stew."

"Hey, he didn't help gather up any of this grub," another hobo protested. "Why ya feedin' him?"

"Just settle down, Joe," Bill said with au-

thority. "I saw this here boy git shot at to bring back two stewing chickens for a gang of us a while back. He can share my stew anytime."

The other man, although not completely satisfied that I should share the meal he helped put together, didn't protest further as Bill handed me a tin bowl filled with a sizable helping from the pot.

"Thanks Bill," I said. "Say, how's old Clarence?"

"Poor Old Clarence," Bill said. "The bull here in the Pasco yard caught up with him last month, ya know Clarence wasn't for movin' fast, bein' older and all. Well, that bull whipped him and worked him over good. His clothes were torn to pieces and his back and face was too. It just stove up Old Clarence somethin' fierce and he never got over that beatin'. He died the third night and we buried him downstream of here before the sun came up."

"Damn you, Pasco Bill," I whispered. My mother and father would have been disappointed that I cursed, but, this time, I meant it.

With so many people out of work and using the rails to try and find work, there was no reason for the bulls to be so sadistic. They had the law on their side, though, and nothing was ever said about the death of a hobo at the hand of a railroad bull.

"Say Mooney, the word is that the work's all done in Yakima, that so?" Bill asked.

"I've never seen so many men tryin' to get so little work. I'm headin' back to Montana or the Dakotas. All I want is a job, so I won't be hungry. Havin' an empty belly is gettin' to me."

"I know where you can have a full belly all the time," another hobo said.

"Where?" I asked, expecting the answer to be a joke.

"Get off the freight in Malta, Montana," he said. "Those people are always looking for someone to herd sheep on the range."

"If there's so much work there, why don't you do it?"

"I can't stand the loneliness," he said.

"I've herded sheep some in the past," I said. "I'd take the herd out in the morning and bring them back at night. I kinda liked it."

"This is different. You're on the range for weeks, maybe months at a time with only the sheep and a herd dog to keep you company."

"Who brings you the food?" I asked.

"There's a man who brings out canned food every month and you'll be able to butcher a ewe whenever you need fresh meat."

"Sounds like that's where I need to go for awhile. When's the next freight leave for Spokane?"

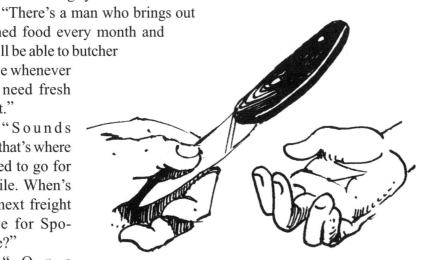

"One leaves in about 20 minutes," Bill said. "If you hurry, you can make it."

"Thanks Bill," I said shaking his hand.

I turned to go, but One-Eyed Bill stopped me.

"Mooney, one thing I know how to do is make knives, and I've just finished this here one," he said, handing the knife to me, handle first.

"I can't take your only knife, Bill."

"Look here, I've got another," he said pulling another from his pocket. "You'll need that knife in your work as a sheepherder. Now get goin', so you don't miss the freight."

I took the knife, shook his hand again, then turned and made for the rail yard at a fast trot. I felt good, like there was a purpose to my life.

When I reached the yard, the Spokane freight was starting to pick up speed. I ran straight for an open boxcar where three men were sitting. Normally, I would grab the ladder at the beginning of a moving car, but one of the men motioned for me to go to the opening. When I was alongside, he extended his hand. I grabbed it with my right hand, but he was not strong enough to pull me into the car.

"Keep runnin', I can't hold on," the man said.

My grip was slipping too, but there was nothing I could do. Even though my left hand was flailing in the wind, trying to grab hold of anything, there was nothing to grab. My hand was slipping from the man's hand and the good thoughts about herding sheep in Montana were forgotten by a good dose of primeval fear. My hand was slipping, but I was squeezing harder and I kept running, but it was harder with each step to keep my footing. My heart was beating faster and I was gasping for breath. Suddenly another hand grabbed my belt at the small of my back and threw me to the bed of the car.

I lay there, face down in a heap, hugging the rough planking of the floor, thanking God that I was alive.

"Look, you two – Next time reach past the hand and grab the forearm," the man who helped me aboard said. "Like this ..."

He flipped me over and made me try the grip with him. Then he went to the other man and showed him. All I could think about was how close I came to death or at least serious injury and this good Samaritan shrugged the event off like it happened everyday.

"Now, do you understand?" he said, looking me in the face.

"Yeah, thanks mister."

"Wasn't nothin'," he said. "Where ya headed?"

"Spokane, then Montana. How about you?"

"I want to get back to Chicago."

"Is there work there?" one of the others asked.

"I used to work makin' cars. Maybe I can do somethin' there again."

We were 10 miles down the track before I could breathe normally again.

The four of us talked all the way to Spokane. The third man was from California and wanted to get far away from there, but he didn't say exactly why. The other was from Florida. He said the job situation was bad there too.

"As soon as I find a job, I'm going to send for my wife and two daughters," he said. "I sure do miss 'em."

This chat helped me to realize that our great country was not doing well, with jobs in short supply. Families were being torn apart, not because they didn't get along, but as a necessity as

one or more adults crossed the country trying to find work.

The four of us hopped off the freight in Spokane. The other three headed for the jungle. I thanked them again and shook their hands; then I walked to the Great Northern line, about a mile away. The train wasn't scheduled to leave for two hours, but I didn't want to miss it or get aboard when it was moving faster than a slow roll.

I found an empty boxcar and climbed aboard. This car had doors on both sides and they were both open. The entire inside was visible because of the open doors, but there were three empty apple boxes near the middle. I arranged them as a barrier and settled into a corner behind the boxes and fell asleep. My thoughts turned to herding sheep in Montana and having a full belly. I felt good.

"Well what do we have here?"

I was instantly awake and looking up at a big man standing just five feet away.

"I like to be friends with young boys like you," he said.

"Where ya headed mister?" I asked trying to sound friendly. "My friends will be along shortly."

"Never mind where I'm headed. Now, why don't you come closer and we can be real friends."

He started to undo his belt and I knew I was in trouble. My hand felt the handle of the knife.

My first thought was to lunge at this pervert and bury the knife blade in his belly, but my second thought prevailed. My position, sitting on the floor, put me at a disadvantage.

"Wait a minute mister, OK, ah, let me get up here," I said as a stalling tactic.

When I was on my feet, the man took a step in my direction with lust in his eyes. The apple boxes that had served to hide me, were viewed by this man as a barrier to keep me confined in the corner. I knew differently; they were but a false barrier of thin wood. I stepped to the right, which made the man step in that direction too. But I was young, agile and fast. I changed directions, moving left, and jumped over the apple boxes. I felt the fingers of his hand graze my shirt and one of his fingers got stuck in the hole put there by Pasco Bill. The shirt ripped more, but the man didn't have a secure hold and I was out the open boxcar door in a flash.

The man was fast behind me as I ran to the end of the car and climbed up the ladder. He followed me and chased me across the roof of that car and the next one, too. He couldn't catch me; I was too fast. Finally he gave up the chase, cursed me and walked away.

I rode on top of the car from Spokane to Montana. I wanted an open view in all directions, to watch out for danger. Two other hobos rode on top of the car behind me and three on the car in front of me, but I rode alone on this trip. I tried to think about something good and turned my thoughts to cooking all the food I wanted and having enough to share some of that food with a sheepdog.

The freight finally pulled into Malta, Montana, and I stepped down from the boxcar ladder looking for a new life as a sheepherder with a full belly.

17

Hired On

Malta, Montana, was a center for sheep and cattle ranchers when I was a youngster. Having herded sheep when I was 7 years old, I thought I was more qualified to be a sheepherder than a cowboy.

"Excuse me, mister, where can I find the sheep ranchers?" I asked a man near the train depot.

"All the sheep men stay at The Great Northern Hotel in this town, sonny," the man replied.

"Where's the Great Northern?" I asked.

"Down there just around the corner," he said pointing.

I walked down the street, around the corner and into the hotel. The floor was polished and the windows were spotless. The chairs in the lobby showed little wear and the brass door knobs shined. It was obvious to me that a great deal of effort was made to maintain this hotel; the finest I had ever seen.

Suddenly I felt intimidated by the beautiful surroundings and a little shy about standing there looking every bit of the hobo I was. After all, I had been riding the rails for some time now and the only possessions I owned were the clothes on my back, a bedroll and the knife given to me by One-Eyed Bill. But, if this was the place to make a connection with a sheepman, this is where I had to be.

"Pardon me, sir," I said to the clerk be-

hind the counter, "Do you know of any sheepmen around who are looking for a herder?"

"Well young man, there is an outfit, the Hensen Brothers, that is looking," he said. "Why don't you have a seat in that chair, over there, and I'll tell Louis Hensen that we have a sheepherder in our lobby looking for a job."

I sat down in the chair. It was soft, with lots of padding and there was a springy feeling in the seat. I placed my bedroll in my lap and tried to sit up straight as I waited, but the chair was very comfortable. I caught myself dozing off a couple times and jerked awake as my head nodded forward. After a few minutes, I leaned against the right side of the chair and my head touched the upper part, my eyes closed ...

"Wake up son, I'm Louis Hensen. Are you a sheepherder?"

The voice jolted me awake, and I was staring into the face of a man standing not two feet away.

"Ah, yes sir," I stammered trying to shake the sleep from my eyes. "I herded sheep when I was seven years old and lived in Rapelje."

"Well, you look pretty young right now, and bein' that young and on the road, you're most likely runnin' from something, but if you want to go out herdin' sheep, I'll give you a try. The pay is 30 dollars a month and your food, but you'll have to cook for yourself."

I had been belly-aching hungry for so long

that I blurted out a lie, "I'm a good cook, sir."

"OK then, we'll leave Malta tomorrow mornin' at four."

"Thank you, Mr. Hensen," I said and started walking for the door.

"Whoa there, where you goin'?"

"I guess I'll sleep in the jungle."

"Young man, ... say what is your name?"

"Monrad Holm, but my friends call me Mooney."

"Well Mooney, now that you're workin' for me, why don't you stay here, in the hotel?" You can have a good supper tonight too. I'll just take those expenses out of your pay when you come off the range."

I thought I'd died and gone to heaven. Mr. Hensen walked over to the hotel clerk and told him to get me a room and that I should get a bath and supper too. I hadn't even seen one of Mr. Hensen's sheep and I already loved them all.

It was early afternoon and I had nothing else to do, so I asked the clerk if I could get my clothes washed as long as I was going to wash my body. He laughed and made the arrangements for the bathtub upstairs to be filled with hot water.

"Now as soon as you strip down, tie all your clothes in a bundle in your shirt and set 'em in the hall," the clerk said. "Take a nice long bath and I'll have your things washed, and that rip in the back of your shirt stitched up too."

I did as the clerk said and placed my clothes, along with my bedroll, just outside the door of the room with the tub. I placed my knife and the only money I had, a quarter, two dimes and five pennies, on a chair within reach of my position in the tub.

It felt good to settle into the hot steaming water. I scrubbed my hair and every other part of my body, then relaxed and lay back. When I had been soaking for some time and figured it was about time to get out, there was a knock at the door, then the door opened. In stepped a boy, not much younger than me.

"Hi there," he said. "Joe told me to get you some more hot water."

He took an empty bucket and dipped it right in the tub and took it out filled with bath water.

"I'll be right back," he said as he walked to the door.

He was back with the same bucket, but this time it was filled with piping hot water.

"Careful now, this is hot," he said as the fresh water began to mix with what was already in the tub.

It was hot and it felt good. I soaked for another 15 minutes and the kid came back.

"My mother said to tell you your clothes aren't done yet, so I should get you another bucket of hot water."

He repeated the task of taking cool water from the bath and bringing back hot water, but by this time, I was starting to feel waterlogged.

"How much longer will it be?"

"Not much," the kid said. "They're about done. Maybe another 15 minutes or so."

I thought about my time on the rails and how dirty and dusty it was. Then I thought about the times I jumped into cold rivers and lakes just to scrape a few layers of dirt off, all the while dreaming of a long, hot bath. I lay back and forced myself to relax. The hot water felt good, real good.

Twenty minutes later the kid was back with my washed and pressed clothes.

"Mother said to tell you she was sorry to take so long, but she wanted to do a good job of sewing up that rip in your shirt."

"You tell your mother that I appreciate her work, and I appreciate you attendin' to me. How do I pay her?"

"The Great Northern will pay us, and Mr. Hensen will pay the Great Northern; then he will take it out of your pay."

I thought that was a great arrangement.

"Say, when's supper?"

"They start servin' in about 30 minutes."

I toweled dry and slipped on my clean clothes and mended shirt. I was clean, body and clothes, and I felt good.

My room was down the hall and contained a bed and a chest of drawers with a water basin and pitcher sitting on top. I lay on the bed and marveled at how good a bed felt. My eyes focused on the ceiling, then closed.

The sound of men walking outside the door awakened me. They were headed downstairs. I was off the bed and out the door in a flash. I didn't want to miss supper.

"I'm working for Mr. Hensen," I told the woman in the dining room.

"I know," she said. "Order anything off the menu."

A sizable bowl of stew and two big slices of bread were the first items placed before me. They disappeared quickly.

"Can I order something else?"

"Anything you want."

I asked for the roast beef and it was brought. I slowed down a bit about halfway through the slab of beef, realizing that if I finished it, I would have no food left.

"I'd like another bowl of that stew, please."

"My, you're a hungry one," the lady said as she brought me a second helping of stew.

I ate the stew, but slower this time. The left over roast beef was placed between the two slices

of bread from the second bowl of stew. I was about to place the sandwich in my shirt, but the woman stopped me.

"Here, let me wrap that up for you."

She took a page of newspaper and folded it around the bread and beef. I thanked her and left. This was the first time I hoarded food. Because hunger is a common sensation experienced by hobos, they have a tendency to always stash a bit of the food they get their hands on and save it for the times they will need it. Hobos know those times might be, and usually are, right around the corner.

I went to my room and locked the door. I folded my clean clothes properly as I took them off, then crawled between the sheets of the bed.

"I like bein' a sheepherder," I thought as my head settled into the pillow.

"The Great Northern Hotel was built by the Sklower family in 1903. It was reported to be one of the finest hotels in Montana, with a ballroom, dining room, a bar, and 31 guest rooms. The two-story structure was known as the meeting place for everyone, including the sheepmen."

Diane Smith, author and historian

18

Traveling to the Sheep

Bam! Bam! Bam!

"Mooney, wake up, it's time to get on the road," Mr. Hensen said as he pounded on the door.

"OK, Mr. Hensen, I'm awake."

I scrambled into my clothes and poured a little water into the bowl on the dresser. The cool water on my face helped wash the sleep from my eyes. I ran my fingers through my hair realizing that was the best I could do without a comb; then I was out the door and down the stairs.

Mr. Hensen was at the counter signing the bill for both of us.

"Tell Sam I'll be in at the end of the month to settle up," he told the clerk. "Come on Mooney, we've got a lot of ground to cover."

It was the first time I had stepped outside the hotel in over 18 hours and I was surprised to see that it had rained during the night. Usually I was aware of all weather changes, but my sleep was so deep from having clean clothes, a clean body and a full belly, that this rain had skipped my notice.

We crawled into his truck and headed out of town. The road ahead of us was nothing more than a trail. Sometimes during the trip to the ranch, I wondered if we were even following a trail or if Mr. Hensen was just heading across the prairie making a new trail as he headed in the direction of his ranch.

The rain had turned the ground into a soggy mess. Eastern Montana is dusty when dry, but turns into a sticky-gooey-gummy mixture of soil and water when wet. The locals coined the term gumbo to describe it because the mixture sticks to everything.

Mr. Hensen snaked his vehicle along the so-called road for a few miles, then, in a low spot filled with water, the wheels began to spin and the truck stopped.

"Time to start earning your pay, Mooney. Get out and give me a push."

I did and we were out of the puddle after a few minutes of me pushing and Mr. Hensen's rocking the truck.

The mud stuck to my boots and more mud became attached with each step. I hesitated before climbing back into the truck with mud covered boots, and dirty pants.

"Just get in and don't worry about that gumbo." Mr. Hensen said. "It sticks to everything, including boots and tires."

Thirty minutes later we were stuck again. This time I was out of the truck and pushing without being told to do so. It was then that I noticed the car tires were bigger because of the gumbo. The stuff didn't help the car get traction and we became stuck many times, and each time I pushed us out of knee-deep water, mud and gumbo.

When I was back in the truck the hunger pains hit. I pulled out the beef and bread wrapped in the newspaper and unwrapped it.

"Mr. Hensen, would you like half of my sandwich?"

"Sally said she wrapped you a sandwich," he said. "Sure, I could use a little of it. I like you Mooney, you're a smart young man. There's no place to get grub when I have to leave so early, and I get mighty hungry by the time we get to the Hog Ranch."

I split the sandwich and gave Mr. Hensen the biggest part.

"What's the Hog Ranch?" I asked as we ate.

"It's a spot on the old Colburn Ranch, now the Matador Ranch, that has a post office and store. That's where I get gas sometimes because it's about half way between Malta and my ranch."

We arrived at the Hog Ranch six hours later. Mr. Hensen bought gas for the car and refilled the two gas cans that were strapped to the back of the vehicle. He also bought several chunks of beef jerky. Then he saw me looking at the jars of hard candy.

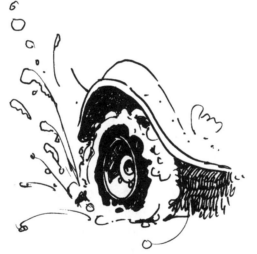

"What kind do you like best?" he asked.

"This horehound kind," I said. "I haven't had any in two years."

"Get Mooney two pieces of the horehound," he said to the store owner. "You might want to save one of those pieces for when you're on the range," he said handing me the candy.

That's just what I had in mind. The first piece was in my mouth before we left the store, but the second piece was in my pocket, to be eaten later.

We climbed into the truck and headed south again. The gumbo was as bad as during the first half of our trip. The car got stuck several times, and I pushed and pushed and pushed. Mr. Hensen gave me a piece of jerky from time to time, but that was the only other food we had that day.

Finally we arrived at the Hensen Ranch at 10 p.m. We had made good time, according to Mr. Hensen. The ranch was situated about 60 miles south of Malta, east of Zortman and just north of the Missouri breaks.

"That's the bunk house, over there," Mr. Hensen said. "You find a bed, and we'll leave for your sheep wagon at five in the morning."

As an afterthought he handed me two pieces of jerky.

"It's too late to get grub tonight. These will have to do."

Then he turned and headed for the main house.

The clouds that brought the rain had dissipated a bit and a full moon provided enough light for me to see a little. I walked to the bunk house, opened the door as quietly as possible, and stepped inside. I took off my boots by the door and left them there. Then I quietly made my way to an empty bunk. I left my clothes on, lay down, pulled my bed roll over me and was fast asleep.

Bam! Bam! Bam! "Everybody up!"

It was Mr. Hensen again.

"You're eatin' in five minutes."

There were three other men in the room. One was already dressed and headed for the outhouse, another was lacing up his boots and the third was yawning and stretching. I rubbed the sleep from my eyes, folded and rolled my bed roll, then put on my boots.

They were an odd bunch. During breakfast, only Louis Hensen and his brother, Paul, said a thing, barking out a few orders.

"Joe, you ride south. There's been a lot of coyotes howling down there, and I wonder if there's some strays down that way. Ken, I want you to head east and look that way. Sam, you stay around here today and finish choppin' the

53

rest of that wood we gathered last week."

I was amazed at the sight around me. While those orders flowed forth from the mouths of the Hensen brothers, no one at the table looked up or even acknowledged the direction given by their bosses. Everyone was eating and eating fast. I did the same, shoveling food in my mouth and swallowing with a minimum amount of chewing.

"You about finished, Mooney?" Louis asked. "We've got to get you to your sheep wagon."

And with that he was up and out the door. I was quick to follow. As we headed down the road, Mr. Hensen gave me an overall view of his operation.

"My brother and I have a big ranch. If a person were to ride across it, he would travel 100 miles, and it takes 100 miles to cover it in the other direction too. We have a herder stationed about every 10 miles in all directions. Once a month, someone will be out to move your wagon so the sheep can eat the grass in another area. Otherwise they starve. These sheep are important to us. Guard them from all danger. Shoot any coyote you come across. You can have an old ewe, that has lost a lamb, to eat whenever you need one, but eat your other food up too. There are a few sage hens around and you can eat those if you can get one, but don't waste your shells. You are not to visit with another herder, unless there's trouble. We want you to keep the flocks apart."

We must have traveled 20 miles when a sheepherder's wagon came into view.

"Howdy, Mr. Hensen," the herder said when we stopped the truck.

"Hi, Willard. Ready to go?"

"Yes, sir. Who's the kid?"

"This here's Mooney. He's going to take over for ya."

"Mooney, let me show ya around. This is the water barrel. I see Mr. Hensen's brought enough water to top it off. Keep the lid on tight, and don't waste it; that's all you've got. Here's the Winchester .33 and five boxes of shells. There's lots of coyotes around, and they can kill a lot of sheep if you don't keep the population down. These sheep know where they want to go in the morning, so just follow them. They'll bed down during the heat of the day and eat more in the afternoon. In the evening you'll have to get them back here. That's where the dogs come in. The brown one is Tom, and the other is Blackie. They're both good dogs, but Tom is the friendliest. Those dogs will alert you to danger you don't see. Oh, and watch out for the rattlesnakes. I'm ready; can we go now, Mr. Hensen?"

"How many sheep do I have to herd?" I asked.

"Three thousand."

Suddenly I didn't know if I could handle the job. There were many more sheep than I had to take care of before. Mr. Hensen must have sensed my apprehension by the look on my face. The other herder was in the car ready to go when Mr. Hensen walked over and stood in front of me.

"By the way, Mooney; if a herder abandons his sheep in Montana, they get an automatic two years in the state pen," he said softly, but firmly.

He then walked to the truck and drove away.

The other herder waved and yelled, "See ya Mooney," as they drove off.

I stood there as if glued to the spot and watched the truck until it was out of sight and I was alone. I wasn't quite sure what kind of pickle I had gotten into at that point. I felt funny about the situation, but my belly was full. Yet something didn't seem right. I jumped at the touch of a wet nose. It was Tom. He licked my hand. I scratched his ear. We were friends.

"Like my time in the bath tub," I reasoned to myself, "maybe it's time to sit back, relax and enjoy what I've got for awhile."

I sat down on the step of the wagon and looked at the herd that was now my responsibility.

"Three thousand," I said in disbelief.

"In the 1930s, the road from Malta to Zortman was merely a trail called the D–Y Trail, which stood for Dominion and Yellowstone. This trail stretched from the Canadian border to

Yellowstone National Park.

 "Gumbo is still the term used for the mud that is formed when it rains around Malta and Zortman. It sticks to everything.

 "The Hog Ranch was a halfway house and store used as a stagecoach stop in the early days of Montana. When the Hensens traveled the area, it was a general store.

 "Louis and Paul Hensen ran one of the largest ranches in Phillips County, Montana. They ran many bands of sheep, several head of cattle, and a haying operation."

Diane Smith, author and historian

19

On the Range

My emotions were mixed during the first afternoon at the sheep wagon. I knew my belly would be full during my time on the range, but there was an indescribable void from the start.

As soon as Mr. Hensen was out of sight, I took stock of my life. My home would be the standard sheepherder's wagon held up by four wooden-spoke wheels with an iron rim on the outside of each one. The wagon was covered with a canvas, just like the covered wagons that traveled the Oregon Trail. Attached to the outside of the wagon was a 50-gallon barrel filled with water and three storage compartments filled with various tools and supplies.

Inside there was a wooden bed area, a small table and a stove. A bench took up part of the right side. The top of the bench was hinged to allow storage underneath it. Most of my food was there, and it consisted of a considerable amount of dried beans, about 25 pounds of potatoes, 20 pounds of flour, a crock half full of lard, about 10 pounds of sowbelly and about three pounds of dried fruit. A cast iron skillet and Dutch oven, without legs, served as my cooking pots. Two spoons, one large

and one small, a table fork and a butcher knife were my utensils. And, I still had the knife One-Eyed Bill gave me.

The sowbelly was important because it was the only kind of meat that would keep without refrigeration. And the slab, also called salt pork, provided the cooking fat I needed to prepare my meals. Any fat that was left in the skillet when I was finished cooking would be poured into the crock for storage.

There was not a can opener in sight and no canned food, as I thought there would be. I noticed a second crock sitting near the stove and found it contained a starter of sourdough.

"Good," I thought, "at least I can make bread and pancakes."

I could see that I was going to have to cook everything from the ground up; from scratch. Water was scarce in this country. My water supply, in the 50 gallon barrel, was the only drinking and cooking water I had, and it needed to last until the next supply wagon came by in about six weeks.

The sheep watered in lakes and ponds, which were alkali water and tasted terrible to me. I didn't have much sympathy for them though, because the water in the barrel tasted terrible after a few days in the hot Montana sun.

I checked the Winchester .33 and again counted five boxes of shells containing 20 rounds each and found another box that was half empty. A little bit of firewood, about one-eighth of a cord, was stacked beside the right front wheel. There were no trees in sight, so I knew firewood was a precious commodity. Mixed in with the larger wood chunks were some pieces of sagebrush.

There was no bathroom facility, except the great outdoors, and not a bit of toilet paper either. I could tell that Willard had been using the pages from an old Sears catalog and an old Farmer's Almanac for toilet paper, but if I used the pages from those two

books, I would have nothing to read.

When a person is alone in the middle of nowhere, with no company except the sheep dogs, any reading material becomes precious. You would be amazed at how well the soft tips of sagebrush will work as a toilet paper substitute. I wasn't about to use up my only reading material for toilet paper when there was plenty of sagebrush around.

I sat on the front of the wagon and surveyed the surrounding area.

What this country lacked in trees, it made up in sagebrush, which sometimes reached a height of five feet.

There were open spaces between sagebrush patches where the lush green of spring-growing bunch grass lured hungry sheep to eat their fill. But also in the open areas prickly pear cactus grew in abundance. Their long, sharp stickers could cause a nasty injury when encountered. There was an abundance of rocks in the area; some small and some large.

It was late afternoon when I took my first walk around the herd. Tom and Blackie followed me; Tom was right beside me, but Blackie stayed about 10 yards away. The sheep were down for the night and were calm, with lambs sleeping next to their mothers. It was a tranquil scene, and it made me feel good.

Suddenly the sheep up ahead, about 80 yards away, started bleating and several got to their feet. Blackie took off in that direction with Tom close behind. I ran too, but could not keep up and stopped on a knoll that provided a view. From 50 yards away, I watched as a coyote let go of the back leg of a large ewe he was trying to bring down, and scoot out of the herd with Tom and Blackie at his heels.

I cursed the fact that the Winchester was back at the wagon and not in my hands.

The three ran away from me and over the edge of a draw 150 yards away and disappeared.

Five seconds later Tom and Blackie were in sight again and still running at top speed, but this time toward me. Now though, the pursuers were the pursued as four coyotes were right behind them. Suddenly another coyote joined the chase. He had been hiding in a clump of sagebrush 100 yards away from where I was, then a sixth coyote jumped from tall bunch grass and joined the hunt.

I was now running in the direction of my dogs, to save them from what I thought was sure death. My line of direction took me off the knoll and into a slight dip for about 10 yards, which caused me to lose sight of the pursuit. When I once again had the dogs and coyotes in view, I noticed a change. While the two fresh coyotes continued to chase the dogs, the other four turned and dashed into the sheep herd and killed a lamb. Then one of them grabbed the neck and another the hindquarters and were making off with it at a fast gallop. I yelled trying to scare the coyotes chasing my dogs who were just 50 yards away now. The tactic worked. They turned and made a quick retreat over the edge of the draw where the other four, with the dead lamb, vanished.

Once again I cursed the fact that the rifle was not with me.

Tom and Blackie were completely winded. Both of them ran past me, stopped, then circled to a position just behind me. Tom came close,

sat down and whimpered. Blackie was closer to me than he had ever been, but he wouldn't stand still. He trotted nervously back and forth, growling.

"Let's go check out that ewe," I said to them, and we started walking into the herd.

The old ewe had punctures on both sides of her left hind leg and her hide was badly torn. She couldn't get up. I figured this was a good time to get some meat for the next couple of days, so I put a stop to her suffering and dressed her. As I pulled the carcass back to the wagon, we, my two partners and I, moved the herd closer to the wagon for the night.

Once there, I skinned the ewe and knew right away that eating this critter was going to be a difficult job; not because there was more than I could eat before the meat spoiled, but because an old mutton does not make good table fare. To put it bluntly, the meat stinks and, as I found out after cooking a mess of it, it tastes like it smells. But I didn't want to waste it, so I forced myself to eat it. To help get rid of it, I fed extra helpings to Tom and Blackie, who ate it with vigor.

I placed the boned pieces of mutton into the crock of lard. I sat the crock next to the stove, which was still warm. The melting lard would provide an air tight seal over the meat, which would be used as a main part of my meals for the next two days. I added flour and some water to the sourdough starter, then set it behind the stove to work during the night. The dogs had been feasting on the bone pile left from the ewe. I noticed Blackie would get a bone, eat the scraps of meat left on it, then find a spot not far away and bury it. Tom did the same, but didn't eat or bury so much.

From my perch on the wagon step, I watched the sun set and the twilight turned to darkness. Tom walked over, sat below me and started to whimper.

"Need a friend?' I asked out loud. "Look at me, not even one day on the range and I'm already talkin' to the dogs."

I climbed off the wagon and lay on my back on the ground. The sky was filled with twinkling stars from horizon to horizon. Once in a while a shooting star would flash across the heavens. I thought about my full belly and how good it was not to be hungry. Then I thought about my mother, my aunt and my brothers and sisters. I became melancholy, but I continued to watch the light show above. I jumped when Tom whimpered close by.

"It's OK boy, we'll get through this."

He was right next to me now and I scratched his ear and ran my hand down the length of his body. He put his head on my belly and sighed.

I listened as Blackie finished gnawing on another bone, then the black dog walked back to where Tom and I lay and stopped.

"How ya doin' boy?"

He turned and walked to a spot near my feet and laid down. He held his head high, looked over the herd one last time, then flopped over on his side. Blackie's hind paws came in contact with my left foot. I gently pushed with my foot and he pushed back. It was the first physical contact between us.

"Well, at least we're all friends," I thought as the three of us fell asleep.

The first coyote howl jolted me awake. It was so far off the dogs didn't even wake up. The singing of a closer coyote a couple of minutes later had both dogs up and barking. Then a coyote, closer yet, began the familiar yip, yip, yip of the wild dog. I stepped to the wagon, lit the kerosene lamp and found the Winchester. I cocked the hammer, pointed the barrel in the air and pulled the trigger: Click. More coyotes were singing now and they seemed to be getting closer. I worked the lever action and again pulled the trigger: Bang!

A few sheep jumped to their feet, but settled down right away. The coyotes continued to yip and sing, but away from the herd. Tom and Blackie seemed to know when the wild dogs were closing to within an uncomfortable distance of the herd. I decided to trust them to let me know when I should be concerned.

I returned to the wagon and put the rifle away, uncocked and with an empty chamber. I crawled into my bed and blew out the kerosene lantern. I listened to the song of the coyotes in the distance, then the soft sounds of Blackie snoring reached me, and I knew the herd was safe. I relaxed and fell asleep.

20

Settling into a Routine

My first morning on the range, I settled into a regular routine. I was up at first light to cook my breakfast of a slice of sowbelly and a pancake. Then I fished two chunks of mutton out of the crock and cooked it in the pan for Tom and Blackie. When I came out of the wagon with the finished product, they were both chewing on bones that were buried the night before. They seemed surprised to get a bite to eat at the start of the day, which led me to think Willard only fed them in the evening.

"We're working together, the three of us, and we all need to eat. As long as I'm out here, you'll eat when I eat."

Then I went back to the wagon and started to put the cooking items away. I stopped and smiled.

"Why not take lunch along," I thought. Another slice of sowbelly was thrown in the frying pan. Another pancake was cooked. The pancake was rolled around the sowbelly and placed inside my shirt. To keep my promise, two more chunks of mutton were cooked.

I was dampening down the fire when I heard the dogs begin to bark. I looked outside and noticed the herd was up and moving. I poured the extra pork fat into the crock, grabbed the Winchester, along with an extra box of shells, and headed out the door to catch up with the rear end of the herd.

The herd headed west, eating as they went.

They seemed to have a destination in mind because their direction was deliberate. Although any one of the critters would stop and eat a clump of bunch grass if it was close to them, their pace was not slow. We were on the move.

I took a closer look at the bunch grass at the side of the herd and noticed the herd had passed that way before. The grass had been eaten during another pass, perhaps the day before or the day before that. Then the herd slowed. We arrived at a place that the herd had not been that year. The bunch grass was abundant and the white fleece balls spread out in what, I was soon to learn, was a normal feeding pattern.

I walked around the entire herd of 3,000 sheep in an effort to see what I was responsible for. It took me over an hour to complete the circle. Then I walked through the animals to learn their condition. There was about a 50 - 50 split of ewes and lambs. Most of them were in good shape, but a few, about five, were limping. I looked those over good and felt their injuries were simple sprains and not serious.

When I finished my assessment, the sheep began to bunch closer together and lay down. It was mid-afternoon and the hottest part of the day. I remembered my lunch and pulled out the pancake and sowbelly sandwich. But before I began eating, I called Tom and Blackie. They again seemed puzzled to get a bite to eat during the day, but they didn't hesitate to consume the chunk of cooked mutton set before them.

"Nice to have a bite during the day, isn't it?" I said to the dogs. "Now back to the flock."

I motioned with my arm and the dogs took off towards the sheep. One circled to the left and the other the right. Each took a position where they could watch over the animals, then lay down as the sheep had done, each about 50 yards from my position.

The shade of a large sagebrush looked inviting, and when I was seated, I ate my sandwich. It was the first time in 18 months that food had passed my lips before hunger pains were intense.

"I could get used to this," I said out loud. I looked over the herd one more time, then stretched out and fell asleep.

When a person is herding sheep, time has no meaning. The animals move to their feeding grounds in the morning, rest during the heat of the day, feed again in the late afternoon and are herded back to the wagon for the night.

I knew the herd was moving again when the dogs began to bark. I wasn't in a hurry because I could catch up to them with a fast walk or a slow trot. I stretched my body to its full length, flexing each of my muscles. It felt good to have a full belly and not have to worry about other people stealing your possessions.

I was startled by movement near my left side and something brushing against me. My mind was instantly alert and I was wide awake as my eyes focused on a large rattlesnake beginning to coil next to my stomach. Don't let anyone tell you that a person can't jump straight up from a position on their back. I know such a feat is possible because I did it. I must have yelled as my

body went from horizontal to vertical because 10 seconds later Tom and Blackie were by my side. We were now about 20 feet from the rattler.

Tom barked and jumped about excitedly. Blackie let out a deep growl that would have made me fearful of him if the sound were intended for me. The black dog deliberately moved in the direction of the snake, which was curled in a tight spiral and shaking its tail in warning.

"Blackie, get back here!" I yelled, then I repeated the command. It was no use. The dog was moving closer and I thought I would be burying him that afternoon. I would have tried to shoot the snake, but the Winchester was on the other side of the fanged reptile, still leaning against the sagebrush where I had left it.

Blackie was still growling and heading for the snake. It struck at the dog, but Blackie was quick to jump out of the way. The rattler had extended about two-thirds of its body length during the strike and that seemed to be what Blackie wanted. He started circling the snake, around and around, in a clockwise direction. The snake lunged in the dog's direction two, three, four times, but Blackie was always just out of reach.

On the fifth strike, the snake didn't bother to regain its coiled position as it had after the other strikes. It started to crawl away and Blackie continued to circle. The snake slithered toward the shade of the sagebrush where I had been laying and Blackie continued to circle. When its entire body was as stretched as it could get and the snake wasn't paying too much attention to the dog, Blackie circled one more time; past the head, past the tail. Then he darted from the tail to the head, not in the circle, but along the snake's body. He bared his teeth and snapped at it just behind the head. The snake began to twist and wiggle and turn in all directions. I thought Blackie was a goner for sure, but then I noticed him sitting down and watching the snake from a safe distance.

The gyrations of the snake began to slow and I saw that Blackie had broken the snake's backbone, near its head, with his teeth. I called him over and patted his head and scratched his ear.

"Good job, boy."

Then he was off, running in the direction the sheep had taken, with Tom on his tail. Killing the snake was equal to saving my life, but to Blackie it was all part of the job, and now he wanted to make sure the sheep were OK.

I looked back at the snake. It was still moving, bringing to mind a saying that a snake doesn't die until sundown. I didn't want to stay and find out, so I turned to go. The Winchester caught my eye, and it scared me that I almost forgot it. I ran past the snake, grabbed the rifle, then past the snake again and in the direction of the herd.

When I caught up to the sheep, Blackie had killed another rattler. Then I noticed a lamb a short distance from the snake. The right leg of the lamb was swelling. The lamb was snake-bit. There's only one thing a herder can do when an animal under their care gets too close to a rattler.

I took my knife out of my pocket and approached the lamb. I grabbed the muzzle and tilted it towards the sky. In one swift motion, I slit its throat from one ear to the other. The lamb stood there, still blatting, with blood gushing from the throat area. I turned and walked away. I didn't want to look into those eyes again. A couple of minutes later, the blatting stopped and a deafening silence en-

gulfed the land around me.

I felt sad and mad at myself because I didn't protect the lamb as I should have. My moment of self pity was interrupted by Tom barking in the middle of the herd. I found him standing over an old ewe. It was dead.

"Oh no, what happened now?"

I looked the sheep over from head to toe and could find nothing wrong. Then I opened her mouth and saw that her teeth were worn considerably. She had died of old age. She had a lamb and it was nearby making a ruckus.

I remembered there was one ewe without a lamb and now one lamb without a mother. I needed to get the two together. I found the ewe at the back of the herd, still looking for her lamb. She sniffed the new lamb, but would have nothing to do with it. This was a real predicament. I didn't want to let the lamb die and it surely would without the care of a ewe.

I thought about what my father would do and my experiences as a herder when I was 7 years old. Then I remembered a procedure called slickering.

I called the dogs to me and told Tom to stay with the herd and had Blackie go with me. I trotted towards the snake-bit lamb, about a mile back of the herd now. When we were about 50 yards from the spot, Blackie started to growl. Up ahead, there was another growl, and another and another, all coming from different animals. Then we heard the yip, yip, yip of a coyote.

I cocked a round in the chamber of the rifle and

walked ahead. Blackie was on my left, but he was behind me. He knew he couldn't take on several coyotes by himself.

At 20 yards, one of the coyotes spotted me and the pack took off. Four ran up the side of a small hill to my right. I got a bead on one and fired. The animal dropped and didn't move again. I worked the lever-action of the rifle, putting a new round in the chamber, but the other three were over the hill and out of sight. Blackie barked; he was looking to the left. A fifth coyote was trying to sneak out of the area, but Blackie's bark had him on the move. I brought the rifle to shoulder, gave him a good lead and pulled the trigger.

The bullet hit the ground two feet behind the song dog. I cocked the gun again, led it more and fired. The coyote hit the ground, twitched a couple of times and died.

We found the lamb partially eaten. I skinned it, taking care to avoid the affected portion of the leg. Then Blackie and I walked back to the herd.

The orphaned lamb wasn't hard to find. It was still hungry and bleating, and the ewe of the dead lamb wasn't about to let it feed. I placed the skin of the dead lamb over the head, neck and back of the hungry lamb and tied it in place. When I released the lamb, it once again ran to the ewe, who once again sniffed it good. It smelled like her lamb, so she let it eat.

I sat back and watched the two, and I felt good.

"At least something good happened today," I said to Tom and Blackie, who sat nearby watching. I looked at the sun. It was starting to drop in the west. "Let's get these critters back to the wagon."

I whistled and yelled "bunch!" The dogs turned the sheep in the direction I was walking. They would nip at the heels of any sheep that didn't want to comply, and we walked at a brisk pace back to the wagon.

I cooked supper for the dogs and me, then walked the herd once more. The sheep were bedding down as the sun set.

"What a day," I said to the dogs as we got back to the wagon again. I sat on the step and looked at the stars. They were beautiful and bright. The coyotes were singing in the distance, no doubt feasting on the lamb carcass.

"I hope they all die of snake poison," I said to Tom and Blackie.

When it was completely dark, I crawled into bed. Sleep came easy after my first full day on the range.

21

Thinking About Life

My belly was full during my time on the range, and I didn't mind the work. It was a nice change to have living creatures depend on me for much of their well-being. A great working partnership developed between Tom, Blackie and me. None of us could have done the job alone. We needed each other to watch out for the sheep under our care. But watching out for the herd wasn't the only reason the dogs were important to me.

If it hadn't been for those dogs, I would have gone completely mad. I talked to Tom and Blackie like they were people, and I was thankful to have them available for that purpose. I even began talking out loud to myself. When  the sheep bedded down during the heat of the day and it was time to eat a sandwich, I was just as likely to say, "Looks like it's time to eat," instead of just thinking about eating. It seemed perfectly normal at the time and I didn't really know I was doing it, but being out of touch with other human beings can do strange things to people.

At least during the day I was busy tending to the sheep and making sure my friends, Tom and Blackie, were not in danger. The nights, on the other hand, were absolutely dreadful. The yearning to visit with another human was so great after a couple of weeks, I started to wonder if being lonesome was worse than being hungry.

I laughed when the thought first occurred to me.

"Am I crazy? First I want a full belly, no matter what, then I consider giving up a constant full belly for the company of another person, no matter if that person is the most rotten person in the world."

The thought and the arguments, for and against, kept my mind occupied for days. My only entertainment was watching the stars at night and using the kerosene lantern to read the Sears catalog and the old Almanac. I read every page, then I read them again. Then I picked out the parts I liked best and read them a third time.

Solitaire was my favorite card game, but I had no cards. I picked the pages of the Sears catalog that I liked the least and made a deck. I spent hour after hour playing solitaire by the light of

64

the kerosene lantern.

It's hard to figure the passage of time when a person is alone without a clock or watch. I didn't even have a calendar. The Almanac had an old one, so I marked the days in that book. It didn't really matter what time of the day or night it was, because the herd was guided by sunlight, and they didn't care if it was six in the morning or nine. The days of the week didn't matter to the animals either. So what if it was a holiday or Sunday? The sheep went about their normal daily activities of walking to the feeding area, eating, resting in the heat of the day, then walking back to the wagon in the evening.

Besides talking to the dogs and myself, I thought about the past and my mother and aunt, then my father and his new wife. I wondered about what my brothers and sisters were doing and if I had any new nieces and nephews. I also began to dream about the future and wondered if God had a plan for me to someday get a good, respectable job and have a family of my own.

"I'm trying to learn what it is you are trying to teach me," I prayed one night.

I don't know why the thought popped into my mind that way; it just did. Maybe it was a theme my father would use when one of his congregation was dealing with the loss of a loved one or having a hard time with another aspect of life. Whatever the reason, the thought - the prayer - allowed me some peace over the course of a few weeks. I did try to learn from my situation. Patience was one part of the job and I had no choice but to be patient, or go to prison for leaving the herd.

I learned respect for animals; especially dogs like Tom and Blackie. We were a great team of three that worked as one to accomplish a common goal: the protection of our sheep. Those sheep had the best care that two dogs and a man could give.

My time on the range also gave me a chance to analyze relationships between people, something I thought little about before. After watch-

ing ewes taking care of their lambs, I better understood the mothering instinct.

If a ewe gave birth to a lamb, that ewe would risk her life to defend it. But if the lamb came from another ewe, she would have nothing to do with it. The lamb could die as far as the other ewes were concerned.

One day I came across a family of sage hens. The mother and chicks were out for a stroll, looking for food; insects in this case. The chicks were so young, they were not yet able to fly. The group was on a hill about 100 yards from where I was sitting as I watched the sheep that were bedded down. I noticed movement through the bunch grass and saw the outline of a coyote approaching the family. When the mother became aware of the coyote's presence, she pretended to have a broken wing and hobbled away from her chicks. The coyote was not fooled, for he had already spotted the chicks, and headed straight for them.

The mother ran back to her family and gathered them under her wings. There she stood her ground, ready to meet death rather than live without her chicks. The coyote walked closer and was about to grab the hen, when I dropped him with a slug from the Winchester. The hen and chicks didn't stick around to thank me. I last saw them running, as fast as their legs would carry them, over the top of the hill.

Now I could better understand why my mother was so close to her children, like the ewe and the sage hen who would do anything to protect one of their offspring. I even tried to apply the example of the ewe who would not accept the young of another as her own to my relationship with my father's new wife. There were some similarities there, but perhaps there was more to this woman that I didn't know about.

While I couldn't resolve the conflict between that woman and me in my mind, I did settle on the fact that life is complicated and, without the entire story, it is best not to judge another's actions.

One evening, just as Tom, Blackie and I arrived back at the wagon with the flock, Tom started barking. I looked west and noticed a horse and wagon coming towards me. I could see it was not the camp tender, but after being so long without human company, I didn't care who it was. I ran to greet the man as he neared my wagon.

"Hi mister, what you doin' out here?"

"Hi there young man. My name's Joe. I came out here to see you, and to show ya my catalogs of fine clothing."

"Have ya had supper yet?" I asked him.

"Can't say that I have."

"I'll fire up the stove right away and get somethin' in the pot."

It was so nice to have some company I was beside myself.

"Whoa there, you've got to settle down a bit," he said after I dropped an arm load of firewood. "We've got all evenin' and night to visit."

I took a deep breath and relaxed. Joe told me what was happening in the outside world as I cooked supper. Then he showed me his catalogs by the light of the kerosene lantern. All of the cloth came from a woolen mill in Minneapolis.

"I'd like to order these pants and this shirt, but I don't have any money."

"Don't worry, whatever you order, Louis Hensen will give me the money and take it out of your pay."

It was a wonderful idea in my mind, so I ordered several clothing items. Joe was such a good salesman that I ordered enough to just about equal the money that I would have coming after my tab at the hotel was paid.

Joe stayed the night. He was much older than me and since I was taught to respect my elders, I gave him my bed and I slept on the floor.

The next morning I thanked him for stopping by and encouraged him to come back again.

"Don't worry, Monrad, I'll be back."

The uplifting feeling that Joe brought me was instrumental in my mental health during the rest of my time on the range and for the rest of my life. When a person least expects it, when a person thinks they are feeling as low as it is possible for a human to feel, something wonderful happens. In this case it was Joe, bringing me the message that there was life after the loneliness of the range.

"... The North Star Woolen Mill Co., an 85-year-old Minneapolis blanket firm, ... stands on the site of the original factory established in 1864....

"The company also makes a complete line of all-wool baby blankets, contract blankets for airlines, railroads, hotels, hospitals, schools and steamship lines, and in recent years has turned out a line of woolen fabrics for men's, women's and children's wearing apparel ..."

Minneapolis Tribune, April 27, 1949

22

A Decision is Made

Time continued to pass on the range. The daily routine didn't change one bit, but my thinking did. Over the next six months, I realized that working as a sheepherder could be a lifetime job for me, if that was what I wanted. The ultimate question facing me was, what did I want to do with my life?

I remembered my family talking about the subject more than once when we were seated around the dinner table. Like the time when Oscar, my older brother, asked my father how and when he would know what he was going to be.

"Will I be a preacher like you, Father, or a carpenter or maybe a rancher with lots of cattle?"

"The Lord will help guide each of you in all that you do in life," my father said, as he made a point to look directly at each one of his children.

"We know that, Father," my oldest sister said, "but how will we know when the decision we make is the right one? When I meet a man, how will I know if he is the one I'm to marry, or am I to become a nurse or a banker?"

Everyone at the table laughed, because in those days, girls didn't grow up to work in a bank.

"I know these are important questions to you Ann, but I don't know the answer," my father said. "All of my children are important to me, so I want you to be happy in all that you do. I believe the Lord will guide you during your journey through life, and He will show you the way. Even during the tough times, when you think He

has forgotten you, those are the times when you may learn the most important lessons of life. Just remember, you can call on the Lord anytime, through prayer, and He will surely guide you."

"Ann, when you meet the man you are going to marry, the feeling will be special between the two of you," my mother said. "When your father and I first met, we both knew our relationship was special, but your father had to convince my father that he was the right person for me."

She looked at my father and asked, "Isn't that right?"

My family enjoyed a good hearty laugh together as we all looked at my father. It was the only time that I saw my father blush.

I was laughing when I became wide awake. It had been a dream, taking me back to the happiest time of my childhood. There was laughter and kidding and everyone in the family was allowed to ask questions and speak their mind.

I missed those times and was sad for a moment, but then I realized my mother could still make me laugh, seven years after we laid her in a grave. Not only that, but my father was still guiding me with his teachings about the Lord.

"The lessons you learn may not be obvious at the time, but the Lord is, no doubt, preparing you for another part of your life during difficult times. Try to make the most of each and every difficult situation. I believe the Lord will help each of you find your place in this world."

I thought about that guidance and the other direction and instruction my father and mother offered. I was thankful there was lots to think about, because there wasn't much else to do while herding sheep.

I came to the realization that the Lord had allowed me time on the range to fill my belly in answer to my plea for more food when I was riding the rails. Without having to ask in words, the question was, "Is that really all you want: a full belly?"

"Is there somewhere in between the hunger and danger of being on the road and having a full belly, but being lonely on the range?" I thought to myself.

Somehow I felt embarrassed and selfish as soon as the thought occurred to me. After all, I did have what I had asked for. Would it be stingy and greedy to ask for more?

"Nothing will just be handed to you," my father had told his children more than once. "You must work for what you get, and that includes improving whatever situation you are in."

Already in this life I had experienced two different life-styles while I was on my own, and neither filled the bill as a lifetime career as far as I was concerned.

I wanted a job that allowed me to stay in one place to earn a living. The thought of having enough money to pay rent by the month for a room in a boarding house appealed to me. There I would have a steady supply of food.

"Someday I'll meet a woman and have a family of my own," I thought out loud.

I laughed again, not only because it was the first time the thought of a future family had occurred to me, but because I was only a 14 year old kid.

No matter how foolish

the thoughts seemed to me when they first popped into my head, a foundation had been laid. All I had to do was build on it.

I figured one way to become more than just a sheepherder would be to get back into school and get more book learning under my belt. I was learning fast about taking care of myself in the world of hobos and being on my own with 3,000 sheep. Book learning was respected by the people who hired workers on steady jobs, and that's what I needed.

Every six weeks, the camp tender would come by to bring me water, food and a few boxes of rifle shells. He was one of the men I met at the Hensen ranch when I spent the night there.

It was his job to make a circuit of all the sheepherders on the ranch and resupply them; those to the north one day, the west on another day. He didn't like to be late back at the ranch house and miss supper, so his stop was a short one.

Although I was eager for his company, the visit was always disappointing. If his stay lasted

two hours, it was a long one. He would always hitch my wagon to his and move it a few miles to a new area, so the sheep would have fresh grass to eat. It was during this move that most of our talking took place. I did most of the talking. The tender, not much for words, would usually just grunt a reply.

One time he brought me the clothing I ordered from Joe the salesman. That was a special day. Another time I remembered that Mr. Hensen said that I was supposed to have canned food.

"Say, where's the canned food?"

"Look kid," the tender said. "This here's all I have for you. Do you want it or not?"

Sure I wanted what he had for me, and I didn't ask again.

Six months after Mr. Hensen dropped me off at the herder's wagon, I was anxious for the tender to make his rounds.

Before he even got off his wagon, I gave him the news.

"Tell Mr. Hensen that I want to go back to school."

"How you goin' to do that and look after the sheep?"

"I'm going to quit."

"I'll tell him, but don't you leave until he brings another herder out here. It's time in the pen if you leave ahead of time, ya know."

It was another two weeks until Mr. Hensen finally brought another herder to the wagon, but the days went fast, because now I was planning for the future, my future.

I was excited when I saw them coming down the trail. I brought my replacement, the new herder, up to date on the herd and showed him around the wagon and supplies. Then it was time to leave. I called Tom and Blackie to me and introduced them to the new herder. I said my good-byes to the dogs. They had been good companions, and it was as hard to leave them as some of the people I had known, but it was time.

I climbed into the truck with Mr. Hensen, and off we went. Tom and Blackie ran alongside the truck for awhile, then turned back to guard their sheep.

"Mr. Hensen, I've worked six months for you and I figure I've got $180 coming."

"That's right, Monrad, but don't forget your night at the hotel and your clothing."

He was right. I owed him some money from my wages, and I was thankful for him extending me credit like he did. In the end, he handed me $30, the total I had coming after settling up. But that was more money than I had ever had, and I felt quite rich.

Mr. Hensen gave me a ride back to Malta because he was headed that way the next day. I was thankful for that kindness too. I shook his hand at the train station and watched him drive off.

I had the money to ride a passenger train to anywhere I wanted, but after spending six months on the range, I wanted to save as much of the money as possible. I hopped the first freight out of Malta and headed east.

My days on the range taught me many lessons. I had a goal to accomplish, and my future looked bright from where I was sitting, inside an empty boxcar during the first part of October, and listening to the clickety-clack, clickety-clack of wheels on track.

23

Back to School

I never actually lived in Peever, South Dakota, but during a family visit there a few years before, I had stayed for a few days with the Henry Hinseth family. They were real good people, and I was invited to spend a night with them when I arrived in Peever. I explained my purpose of looking for a way to continue my education. They told me of a family who lived not far out of town who needed someone to do chores.

"In the morning, why don't you stop by the school on your way to check on the job," Mr. Hinseth said after supper.

I thought that was a grand idea and felt good that evening as I fell asleep.

The next morning I walked to the school and explained my situation to the principal.

"Well, school's already started, but it sounds like you're sincere about your studies, and I admire you for wanting to continue," he said. "I'll help you all I can. Go check on the job, and you can start school when you get settled."

When I left the school that day, the world seemed good, and I felt things were really looking up. I walked to the ranch, a distance of about three miles, with confidence and felt nothing could stop me from completing my education.

"Mr. Hinseth said you might need someone to help with the chores," I said when the woman answered the door.

"Yes, we do need a hand around the ranch," she said. She called her husband, who was in the barn.

The woman told me to stay where I was and walked half way to the barn to meet him. They talked for a few minutes, then motioned for me to join them.

"You can work for me for your room and board, but because you're so young and not able to work like a grown man, you'll have to pay us $1 a week," he said. "That will make up the difference from what a man could do and what a boy, like you, can do."

I didn't like the arrangement. I was a hard worker and my work output would measure up to or surpass most of the men I had worked with. But I didn't want the opportunity of going to school to be put in jeopardy, so the agreement, under their terms, was sealed with a handshake.

The work expected of me on that ranch was, no doubt, harder than almost anything I have had to do before or since. They got me up at five in the morning, and I helped milk a barn full of cows. Next I fed the hogs and chickens, then cleaned the chicken house and hog pen. Following that, I split a supply of wood and took some to the bin in the kitchen, and the rest to the storage area near the barn. My last job of the morning was to separate the milk.

After completing a day's worth of work in three hours, I would walk to school. The situation didn't change after I returned to the ranch after school: I would husk corn and do other chores until dark and the cows came home. That barn full of cows had to be milked in the evening too, with the help of kerosene lanterns. Saturdays and Sundays were full work days, from sunrise to well past sunset.

The only bright spot in this experience was my journey to and from school. As I was walking back to the ranch after my first day in the classroom, a Model T Ford stopped beside me at the edge of town.

"Hi Monrad, I live just past the ranch were you're staying," the driver said. "I'll give you a ride."

She was an older girl who was attending the same school as me. I appreciated her kindness, and the gesture saved me many miles of walking, but that didn't stop a fast approaching dilemma.

The problem with working for these people and going to school was I needed more sleep. The only time to make up the sleep I needed was at school. Still I tried my best to stay awake. I was lucky; the teacher and principal were compassionate towards my needs and didn't hassle me.

This routine continued for about six weeks. Then, one afternoon, the neighbor girl had to stay after school for about 1 1/2 hours. I stayed too, sitting on the step waiting.

Upon my arrival at the ranch, the woman confronted me.

"Mooney, we can't put up with you being late," she said without asking for an explanation.

I got mad and went up the stairs. I packed my suitcase and started down the road to town.

"Mooney, Mooney, if you will stay, you won't have to pay the dollar a week," the woman said as she ran after me.

I was so tired from being taken advantage of that I never looked back. I just kept walking.

"Even herding sheep was better than this," I thought. Then I laughed at the thought.

When I got to town, I went to the pool hall and sat down to ponder my situation. I wasn't there long when a young man named Clarence

Holland walked in. He and I had become friends, first by exchanging friendly waves, then during short visits on my way to and from school. His father owned one of the grocery stores in Peever.

"What's going on Mooney?" he asked. "Ya got all the chores done?"

I explained the situation.

"We all wondered how long you would stay out there. What are ya gonna do now?"

"Guess I'll catch the next freight and go lookin' for work. I want to stay in school, but I don't know what else to do."

"Let me talk to my father and ask if you could help around our grocery store. That way you'll be able to finish this year of school."

"I sure would like that," I said as he left to talk to his father, but, in my heart, I thought my luck had again run out.

Clarence was back in 10 minutes. "You start tomorrow," he said.

The news caught me by surprise and I almost cried right there, but instead, only a silent prayer escaped me.

Even though I had been on a ranch close to Peever for about six weeks, I never really had a chance to look around the town. It was a typical town for the times, with a barber shop, two grocery stores, a pool hall, a cafe, a gas station and a few other stores that sold general merchandise. The population of Peever then was about 350 people. Many of them were real nice to me, and the Hollands were tops. Working in their grocery store was my first indoor job.

Mr. Holland handed me an apron and showed me around the store. It was similar to other groceries in those days, but I had never been on the other side of the counter. Customers entering the store didn't have access to the merchandise. Instead, they would have a list of things they needed, like flour, coffee and beans. My job as clerk was to get those items from the shelf and give them to the customers. The shelves were at least 10 feet high, and a ladder was needed to reach many of the items.

Very seldom was cash actually exchanged when items were purchased. Most people carried a tab for the month or, in the case of crop farmers, the season. And some of the business was completed on a barter system. When a customer gave me a list of items, and those items were set on the counter, I would add them to their tab.

When the customer brought in extra eggs or cream from their farms, the value of those items

had to be decided. This was determined by testing the cream and counting the eggs. The difference was either added to the tab, if the eggs and cream money didn't equal the amount due, or the customer was given the cash they had coming.

I had been working at the store for two months when the rancher and his wife who had nearly worked me to death came in the store. I was in the back room, out of sight, but I could hear them talking.

"Mornin'," Mr. Holland said to them.

"Mornin'," the rancher said in return. "We do our business at the other store, but the wife wanted to look at your cloth."

"There's a few bolts over here," Mr. Holland said pointing to one corner, then walking there.

He was showing them the cloth when another customer walked into the store.

"Monrad, would you help Mrs. Smith?" Mr. Holland called to me.

"Yes, sir," I replied.

"What's he still doin' in town?" the rancher's wife asked.

Mrs. Smith and I stopped and looked at the woman. Clarence came from the back room to see what the commotion was all about.

"Oh, you mean Monrad?" Mr. Holland asked. "Let me tell you about the boy. He's the best clerk I've ever hired. He works as hard as Clarence and I, and he's courteous and kind to my customers. It just goes to show ya what a worker'll do if he's treated properly, instead of bein' worked half to death."

The rancher and his wife, justifiably insulted, left the store in a huff. Despite being stunned at what the store owner had said, I returned to my job of getting the groceries Mrs. Smith requested. Later, at the end of the day, I asked Mr. Holland about the incident.

"Everyone knows those people," he said. "They work a hand until they can't take it anymore, then they try to find another. You worked on their ranch longer than most. Judgin' from the way you work for me, I know ya did a good job for them too. I'm not one for runnin' off business, but since they're doin' business at the other store anyway, let them do all their business there."

"Thank you, Mr. Holland."

"You're welcome, Monrad."

The businesses in Peever started showing a loss as the depression gripping our great nation continued to deepen. I worked in the store for another two months and realized Mr. Holland didn't really need me. He was being good to me, like a father would care for a son, but I didn't want to be a burden to him and his family.

I went to the principal, explained my situation and asked him if he would pass me for the year because I had to get on the road and look for work.

"I sure will, Monrad," he said. "But I want you to promise me that you'll come back and get a diploma."

"I'll sure try, sir."

I thanked the Hollands for their kindness. "I feel like family here with you," I told them.

"You are like family to us," Mr. Holland said.

"Like family," Clarence repeated, shaking my hand. "Where ya headed?"

"I don't want to herd sheep again, so I guess I'll head for Chicago."

"Don't get lost in that big town," Mr. Holland said as I started walking toward the tracks.

That afternoon I hopped the local freight headed for Chicago. I was back to riding the rails, yes, but my accomplishments were many during my time in Peever. Another year of schooling was under my belt, and I had made lifelong friends in a town where I knew few just months before. Anytime I wanted, more schooling was available to me.

I was a hobo again, and every hobo knows that life on the road is uncertain, but even I could see that the foundation was being formed for a solid, respectable life in the future.

24

Looking for Work

When I stepped off the freight in Chicago, the thought of being in a large city held the dream of finding work. This was my first visit to any city that was considered big, and a kid from Montana sure can get lost in a city like Chicago.

Despite what other hobos had told me a year before about there being no work in the cities, I had to see for myself. Work was scarce in the small cities and towns I visited, so there must be work in the larger cities. At least that was my reasoning during this time.

Word on the road was to go to Madison Street when in Chicago. I had no trouble finding Madison; a person just had to follow the crowd of hobos walking downtown from the rail yard. I was shocked at the number of people who were together in that one area. Their number seemed greater than the population of most of the towns I had called home during my short life.

When I inquired about a place to eat, I was told that there were two missions in the area. I went to one and was directed to a room full of other hobos. A preacher stepped to the pulpit and commenced to delivering an hour-long sermon about the dangers of alcohol, tobacco and women.

I could understand the alcohol and tobacco dangers because I had heard my father preach similar sermons all my life, but I didn't understand the dangers of women. Most of the women in my life, my mother, aunt and sisters, were car-

ing and loving. The subject was of passing interest only and didn't occupy much of my time, because my belly was empty, and the hunger pains were intense.

When the preaching was finished and those present were allowed to get a plate of food, I approached the man in charge.

"Sir, my father is a Lutheran minister and I truly enjoy a good sermon," I told him. "But wouldn't the message be better accepted by those listening if they were fed first and had a full stomach?"

"No, it's better if the sermon is preached first young man," the man said. "We tried it the other way, but after these people eat, they either leave or go to sleep."

After the explanation, the reason for the sequence of events made sense. Still it was hard for me to understand why people would be so rude as to leave before, or to fall asleep during, the sermon, if the agreement was to attend.

After a few days on Madison Street in the great city of Chicago, the reason was obvious. Most of my time was divided between finding food and looking for a place to sleep. That left little time to look for work. When I did ask store owners for work, they flat out told me there wasn't any work and not to come back.

I decided to leave and headed for Cicero on the west side of town for two reasons: First, Cicero was the place where a person could catch freight trains out of town. Second, word on the street was the bread line there was one of the best in the nation. After waiting in line and getting an ample amount of soup along with a reasonable hunk of bread, I sat down to eat what I considered a feast.

"This is great food," I said to another hobo seated near me. "How come this bread line is so good and the others aren't?"

"This here's run by Al Capone, and he runs most of Chicago," he said. "He's always treated a man who's down and out with respect, and he has the money to make sure this bread line is well supplied. Look, there he is now, the third one back."

Glancing up I could see six men in suits walking through the room. The third man in the bunch didn't look much different from the rest, and I continued with my meal.

I ate at Al Capone's soup kitchen twice a day over the next few days, but I still couldn't find any work. I didn't want to wear out my welcome, so I decided to leave.

Chicago has one of the largest freight yards in the country, so catching a train wasn't a problem. Catching a freight going where a hobo wanted to go was the problem. It's sure not like a passenger station where departure times and destinations are announced so passengers can get to the appropriate train before it pulls out of the station.

In a smaller freight yard, everyone would know where each train was heading and when that train was scheduled to roll. Not so in Chicago: There were so many trains getting ready to pull out, it was just a guess as to their destination. Only the railroad staff knew for sure.

Not long after the train I selected started its run, word passed among the hobos that we were headed for Peoria, Illinois. The destination was fine with me. At that point, any destination was as good as the next. It was a nice day, and I was sitting in the open door of a boxcar with a hobo on my right and another on my left. The three of us were dangling our feet over the side of the car and enjoying the warmth of the sun and the scenery as we talked about where to find work.

In an area where one would not expect to find a lake, a lot of water was near the tracks. I had never been in a flood before and found it interesting to see water covering roads.

Suddenly we heard a yell from one of the cars ahead of us. Then another and another. We strained to see, but the train was in a shallow bend to the left and we couldn't even see past the front of our car.

With no knowledge of what had happened, we relaxed again. The man to my left pointed.

"Look at those ducks," he said, and the three of us looked at the water.

Just then his lower legs hit mine and mine hit the legs of the man on my right. A post, with a warning sign attached, was placed too close to the tracks. The post caught the lower legs and feet of all the hobos on our side of the train. We were traveling about 40 miles an hour and the results were devastating to many.

The man to my left, who was not wearing shoes at the time, ended up with two broken feet, but the impact only bruised mine. They were spared more serious damage because I was wearing the boots I purchased from Joe, the clothing salesman. Now those boots were worth their weight in gold. Suddenly the loneliness endured during my time as a sheepherder didn't seem so bad. The boots saved my feet. Although bruised, I was able to walk, while many other hobos on that freight suffered broken bones like the one next to me.

When the train stopped, I found a conductor and told him about the hurt man in our car.

"There's about 20 others like him on this train," he said. "We'll find care for him in town, and we'll pull up that damn sign post."

"Any work around these parts?" I asked.

"None, better keep movin'."

I was on the next freight headed for Kansas City. That place was crammed full of hobos, which meant little work or food. And the bulls were on the mean side, so I set my sights on Denver, Colorado.

It was early spring, and I soon found out what a foolish decision I had made. Being a mile high, Denver was cold, and hobos were thick in the thin air. Again it was hard to get food and there was no work. I looked west and headed for Salt Lake City, Utah.

Another hobo and I hopped a freight of the Denver Rio Grand Railroad and headed for the setting sun. The train climbed the mountains to the Moffet Tunnel, which is over 10,000 feet high. Along the route, we had to stop for a long time, but we never knew why. Some of the hobos decided to build a fire and boil some coffee in an effort to restore body heat. A fire was started and a pot of water was placed over the flames. Warmth of the fire felt good, and so did a sip of coffee

The train again started and there was a scramble to get aboard. In Salt Lake the story was the same; no work and lots of hobos.

I had traveled throughout much of the country and found the story the same everywhere I went. The country was suffering from a depression, but the depth of the distress was a surprise to me. I was a hard worker and willing to work long hours for an honest wage. Yet, it seemed that for every job I asked about in small towns, there were 10 other men ready to take it. In the big cities, there were 100 men for every job. I wasn't the only person in a tough situation, but I was on my own, and now it was time for me to make another decision: Where to go from Salt Lake?

"Montana has been good to me," I thought. "I'll go back there, but not to herd sheep."

I caught the next freight to Butte, Great Falls and Havre. Then I traveled east on the Great Northern. Two other hobos and I were in a boxcar when a blizzard rolled in. It was cold, with the wind blowing hard, pushing the snow through the cracks in the car. The train stopped at a couple of towns, but it was night, and not one business was open. If there would have been, we would have stayed where we were and spent the night. The stops were just to allow the train crews to take off or add a rail car or two. When we couldn't find a place to get out of the cold in the town, we climbed back on the boxcar when the train started rolling again.

I was lucky that the two other hobos sharing the car were older and wiser than me. They realized we were in trouble.

"Must be 20 below," one said.

"At least that," said the other.

"I just want to sleep," I told them. "I'll just curl up in the corner here."

"Nope, we can't let ya do that, Mooney."

And they slapped me and punched me to keep me from falling asleep. They knew that if I fell asleep, I would freeze to death.

"On your feet kid," I heard one say as my eyes slid shut. "We've got to get him up and movin'."

They did just that, and it saved my life.

The train stopped at the next town, and the conductor happened to walk by our boxcar and

noticed us.

"What are ya doin' in there?" he said.

"I won't be any trouble," I said. "Just let me stay here and sleep."

"The kid's half frozen," one hobo told the conductor. "He's been delirious for some time now."

"Well, you're all going to freeze to death in that boxcar. Get out of there and come back to my caboose."

In those days, each conductor was assigned their own caboose and they took care of them as if they owned them.

The trip from the boxcar to the caboose was not an easy one. I remember we had to walk real close to the train because the blizzard made it impossible to see more than 10 feet in any direction. Traveling away from the train meant getting lost, and that meant certain death. One of the other hobos put my arm around his neck and helped me walk. When we reached the caboose, the three other men helped me climb inside. It was warm and no wind could touch my body. I laid down on the bench and was fast asleep.

I woke up alone the next morning in Williston, North Dakota, which was a railroad division and the end of the line for the conductor and his caboose. That conductor took pity on a young boy, and no doubt my life was saved for the second time in one night. From that time forward, I have considered a caboose a friend.

I traveled around a bit more, mostly in Montana, but I found no work and always lots of hobos. Hunger was once again a constant factor in my life, as it had been since about three days after leaving the employment of Louis Hensen. Once again I was having to decide which was worse: an empty belly or being lonely.

My thoughts drifted from loneliness to hunger as I mentally discussed which was the lesser of two evils. In the end, the rationale was easy, "From this side of the fence, I'll trade the loneliness for a full belly."

That was it, the decision was made. I would go back to the range and look after a flock of sheep once again. The job isn't really what I wanted to do, but it was steady work with all the food I could eat, and the pay was $30 a month. I was inside a boxcar on the next freight headed for Malta, Montana.

25

Back on the Range

I stepped off the freight with confidence as it slowed to a stop in Malta, Montana. Unlike my first visit to the town 18 months before, I knew where the hotel was and whom to ask for.

"Is Louis Hensen in town?" I asked the clerk.

"No, but I'm sure he will be here in a couple days. Say, I remember you. He hired you before."

I looked close and recognized the clerk as Joe, the same clerk who was there before.

"That's right, and I'm ready to work for him again."

"Well you know the way Mr. Hensen lets his herders stay here and use the restaurant. Here's the key to your room. It's the second one on the right at the top of the stairs."

I was fully aware of the cost of staying at the hotel and eating at the restaurant. It wouldn't cost me a thing now, but my time on the range would pay for my expenses at the hotel.

"Is there a room that doesn't cost as much as the one at the top of the stairs?"

"Don't worry, Mr. Hensen will pay for your room."

"And take the money out of my pay later. Is there another room?"

"Well, let me see ... There's a little room near the kitchen that isn't rented much because there's a lot of noise near there, but I can let you use it at half the price of the other room."

"I'll take it."

I stayed there three days and two nights.

There was a considerable amount of noise, but it didn't bother me enough to pay more for a room. I was careful of my meals this time too. I ate a large breakfast, skipped lunch and ate a bowl or two of the stew and bread for my evening meal.

I indulged myself in a hot bath, like I did when staying at the hotel before. I had my clothes washed and mended too. It made good sense to get ready for time on the range.

A couple days later, while I was having my evening meal, in walked Mr. Hensen.

"Mooney, it's good to see ya," he said extending his hand.

"I was wonderin' if you had a need for another herder for awhile?"

"Sure do. I'll always have a place for you to work, Mooney. You're one of the best herders I've ever had and besides, one of my herders tells me he's had his fill of sheep and bein' on the range."

So, the next day I went back to the Hensen ranch with Mr. Hensen. Like before; we spent one night at the ranch, then I was taken to the same wagon and herd. A different herder walked from the wagon to the truck as we drove up. As soon as I was out of the vehicle, he was in with the door shut.

"I'm ready to go, Mr. Hensen," he said, wanting to leave right then.

I was instantly suspicious.

"Mr. Hensen, aren't you goin' to top off the

water barrel?"

"Oh, right, Mooney."

I took a fast look in the wagon and found it a mess.

"Stay here till I have a look at what's going on," I said to Mr. Hensen.

He looked inside, then at the truck, then back at the wagon.

"I've never seen such a mess. You get out of that truck and come over here."

The herder reluctantly walked back to the wagon.

"What you been doin' here? There's flour and beans spilled all over and ..."

"And there's no coffee left," I said from the inside.

"Yeah, that's one of the reasons I want to leave," the herder said. "I'm about out of supplies."

"I don't short supplies on my herders," Mr. Hensen said. "Every six weeks you were supplied with enough food to last for another six weeks or more. You've wasted food by spillin' it and usin' more than you needed. You'll never work in Montana again."

"That's fine with me, Mr. Hensen," the herder said. "I don't mean no disrespect, but herdin' sheep is not for me."

"Where's the shells for the Winchester?" I asked from inside the wagon.

"I used them all up."

"You what?"

"I shot lots of coyotes, Mr. Hensen," the herder said, with his hat in his hand and looking at the ground.

"Let's see those coyotes." Mr. Hensen said.

"Well, they're scattered all over."

"Just show me the one closest to here."

The herder started fidgeting and shuffling his feet in a nervous manner, but he didn't move.

"Mr. Hensen, I want you to walk the herd with me," I said.

"I think you're right, we better have a look around. You come with us," he said to the herder,

who did not want to do so.

"Where's the dogs?" I asked the herder.

"They don't come around much," he said. "They just stay with the herd."

Fifty yards from the wagon we found out where the bullets went. It was obvious that a rock was used as a target. It had the markings of several hits and the ground near it was torn up by bullets missing their mark.

The herd was another 50 yards distant - to far away for a herder to effectively control the sheep, not to mention help the dogs if they were in trouble.

"You were not watchin' my sheep properly," Mr. Hensen said.

The herder simply looked down.

I noticed movement to our right. It was Tom and Blackie. They circled around until they were downwind of us to catch our scent. Both let out a bark and ran to me. The two squirming fur balls licked me and whimpered and wagged their tails. It was a reunion of three old friends. Then I noticed that they were just skin and bones.

"You've mistreated these dogs," I said as I turned to face the herder. Tom and Blackie looked at the herder and growled.

"When's the last time they were fed?" I asked.

"They just seem to take care of themselves."

"Mr. Hensen, if you don't get that sorry excuse for a man out of my sight soon, I'm goin' to let Tom and Blackie take him down."

This time the herder started to whimper. The dogs continued to growl.

"Let's look over the herd first," Mr. Hensen said.

Like the dogs, the herd was in sad shape. They had been allowed to find their own food during the day, and the dogs had brought them back near the wagon in the evening.

"When's the last time you were out here?" Mr. Hensen asked.

The herder whimpered again.

"When?!"

"It's been two weeks, Mr. Hensen. I got real scared and the coyotes got real close and ..."

"So you let the coyotes have as many of my sheep as they wanted."

"No, that's the dog's job."

I stepped in the direction of the herder and started to swing, but Mr. Hensen caught my arm.

"Stay here," he said to the herder. "Mooney, this isn't the worse I've seen. Sometimes a herder will go completely crazy and shoot the dogs and some sheep. I've got some extra grub and shells in the truck that will last ya a couple days. I'll send the tender out for a special trip tomorrow or the next day. You do what ya have to and get this herd in shape and take care of the dogs. I know you'll do a good job."

He talked as we walked through the herd. The dogs had done what they could to protect the sheep, but the coyotes had killed several and there were a few that were wounded and needed to be destroyed.

When we were back to where the herder was standing, Mr. Hensen motioned with his hand.

"You get to the truck," he said. "And sit in the back. I don't want ya up front with me."

The man scurried off like a forlorn puppy.

Mr. Hensen and I unloaded the little bit of grub that was in the truck, along with a few shells and five gallons of water.

"Mr. Hensen, that water barrel is empty. These five gallons aren't goin' to last me very long."

"I know Mooney," he said as he climbed in the driver's seat. "The tender will be along in a day or two and I'll be out here soon to check on ya myself."

The herder, seated in the back of the truck, was still whimpering and crying.

"Quiet back there, or I'll leave ya here with Mooney."

The man's eyes got big and an anguished look appeared on his face, but he didn't utter another sound. If it wasn't such a sad situation, I would have laughed.

Tom, Blackie and I watched the truck until it was out of sight. Then we moved the herd closer to the wagon. I killed a fine ewe and fed the dogs their fill. A tender lamb was my evening meal.

I was able to kill a coyote that didn't realize another herder was on duty. That kept the others at a reasonable distance during the night.

I started to clean the wagon, but darkness arrived before I could complete the job. It was so filthy, I slept on the ground with the dogs that night.

"We're a team again," I told them. I swear they both smiled at me.

"Well, things could be worse; at least I have a full belly," I thought to myself.

"More than one sheepherder has gone crazy while herding sheep. Most herders were bothered by the loneliness of the job, but a few couldn't stand being alone to the point where they went off the deep end."

Diane Smith, author and historian

26

Regaining My Strength

Mr. Hensen was true to his word. The tender arrived the next day in the early evening.

"What are you, special or somethin'?" he asked. "Mr. Hensen made me come out here when you weren't supposed to be resupplied for another three weeks. What happened out here?"

"Did you see that last herder who was out here?" I asked.

"Yeah, that was a strange one. Mr. Hensen didn't even let him spend the night or drive him back to town. The guy had the nerve to ask Mr. Hensen for his pay and that's when Mr. Hensen pulled out his rifle and started yelling at the man. 'I want you off my land, now!' Mr. Hensen told him, then 'bang!' he fired a round in the air. The man started running down the road. 'You let the coyotes have my sheep!' Mr. Hensen yelled, and then he fired another round in the air. And the man ran faster. Do ya know what that's all about?"

"That herder didn't take care of the dogs or the sheep. He wasted food and the bullets for the Winchester. Without bullets, the coyotes ganged up on the dogs and killed a bunch of the sheep. I'm just starting to get the camp and the herd in shape."

"Well I've got extra water and supplies for you, and Mr. Hensen said to move you to a different spot with more feed for the sheep."

"We'll do that in the morning. I'll cook us up a lamb for supper."

The tender hitched my wagon to his the next morning and moved my camp about five miles to the south.

"See you in about six weeks," the tender said as he rode away from my new camp.

The sheep were content to stay close to the wagon the first couple of days we were at the new camp because there was plenty of grass nearby. That gave me time to watch the herd as I cleaned the wagon from one end to the other. The extra water helped in the cleaning process.

Mr. Hensen drove up at noon on my third day there.

"How's it goin', Mooney?"

"I've about got the wagon cleaned up. Five sheep were in bad shape and I had to shoot them. Three others that might not make it, but I'm nursin' them along."

"Do what ya have to do. I know you'll do what's best for the herd. I trust your judgment."

"I want you to know up front that I killed a lamb the other day for my meat and a ewe for the dogs. I just can't stomach the old ewes, Mr.

Hensen."

"Usually I don't allow herders to kill lambs for food and certainly the herd dogs don't get to eat ewes. But, I can see the herd is already doin' better than a few days ago. If it wasn't for you, Mooney, there might not be a herd left to take care of. You do what ya want, eat what ya want and feed those dogs what ya want. There's more supplies for ya in the truck."

Mr. Hensen must have wanted to take good care of me because when he left later that day, I was better supplied than any other herder in Montana. I spent the next five months in that area and the tender made

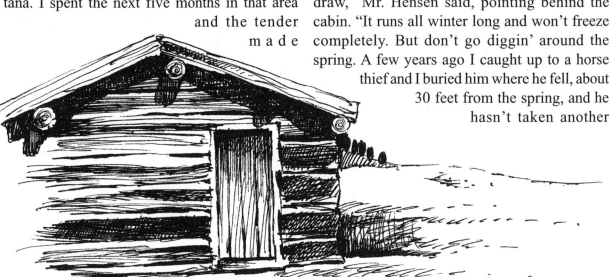

four more trips to resupply and move me instead of the usual two. When he stopped at the camp in the late fall, there were two other men with him. Mr. Hensen arrived in his truck a few hours later.

"It's October, and that means winter will settle in soon. I've got a special place for ya to winter the sheep. Get all your supplies out of the wagon and I'll take ya there. These two will get the sheep to ya in a couple of days."

I cleaned out the wagon and placed everything, including the sourdough starter, in the back of the truck. We traveled at least 25 miles to the north before Mr. Hensen told me that we were about there. He stopped next to an old log cabin.

"This here's your home for the winter,

Mooney. Ya have to get the sheep out to eat every day or they won't survive. If the snow gets too deep, ya feed them the hay and cotton seed cakes over there, but only if ya have to. I'll have some more sent to ya. By the way, Charlie Russell spent some time in this cabin."

"Who?"

"Haven't ya heard of him? He's just about the most famous painter from Montana there ever was."

"Oh yeah, now I remember."

"There's a spring about a half mile up that draw," Mr. Hensen said, pointing behind the cabin. "It runs all winter long and won't freeze completely. But don't go diggin' around the spring. A few years ago I caught up to a horse thief and I buried him where he fell, about 30 feet from the spring, and he hasn't taken another horse."

Mr. Hensen let go with a hearty laugh. It was the first time I had seen him show any tendency towards humor, and I laughed at him laughing.

"You'll be just fine here. Your herd will be along in a couple of days and the tender will stop by every four weeks in the winter. But if the weather is real bad, he might not make it out on time. Watch your food and ammunition. The tender is bringing more wood too."

He helped me transfer my supplies to the cabin, then he climbed in his truck and started the motor.

"See ya, Mooney," he said as he drove off.

The two days without the sheep allowed me

a chance to clean the cabin and explore the surrounding area. The cabin was well built. It measured 12 feet wide and 16 feet long. It had a board bunk along the back wall, a stove for heating and cooking, a wooden bench by the table and a kerosene lantern. There was a pile of wood along the north side, but there wasn't enough to last three weeks. I looked for an outhouse, but there wasn't one. I dug a pit about 50 yards from the cabin and grubbed out a trail to it that would be easy to follow at night. That would be my toilet.

The men and sheep arrived two days later. They were anxious to get back to the ranch house, so as soon as the sheep were under my control, they headed out.

"Hey aren't you goin' to stay and visit awhile?" I asked while walking alongside the wagon.

"Nope, we want to get back to some good grub," one said.

"And some baked apple pie," the other man said.

"The least you could do is visit for awhile."

"We've got to get back."

I thought about saying more, but stopped and watched the wagon disappear.

"They could have stayed for a little bit. Yeah, it wouldn't have hurt them," I mused out loud.

The fact that I was talking to myself and answering scared me a little. Maybe I would be a sheepherder all my life. After all, I was becoming suspicious of every person I met. And, at least at the moment, I was getting along better with the dogs and my herd of sheep than people.

I had lots of time to think about the situation and my relationship with other people and the animals as the winter storms covered eastern Montana. Every day, Tom, Blackie and I would take the sheep to a spot where they could graze. It was cold. In those days there was no insulated clothing and the cold wind seemed to fly right through mine. The cold I was feeling could be compared to the hunger I felt when on the road. I spent several weeks pondering the question of which was worse, and never reached a convincing conclusion either way. I did know that eight months on the range was enough. Around the first of December, I told the tender that I wanted to quit.

"I hate to lose ya again, Mooney," Mr. Hensen said. "But I guess you've got your reasons. Are you going back to school?"

"Not this year."

"Well, you're one of the best herders I've ever had. You can work for me anytime ya want. Here's the pay ya have comin'."

He handed me $40. That's all I had coming after he took out for some more clothes I ordered from the man from Minneapolis and my stay at the hotel in Malta eight months before.

Mr. Hensen once again took me to Malta and I stayed a couple nights at the hotel there. After supper on the second night, a couple other men invited me to join their poker game. I promptly lost $10 and quit the game. But I did meet a man who was driving to Miles City, Montana, the next day and he offered me a ride. I accepted. The Milwaukee Railroad goes through Miles City and my goal was to head east to Minneapolis, a place where, I was told, there were jobs for willing workers.

I thanked the driver for the ride and walked to the rail yard. There I climbed in a boxcar and snuggled in a corner as the freight headed east.

I didn't consider my luck to be bad at that point, except for losing the money in the poker game, and I tried to think of the positive side of my life. I had been a sheepherder twice and this is my third time on the road. I didn't want to be either cold or hungry anymore. My thoughts and hopes centered on finding a job in Minneapolis.

27

Cold Weather is Hard on Hobos

The trip from Miles City, Montana, to the railroad division town of Aberdeen, South Dakota, was uneventful. I was cold when I climbed out of the boxcar, but being cold was just a fact of life for me at that point.

"When's the next freight to Minneapolis?" I asked the first hobo I passed.

"That there one that's just startin' to roll is headed east. Better hurry if you're goin' to catch her."

I intercepted the moving train and hopped the first car in front of me. It was an open flatbed carrying a load of large wood poles, like telephone poles. An open car was no place to ride during the winter, and I knew that, but once on the train, my plan was to move forward or backward until I found a boxcar.

I advanced to the front of the train until the engine was in sight, but saw nothing but flatbeds, all loaded with wood poles. I traveled to the rear of the train and saw that the entire train was made up of flatbeds hauling the same cargo.

The realization that I was in a serious pickle began to sink in as the wind and cold cut through my clothing to the skin. Just once I considered jumping,

but the train was traveling too fast for a safe dismount. Besides being off the train in the middle of nowhere wasn't a good idea either.

I went to the end of the pile and found one pole on top of the stack sticking back a little farther than the rest. I sat under that pole with the ends of the other poles to my back. The wood didn't provide much protection because the wind swirled around the back of the stack like an eddy around a rock in a river.

I was colder than I had ever been before in

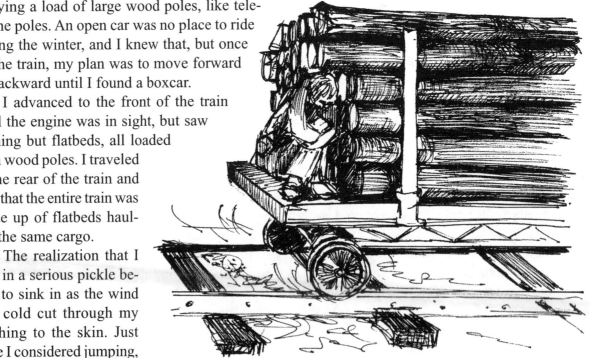

84

my life. I'm sure the temperature was well below zero, and the wind from the moving train made it seem much colder.

My spirits lifted when I heard the train blow its whistle.

"Good, we're going to stop," I thought to myself. But the train didn't slow down a bit. I watched as the lights in the small town faded in the distance. A few miles down the track there was another whistle, and again I thought this train ride through frozen hell was about to end. Again the train didn't change speed. We passed through town after town until, 90 miles later, the train yard in Milbank, South Dakota, came into sight.

When the train was completely stopped, I stretched one arm, then the other. It took me a few minutes to stand up because I was stiff from the cold. I climbed down from the car and started walking to the station.

My lower legs and feet didn't want to work properly. To others, my walk no doubt resembled a stumble, and some people might have thought I was drunk. Moving helped thaw out my feet, but then they started to hurt.

I passed another hobo, and he grabbed my arm to stop me. I pulled away thinking I was about to be robbed.

"Whoa there kid," he said. "You got trouble with them feet. Better get over to the jail, and they'll let you stay there."

"Oh I'll be all right."

"Now ya listen to me kid. Your feet is frozen and if they're too bad, they'll have to ... Well you just get over to the jail; that's it right there down the street, the red brick building."

So I hobbled over to the jail, opened the door and stumbled in.

"Looks like we got ourselves another one, Sheriff," a man in uniform said when he saw me.

A second man in uniform looked up from the newspaper he was reading.

"Put him in with the others."

"This way," the first man said as he grabbed a ring of keys and opened a door.

I walked through the door and into an area containing two jail cells. The jailer used a key to open one cell occupied by six other men. I shuffled through the door and heard it close; then the key moved the lock in place.

"Sit over here, son," an older man said as he patted a spot on the bunk next to him. "We've all got frozen feet."

"Yeah, we've all got the same problem," another said.

"But they hurt so bad," I said.

"Frozen feet hurt; that's a fact of life. They'll stop hurtin' in a day or two, but they'll hurt again every time you get in cold weather, and I mean for the rest of your life."

I was about to fall asleep sitting up, so the others made some room for me to stretch out on the bunk.

The jail in Milbank was my home for 10 days, giving me a chance to recover from the near-fatal train ride. I saw other hobos come and go during my stay. The sheriff was a good-natured man who saved a bunch of lives by letting hobos stay in his jail for as long as they needed to recuperate from time in the bitter cold.

One old hobo arrived five days after me. His feet were frozen so bad that they were black.

"I've got to get home," he said to me on the third morning he was in the jail.

"Better stay a bit longer," I said. "Until those feet heal up."

He looked at his feet, then at me.

"Just a couple hundred miles to go, I've got to get home."

He shook the jail door, and the jailer appeared.

"What d'ya want old timer?"

"I've got to catch the next freight; I've got to get home."

"Sure you don't want to let those feet heal first?"

The old man looked at his feet, then at the jailer.

"Please, I've got to get home."

I said a silent prayer for him as he walked out of sight.

My feet were feeling better. The pain had subsided, and I was able to walk normally again. The time behind bars saved my life, but I couldn't stay there forever. I thanked the sheriff and jailer, then headed for the rail yard. Along the way I found two gunny sacks and wrapped them around my shoes for added insulation.

I was on the first freight heading for Minneapolis. There were five hobos in my boxcar and not one of us was dressed properly for cold weather. We were strangers before we climbed into the car, but we huddled close together in one corner to share body heat.

The freight pulled into the Minneapolis yard in a blizzard a couple of days before Christmas. The hobos in my boxcar split up, since we were heading for different parts of the country. I had to cross several tracks to get to the edge of the yard and into town. Five railroad men were gathered near the back of a tender, so I walked closer, so I could hear what they were talking about and to see what was happening.

"Poor guy, he didn't have a chance," one of the men said.

"Is he dead?" another asked.

"Of course he's dead, you idiot. Look how thick that ice is coverin' him."

"How long you think he's been there?"

"Must have been at least four hours. That's when we took on water at the last stop. Some must have spilled over and froze him in place before he could move."

"Get the hammers and let's get him off there."

Three of the railroad men started hitting the chunk of ice that had a man inside. I said a silent prayer for that hobo too, then turned and headed into town in search of the two things a hobo is always in need of: a meal and a place to spend the night.

28

Christmas in a Bread Line

Snow stung my face as I walked into the city of Minneapolis. The blowing wind of the blizzard made the ice crystals move parallel to the ground instead of drifting straight down from sky.

"Where's Hennepin Street?" I asked a man standing in a doorway.

"The street's five miles long; what part do you want?"

"Where it joins Washington Street."

"You're almost there," he said. "Two blocks ahead and four to your right."

Every large town had a skid road, and Minneapolis was no exception. It was the area of town where all hobos were welcome. I found Hennepin Street and turned to the right. The buildings were old and deteriorated; some to the point they shouldn't be used anymore; yet people still used

them for shelter.

I noticed a line of men leading to the door of one building. I walked past the front of the line to the end of that block. There I found Washington Street.

"What is this place?" I asked a man in line.

"The St. James Mission."

"Why is everyone waitin' in line?"

"They feed all hobos and anyone else that's hungry," he said.

As usual, I was hungry. Getting some food to my stomach was my top priority. I turned the corner and walked down the street. I passed men with sunken eyes and blank looks on their faces indicating the only future they were thinking about was a meal.

I turned the next corner but still no end was in sight. Not until I was halfway down the fourth

side of the block did I reach the end of the line.

"Is this the line for the St. James Mission?" I asked the last man in line.

"Yes."

"Is this space reserved?" I asked, pointing to the spot behind him.

"No."

The line moved slowly. I figured the people of the mission must feed real good to get men to stand in line for so long. Two hours later, I made the first turn. It was three hours before I negotiated the second. And all the while, as I made progress toward the front of the line, it continued to grow in length behind me.

It was another two hours before I turned right and could see the front of the line, one-third of the way down the block. The anticipation of eating made my hunger pains intensify to the point that my stomach was growling. The men in front of, and behind, me felt the same way. This was the highlight of our day and the mood turned as joyous as possible for people in our condition.

Finally, I was inside the door. There was a man standing behind a large kettle on a table. There was a second man standing beside the first.

When it was my turn, the first man picked up a bowl and filled it with a dipper full of soup. The next man handed me a slice of bread and a spoon. I took a place at one of the long tables and used the spoon to shovel the soup to my mouth.

There was no talking at the table. All of the men were busy providing their bodies with much needed nourishment, meager as it was. In a matter of minutes, there wasn't enough soup left to fill my spoon. I used the last bit of bread to wipe up the final drop from the bowl.

I was thankful for the food, but what I had eaten in no way caused the hunger pains to cease. I could have eaten many more bowls of soup and an entire loaf of bread. I took my bowl and spoon to the dishwashing area and put it on the pile with the others.

"Bless you," the man standing by the door said as I walked out.

"Thank you," I said in reply.

I walked the short distance to the end of the line and was surprised to see that it was just as long as it was when I got in it the first time.

"Is this spot reserved?" I asked the last man in line.

I was shocked when the same man who had been in front of me before turned and said, "NO."

The line slowly circled the block again, and I shuffled along with the others, through snow, for seven hours to eat another bowl of soup and bread. I could see that if I was going to stay in Minneapolis long, I would not be able to do anything but stay in line in order to eat. I wanted to look for work, but that was impossible to do when standing in such a long soup line.

On my third trip around the block, I asked another man where a hobo could find a place to rest for the night as it was too cold to sleep outside.

"There's a place called the Washington Annex down two blocks on Washington Street," he said. "It's up a flight of stairs on the second floor. Maybe you could stay there."

I found the door to the stairs under a sign indicating it was the Annex of the St. James Mission.

"Sir, would you have a place for a hobo without any money to spend the night?"

"When did you get to town?" the man behind the desk asked.

"I got here after midnight on a freight and have been standin' in the bread line all day."

"We'll put you up for the night, but we'll have to delouse you first," he said.

The thought of any critter being able to live on me instead of being frozen stiff struck me as funny. I almost chuckled out loud, but kept my thoughts and feelings to myself.

The process of delousing was quite simple. First I took off all my clothes and placed them in a bag. A man pointed to the shower room and took the bag, containing my clothes, out of the room. It felt good to scrub a month's worth of dirt off my body. Then I sat on a stool, naked, until my clothes were returned over an hour later.

"Now go back in that room and find a place to sleep," the man that brought back my clothes said.

I put my clothes on, then walked through the door he pointed to and entered a large room full of cots, most of them occupied. I walked up and down the rows, passing cot after cot. I knew the man in charge wouldn't send me to the room if there wasn't an empty cot. But it wasn't until I was half way down the second-to-the-last row that I found one.

I fell to the cot tired, hungry and weak. I wouldn't dare take off one article of clothing or my shoes, for fear they would be gone when I woke up.

Everyone had to take a shower before they slept there the first time, but it was obvious that many of them had not taken one since. The body odor in the room, along with the snoring and other noises and smells that come from old men, and they were mostly old men, made it one of the most miserable places I ever stayed. Still I was grateful. It was warm in the room and I was out of the wind and snow.

The next day I spent another 16 hours in the bread line. There wasn't anything else for me to do. I wanted to look for work, but I couldn't afford to lose my place in line. I was a guest of the Annex the next night too. And for a third day, I was in the bread line. The line was longer this day than during the two previous days. When I got to the front of the line for the first time that day, the reason became clear.

"Merry Christmas," he said.

"Merry Christmas," I replied. "And bless you."

The realization that it was Christmas caught me off guard. The soup this day held more vegetables and meat. There was also more bread. The extra people in line were counting on a better-than-normal meal. Although no one grumbled about the lack of food being served, the faces I saw in line were somber, melancholy and depressed.

During my wait in line for two more meals of soup and bread, during my first Christmas in a bread line, my thoughts turned to my mother and my family. Oh, we would have fun on Christmas Day. First my father would lead us in a prayer, then everyone was given a present. My mother and sisters spent a good deal of time in the kitchen preparing a turkey and other food for the afternoon meal.

I remember sneaking in from outside, where I would play with my brothers, and Mother giving me a small sample of the turkey or other dish. When all was prepared and placed on the table, we would hold hands and my father would thank the Lord for our family and the food we were about to eat. It was the best eating and most fun meal of the entire year. We would laugh and tell stories and laugh some more.

"Hey there, move along!"

The yelling jarred me from a trancelike state. There was a six foot gap between me and the person in front of me. My daydreaming was holding up the rest of the line.

"Sorry," I whispered.

Two hours later I entered the St. James Mission for the third time that Christmas Day. I sat down and placed the bowl of soup and bread on the table in front of me. I folded my hands together in my lap, bowed my head and closed my eyes.

"Lord, thank you for this food, that it might nourish my body in order to serve you as you see fit. Bless the others in this room that are in need of your help and watch over my family until we can be together again."

With each spoonful of soup I lifted to my lips, I saw an entire Christmas dinner like Mother would make years before. There was turkey and dressing, potatoes and gravy, milk and apple pie in that bowl of soup, at least in my eyes.

I looked across the table and watched as an old man finished eating his soup and bread. He looked up at me when he finished and I was looking into the eyes of a man who was malnourished and still hungry. I looked at my bowl, still half full and my bread laying on the table. I poured half of my remaining soup into his bowl, then handed him my bread. He smiled.

"Thank you, sonny," he said. "Merry Christmas to ya."

I walked back to the Annex feeling better about myself and life in general than I had since the happy times my family enjoyed when I was a little kid.

"When I get settled and on my feet, I'm going to make sure everyone I meet gets something from me, even if it's just a smile or a handshake," I vowed as I fell asleep in the room full of men sleeping on cots.

"Through the doors of the Union City Mission, the unemployed labor of the Northwest flows. ...

"The mission is located in the building adjoining the St. James Hotel which it owns. It is equipped with bathing and fumigating facilities, both so necessary to arrest the spread of disease.

"Except for a minimum contribution from its only supporting agency, the Community Fund, the Union City Mission has been self supporting until the depression years when activities were expanded to include six additional lodging houses.

"The demand upon the Mission rose to a maximum in 1934 when 2,614,333 meals were served and 890,581 lodgings furnished."

Union City Mission pamphlet, circa late 1930s

"His meal finished, the stranger paid a wandering visit to the Rosemont, the Grace, the Manx and the Home, the four hotels controlled by the mission and used entirely to take care of the overflow at the mission building. No meals were served at these hotels. Residents there go to the mission dining room.

"The Union City Mission is overcrowded — but it is clean and the food is wholesome."

Minneapolis Journal, February 25, 1934

29

Stuck in the Bread Line

The winter in Minneapolis was extremely cold, with lots of snow, and I was always hungry.

"If I ever get to where I can afford it, I will eat all I want and whatever I want," I would say to myself over and over while standing in the bread line.

I don't know of anything worse than being a hungry kid and having to go to bed with that empty feeling every night.

In order to better my position, I ventured outside of the skid road area of the city trying to find work. But that could be risky, because I couldn't be gone from the bread line too long and miss a meal. I was willing to miss one of three meals available each day, but if I missed two, and that occasionally happened, I would become weak. I knew that wasn't good when the snow piled up on the streets, and the temperatures plunged below zero.

From experience, I knew how far I could travel from the mission in order to return in time to stand in line and receive three meals of soup and bread a day. If I could rustle up a job for a couple hours within a five-block radius of Washington and Hennepin Streets, I would gladly take it. But those jobs were few and far between. Not only that, but there were fifteen hobos trying to get every job that became available.

It became apparent to me that the only accomplishment I could expect by staying in this city would be standing in the bread line three times a day. There was nothing else I could do; I was stuck. I was afraid to get on a freight, even in a boxcar, because it was so cold. The only smart thing for me to do was to stay put: stand in line three times a day and sleep on a cot, thanks to the good people of the St. James Mission.

There are towns where hobos are welcome for only a few days at a time. Thank goodness Minneapolis did not have such a rule. Or, if they did, it was nice of them to suspend it for that harsh winter.

I spent many an evening looking out the window from the small lobby of the Annex after finishing my last bread-line meal of the day. The view was of Washington Street, and it wasn't a pretty sight.

Vendors would try to sell a few vegetables and fruit; women would sell their bodies. Neither business had many takers because few people had money to spend. If I happened to find a short duration job, I would use the money to supplement my diet. Two hours of work might provide me enough money to buy an apple. That's about all a penny or two would buy.

One evening I was watching the street from my perch in the Annex. Everything was calm and most of the vendors were packing up and heading home after a long day of selling. I watched as an old Greek man I had met and considered a friend began putting his produce into a box. A buyer walked up and started picking out apples

91

like he was going to pick one to buy. My friend seemed happy that the man was going to buy one, but when the man tried to walk away with the fruit in his hand, the old man grabbed his arm. The man shoved my friend to the ground. The vendor was up and yelling at the man as he ran after him. The other man pulled out a gun, turned and shot him. My friend died on Washington Street in the cold of a Minneapolis winter because of an apple worth a penny. The gunman started to run, but the police arrived and arrested him.

table when I was young, my father would sometimes talk about his family back there. More than once he talked about a relative who lived in St. Paul. He had a business there named The Holm Tire Company.

One day, when I was feeling particularly low in spirits, the thought occurred to me to go to St. Paul to look up this relative. Perhaps there was a good meal in the venture. After all, that's what my father and mother would offer any relative who wandered in from the cold. At the very least, there was a possibility that I would meet and visit

I was sad about my friend, but I felt thankful about my situation, appalling and grim as it was, because I could see others, every day, who were in a worse predicament. It's bad enough to be down and out in the world and not be able to find work because there were so many others looking for the same job, but the world seems hopeless when a person is stuck in the middle of a dreadful winter under those conditions.

I had to break out of the frozen hell that Minneapolis had become for me that winter, or at least try to make life better. My father was from Minnesota. When we were seated around the

with a member of the Holm family.

Although my feet were still a bit tender from being frozen during my trip into town, I felt well enough to try to make contact with my relatives. I asked the man at the front desk to wake me at 5 a.m., which he did. I followed his directions to the outskirts of Minneapolis and walked the other 20 miles to the Holm's Tire shop in St. Paul.

It was about 3 p.m. when my hand turned the knob on the shop door. Inside there was an old desk and an elderly man seated behind it.

"Are you Mr. Holm?" I asked. "I'm a Holm, too. My father is the Reverend Holm."

"I have a cousin by that name," he said. "Sit down, young man. What are ya doing here?"

"I'm lookin' for work in Minneapolis and eatin' in the bread line. I'm flat broke, but I'll take any work I can find."

"Times are sure tough aren't they?" he asked.

"Oh yes," I said, excited that there was another man who understood what I was going through.

We continued our discussion for another two hours, covering family information and the hard times experienced by our country. Abruptly at 5 p.m., my father's cousin stood up and fumbled in his pocket for his keys. I also stood up, in an act of respect, as I had been taught by my parents. We walked to the door and both went outside.

"Well, it's been nice talkin' to you, Monrad," he said while locking the shop door. "I've got to get home now. Thanks for stoppin' by. Oh, and give your father my best."

I stood beside the shop door and watched him walk down the street until he turned left at the end of the third block. He hadn't offered me a bite to eat or a dime. And I was too proud to ask.

I turned and walked the 20 miles back to Minneapolis, arriving at my cot cold, hungry and weak from missing my bread-line meals for the day. Although I was very tired, sleep did not come easy.

I came from a family who opened the door of their home to friends, relatives and many strangers in need of a meal, and many strangers had treated me kindly during my time on the road.

The attitude of my relative was difficult to understand. Perhaps he was also suffering during this nationwide depression. But I knew he wasn't suffering much because he was carrying a few extra pounds around the middle. Both sides of the topic circled my mind during the night with no resolution.

30

The Riot

Usually I was wide awake and out of bed before most of the others in the room full of cots opened their eyes. This day I was the last. My forty mile journey during the prior day made me extra tired, and I didn't wake up until the others had left the room to join the bread line. Stomach pains reminded me that I hadn't eaten in two days.

I staggered out of the building and into the below-zero cold to the end of the line. During my stay in Minneapolis, the hobo population continued to grow in the skid road section of the city. The wait to get to the front of the line and a meal of soup and bread now became an eight-hour ordeal.

The men in the line shuffled forward when space appeared ahead of them. When viewed from one end of the block, the line seemed to be a living being, like a snake crawling through the grass. If times weren't so tough, I'm sure many of the things that happened in the line would have been considered humorous.

Instead, humor was not on anyone's mind. We all thought about making it to the front of the line, being able to sit down for a few minutes and gulping down the food offered. Staying alive was serious business.

When times are tough, people resort to tactics they normally wouldn't think of doing. The bread line was proof. While making the pilgrimage from the back of the line to the front, men would offer items for sale, like jeweled railroad watches for 25 cents and overcoats for a nickel. No one asked where the items came from, because most of them were stolen. Still, these things were hard to sell because the men in the line didn't have much money, if any.

One day a man approached the line and singled me out.

"Hey kid, look at this," he said holding an object in his hand that looked like a knife handle.

"What is it?" I asked.

"Watch this," he said, pushing a button on the handle.

I jumped back as a knife blade popped out. The man then made a swipe at my throat with the knife.

"A kid like you could make a lot of money with a knife like this. I'll sell it to ya for only a nickel."

Frightening and hurting people was so far from my way of thinking and living that the thought made me want to throw up. I probably would have done just that if there would have been anything in my stomach at the time. My head snapped away from the man and I grabbed my stomach. When I turned back around a few seconds later, the man was gone.

Once again I thought about leaving the city, but the idea of riding the rails in midwinter stopped me. I would think about being caught on the road without a place to spend the night and with no food. As bad as it was for me, Hennepin and Washington Streets were my home for now. Time has a way of dragging on when most of it is spent in a line with hundreds of other men.

January and February slipped by, and I was still standing in the bread line in March. Word circulated on the street about a group of people getting together at the county courthouse to talk about food. I was a curious kid, and hungry. Naturally, if there was going to be an event about food, I wanted to be there.

On the morning of the get-together I arrived early, just in case food was available, but many others must have had the same idea. Hundreds of people were already there. I was standing at the back of the group which was in the middle of an intersection. I could see the top of the courthouse, but not much more. A noise to my right distracted me. Looking down that street I saw a wall of people heading for the spot where I was standing. I looked to the left and saw the same thing. I turned around to run, but a third wave of people was marching in my direction. I was trapped in the middle of what seemed like thousands of people and they were all mad. I was just hungry.

The people coming from the right and left turned toward the courthouse when they reached the intersection. The people coming from behind me didn't stop, and I had to move forward or be crushed. A man nearby fell, but the crowd didn't stop. They walked on him and over him. Then there was a man on the ground in front of me, and I tried to step over him, but was pushed from behind. My right foot landed on his left hand and a man to my right stepped on his midsection. The man on the ground was yelling, but no one could stop to help him.

The crowd continued to surge forward, then it drifted right, then left. I was forced to go where the crowd went. We passed a truck loaded with coal parked by the curb. Two men climbed up on the truck and started throwing lumps of coal at

the policemen standing on the curb. Sometimes the throwers missed their target and the coal hit the people in the riot, bouncing from head to head before falling to the ground. The policemen began throwing pieces of coal back into the crowd. It reminded me of a bunch of kids throwing dirt clods at each other, like I had done in Rapelje. The situation would have seemed funny to me if lumps of coal weren't bouncing off my head.

The huge group continued to surge in different directions and I wanted to get out of the mess and back to the Annex. After making several attempts, I found it was impossible to exit a riot if a person was caught in the middle.

I saw a spray of water in the air near the courthouse and knew the fire department was using fire hoses to soak the crowd. During a cold winter, just the water alone would be enough to make everyone want to go home. But I also saw a can tossed into the air by a policeman that was trailing what looked like smoke.

"Tear gas!" someone yelled, and the crowd surged backward, then forward again.

From my vantage point, I didn't know what was going on except that I was afraid for my safety. The canisters of tear gas were thrown back at the police who threw them back at the crowd. I tried to anticipate the way the crowd was going to move next and make sure I didn't stumble and fall. At one point I was going along with the crowd and moving forward, toward the courthouse, when I noticed those in front of me backing up quickly. Then the man in front of me turned to face me and tried to run. I turned too, but there was little room to run. We were all basically running in place and making as little as six inches of progress per step.

As one mass, the crowd moved away from the courthouse. I heard the screams of men falling and being trampled. I could only watch out for myself at that point and I concentrated on keeping my feet under me. We moved as one for about two blocks. It took that long for the compact mass to disperse a little. I then had room to stretch my legs and everyone was running and we scattered in all directions.

I went straight to the Annex, curled up on a cot and lay there for an hour as I tried to overcome the fear that was still gripping me. Hunger finally caused me to get up and head for the bread line, but there was only enough time for me to get one meal. The men in the line were talking about the riot, saying that some people were killed, others injured and several arrested.

"Why did that happen?" I asked.

"Here, read this," one said as he handed me a newspaper.

There was an article about an assistance program for families that the government was going to stop funding. The three-hour riot resulted from a march that was planned to protest the funding cut. I was relieved to find out later that no one was killed.

I shuffled along with the others in the bread line and ate once that day. But I was thankful for the soup and bread and that I made it through the riot with only a couple bruises and a few lumps on my head.

"Thousands of unemployed stormed the city hall today ... Meeting quietly at the Minneapolis auditorium, several thousand paraded through the loop, gathering additional marchers as they went. They approached the city hall from the fourth street side, ...

"A policeman tossed out a black cylinder. When it struck the sidewalk, a hazy cloud arose.

'It's tear gas,' someone shouted."

Minneapolis Star, April 6, 1934

"What started as an orderly parade of unemployed to present requests to the city council today ended in the most serious rioting in the city's history.

"A crowd of 6,000 men and women, the great part of them orderly and law abiding, massed about the courthouse. ...

"Throughout all of the fighting the legitimate unemployed, making up at least 75 percent of the crowd, took no hand in the rioting. ...

"Another truck, containing coal, also fell prey to the rioters. Soon large chunks of coal and bottles were being used. ...

"Chief Johannes said he would ask Fire Chief Trager for men and that if the 'water cure' failed to work he would order machine guns distributed to certain officers. ..."

Minneapolis Journal, April 6, 1934

31

Not All Food is Healthy

Holidays were special to my family when I was a little guy. My mother would fix great meals using the best food my parents could afford. Each one of those special days were filled with visiting, playing with friends, and with lots of love mixed in.

Easter and Christmas were extraordinary holidays because my father was a minister. Besides the love and fantastic food on these days, we celebrated a religious event too.

As Easter approached in the spring that I was in Minneapolis, I was determined that I would not eat Easter dinner in the bread line. The day before Easter, I went in search of work so I could buy a meal at a restaurant.

I started walking away from the skid road area of the city, zigzagging along the streets, trying to find a job within a reasonable distance of the Annex. The only job available that spring, the only one I asked about, was shoveling snow. After about 20 miles and hours of walking around town, and asking for a job at every business I passed, an old man said he could use some help clearing the snow from the front of his store.

The snow was deep that year and this man hadn't cleared away the prior snow that had fallen. People had just walked on top of what was there. I worked for four hours clearing the compact snow and ice from the front of his business.

"Nice job young man," the businessman said

as he dropped 25 cents into my hand.

"Thank you, sir," I replied.

I was a long way, at least 15 miles, from the Annex and extremely tired. I walked a few blocks, when I noticed a street car heading the same direction as me. It stopped a half block away and I ran to the open door.

"How much to Hennepin and Washington?"

"Twenty cents," was the reply.

My exhausted condition warranted the expenditure and I climbed aboard.

The street car dropped me off four blocks from the Annex. I missed my meals in the bread line that day and collapsed on a cot tired and hungry.

"Well, maybe Easter dinner at the mission will be better than other meals," I reasoned while drifting off to sleep.

Because of my weakened condition, I slept longer than usual once again. But  once awake, I was up and out the door. The line was longer than normal because the day was a holiday and others, besides me, were anticipating a fine holiday meal. Our excitement increased as word drifted back from the front of the line that ice cream was being served along with the meal. I hadn't tasted ice cream in over two years and my stomach growled and my mouth watered at the thought of placing a spoon full of the cool and creamy confection in my mouth.

All of a sudden I didn't feel as bad about having to stand in line as I usually did. I was going to eat ice cream on this Easter Sunday and that made the day special, just like it was when I was with my mother and father years before. Usually there was not one smile on any face in line, but today everyone was smiling. So, the other men and I shuffled along together with lifted spirits, just like an Easter Sunday should make all of us feel.

Ordinarily there was little conversation between people standing in line, but when we turned the last corner and the door to the mission came into view on this special day, the men chattered freely. Instead of being without a focus or a purpose in life with nothing to look forward too, these men were excited about getting a little bowl of ice cream. The dish represented more than just something extra that day. It represented hope for the future, for if we were to get ice cream today, maybe there would be more meat in the soup tomorrow and eventually maybe there would be a job for each and every one of us.

With only 100 people ahead of me, I felt good and talked about past holidays with the man in front of me. Then there were only 80 and the man behind me asked about life as a preacher's son. When there were only 40 men ahead of me, I listened to a man tell three of us about his family of three sons and two daughters. When there were 20 men in front of me, a man from the mission stepped out of the door and climbed a snow bank near the street. He held a large spoon in one hand and a pot in the other. He banged the pot with the spoon to get our attention.

"I'm sorry to tell you this, but all of the ice cream is gone."

It was as if he had taken a dagger and plunged it into the spirit of the line and killed the happiness that had preoccupied us for the past three hours.

"But we still have plenty of soup and today everyone gets extra bread."

I shuffled to the door like the rest and ate my food. When I left the building, I again headed for the back of the column for another trip through the line. I was disheartened about missing the ice cream that made today's wait in the bread line special. And I was depressed and discouraged about my purpose in life and about life in general. I turned the corner, expecting to see the end of the line, but was surprised to see that there was no line at all. I hurried to the next corner and, again, the line that usually snaked around the building was not there.

The end of the St. James Mission bread line extended around only one corner of the block, instead of the usual three corners. My spirits were once again raised a notch because I would get my next meal after a two hour wait instead of the normal eight hours.

"Where are the rest of the men?" I asked the man ahead of me.

"I don't know and I don't care," he said. "I'm hungry and could sure use more food."

I agreed with him about needing the extra food, but something was wrong, dreadfully wrong. I felt awkward about the man saying he didn't care about what happened to the other men that usually waited with me in the line. On one hand I would get more food, but I just couldn't shake the need to care about my fellow man.

When we reached the front of the line, I asked about the others.

"Some of the ice cream was bad," the man serving the soup said.

Apparently all of it was bad, because every man who ate even a little bit became sick with food poisoning. Someone said it had been thawed out and refrozen several times from the time it was made until it was served to the men in the bread line. The people who gave it to the mission were well intentioned and didn't know it

98

had spoiled, and neither did the people at the mission. Since fewer men were standing in line looking for food, I was able to go through the line two more times.

I was grateful for having the chance to eat two extra meals that Easter Sunday, but I was more thankful for not having a chance to eat the tainted ice cream. Many of the men who became sick were staying at the Annex with me. It was four days before many of them could stand again.

With the line shorter, I was able to get four and sometimes five bowls of soup a day. I was malnourished and needed to regain my strength, but after one day with extra food, I felt guilty. The only reason I was able to eat more was because someone else was too sick to stand in line. On the second day, I asked the men at the mission if I could take my second bowl of soup and slice of bread to the Annex. After explaining the situation, they were still skeptical, but let me leave with a full bowl.

I fed part of it to an old man who could only take a few sips of the soup and a bite of the bread, then gave the rest to another man. When the bowl was empty, I noticed a man from the mission standing by the door. He was checking up on me; making sure the soup and bread was going to the needy. I said hello to him as I left the room, then resumed my position at the end of the bread line. My feelings were again lifted. I felt good, better than I had in years.

Two hours later I again entered the mission holding the dirty bowl I had been allowed to take with me. I took it and the spoon to the dishwashing area, then got some more food for myself. When I was about to leave, the man who watched me at the Annex gave me another bowl of soup and slice of bread.

"Would you take this to someone like you did before?"

"Sure."

I split the bowl between two other men, but made sure the old man had a couple of sips first. I continued this practice for two more days. The men at the mission gave me extra soup to eat and a full bowl to take to the Annex each time I went through the line. I stopped when most of the men were able to stand in the bread line again. The experience boosted my self-esteem and the extra soup they gave me to eat boosted my strength so much that I felt better than I had in months.

Two weeks later I entered the mission and was given a large hunk of the nicest looking ham ever produced. Meat was scarce during those days, so I thought I was getting something special. Then I noticed that all the men in the room had a large hunk of ham just like me. I tried to cut it but couldn't. It was like rubber. I looked around and noticed others were pulling it apart with their hands. I did the same and placed a small piece in my mouth. The ham was impossible to chew and actually seemed to grow in size the more I chewed it. I watched the man sitting across from me try to chew a piece of the meat as I was doing. Finally, he just swallowed it and I could see he had a hard time getting it down. I watched another man do the same thing.

I couldn't bring myself to swallow a piece of meat that was not chewable. I took the piece out of my mouth and placed it on my plate. I offered the rest of the meat to the man next to me. He took it and thanked me. I headed out the door of the mission and stopped at the back of the bread line, which was once again as long as it was before Easter.

32

Riding Inside With High Hopes

I had been in the great city of Minneapolis for almost four months, but, while spring was trying to break the grip of a nasty winter, the cold would not allow me to safely move to another destination. I decided to stay in the bread line until I could move to another place to look for work without fear of freezing to death enroute.

The men seemed a bit more cheerful as the shining sun began to melt the piles of snow that surrounded us as we stood in line, day after day. There was more talk about families and the prospects of work in different parts of the country. I was listening to all of the talk, but not all of it was pleasant.

Conversations would drift along the line as men talked about wives and children, and their pride would be evident in the smiles on their faces.

"I'm going to be with 'em soon as I can find a job and bring 'em here. Then we'll be a family again," was the gist of much of the talk.

Listening to such talk caused me to think about life with my mother and father, and how we were a happy family before my mother died. It made me sad.

However, the talk about the prospect of finding jobs in different parts of the country excited me. A steady job was the only way I was going to get ahead in the world, and I was determined not to stay a hobo or a sheepherder for the rest of my life. So, when there was talk of several jobs

down south or in the east, I listened and asked questions about the conditions there. Most of the time I was able to see through the idle talk and recognize the risks of traveling hundreds of miles just because one or two men said there were jobs waiting for hungry men.

I listened to all of the rumors and I was considering one or two directions to travel as soon as the weather broke. Two men who were staying at the Annex were headed south in a day or two. Five others wanted to head east in a month. I still wasn't convinced that traveling in any direction would be in my best interest right then.

"I'm going to head back home to Arizona," I overhead a man behind me in the bread line say one day. "But I wish I was from Montana."

"Yeah," the man in front of him said, "they're the lucky ones."

I gave up five places in line to talk to these guys.

"What were ya sayin' about Montana?"

"People from Montana have the priority on gettin' jobs on a new project there," one told me.

"Yeah, I hear it's up around the Fort Peck area," another said.

"Well, I'm from Montana," I told them.

"What are ya doin' here?"

I wondered that too, as I waited another four hours in line for soup and bread. Traveling during the cold weather was still my primary concern. Although my health was better because of the little extra food I had received just after Easter, I knew my body was not up to its normal strength.

I had seen the man in charge of the Mission several times. He seemed like a nice man who was sympathetic to the people who visited his feeding station. I saw him walking through the building as I was finishing my soup one day. I followed him up the stairs to his office, approached him and introduced myself.

"I know who you are," he said. "You helped feed the men at the Annex."

I explained my job prospect to him and my concern about my physical condition.

"I would normally just hop a freight to Glasgow, sir, but I don't feel my body's up to it right now."

"I don't know, this is highly unusual, but I'll see what I can do for ya," he said. "Come back in two days and I'll have some news."

I spent two more days circling the block near the mission for soup and bread, then walked up the stairs again.

"You are a lucky young fellow," he said. "I have a pass on the Great Northern for you to Glasgow. Now, do ya have enough money for food during your trip?"

"No, sir. I don't have a penny."

He sat down at his desk and scribbled something on a piece of paper.

"You take this to the kitchen for some sandwiches."

"Thank you, sir," I said. "This means so much ..."

Tears filled my eyes and I couldn't continue.

He walked around his desk and walked me to the door.

"Young man, these are tough times for all of us. I've a feeling helping you now will benefit others in the future."

I shook his hand and thanked him again. My faith in the goodness of my fellow man was renewed and I wanted to tell him of my feelings, but he wouldn't let me.

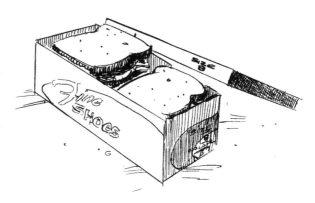

"Now get going to the kitchen, so ya don't miss that train — and good luck."

I turned and headed down the stairs to the kitchen. A man there read the note and started making sandwiches. When a shoe box was full, he handed it to me.

"You must be somethin' special," he said.

"No, I've just got a job prospect."

I hadn't formed many friendships in Minneapolis, but there were a few. I went to the Annex to tell them good-bye, then I walked to the train station.

It was nice to ride inside, but it was a strange and unpleasant trip for me. I couldn't put the thought out of my mind that there were many other boys and men riding on top of the cars or on the rods, under the cars. For three days I watched the countryside pass by my window, ate my sandwiches and dozed off from time to time.

The conductor finally called out "Glasgow, Montana," three times as he passed through the car.

I stepped from the train with high expectations.

"Where's this Fort Peck Dam at?" I asked the first man I saw.

"Go down three streets, then take a right and follow that road to the dam."

"How far?"

"Seventeen miles."

With no money in my

101

pockets and there being no other way out there anyway, I decided to start walking until a car or truck came along, then I would thumb a ride.

After walking the entire 17 miles without a single vehicle willing to stop for me, a fascinating sight came into view. There were machines operating, vehicles moving and men scurrying all over the place. The typical six inch deep Montana dust was evident: clouds of fine dirt hung in the air from all the work. I found the office and rushed up the steps, eager to join a crew and start work.

"Hello, I'm here for my job, bein' from Montana and all."

An older fellow stepped in front of me and looked me up and down.

"Well sonny, I can't hire everyone in Montana, now can I? But if you're an engineer, I've got work for you."

I relayed my railroading experiences, but told them I've never been allowed to be the engineer on one. The man chuckled and commented about there being different kinds of engineers.

I stepped out of the office with my hopes once again deflated. The work site didn't look like a good place to spend the night, so I headed back to town. Once again I walked the 17 miles without getting a ride. It was cold in Glasgow, just like it had been in Minneapolis. I headed for the hobo jungle in search of a place to sleep. Several men were hunkered around three fires, planning to stay the night. There wasn't room for another man, if they all were to stay warm. They told me that the hostler at the roundhouse would let hobos sleep near the boiler, and all of them had accepted his hospitality from time to time.

The hostler was a wonderful man. I didn't ask him, but I'm sure he was once a knight of the road, like me, because this was the most considerate hostler I ever met.

The good folks of Glasgow had big hearts and they realized what a tough time the hobos were having. They had an assistance program where a person could work on the street for two

hours a day, shoveling dirt where needed, cleaning the streets or doing other odd jobs. In turn, the person would receive 60 cents in the form of a meal ticket for a restaurant or a voucher for a grocery store. I felt the groceries would do more to keep my belly full than visiting a restaurant, so I always took the grocery voucher.

At the jungle, I met several other men who had the same idea. We pooled our food and prepared some of the best hobo stew ever made. After about two weeks of working for the city of Glasgow for two hours a day, eating stew with the others and sleeping on a bench next to the boiler in the roundhouse, I felt my body strength returning. There were two reasons for my recovery: First, the days weren't as cold as my days in the bread line in Minneapolis, so I wasn't shivering off calories, and, second, I was eating my fill of good meat and vegetables in the stew each day.

While I was thankful to the City of Glasgow, that didn't stop me from trying to make my life better. One day another hobo asked 10 of us to consider a plan.

"What if we go back to where we got these grocery vouchers in the afternoon, when there is a different girl at the desk, and see if we could get another voucher."

"Oh, I don't know if I like the idea," I said. "It's like stealin' somethin' from a town that's helpin' us."

"Monrad think of it like this: What if you worked another two hours a day, wouldn't you expect to get paid the same amount again?"

I told him I would. They told me to do twice the work then, if I wanted.

We discussed the scheme for a few minutes and decided it was worth a try. For a few days, I believe we were the best fed hobos in the country. We were collecting $1.20 every day and eating like kings. We were even eating strawberries out of season and having steaks on a regular basis.

I tried to work twice as hard during my two hours on the job each day, in order to justify collecting twice the pay. The distinction was important to me, but I don't think it mattered to some of the others in our group. Some of them hardly worked at all during the time they were expected to earn their pay.

After two weeks of this high living, I began to think we had developed a nice life for the 10 of us. One evening we were finishing off a batch of steaks when we noticed a truck driving towards the jungle. I saw that it was a city truck and the thought occurred to me that perhaps they were now delivering the food to us, but that was not the case.

The driver got out and called out 10 names of which one was mine. We were ordered to climb into the back of the truck. When we hesitated, a city policeman waved to us from the passenger side of the truck. The truck drove us outside the city limits of Glasgow and stopped. We were ordered out of the truck and told that we were not welcome in the town any more.

"We caught on to your little scheme, boys" the man said.

The group of us started walking west with full stomachs, but those full stomachs soon were empty. Montana towns are not close together and that didn't help our situation. We split into smaller groups and, after a couple days, I was again a hobo alone looking for food and shelter.

I wasn't proud that Glasgow thought I was taking more than my fair share. I, of course, felt my work deserved the extra pay. I am thankful to the City of Glasgow for giving me a chance to regain my strength so I could continue my journey in search of a steady job and a permanent place to hang my hat.

33

A Trip Home

About this time I had a strong urge to go home to see my father. I knew he had received a new assignment with the church that required him to move the family to Strool, South Dakota. I checked around the local jungle and found the depot closest to him was at Hettinger, North Dakota, 52 miles from Strool.

I had an uneventful trip to Hettinger, stepping from the freight at about 6 a.m. The town was starting to stir, with the most action occurring around the livery stable. After asking directions to make sure I was on the right road, I started putting one foot in front of the other. It took me two days to walk to the city limits of Strool. I spent the night sleeping in a haystack, and ate a sandwich and some other bread I had begged at a house before I got to Hettinger.

Although I could have walked around the small town until I found my father's church and the parsonage, I asked directions at the first business I came to.

"Could you please show me the way to the Lutheran church?" I asked two men at a filling station and garage.

"Ain't no Lutheran church in Strool, but the preacher's parsonage is down that way and to the right," one of the men said. "But they ain't home right now. They were by here and gassed up about three hours ago — said they'd be home later this evening."

At first I was disappointed that I had walked all that way just to find my father out of town, but then I realized that it gave me a chance to see the town and eat a meal. I found a cafe, ordered a bowl of stew and ate it, then ordered a second bowl and finished that off, sopping up the last drop of liquid with bread. I felt full and content for the moment.

As I walked out of the cafe, I noticed a general store across the street. It had been 18 months since I had seen my sister Ruth, and I wanted to give her a present. I looked around at the different items in the store and considered buying either a few pieces of candy or a doll. The candy was within my price range while the doll was just beyond what I figured I could afford. Yet, I had a hard time giving up on the doll and picked it up for a closer look.

"She's cute, isn't she?"

The voice startled me and I turned to find a man standing near me with an apron on.

"Ah, yes sir, she's a beautiful doll," I said. "My sister would like it, but I can't afford her. Guess I better just buy a couple pieces of candy."

"You want to buy this for your sister?"

"Yes, sir, Ruth Holm."

"Is the Reverend Holm your father?"

I nodded and set the doll down.

The man introduced himself as Mr. Ogard, the store owner and postmaster of Strool.

"Your father's a fine man, and does a lot of good for this town, I'll tell ya. Say, why haven't you been around before?"

"Well," I said, shuffling my feet a bit and looking down. I didn't want to answer, but the man kept looking at me, waiting.

"I've been on the road a bit," I finally stammered.

"As your father says, 'We've all got our cross to bear,' and that applies to a preacher's son, too," the man said, then he reached around me, grabbed my shoulders and pulled me close to him in a half hug. "Now let's talk about this doll — I know Ruth would like it, too. Let's see, five pieces of candy would cost you two pennies, so that's what I'm gonna charge ya for the doll."

"But ... ," I protested.

"I'll not discuss it further," he said. "Look young man, your father has been very kind to me and my family, and if the truth were known, I owe him more than you'll ever know. Now, this here doll is yours to give to Ruth."

He handed me the doll and I turned to leave when he stopped me.

"Aren't you forgetting something?" he said. "You owe me two pennies."

I was embarrassed that I had forgotten the deal struck just a minute ago and reached into my pocket for the money. When I handed him the pennies, he bent down and got close to me and asked, "What kind of candy do you like?"

"The horehound, there," I said pointing to a jar.

The man dug five pieces out of the jar, put them in a sack and handed them to me.

"Thank you, sir," was all I could say.

"Oh, now be off with ya," he said smiling. "Go visit with your father."

I would have protested again, but it was obvious that the man was proud of his kindness. My father's message of generosity had reached him, and I wouldn't take that away from this man or my father.

I walked to my father's house, but it was clear that he had not returned home, so I walked around the town for a couple of hours. The people of Strool were a friendly bunch, and it wasn't hard to strike up a conversation with an old man sitting on his front porch or the young couple taking their child for a walk. Whenever the Reverend Holm was mentioned in a discussion, people smiled and talked of him as a teacher and guide in their lives.

I returned to the parsonage and circled it twice, looking it over. Both buildings, the parsonage and the garage were freshly painted; the windows were clean and the picket fence was level and straight. My father's influence was apparent at the parsonage as well as throughout the town. I was proud of my father and the positive influence he had on others.

The sound of a car approaching caused me to turn. I could see my father at the wheel, his wife in the passenger seat and little Ruth peaking out the side window. I hurried to open the car gate, and my father drove into the yard, stopping in front of the garage.

As soon as he opened the car door, little Ruth was out of the car and running to me. I knelt down, and she ran into my arms with such force that we almost tumbled to the ground.

"Monrad, I've missed you," she said.

"I've missed you, too," I said. I held out the doll and said, "Here, I brought this for you."

Ruth took the doll and gave it a big hug too.

Then my father was standing near me. I stood up, not knowing his attitude about me leaving his house, then returning like this.

"Oh, Monrad," he said as he put his arms around me

in a bear hug. "It's nice to have you here."

My father held me for a minute or more, squeezing hard all the while. I hugged him back for all I was worth. Then we went into the house and sat at the dining room table. We drank coffee and visited as little Ruth sat on the floor nearby and played with her new doll. My father wanted to know everything. I told him only the good parts of my adventures. I asked about my brothers and sisters and was brought up to date about our family. At one point, my father glanced at his watch and jumped from his chair.

"Oh my," he said. "I've got to visit Mrs. Nelson, Monrad, before it gets too late. She's one of my flock."

I looked at the mantel clock and noticed my father and I had been talking for two hours.

He turned to me and grabbed my shoulders. "Monrad, I'll be home in an hour or so, and we'll have supper and talk some more." His hands squeezed my shoulders and he bent down, putting his face closer to mine. "It's good to have you here, son," he said. I felt good and warm inside as I watched my father leave the house to visit one of his flock: an elderly woman who was sick.

Ruth was still playing with her new doll and some of her other toys. She had grown from just a toddler into a cute 4-year-old. I sat down on the floor beside her and we chatted and played with her toys.

I could hear my father's wife in the kitchen as she began to prepare the evening meal. We had not said one word to each other, but that didn't bother either of us. Suddenly she was standing beside me and pointing out the window.

"Father Hoyp is coming," she said.

She was obviously upset, but I couldn't figure out why a priest walking down the street would bother her. She looked at me, outside at the priest, then at me again. I looked at my clothes and couldn't see anything wrong. Granted they were a little tattered, torn in spots and a bit dirty, but they were in great shape for someone who was on the road as much as I had been.

Her distress grew as Father Hoyp crossed the street and approached the front gate. She turned to me and put her hand on her hip. She was in charge now and she knew what she wanted.

"Monrad, I'm ashamed of you," she said. Then she walked to a closet door. "Now, I want you to get in there and stay until I let you out."

I looked at my sister Ruth, who was still playing with her toys, seemingly unaware of what was going on, then at this woman who was ashamed of me. I stepped into the closet as the priest knocked on the door.

I stood in the darkness of the closet and listened, but I could hear only parts of the conversation.

"Afternoon, Mrs. Holm. Is the Reverend Holm in?"

"No, Father Hoyp. He went to visit ..."

"Father Hoyp, look at the doll my brother brought me."

"Oh that's nice Ruth," the priest said. "When do you expect him to return?"

"He should be back within the hour."

They talked for another five minutes or so, then he left, saying he would be back in the morning.

The closet door remained closed for a few more minutes, until the priest was out of sight, I supposed. When the door opened, I remained still for a few seconds, looking at my father's wife.

"You'll never be ashamed of me again," I said, and I walked straight for the front door.

I noticed Ruth looking at me and I stopped, knelt down and opened my arms to her. She came over and gave me a big hug.

"No matter what, Ruth," I said. "You remember that I love you very much."

"I love you too, Monrad," she said.

Then I stood up and opened the front door of my father's house and stepped outside.

"You'll never amount to nothin'," my father's wife shouted after me. "You'll always be on skid road."

I stopped, turned and looked her in the eye, then smiled. I turned back and walked through the gate, whistling as I went. Without knowing it, this woman had just given me a goal to shoot for. How I was going to achieve it was unknown, but I had no way to go but up.

I walked a couple of blocks until I was out of sight of my father's house, then stopped. I didn't want to leave Strool until my father and I had a chance to visit again. An explanation about why I left his house the first time and why I left before he returned this time seemed the proper thing to do.

Then I thought about Ruth. She seemed happy and her life was good. I didn't want anything to change that, especially me. I turned and walked out of town.

"My father was the Lutheran Minister in Strool, South Dakota, for seven years. He was respected and loved by his congregation and all of the townspeople. My mother was a nurse and served the entire community, day or night.

"The day Monte came home, when I rushed into his arms and he gave me the doll, is still vivid in my mind."

Ruth Holm Sawyer, Monte's sister

34

The Century of Progress Exposition
Chicago (1933-1934)

Although my main focus in life at this time was to find a respectable job and settle down, I was led astray just once: I was distracted from my goal by the Chicago World's Fair. Several hobos I traveled with mentioned it, and the subject was brought up more than once during the time I spent in Minneapolis.

County fairs were common in those days, but I only visited a couple during my childhood. I enjoyed the two I did attend; they were fun and had many exhibits. However, I couldn't imagine what could make me face the dangers of riding the rails to Chicago just to see exhibits like those offered at the various county fairs around the country.

Then one evening in a Montana hobo jungle, I talked with a traveling man who had just returned from the fair.

"There's a glass house there," he told me.

"Why would anyone build a glass house?" I asked, but didn't get an answer.

"You can see how a radio works, and a telephone."

I wouldn't mind learning how those marvels worked, but that alone wasn't enough to entice me to make the journey.

"In one room, there's a bunch of jars and each jar has a baby in it. It's small at first, but then each jar has a bigger baby, just like a baby grows in a woman."

"You mean the baby's alive?"

"No, it just shows how a baby grows as the months go by."

"What else is there?"

"Well, I saw a great German airship. It was a Zeppelin."

"I've already seen an airplane."

"This was an airship, not an airplane. And there was the Sky-Ride that takes people from one part of the fair to another."

I still couldn't justify the trip in my mind. The next day another hobo talked about visiting the fair, then another and another. The discussions made me try to rationalize such a trip. If so many people were visiting the Chicago World's Fair, maybe there's something special about it. I decided to go.

I sacrificed by not eating a few meals and worked long hours at several laborer jobs that no one else wanted. It's not that I didn't take the jobs before because I thought the job was beneath me, but there were employers who offered ridiculous wages, like 10 cents a day, and they knew someone would eventually take the job for whatever reason. I worked at a series of such jobs until I had $5 saved up. I sewed the money into my belt lining and hopped a freight to Chicago. On the way, I couldn't help but think how unimportant the trip was. I played the argument inside my head both ways, "Why am I travelin' to a big city just to go to a fair?"

"Because there are many things to see there."

"But it's dangerous to ride the rails and I'd be better to stay put and continue workin'."

"Because it will be fun."

"There will be lots of men out of work, and I'll be hungry most of the time."

"Who cares about a little hunger when you can visit a once-in-a-lifetime fair?"

Before I knew it, my freight was pulling into the yards of Chicago.

"Which way to the fair?" I asked the first person I passed.

"That way," he said pointing.

I walked in the direction the man pointed, for several hours. I asked directions again and walked some more. At dusk I slept in the doorway of a building. I was hungry, but didn't want to spend any of my money until I was at the fair.

At sunrise, I continued my trek through the city of Chicago, asking directions as I went. It was late morning when the gates to the fair were before me and I tried to open them.

"Wait a minute there, son," a guard said. "The fair doesn't open for another 30 minutes."

"Oh, where can I see the glass house?"

"It's over that way," he said gesturing with his hand. "And the Ford building is over there."

"The Ford building?"

"Yeah, that's where they make a car as you watch."

I waited until the gates opened, then cut the thread on my belt and took out my money. It cost me 50 cents to get in, which I thought was expensive, but I was sure the chance to see the glass house and a car assembled before my eyes, would be worth the cost.

There was an industrial section to the fair and an entertainment section. I headed for the entertainment section and found an exhibit called Hollywood. A poster showed a lady named Sally Rand performing a dance with two fans. I didn't know there was such a dance, but decided to see the act. The schedule on the door indicated the fan dance would not take place for another four hours.

I was hungry and started looking for something. There were carts and booths set up along the walkways with people selling all kinds of food. The prices were outrageous. I continued to walk along the avenues of the fair until I spotted an old man unloading a wagon. It was obvious that the job was a hard one for him and the teamster was getting anxious to move on to another vendor.

"Can I give you a hand, mister?" I asked.

"Thanks, I could use some help."

"See Joe, I said youse should get a kid to help with the business," the teamster said from his seat on the wagon.

I helped him unload the wagon and set up his booth. He asked about me; where I was from, what I was doing there and where I was headed next. I told him about my life and that all I was after was a steady job and a place to settle down.

"There ain't no work here, kid; very little anyway," he said. "Chicago has a skid road just like you saw in Minneapolis. Now you go see the fair and be careful with your money. I'll be here until 10 tonight. You be back here at 9:30."

He then gave me three sandwiches. I ate one immediately.

"Space those others out during the day," he said. "Now get goin', and have fun."

I did as he said. My time at the fair was enjoyable. I walked to the industrial section and saw a building that must have been 1,000 feet long. It was the Ford Motor Company building. I went in and was amazed to see a large globe that indicated the operations of the company around the world. There was also an actual automobile assembly line and I saw how an automobile was put together. I walked out of the Ford building with a deeper appreciation of how much work it takes to build motor vehicles.

Other exhibits in the industrial area included an oil refinery and assembly line demonstrations, like how toothpaste was packed inside a tube. I went to every exhibit and demonstration that was free, then headed back to the entertainment part of the fair.

I saw the Sky-Ride shuttle passengers from one part of the fair to another, but I didn't want to ride it because I felt the fare was excessive. A poster of a Midget Village where the little people performed plays caught my eye. I had never seen a midget, and couldn't quite understand the interest in seeing them perform.

"What do you think?" came a voice from nearby.

"I don't know," I said, without looking to see whom I was talking with. "I've never see a midget."

"Look here."

I looked right, then down. There beside me stood a man, but he was very short.

"Now you have," he said. "Are you going to see the show?"

"I would like to, but I can't afford it."

"Come on in and meet the gang," he said. "We're having a rehearsal in 10 minutes. By the way, my name's Sam."

I took his small hand in mine, "I'm Monrad, but my friends call me Mooney."

I followed Sam into the theater and up some stairs. A group of people, all but three of them midgets, were in front of a row of curtains.

"Hi gang, this here's Mooney," Sam said to the group.

They all said hello, then Sam told me how I could help him out.

"Go down there and sit in the middle this way and halfway up that way. Let me know if you can't hear us."

I hadn't realized it, but we were on the stage of an empty auditorium. I walked down the stage steps and sat in the middle of the theater. Those little people sang and danced for two hours, rehearsing for a show scheduled to start that evening. I clapped after each number and thought their show was very enjoyable. I heard every word.

When I left the little people, it was time to see the fan dance. I bought a ticket and entered the building. The place was three times the size of the theater used by the midgets and it was crowded with adults of all ages. The lights dimmed and the audience was entertained by three vaudeville acts before the main attraction was announced.

At last Sally Rand walked on stage with a large, white fan made from feathers in each hand. The fans moved to the music and so did she, but the only parts of her body visible were her feet, head and hands. Her visible skin was painted a beautiful white, like the color of the fans.

She danced for ten minutes, twisting and turning around the stage, moving the fan to her front and back, but not allowing a single glance at the rest of her body. Then the music slowed and Sally Rand slowed her movements, until she stopped. Her arms then slowly raised the fans above her head and she stood there, naked in front of the entire audience.

I was surprised, but not disappointed. She was beautiful.

The curtain closed and I blinked for the first time in minutes. The lights were turned on and the audience shuffled out of the building. I went back to the vendor who gave me the sandwiches.

"Well, did you like the fair?" he asked.

"It was wonderful."

"What part was your favorite?"

"It was all great and there was so much to see, but Sally Rand and her fan dance was the best."

We chatted for a bit longer and he made me five more sandwiches.

"You'll need these for your trip back to Montana."

I hadn't heard another person approach us, but suddenly, from behind me, came a female voice.

"Hi Joe, how's it going for you today?"

"Just fine Miss Rand, and you?"

"Now Joe, I told you to call me Sally. Who's this young man?"

"This is ... What is your name?"

"My name's Monrad."

"It's nice to meet you, Monrad," she said as she held out her hand to me.

"Monrad says your show is the best of the whole fair."

"That so?"

"Yes ma'am."

"You can call me Sally, too."

"She stops by every night for one of my sandwiches," Joe told me after she walked away.

I thanked Joe for his kindness, then left the Chicago's World Fair. The one-day experience had been an expensive one for me, but it was rewarding too. I spent hard earned money to see and do things that I didn't need to see or do. However, the day had been like a breath of fresh air.

After visiting several exhibits, some free and others that charged an entry fee, and the Sally Rand performance, I still had 20 cents in my pocket and that was enough to ride a street car to the freight yard. Within an hour I was on the midnight freight heading west and back to the reality of looking for work during the Depression.

"The Century of Progress Exposition in Chicago (1933-1934) is a good example of a world's fair designed to help alleviate the Depression. ...

"The Ford Motor Company built a 5 million dollar, nine-hundred-foot-long building with a rotunda displaying a twenty-foot globe ... featuring an automobile assembly plant ...

"The Sky-Ride, a two-hundred-foot-tall transportation system, shuttled visitors around the fair ...

"... and the Midget Village starred sixty midgets in plays and other entertainments. Sally Rand was the greatest headline grabber of the fair. Rand was a burlesque dancer who starred in a notorious fan dance that featured her nude body, made up to look like an alabaster statue, behind two large, feathery fans.

"... all waiting for the divine moment when the two fans were held aloft and the naked body was fully revealed. No one could deny the beauty of the spectacle ..."

Comments from people who visited the fair

35

Continuing My Education

After visiting Chicago and the World's Fair, I felt like there was hope for me to find a steady job and settle down. But I was in for a rude awakening. I traveled west a bit, then south, west again, then south and east again, but there was no work to be found. Everywhere I went, the people in charge of hiring would hire their friends or relations, but not a kid like me.

My meals were begged from the people of whatever town I was in. I shared what I had with my hobo friends, and they shared with me. We would cook our meals over the campfires in the local hobo jungle. But there was never enough food and the hunger pains were always present.

As 10 hobos gathered around a cooking fire one evening, a group of 15 men approached and took up positions surounding the group.

"Any IWW members here?" one of them asked.

"I am," a hobo said.

"Me, too," said another.

"Got your cards?"

The hobos reached in their pockets and pulled out a piece of paper.

"What's IWW?" I asked the hobo next to me.

"Industrial Workers of the World," he said. "They're wobblies."

"Hey kid, you got a card?" one of the IWW men asked as he grabbed my arm.

"No, why Should I?"

"Because we want one big union to help the workers," he said, releasing his grip on me.

Naturally I was interested in any group who was going to help workers, but I wasn't prepared for the cost.

"I need a dollar for ya to become a member."

"But I only got a dollar and four bits to my name," I protested.

"Give him the dollar, Mooney, or there'll be trouble," the hobo standing beside me said.

"But . . ."

"Give me the dollar, kid," the IWW man said sternly.

Three of the other IWW men closed in on me and I gave them the money they wanted and they gave me an IWW card. The group didn't ever do me any good as a worker, as far as I know, but I carried that card so I wouldn't have to pay another membership fee.

One evening, after I had shared a hobo stew consisting of one chicken and a few vegetables with 10 other men, I sat and watched the sun set over the Colorado Rockies. My situation wasn't a good one, but I realized it could have been worse. The cooking chores were mine that day and that assured my share of the stew, but one chicken and a few vegetables doesn't go far when that many people are sharing the pot.

The hunger pains returned in less than an hour, and although I had tried to keep such thoughts out of my mind, I knew there was one place where I would be able to cook and eat as much as I wanted. The next morning I was on a freight headed for Malta, Montana.

I walked into the Great Northern Hotel without a penny, and the same clerk was there. We called each other by name, and he assigned me my favorite room. I had a bath and my clothes washed; then I headed for the restaurant. There I ate two dinners of beef stew and bread. My belly was full and I slept well that night and the next two nights. Louis Hensen came to town on the fourth day. He was in need of a herder, so back to the range I went, to the same sheepherder's wagon and the dogs, Tom and Blackie.

This being my third trip to the range, I knew what to do and how to pass the time without going nuts. It was a time to recharge my batteries, so to speak, and a time to eat as much as I wanted to eat and to enjoy my friendship with the dogs.

As before, we were a good team and the sheep under our control did well. We ate good too. I always had lamb, and the dogs fed on the meat of a fat ewe, then chewed on the bones for dessert. The Winchester .33 and I renewed our friendship, too, and I could vary my diet by shooting a sage hen from time to time.

Besides resupplying my body with needed nutrients, I used this time on the range to think about what to do with my life. I thought about going into the trades, like carpentry or masonry, but neither of these occupations appealed to me as a lifetime endeavor. For some reason, completing my education would always enter my mind when I was thinking about different jobs.

After about six months on the range for the third time, and it being late September with winter approaching, I decided schooling was the way for me to go to make a better living than I was used to at that point in my life. The next time Mr. Hensen stopped by the wagon, I told him about my plans and that he would have to get another herder. He said my idea was a good one.

"Monrad, I've told ya before, you're the best herder I've ever had, and that's still true. You go

and get your education. Then you can come back and herd sheep for me again."

It took him about a week to find another herder. I said my good-byes to the dogs and rode with Mr. Hensen to Malta again. After taking out the money for my clothes, along with my stay at the hotel when I arrived in town six months before, he handed me $90. It was more money than I had ever owned. I had been careful with the money I spent on my clothing and the food I ate at the hotel, but, still, I was surprised at the amount placed in my hand. For the first time in my life I felt rich.

The thought of riding a passenger train to Peever, South Dakota, crossed my mind.

"Why not travel inside, where it's safe?" I said to myself.

Then I checked the ticket price and decided it would be smarter to mail the money ahead and ride the freights east. The $90 would be better spent toward my room and board once I arrived in Peever.

By this time, I was more savvy to the ways of the rail and, although no trip on board a train without a ticket could be considered safe, the trip to South Dakota was relatively uneventful.

I arrived at Peever in the afternoon and went directly to see the school principal. He remembered me from my time there a couple of years before.

"How are you doing, Monrad?"

"I'm all right, sir. I've been herdin' sheep again and have saved up my money so I could go to school without doin' much work at the same time."

"Well, I'll help you in any way I can. You're welcome to come to school whenever you would like."

"I'll be there tomorrow mornin', if I can find a place to stay."

He suggested a couple of places and I checked with them, but they were full with boarders. This being a small town, it was not easy to find a place, but one house did have a room to rent for $3 a month. I could not help but think of the miles I had to chase sheep in Montana for $3, but being unable to find another place to stay, I told the landlord I would take the room.

I went to the post office, retrieved the letter I had mailed to myself at general delivery and returned to the landlord. I handed over $18 to pay for six months' rent in advance, so I would have a place to stay in case I went broke before school was out for the year.

There was no place to cook in the room; it just had a bed and a dresser. My next mission was to find a place to eat. The most logical place to begin such a search was the pool hall, as it was the information center for the town.

Upon entering the building, I noticed a nice-looking old man standing behind the counter. I explained my situation and asked if he knew how I could solve my problem of finding a place to eat while attending school.

"If you want, son, you can cook here for me and several other men who come for dinner. Then you can eat some of the food yourself. Say, what's your name?"

"It's Monrad, but my friends call me Mooney."

"Well Mooney, we expect to be eatin' in about an hour."

And that's how I started work as a cook.

After the first meal, the man came back to the kitchen where I was cleaning up.

"Say, that was some mighty fine food, Mooney. How did you learn to cook like that?"

"I've spent some time over a fire in the jungles, and there was no one else to cook for me when I was on the range with the sheep, so I learned because I had to."

"All the guys liked it, so you can consider yourself our cook. Come by and fix yourself somethin' in the mornin' before school if ya like. Oh, and by the way, there's a dance in the city hall every Saturday night. If ya want, you can make hamburgers and coffee to sell and then keep the profit. No one else in town wants to mess with doin' it, but there's lots of people who wish someone would."

And that's how I started selling food at the Saturday night dances.

I felt that my life was beginning to turn around. I had all the food I could eat, and I didn't have to be alone on the range to eat that food. Plus, I was continuing my schooling and making $3 or $4 every Saturday night.

After dinner one evening, an old man who was one of the regulars at the pool hall came into the kitchen. He asked if I would consider him as a roommate and that way we could share the rent. The idea sounded great to me, and we shook hands on the deal. After we fell asleep the first night, I was sorry the deal was set. The old man — he must have been at least 75 years old — snored louder than any other person I've heard.

Over the course of the next two months, I tried all sorts of ways to shut out the noise, but it was no use. I wasn't getting the sleep I needed and when he fell asleep when I was studying, I couldn't concentrate because of the noise. The lack of sleep affected my school work too. Finally I got up the nerve to approach him and explain the problem. He offered to move, and I was grateful.

Another month went by. Then one day, I noticed one of the men who came for supper talking to some children who wore nothing but rags for clothes.

"Who are those children?" I asked him one day.

"They're my children," he said. "I have eight, ya know?"

"But they look hungry, don't ya feed 'em?"

"They do just fine on their own. I give 'em a place to sleep ... and what business is it of yours anyway?"

I walked away before I had a chance to lose my temper. I didn't sleep well that night just thinking about eight children going hungry while their father ate good meals that I was cooking each day.

The next morning I went to the pool hall operator and told him how I felt. It didn't seem to bother the man, and that made me feel worse about the situation.

Sometimes a man has to stand up for what he feels is a moral and ethical way to live. If those around him don't fit that standard, the person has to make the decision to either live with the situation or protest and that's what I did in the only way I could.

"If this man eats one more meal here I'll quit. What he's doin' isn't right, and I won't be a part of it."

The man arrived at the pool hall in time for the evening meal. I cooked the meal, then told the man in charge that, although I was grateful to him for all his help, I couldn't work there anymore and walked out.

I counted $75 in my pocket and figured that I had enough to finish high school while eating in the one restaurant in town. At the time, meals were cheap, and just a bowl of soup was cheaper yet. I ate lots of soup.

36

Death on the Range

The next few months presented a different kind of life to me. I wasn't concerned about my room and board because the money I had saved was enough to cover those expenses. The power of having money available made an impression on me. Watching my money wisely let me concentrate on my schoolwork, and that's what I did.

As the cold of the South Dakota winter raged outside my room, I studied. I viewed my schooling as a ticket to a better life with a steady job, so I allowed nothing else to occupy my time except my all-important schoolwork.

Attending school and studying in my room, with a meal or two of soup each day, was my life during that winter in Peever. It was cold outside and my clothing wasn't adequate for the winter weather. I wanted to make sure I didn't get sick, but I wasn't overly worried because I didn't have to spend much time outside. Every morning I would run to the schoolhouse. In the evening I would run to the restaurant to eat and then run back to my room. My total time outside was a matter of minutes. I felt good, physically fit, and my attitude was good too, because I was building a solid foundation for my future life by finishing my education.

But all of this came to an abrupt halt in February. I didn't feel well one day, but I simply blamed the feeling on too much late night studying. I went to bed early that night realizing my need for extra rest. When I woke up the next morning, the sun was shining and it was well past the time I was usually out of bed. I tried to get up, but couldn't. I was having trouble breathing too. Then sleep overtook me again. During the day I woke up a few more times, but would drift off again without being able to get up.

It's hard for me to recall much about the delirium I suffered, but I do remember some parts. I know it was two days before someone came to see why I hadn't been in school. The landlord later told me the school principal sent for the doctor. There wasn't a doctor in Peever at the time, so one from the next town, 15 miles away, was summoned.

I remember the doctor examining me, but I couldn't talk or get out of bed. I overheard what he told the landlord and the principal, who were also in the room.

"He has double pneumonia and it has progressed to the point that there is little I can do for him. I'm afraid there's little hope."

Hearing that made me determined to beat this illness. I hadn't worked so hard during the past few months just to roll over and die. I wanted to find out if there would be better days for me instead of life as a hobo riding the rails or as a sheepherder on the range. I lay there and said a prayer, then drifted back to sleep.

The landlord and the principal tended to me, giving me food and water. Without their help I wouldn't have made it. From the day the doctor was there, the same day I said the prayer, I stabilized and my condition steadily improved. After three weeks, I felt good again and wanted to get back in school, but the principal wouldn't let me until the doctor checked me out again.

"I'm surprised you're still with us," the doctor told me. "I thought for sure you were a goner."

"I've got too much livin' to do Doc," I told him. "I want to find out what else the Lord has in store for me before I depart."

The doctor laughed and cautioned me about trying to do too much before I had completely regained my strength. I started school again, but I also took his advice and made sure I had plenty of rest.

By the end of March I assessed my financial situation. It was not good. I could not continue to eat at the restaurant and sleep at the house without extra money. I was faced with a couple different avenues to approach the problem. I could try to find work in Peever in order to complete the school year or ask the principal to pass me because of the amount of schooling I'd already had.

"Sir, I think I've learned enough to graduate from high school now instead of in June," I said to him in the office at the school. I didn't want to tell him the real reason I needed to move on was a lack of money. But Peever was a small town and I'm sure he was well aware of my financial situation.

"Monrad, I'll give you the tests tomorrow, if you wish, and, if you pass, I'll see to it that you get your diploma in June."

The next morning, I was given a battery of tests about all the subjects I had studied during the winter. I passed with flying colors, but the tests were easy. We talked for quite awhile afterwards, and I thanked him for all he had done for me that year.

"You've had it hard these past few years," he said. "I expect you to make something of yourself in this world. I know you will."

I left his office feeling good and realizing that he would not have let me fail no matter what.

"Now I won't have to spend the rest of my life herdin' sheep and ridin' the rails," I thought to myself.

But I had no money to get started, so I spent another stint on the range. Hunger was another reason for returning to the range. I was tired of standing in bread lines, and with the sheep, I would always have a full belly.

I had written my sister, Ann, a couple letters while I was in Peever, so it wasn't a surprise when I received a letter from my brother, Gary.

He asked about my plans. I wrote back that I was headed back to the sheep range in Montana and asked if he wanted a job with Hensen, too. So he joined up with me, and we hopped a freight that took us through North Dakota on its way to Montana.

I experienced difficulty in breathing during this trip and was afraid the pneumonia was returning. When the train stopped in Minot, North Dakota, I could see a hospital from the floor of the boxcar where we were sitting. The hospital was beckoning and I wanted to go so bad, but there was no way I could pay for the care I needed.

Gary and I looked around the rail yard in Minot and found a pail, put some dirt in it and scrounged some wood to use as fuel. We fed the fire in that pail during the rest of the trip.

Three days later we were in Malta. Gary and

I walked to the Great Northern Hotel, and I introduced him to the clerk. We stayed in my favorite room again to save money, ate at the restaurant and visited for three days, until Mr. Hensen arrived in town. I introduced Gary and asked about jobs for both of us.

"Yes," he said. "But I can see your brother is no sheepherder; he'll work at the hay ranch."

The three of us rode to the Hensen ranch. Gary was assigned to the haying crew, and I was taken back to the range; to the same wagon, with the same Winchester and the same two dogs, Tom and Blackie.

Having been on the range three times before made this experience easier to bear. I didn't like the time alone, but it was tolerable with a full belly. Gary arrived at the wagon with the tender after I had been there for about two months.

"I guess workin' at the hay ranch isn't the life for me," he told me.

He spent one full day and night with me. The tender was going to pick him up on his way back to the ranch. That evening I fixed us a supper of fried lamb, sage hen and sourdough bread. After we finished eating, we sat by the fire and watched the stars in the sky.

"Monrad, do you remember our mother?"

"Sure I do."

We then talked about our mother, our aunt and the rest of our family for several hours. It was nice to have Gary with me, but the talk about family was making me sad. After catching up on what everyone was doing and learning that everyone was in good health, I got up and walked around the herd as a means of changing the subject. Gary followed me, but he realized that thinking about family bothered me.

"I don't understand how ya can stand it out here all alone with just the dogs and sheep."

"Well, the main reason is hunger," I told him. "I've been hungry so many times that a chance to have as much food as I want is a good reason to be here. Besides I have lots of time to think

about life and what to do with mine. It isn't much money, but when I leave here, I expect to have enough to get me started in another town. I want to settle down, Gary. I don't want to be here or in bread lines all my life."

He said he understood, but I'm not sure he really did. Unless someone spends time with an empty belly or alone on the range, there is no way they can understand what the experience is like.

The next day, about mid-morning, the tender was back at my wagon. Gary and I shook hands and he climbed up to sit next to the man holding the lines. I watched until the wagon was out of sight.

I had been on the range for about three months when one day I noticed a band of sheep, about a mile away, coming toward my flock. I knew that there was another sheepherder to the east and figured these must be his.

"He sure has nerve to let his sheep get into my territory," I thought.

Before I could get to my band and turn them away from the others, the two bands merged into one.

One flock of 3,000 sheep is a handful, but manageable. Six-thousand sheep, however, is a nightmare. I expected the other herder to be with his sheep and continued to look out for him. I spent the rest of the day chasing the 6,000 sheep and looking out for the other herder, who never did show up. I was not able to leave the sheep during the day, so I decided to wait until dark, then walk to the other herder's camp.

At that time, a ten mile hike was nothing to me. I was more concerned about the other herder getting in trouble for abandoning his sheep and having to serve two years in prison. One thing a herder or a hobo likes is freedom, and I didn't want to think about any herder going to jail.

When the sheep bedded down as night fell, I instructed Tom and Blackie to stay with them. I couldn't let the coyotes have a chance at the large flock. The two dogs would stay busy keeping pesky varmints away from the young lambs. When the stars came out, I started for the other sheep camp.

There was a full moon that night, so I didn't take a lantern with me. It took me about two hours to walk to the other camp. I first noticed that there was no light in the wagon. I called out, then en-

tered the wagon and found it empty. Then I started looking around.

I started at the wagon and walked in ever-increasing circles. After searching for about an hour, I came upon a dead sheep. I approached it with caution, not knowing what might have caused it to die. There was no obvious cause of death, so I looked around some more. Nearby I found another dead sheep, then another and finally I counted 20 in all. I circled the dead sheep twice before I found the herder. He was also dead.

I studied the pattern of the dead sheep and herder and found burn marks on some of the sheep. Then I remembered watching a thunderstorm from my wagon a couple of days before. It appeared that lightning had struck the ground near the herd, killing some of them and the herder.

I returned to my wagon without burying the herder. It was important to leave everything as it was in case someone was to question what had happened. My hands were full watching after 6,000 sheep. It was the busiest time I spent on the range. About 10 days later, Mr. Hensen came out to check on me, and I told him what had happened. He went to the other camp and investigated. When he returned, he told me about the herder.

He was a happy man who had been working for the Hensens for sixteen years. He was a Basque. He stayed on the range most of the time, earning and saving his money to take home to Europe and his family. The man was scheduled to go home that fall after working and saving his money for 16 years.

I said a prayer for the man that night. When I was young, my father taught me to accept life as it comes. After thinking about the dead herder for a day or two, the only good that I could make of it was that he died happy, with thoughts that he would soon be home with his family.

In a few days, Mr. Hensen hired another herder, so we could split the large herd into two smaller ones again.

37

To North Dakota
I Meet Matador Bill

It was a dry year in Montana and it was becoming increasingly difficult for me to find enough grass and water to satisfy the sheep under my care. I was becoming more and more concerned because some of the sheep were looking thin from not getting the feed they needed.

I wanted to talk to Mr. Hensen and let him know about my predicament. Then I realized that the other herders must be experiencing the same problems as I and surely Mr. Hensen was aware of what was happening.

The tender stopped by a few days later, and before I could ask him about what the other herders were doing, he told me Mr. Hensen was coming to see me soon. The seriousness of the situation was real, as I had thought, and I was anxious to alleviate the suffering of the sheep under my control.

Mr. Hensen arrived at my camp early the next morning.

"Mooney, as you know, things are tough for the sheep here. I've got to get 'em out of here, to a better place for the fall and winter, and I need your help."

"I'd be willing to help, if the new place has enough feed for the sheep."

"You'll be taking your herd to North Dakota where there's plenty for them this year, and lots of water too."

"You've got a deal, Mr. Hensen."

"Thanks Mooney, I knew I could count on ya."

We shook hands and walked to his truck. We unloaded a bunch of supplies he brought me for the trip.

"It's 70 miles to the siding at Malta. You'll need all of these supplies," he told me as the last bag of flour was placed in my wagon.

He stopped before he climbed into his truck to leave and turned to face me.

"I'm sending a tender — the name's Matador Bill — to help you make the trip. He's a great man. He'll move your wagon each day and do the cookin' too."

The next afternoon, Matador Bill arrived at my camp. An introduction and a handshake began a lifelong friendship.

Each morning, after breakfast, Bill would hitch the horse to the wagon, climb aboard and start moving in the direction of the railroad sid-

120

ing. The dogs and I would try to keep the sheep headed in the right direction, but that was an impossible job.

Those critters would head down every coulee we passed, thinking there must be water and grass at the bottom. In a normal year, they would have been right, but in this dry year, there was none. Still, they wanted to go to the bottom and find out for themselves. The dogs and I would go after them and bring them back to the top of the hill. After midday, the dogs would be played out, and it was up to me to do all the chasing.

In the late afternoon I would find my wagon and Matador Bill waiting for the sheep, the dogs and me. As Mr. Hensen had told me, Bill was a great man and friend. As soon as the flock was bedded down, Bill would have supper ready. We would eat, then Bill would tell me colorful stories about the good-old-days when he was part of several cattle drives to Montana. I loved his stories and listened for hours. Then we would go to bed and continue the journey the next day.

It took us a week to travel the 70 miles to Malta, but I walked many more than that because of all the trips into and out of the coulees while chasing the sheep.

Matador Bill and I could see the lights of Malta in the distance from our last camp. While I didn't enjoy all the walking involved in getting the sheep to the railroad, visiting with Bill had been delightful. He made the trip as bearable as any 70 mile trip could be while chasing sheep.

We were in Malta by mid-morning of the next day, where I was to meet up with three other herders and the ranch foreman. The four bands of sheep would make up an entire trainload. We found the other herders all right, but they had gotten drunk the night before and were still drunk when we arrived. They were in no condition to help load my sheep or their own.

Matador Bill, the ranch foreman — Luger Henderson — and a couple of railroad men helped me get the sheep into the rail cars; then we put the herders aboard and were ready to pull out of Malta 30 minutes later than planned.

"Thanks Bill, I appreciate all your help and enjoyed visitin' with ya," I said as we shook hands.

"I enjoyed it too, Mooney," he said as the train started to roll.

I found a spot to sit in the passenger car, and with Tom and Blackie at my feet, fell asleep to the rhythm of train wheels on track. The next morning, the train started to slow, and I knew we were going to stop at a small town as we entered North Dakota.

I asked the conductor if there was time for me to go uptown and get a cup of coffee.

"Sure, we'll be here for at least half an hour," he said.

I told Tom and Blackie to stay and walked into town. I was two blocks from the train station when the train whistle sounded. I looked back and saw my train leaving the station. I ran as fast as my feet would carry me, but the train was going too fast for me to catch it. The depot agent didn't have much sympathy for me. I only had 50 cents with me, but told him that Mr. Hensen would pay my fare if he would let me ride the next train.

"That would be fine, young man," he said. "The next train will be here in about 10 hours."

I could have waited to ride that train, but felt it my responsibility to get to Devils Lake at or before the time my sheep arrived. But how? My hitchhiking experiences to date had not been good. That luck changed when the first car that came by stopped when I stuck out my thumb.

"Where ya headed?"

"Devils Lake."

"Get in, that's where I'm goin'."

We arrived at about 8 p.m., long before the train was due. I thanked the man for giving me the ride and walked into the first hotel I found. I looked in the restaurant and saw Mr. Hensen sitting there having dinner.

"Where did you come from?" he asked.

I told him the story and he chuckled.

"You made good time," was his only comment about my little adventure.

He said the train would be pulling into a little town named Warwick at 4 a.m.

"You had better sleep here too," he said. "That way, we can get an early start, so we can be at the station in Warwick before the sheep arrive."

I had dinner, then went to the room and was fast asleep in no time. Mr. Hensen was pounding on my door at two. I was up and in the truck in five minutes. We arrived at Warwick just before the sheep train arrived. When the train stopped, we started walking towards the caboose. The ranch foreman jumped from the train and ran towards Mr. Hensen.

"We lost a herder yesterday and haven't been able to find him. We even sent a speeder back to look along the tracks for him, but we never found ... ."

I had been walking at Mr. Hensen's side and out of sight of the foreman. When I came into view a second later, the foreman was furious.

"You ..., you ..., how ...?" the foreman stammered. If looks could kill, I would not have lived a second longer.

"Now, now, the young man has a good reason for missing the train, and he didn't miss it on purpose," Mr. Hensen said. "Besides he's here now and that's what counts."

Then Mr. Hensen turned to me and whispered so no one else could hear.

"We'll unload your sheep first, so you can be on the range before the rest are unloaded. I'll keep the foreman busy until you're miles away. You should have an easier time of it with just 1,500 lambs to watch over."

I thought it was a reasonable idea and hurried to help unload my band of sheep. When I counted out the sheep and made sure Tom and Blackie were with me, I turned to Mr. Hensen.

"Thank you, sir. Now, which way do I go?"

"That way," Mr. Hensen said pointing into the foggy darkness of a September morning.

I whistled for the dogs and started walking in the direction my boss pointed. For once, I was anxious to get away from town — and the foreman who wanted a piece of my hide.

"Matador Bill (Rorex) was a well known cowboy around the Malta and Zortman area of Montana. He was well liked by everyone and was a comic. He drove cattle from Texas to Montana and finally settled down and went to work on the Hensen ranch."

Diane Smith, author and historian

38

A Tent in a Wheat Field

The fog closed around me as I walked away from the railroad siding in Warwick. The dogs responded quickly to my commands, and it was easy to get the band of lambs under control. We hadn't traveled 100 yards when the lights at the siding disappeared, the fog was that thick. That's when the realization settled in that I didn't know the area. It was dark, foggy and I was lost. I didn't have a choice but to keep heading in the direction I thought was west, the direction Mr. Hensen wanted me to travel.

Slowly the early morning darkness gave way to the first light of day, and the sheep, dogs and I continued to walk west. We traveled about five miles when the dogs started barking at the front of the herd. I continued to walk with the sheep at the rear of the herd thinking the dogs were just trying to make some stray animals get back with the rest. As I continued to walk forward, the barking of the dogs became louder, which indicated they weren't moving. Then the sheep began to get closer to each other and bunch up, which was another indication the herd was slowing or had stopped.

"Quiet down or I'll shoot ya."

It was a man's voice. I ran forward.

"Tom, Blackie!" I yelled, and the dogs stopped barking.

As I reached the front of the herd, the outline of a ranch house became visible, and I saw a man standing on the front porch. My herd surrounded his house and they were eating and trampling the plants in his vegetable garden.

"Get your sheep out'a my yard!"

"Sorry sir, my name's Mon..."

"I don't care what your name is, get those damn sheep out'a here."

"I'm a newcomer to the area and didn't know you were here," I said, trying to explain and apologize at the same time.

"I don't care how long you've been in the area; let's get these sheep movin'."

So with the farmer's help and persuasion, we forced the herd out of his front yard and garden and moving west again as the sun made a full appearance, and the fog began to lift. That farmer continued to yell at me and the sheep until we topped a hill and dropped out of sight.

After traveling about seven miles, Mr. Hensen drove up in his truck.

"How ya doin', Mooney?"

"I'm sure glad the sun is up, so I can see where I'm goin'."

I explained the experience with the farmer, and Mr. Hensen said he would go settle up with him.

"You can camp here and feed the sheep on this harvested wheat field. I've brought you a tent and other supplies. Sorry, I don't have any sheep wagons out here for ya."

We unloaded a small tent, a couple of blankets, a one-burner kerosene stove, a lantern and some food. Along with the usual flour, pork belly, coffee and water, I was surprised when two boxes of canned vegetables were placed on the ground.

Living in a wheat field with only a small tent for shelter was a drastic change from a sheepherder's wagon. First of all, I had no oven; I had to fry bread if I wanted some. Secondly, I had no choice but to sleep on the ground. I didn't like the situation, but what was I to do? The tent, called a pup tent by Mr. Hensen, was square, about 6 feet to a side and the sides sloped from the ground to a point in the middle that was six feet high.

This was the first time I had canned vegetables available, and they were a blessing. While I still killed a lamb once a week for my meat, I didn't care for bread cooked in a frying pan. That, coupled with the fact that cooking in a small tent was a difficult chore, made the canned food better. Opening a can of vegetables and placing it right on the one-burner stove was a convenient and fast way to cook.

The dogs and I settled into a routine, just as we had during our other times on the range: wake up and take the sheep to food and water for the day, then back to camp at night. Since I was sleeping on the ground, I knew a rainstorm could cause my supplies and my sleeping area to get wet. So I carved a trench around the tent and made a little ditch from the trench leading downhill to carry the water away.

My efforts paid off about two weeks after I set up camp. The rain started to fall just as I climbed into bed. The sound of the raindrops hitting the tent was soothing, causing me to quickly drift off to sleep. I must have been sleeping hard, because I was slow to wake up, despite a persistent feeling that something was crawling on me. My first thought was that I was dreaming, but the feeling continued and finally I was forced to open my eyes. There, walking up my arm and staring me in the face, was a lizard.

I was out of that bed in a flash and started the lantern. I pulled my bed apart and counted 21 lizards who had been sleeping with me. Then another one dropped on the bed from the tent flap that covered the opening. I don't know what kind of lizards they were, but they would come out of their hiding places during a rainstorm in search of dry land. For some reason, they were attracted to my white tent. When they reached the tent, they would climb up the sides looking for a way inside. Some of them found the flap and were successful. The lizards didn't seem to want to do me harm; they could have chewed on me while I was asleep if that were the case. Still, they made me uneasy and I didn't want them around, just in case they were poisonous. I felt I had to kill every one of them, but how? Stomping them was effective, but also exhausting. Finally I hit on the idea of placing a lizard head between two vegetable cans and pushing hard. The effort cut the head off. It was a fast way to exterminate them. By the time the sun came up and the rain stopped, there was a sizable pile of beheaded lizards in one corner of my tent.

It was a miserable night, and I surely would have quit right then and there if I could have turned the sheep over to another herder, but I was stuck doing my job — protecting the sheep to the best of my ability. I tried to think about good things and not why I had to live under such miserable conditions.

My thoughts turned to the life I knew when my mother was alive and the fun we had as a family. At first I was sad, but soon afterward realized that thinking about the fun back then gave me a speck of hope about the future. After all, I had been through some tough times already, some of them worse than what I was experiencing right then. I spent several days debating in my mind which was the worst time of my life to date, but it was not clear. What was apparent was that all the bad that had happened to me could have been worse, and that there would be better times in the future. That little light I could see at the end of the tunnel gave me a little warmth. It also gave me the strength I needed to continue being the best sheepherder in North Dakota.

"When it rains in Montana and North Dakota, lizards are known to appear, either to find a dry area or to get the moisture they need."

Diane Smith, author and historian

39

Moving South of the Cheyenne

After about six weeks in the harvested wheat field, the available fodder for my flock became scarce. Each day I would take the sheep to a different area of the large field, but, finally, I had covered all of it. Just when I was becoming concerned about the welfare of the animals, Mr. Hensen arrived at my camp.

"How ya doin', Mooney?"

"I'm out of feed for the sheep, I don't like sleepin' on the ground in a tent and I don't like not havin' an oven to bake my bread. Other than that, I'm doin' just fine."

Mr. Hensen chuckled.

"Those are the first words I've ever heard ya say that weren't of a positive nature. I'm sorry there aren't better accommodations for ya out here, but this is all I've got. We're goin' to move your flock to a place with more feed, about 25 miles from here.

"Here's the plan, Mooney: I want you to move the sheep south of the Cheyenne River where there's good grazin'. It'll take you most of three days, maybe four, so I want you to take the tent and what you'll need for food and pack it on your back. I'll take the rest of your supplies and meet up with ya when you're across the river. I've got to meet with some other ranchers and herders, but I'll be waitin' when ya get there."

I loaded up the truck with the supplies that I wouldn't need for the trip, and Mr. Hensen drove away.

"See ya south of the Cheyenne, Mooney," he said with a toot on the horn and a wave.

The next morning I folded the tent with my food and other supplies inside. I used a rope to make two loops that would fit over my shoulders and, with the crude backpack in place, started walking south.

The hike was pleasant. The fall weather was cool, which was a relief from the scalding heat of summer, and I was excited about the prospect of having enough feed for my flock. The ill-fitting backpack was the only disagreeable part of the walk.

The ropes cut into my shoulders and hurt something awful. I dug out my blanket and used one end of it to pad the rope on one side, then I looped the blanket over my neck and used the other end to pad the rope on the other side, which solved the problem.

On the third day, we arrived at the Cheyenne River, turned right, as instructed by Mr. Hensen, and walked about two miles. There I found a road and a bridge. The sheep, dogs and I crossed the river without a hitch, and found Mr. Hensen waiting for us on the other side.

"Mooney, I want ya to take your flock three miles in that direction," he said pointing southwest. "Just follow my tracks. I'll meet ya there in a few hours."

Off he went, heading southwest. I whistled for Tom and Blackie to get the sheep moving, and we followed the tire tracks for three miles. Mr. Hensen was waiting for us at the top of a small knoll. He had unloaded all of the extra supplies and looked anxious to get headed back to the nearest town.

"This is it; you can camp here till I return in about 10 days."

"Where should I take the sheep? I don't want to get in trouble again."

"You can herd any place around here ya want to."

I watched him drive off, then set up the tent and dug another trench around it. I arranged my supplies in the tent and prepared for a lengthy stay. I killed a lamb and prepared a supper of fresh leg of lamb and canned vegetables. Tom and Blackie got a side of ribs each. I felt good about this new range. There seemed to be lots of grass around and some water too.

I settled into a herder's routine of getting up with the sheep and herding them in the direction I wanted them to go for the day, then taking them back to the campsite for the night.

On the third day, I woke up and found that my flock had disappeared. This had happened to me a couple of times before during my time as a herder, but it always made me uneasy. As before, I simply picked up the trail of the 1,500 sheep and followed it. After covering a couple miles in an easterly direction, I came upon a large corn field.

The herd's trail lead right into the corn and out the other side. When I reached the far side, I saw a house and my sheep near the house. Two men were standing in the front yard with my sheep wandering around them. I walked towards them cautiously, thinking about what to say.

"You, sheep?!" one yelled in a heavy Russian accent.

"Yes, sir, they're mine, I mean they belong to Mr. Hensen, I'm just the herder."

"Ruin corn, now what?!" the other shouted as he walked over to me, stopping just two feet from me with his hands on his hips.

"I'm sure Mr. Hensen will take care of the damages and ..."

"Hensen have 40 acres only, where you camp. Go, go now!" the first one said raising his rifle above his head and shaking it. They were the most angry men I had ever seen. I'm sure if I had not been just a boy, they would have shot me right there.

I whistled for the dogs to get the flock headed back to camp and they finally started moving reluctantly. When I was 30 yards from the house one of the Russian ranchers yelled to

me, "Sheep come back, bang!, no sheep; maybe you too!"

I understood his intentions, and I planned to stay away, but I also knew that once sheep had a taste of corn, they surely would try to find it again.

On the way back to camp, I became angry at Mr. Hensen. He knew it was impossible to hold a band of sheep on 40 acres and expect them to find enough feed to sustain them for any length of time. I had a problem and I knew it. I didn't sleep well and was up at 4 a.m., well before I expected the sheep to be up, but I was wrong. The sheep were gone.

I knew where they were and started running for the corn field. I was right. The sheep were there, but they had not penetrated to the other side. I quietly called Tom and Blackie and told them to stay with me. We circled around the sheep and herded them out of the corn and back to camp. I didn't get much sleep during the next week and when I did close my eyes, it was just for an hour or two at a time. It was a relief to see Mr. Hensen drive up.

"I've got ya some more supplies, Mooney."

I told him what had happened.

"We better get these sheep a bit to the west," he said.

So he took the tent and my supplies and I walked with the herd, following the tracks of his truck, until we were five miles west of my initial camp.

"You should be fine here," he said when I met up with him again.

"Mr. Hensen, I don't like gettin' in trouble with the ranchers. Are there other ranches around that I have to stay away from?"

"There are a few, Mooney. You'll know when ya see 'em. Just don't let the sheep get into the fields where the crops are."

With that, he was in his truck and driving off before I could protest. It was then clear to me how Mr. Hensen was working his sheep operation in North Dakota. He would lease a small parcel of land here and there, knowing full well the sheep wouldn't stay on that little spot of land. When the herd would wander off the leased land, it was the poor herder who caught the full brunt of the blame. As a result, Montana sheepherders were very unpopular with the farmers in that part of North Dakota.

"It was not unheard of for a sheep rancher to rent only a small parcel of land, knowing full well that the land would not be able to support the number of sheep in an average band. After a day or two, the sheep would go off the rented land to find food, and the ranchers were fully aware of that fact."

Diane Smith, author and historian

40

Winter on the Range

Fall was pleasant that year. The summer bugs were gone after the first frost, and I was as comfortable as I could be in the middle of the North Dakota countryside. I would have preferred a sheepherder's wagon, instead of the small tent, but I did the best I could with what I had. At least my belly was full.

The mild fall weather continued into the first week of December, but anyone who has ever spent time in North Dakota knows pleasant weather can turn nasty and harsh in just a few hours. That kind of weather can become life threatening to both sheep and herder alike.

Mr. Hensen arrived at my camp at the beginning of the second week of December with fresh provisions.

"How's it goin', Mooney?"

"I'm fine, Mr. Hensen. Say, don't ya think we better be movin' the sheep to the feeding sheds soon?"

"Oh, if it's the weather you're thinkin' about, we could have lots of nice weather yet, but I'm leavin' you a few extra supplies just in case."

"I know, the weather's been great, but we could have a storm and ..."

"If we have a storm, you better start north with the sheep."

"Fine, I'll do that."

That was the extent of our conversation. He spent a total of 15 minutes at my campsite, unloading my supplies all the while. Then he was in the truck and headed down the road.

"See ya in a couple of weeks, Mooney," he said with a wave.

I waved back, but my heart wasn't in it. Until this trip, Mr. Hensen had been a good boss, but now he didn't seem to care much about my welfare. The situation gave me something to think about for the next two days. I concluded that there must have been circumstances I didn't know about that caused Mr. Hensen to keep me on the range.

The third day after Mr. Hensen left, it started to snow. It continued to snow for an entire day and

into the next night. When I stepped out of my tent the next morning, over 12 inches of white powder covered the ground. Then it got cold; the temperature dropped to well below zero.

My choice of action was clear: I had to head north, in the direction of the winter feeding sheds. I broke camp and packed half of my supplies into the tent. Once again I folded the tent to form a backpack, using rope for the shoulder straps.

Herding sheep in a foot of snow is a difficult chore. Although some of the ground had been blown bare by the wind, that same wind had created deep drifts in other spots. I had to break trail for them through deep drifts. It was exhausting work as I walked a mile or so with the sheep right behind me, strung out in single file. When we reached an area where enough grass was exposed to keep the flock busy for awhile, I walked back to the previous camp to get the rest of my supplies.

I then returned to the sheep and set up a new camp. The rest of my day was spent scraping snow from grass. Animals need more to eat when it's cold, so I worked until the sheep started to bed down for the evening, indicating they were satisfied with the amount of food they had taken in.

When my flock was content, I retired to my tent. The one-burner kerosene stove was my only source of heat as well as my cook stove. It was crowded in that six-foot-square tent, but I would get Tom and Blackie in there with me and start the stove. I ate lots of lamb during that trip and fed the dogs an extra share, for we had to keep our strength up too. After eating the evening meal, the three of us would check the flock one last time. Sleep came easy after a day of fighting snow.

We continued north for nearly two weeks, when I noticed Mr. Hensen's truck headed our way as I was about to break camp one morning.

"How's it goin', Mooney?"

"I'm about froze to death, Mr. Hensen. I can't take much more of this."

"Well, you're only about three miles from the sheds. You can make that just fine, can't ya?"

"That's two, maybe three, more days. I'll try, but I've been thinkin' about an easier way. Why don't ya attach a board to a small sled. Get a team of horses to pull it from the sheds to us here. That way, the herd won't have to walk through so much snow."

"Ya know, Mooney, I never thought about that. You scrape some more snow for the flock here, then rest in the tent for awhile. I'll send someone back for ya this afternoon."

Then he was in his truck and gone. I spent three hours scraping snow so when finished the sheep could get to more grass. As usual, I was tired by the time I finished and crawled into the tent to start the stove.

Although I was anxious to warm up and get some good food at the feeding sheds, I had been told to stay put. I was thankful for the extra rest during the day and fell asleep. Barking dogs startled me and I was wide awake in a second. I grabbed the Winchester and stepped outside the tent expecting trouble. Instead the sight of a team of horses greeted me. As it neared my camp, I could see a sled with a four-foot-wide scraper attached behind the horses.

When the plow broke through to the area I had scraped with my feet, the sheep started to run to the green grass uncovered by the scraper. When sheep are hungry, they won't just stop where there's food and eat their fill. They eat a mouthful or two, then run ahead for a few feet and grab some more grass.

"Throw you're supplies on the sled and follow along," the teamster said.

I broke camp in a hurry, placed my gear on the sled and watched as the driver maneuvered the team of horses in the snow until he was ahead of the flock and following the same path he used coming out. He was uncovering more grass on the second pass, so the flock was moving even faster. We traveled those last three miles in about 90 minutes saving me a good two days of work in subzero temperatures.

"Welcome to the feeding sheds, Mooney," Mr. Hensen said from the door of the cooking shack. "Come on in and warm up."

He introduced me to the rest of the crew as I warmed my hands by the stove in the middle of the room.

"Joe, show Mooney where to throw his bedroll, and see that he has water for a bath."

Joe took me to the bunkhouse and he made sure I had three full buckets of water to fill the small tub used by the crew for weekly baths.

"We'll have dinner in 'bout an hour," Joe said. "Just come on over when ya finish here. Fill the buckets when you're finished and place them by the stove to warm for the next herder."

When he left, I called Tom and Blackie in to lay by the stove as I cleaned up. It felt good to sit and soak off a couple months of being on the range.

I was late getting back to the cooking shack, and Joe came looking for me.

"Ya better hurry," he said. "The cook's about ready to put the grub on the table. It'll disappear in a hurry. Say what are those dogs doin' in here?"

"Those dogs can stay in here when I'm in here," I said with authority and Joe didn't question me.

He left quickly, not wanting to miss the meal. I finished dressing and followed Joe three minutes later.

"Let's go," I said to the dogs as I left the bunkhouse.

When I opened the door to the cook shack, the men were already eating.

"Hey, Mooney, come sit by me," Mr. Hensen said. "Why don't ya stay here with us and help feed the sheep until spring?"

"I appreciate your offer, Mr. Hensen, but I've been cold for so long I want to be warm for awhile. I've got my eyes set on the southern states; maybe Texas."

"But Mooney, you can stay here," he said. "You'll be warm in the bunkhouse and eat good grub like this every day in this warm cookin' shack."

"But I'll have to go out in the cold and feed the sheep. Don't think I'm not grateful, but I want to go where I can thaw out, where it's warm outside durin' the day and at night too."

"I hate to lose you, Mooney. You're a good worker, but I can see there's no changin' your mind."

I asked him to drive me to Devils Lake, and he reluctantly agreed to do so.

"I hate to drive anywhere for any reason this time of year because the roads are so bad, but I've got to head into town in a couple days on other business. I'll take you then."

The next two days were pleasant for me. I did a little work with the sheep, but generally stayed out of the other workers' way. Tom and Blackie stayed by my side, except in the cooking shack. Then they stayed outside, by the door, until I brought them something to eat. At night they slept by my bunk.

I placed my bedroll in Mr. Hensen's truck on the morning we were going to leave, then headed for breakfast.

"Mr. Hensen, I have one more request," I asked when seated at the table.

"What's that, Mooney?"

"Tom and Blackie are the best sheep dogs any herder could ask for and ..."

"Do you want to take them with ya?"

"No, I can't do that. There's no place for 'em on the road. They belong on the range. But I think they would make good dogs for you."

"You may be right. Let's take 'em with us today and see how they like ridin' in the truck."

We headed to Devils Lake with Tom and Blackie riding in the back of the truck. I looked in the back once and noticed there was one dog looking around the cab on the left and the other on the right.

"I think they like the truck," Mr. Hensen said.

"Yes, sir, looks like you've got yourself a

couple of good dogs, but if I come back, I get to use 'em."

"It's a deal, Mooney."

At Devils Lake, Mr. Hensen paid me off. We shook hands, I said my good-byes to the dogs, and I watched as they disappeared down the street.

I wanted to ride inside the train and checked on the price of a ticket. I had enough money, but would have had very little left when the train arrived in the great state of Texas. Hopping a freight was my only other option.

That night I climbed aboard an empty box-car, wrapped my bedroll around myself and fell asleep. As the train headed south, I dreamed of the warm days of a southern winter.

41

Riding the Rods

Being on the road during a North Dakota winter is down right miserable. It didn't take long before I questioned my decision not to ride inside a passenger train. The cold was sharp, and my clothing didn't stop it from penetrating to the bone.

The trip south from North Dakota to Phoenix, Arizona, required me to change freights five times. I knew my direction of travel was south by watching the sun cross the sky, but the weather continued to be cold as I passed through Wyoming. It was so cold in Colorado that I considered building a fire in the boxcar, but didn't for fear that the car would burn up with me inside. My feet, injured by the previous frost bite incident, were aching and extremely painful. I again questioned one of my earlier decisions: This time, Mr. Hensen's offer of work for the winter.

On one stretch there were two other men in the car with me. One suggested that we sit close together. I looked him over and noticed he was a small man and would not be able to overpower me. The second man was cautious, too.

"Why do you want to sit close to us?" he said.

"I learnt this when I was in the Army. Two or more can keep each other warmer than one alone."

"I've done this before," I said.

"OK, let's get into that corner there and sit in a close circle," he said. "We'll wrap our bed rolls around us so we have more blankets covering us."

We did as the man suggested and discovered the move was a good one. One of the men had two large blankets that covered the three of us at the shoulders. This arrangement, coupled with the small blanket each of us had and the combined body heat, made the trip tolerable, but not completely comfortable.

Northern New Mexico was cold too, but as we descended from the mountains the temperature warmed. By the time the freight pulled into Phoenix, I felt good about being south and in warmer weather.

My first task was to rent a room, and I found one for a dollar a week. Although I could have slept in a city park, on the street or in the hobo jungle, I felt the money spent on the room was a good safety measure.

My initial walk around the city of Phoenix revealed hundreds of hobos looking for the same things: work and food. Facing near-impossible odds, most of my time was spent looking for work; I was not successful. My advantage was the few dollars I had in my pocket, but I didn't let on that I had any.

I joined other hobos outside the county courthouse, next to the post office or under the orange trees in the city parks. Just soaking up the sunshine was worth money to me after spending time in a Montana winter. One day I was visiting with a pharmacist who had lost his job back east before hitting the road. He was flat broke

133

and hungry.

"Why don't you eat a few of these oranges here, Sam?" I said as I reached for one hanging on a nearby tree.

"No!" he said, grabbing my hand. "The cops will put ya in jail."

"For takin' an orange?"

"That's right, just for takin' an orange. The city says the oranges are their property, and they want their property protected."

"That's the most stupid thing I've ever heard. There are hundreds and hundreds of people out of work and hungry. There's food within reach of the hungry people, but they can't help themselves?"

"I agree, but that's the way it is. If a bunch of oranges are missin' from the trees, the cops will run us all in. That's why those of us who sleep here want the new 'bos to understand the situation."

"You sleepin' here, Sam?"

"Have been for about a month now."

"Listen, I have a room. It's not much, but it's a safe place to sleep. You're welcome to sleep on the floor."

Sam stayed with me for the next two weeks, after which my rent was due again. Even though I trusted Sam more than most hobos, I didn't want him to know I had any money. We went to the mission together for our meals and talked for hours in the parks or while sitting on the benches in front of the post office.

The day before I was to check out of my room, we were walking to the park from our morning meal when Sam said he was heading for California. He thanked me for letting him stay in my room; we shook hands, then he turned and walked toward the railroad yard.

At the park that day, another hobo asked me if I wanted to go to El Paso, Texas, with him.

"I hear there's plenty of work there, and the people treat hobos good," he said.

"Sure," I said. "I'm not doin' any good in Phoenix and I was headed for Texas in the first place."

"My name's Herbert, but my friends call me Herb," he said extending his hand. "Let's leave on the 8:30 freight in the mornin'."

The next morning I gathered my bedroll and the few extra clothes I had. All was there, except for a sweater I had bought with my sheephearding money. I searched the room twice, but it was nowhere to be found. Apparently Sam had taken the sweater.

I found Herb near the railroad yard. He had looked over a freight and found an empty boxcar. The trip from Phoenix to the next large city, Tucson, was uneventful. Herb suggested we stay there a few days, "to get some food in our bellies."

I thought that was a great idea, but the reality of a hobo's life in Tucson did not include work. The city was quite small then, and the cops and townspeople made it clear that no hobo lives there; they are merely passing through, and the sooner the better. We were able to beg a little food, but stayed as hungry as when we arrived. A little out-of-the-way spot in the Old Southern Railroad Depot beckoned, and we tried to sneak in there to sleep the first night we were in town.

I was sound asleep when Herb let out a yell. I was on my feet in a second. A railroad bull had kicked him in the side and was about to kick him again.

"Hey!" I yelled.

"Oh, you want some too?"

"No, sir, but ya don't have to kick him."

The distraction gave Herb time to get to his feet and begin moving toward the door. We ran out of the depot with Herb holding his side and the bull cursing at us. That bull patrolled the yard with a sharp eye. We dodged him for the rest of the night as we waited for a freight heading east.

The freight heading for El Paso pulled a full load. We couldn't find a boxcar to accommodate us, and the bull from the yard teamed up with the one riding the train to check the tops of the cars regularly. They conducted a final check just before the freight was scheduled to depart and kicked off two hobos, lashing one severely with a whip until blood was staining his shirt.

"What are we gonna do, Mooney?"

"Well, we can't stay in this town. Looks like we'll have to ride the rods."

"Oh, I don't like that."

"Me neither, but what else can we do?"

We needed a support and found some wooden doors from a car used to haul grain and positioned ourselves near our train, but out of sight on the side of the train away from the depot. As soon as the train started to roll, we ran to the car and placed a couple of the doors on two rods running under the car, front to back. The rods are just a few inches off the ground which makes them the least desirable and most dangerous spot to ride. Any hobo who falls asleep will surely slip beneath the train wheels and be crushed or cut in two.

I noticed another hobo on the rods of the boxcar in front of me and Herb was under the car behind me. As the train picked up speed, the noise also increased. The usual soothing clickety-clack of the wheels on the tracks was uncomfortably loud when riding the rods. Then I heard another sound, that of metal hitting metal. I quickly positioned my bedroll in front of my head and carefully scooted the wooden doors, with me on them, as far back toward the tail end of the car as possible.

I consider all railroad bulls to be mean and sadistic, but some of them are sick beyond sadistic. This was obviously a sick one. He had taken a chunk of metal, possibly a coupling pin, and tied it to a long rope. The bull was at the front of the car in front of me letting out rope so the pin would bounce off the ground and up to the bottom of the boxcar.

The force kicked up gravel from the railroad bed spraying rocks against the underside of the car. This was very dangerous for hobos, for even a small rock hurts when it hits a person at 50 miles per hour. If the bouncing pin hit a hobo,

it could kill him outright, cause serious injury or knock him off the rods and under the wheels.

The sound of the bouncing pin continued until there was a dull thump and the hobo on the forward car yelled. This seemed to please the bull because he worked the pin in that area for several minutes. The hobo continued to yell each time the pin made contact. I could see him trying to dodge the pin, moving to the left, then right, but there was no predicting where the thing would hit next. I saw the pin come up and the hobo dodge right, toward the wheels. He slipped and fell off his board. His scream was cut short when he fell under the wheels. I felt something hit my head and discovered that I was splattered with blood.

I said a fast prayer for him and then one for myself because I knew what was coming next. I watched the front of the car and waited for the bull to drop the pin in my direction. It wasn't a long wait. I buried my head under the bedroll and tried to protect my hands there too. I pulled my body as far back, towards the back end of the car as possible.

Rocks bounced around me, but most of them hit the bedroll. Some that bounced off the underside of the car hit me in the shoulders, back and legs, but they didn't do the damage that a hit in the head would cause. I could hear the pin getting closer to me, first hitting the ground, then hitting the bottom of the car, then back to the ground. It moved back in my direction at a steady pace as the bull let out more rope.

I jumped when it hit the wooden door just in front of my blanket. The bull knew by the sound that he was close to me. He moved the pin up and back a little at a time hitting the wood every now and then'.

"I know you're down there, kid!" he yelled. "The other bull saw you climb aboard, then he signaled me. I'll keep this up till I get ya."

I knew my chances of escaping were slim as the pin continued to bounce around the end of the wooden door. It hit the wood, the bottom of the car, the wood again, then the ground and back to the wood. The pin hit my bedroll, just an inch from my hand and I yelled.

"That's what I wanna hear!" the bull bellowed.

I realized the situation had gotten worse, and I began to panic. I looked up and was instantly pelted with several rocks. I buried my head again and tried to think of a solution to my problem. I said another prayer and took a deep breath. All of a sudden the answer was clear. I would give the bull what he wanted.

Each time the pin hit the blanket, I would yell. After several hits and yells, I let out a blood-curdling scream and cut it off sharply. The bull retrieved the pin and headed for his next victim. I swear I could hear him whistling as he walked across the top of the car.

I looked back at Herb. He smiled and moved back on the rods as I had done. He mimicked my behavior with the same results. When the train slowed at the next town, Herb and I slipped off the rods and ran for nearby bushes. We both had cuts and bruises, but we were still alive.

42

Death of a Bull
On to El Paso

Three empty cattle cars were added to the freight. When it began to roll again, Herb and I sprinted for the first one and climbed aboard to continue our journey to El Paso.

"This is sure better than ridin' the rods," Herb said.

I just smiled and thought about the man killed a few miles back. There was no reason to kill hobos like that. It's a miserable life traveling and trying to find a job with little or no money in your pocket. Only bad bulls would find joy in maiming and killing hobos.

"Howdy, boys," The bull said as he jumped into the car from the top. "What are you two doin' on my train?"

"Look, we just need to get to El Paso to look for a job," I said.

"That's fine with me, but ya can't ride my train. Now do ya wanna jump or do I get to throw ya off?"

The train was now running at full speed so jumping was not an option and being thrown off would mean serious injury and maybe death. Herb and I ran to the other door and scrambled up the outside to the top of the car, using the slats on the side of the car as a ladder. The bull was fast behind us. I headed towards the front of the train and Herb ran to the back. I glanced back and noticed that the bull chose to follow Herb. I stopped and sat down to watch from three cars away.

The bull pulled out his whip as Herb neared the caboose.

"Crack!"

The first swing hit Herb in the right shoulder and made a hole in his shirt that even I could see from my vantage point, but he didn't slow down as he scrambled down the ladder at the end of the caboose. The bull gathered his whip and stepped to the ladder with an arrogant swagger. He unleashed his whip again, and again, and again. I could hear the crack as the tip of the whip found its mark.

But there wasn't a crack on the bull's fourth throw. Instead, he pulled, once, twice and it was evident the whip was wrapped around something: the caboose railing; Herb's arm; something. The bull pulled and pulled again, then he relaxed and stepped forward, expecting the slack to undue the tangle. But there was no slack, and the bull's step forward turned into two, three and four, and he ran right off the back of the caboose. His scream stopped when he hit the tracks. I was surprised at the turn of events, but not sorry.

I ran to the back of the caboose to check on Herb. He was retrieving the whip, pulling it in as he lay on his back.

"Want a whip?" he said with a smile.

I scrambled down the ladder.

"You all right? I thought ya were dead."

"I'm just fine now. The bull cut me a couple times, but there's no serious damage."

"What happened, anyway?"

"He missed his mark, and the whip wrapped around my arm. When he took a step in my direction, I pulled and he just kept coming. That bull didn't let go of the whip until he hit the ground."

"I don't like seein' anyone get killed," I said. "But I think you just saved a lot of lives, mine included."

I helped Herb up and we climbed into the first cattle car. I was still keyed up about everything that had happened, yet I was exhausted at the same time. I tried to relax and fell asleep, not worried about being rousted anymore. When the train began to slow at the next stop, I woke up. Herb and I were getting ready to jump off the car when another bull appeared with a whip on his belt. He was a young man in his early 20s.

"Did you two see another bull on this train?"

"Yes, sir," I said. "He got off a bit ago."

"That's strange, he usually stays around till I have a chance to talk to him before he goes home. And I know he wouldn't let ya ride in here."

"He's been chasin' us around, sir. I guess he had things to do."

"Well, ya can't ride this freight anymore."

"We're just goin' to El Paso. How far is it?"

"About 15 miles, now get off the car and go back to the caboose."

Herb and I walked ahead of the bull to the end of the train.

"If you two are seen on my train when it pulls into El Paso, I'll get in trouble," he said.

The young bull stood on the caboose platform and watched us until the train started to move, then pick up speed.

"If I catch you on my train again, I'll use this whip on ya."

We watched until the train was just a dot in the distance, then we started following it, one step at a time.

"And I was beginning to think that bull was an all-right guy," Herb said.

"No, I just think we caught him on a good day; all bulls are evil. This one's just learnin'. He'll be as bad as the others in a few years."

We made it to the El Paso rail yard four hours later. In order to reach the town we had to cross several sets of tracks and weave our way over, under and around several freights that were sitting idle, waiting for their next assignments.

"Let's head for a park and talk to some 'bos about the work around here," Herb said as he walked ahead of me and to my left.

"Sounds good to ..."

"Crack!"

I felt the lick of the whip on my back, but didn't turn around. I knew what was happening and was running at top speed in an instant. Herb, still ahead of me, was doing the same.

"Crack!"

The second throw was six-inches short as the distance increased between the older, slower bull and me.

"Get out of my yard and stay out," he yelled after us.

Our pace slowed as we neared the end of the yard. I was so winded that my side ached, but I kept moving. Herb stopped, placed his hands on his knees and took deep breaths.

"Come on, we don't wanna stop here," I told him. "Let's keep goin'."

The first group of hobos we came across told us that work was scarce in El Paso, and that the community did not greet men like us as well as we had heard.

"Well, this is a fine situation, Mooney. We're no better off than we were in Phoenix, and I thought ..."

"At least it's warm."

"What do ya mean by that?"

"Oh nothin', just don't believe everything ya hear, Herb."

Looking at the expression on my friend's face made me wish I could take back that last comment. I shouldn't have said what I did, but it demonstrated how desperate and hopeless people were feeling during the depression. Men were willing to travel hundreds or thousands of dangerous miles on the slim hope of finding work. Finding and holding down a job could be the beginning of the dream most hobos harbored of once again regaining self-sufficiency, satisfaction, respect, and happiness.

"Look, Herb, we're better off than a lot of the 'bos. Don't ever forget that, and keep tryin' to better yourself while doing right by others."

"Mooney, you have a way of makin' me feel better, even when I've reached the end of my rope. You a preacher or somethin'?"

"No, but my father is."

"Well, what are we gonna do now? I've heard of 'bos being picked up for vagrancy in this town, and some of them never see freedom again."

. "If we had a room we would be legal residents, wouldn't we?"

"Yeah, but we don't have any money."

"I've still got a little left from my last time on the range. Let's see what we can find."

The best available place in our price range was a small room renting for one dollar a week.

"Mooney, if you pay for the first two weeks, I'll pay for the next two."

I thought that was fair and agreed to the arrangement. I didn't know where Herb was going to come up with his

share of the money, but that was his worry, not mine.

We looked for work together during the first couple of days, but it's hard enough for one person to find work, let alone two. We decided to split up and look on our own. Every evening, we would meet back at the room and compare experiences. I looked all over El Paso, but couldn't find even one hour of work. After two weeks, I mentioned to Herb that it was time for him to pay his share of the rent.

"My, doesn't time go fast?" was his only comment.

I still didn't worry about him not meeting his obligation. However, my concern elevated to one of alarm after talking with another hobo.

"Whatever you do in El Paso, don't skip out on your rent bill," he told me.

"What's it cost, 30 days in jail?"

"Not down here in the south. Here they take ya to the country and put ya on a chain gang where you'll be building county roads without pay for 90, maybe 180 days."

After another week, I confronted Herb again.

"Mooney, I haven't been able to find a bit of work. I just don't have the money."

In bed that evening, I tried to rationalize my predicament; I didn't owe any rent, Herb did. But I knew the authorities wouldn't think of it that way when they arrested me. I drifted off to sleep thinking about a ball and chain fixed to my ankle.

I awoke with a start and looked around the room. It was 2 a.m. and Herb was asleep in his bed. I'm a sound sleeper, so waking up in the middle of the night was unusual for me. I lay there for awhile and continued to think about the situation. Finally I decided that this was a good time to move out. Herb could figure out, on his own, what to do about paying his share of the rent.

As quietly as possible, I gathered my gear and started for the door.

"Mooney, that you? Where ya goin'?"

"Yeah, Herb, it's me. I'm movin' out."

I quickly closed the door behind me and went down the stairs to the street. From a vantage point in a nearby alley, I watched to see if Herb would leave the room or stay to fulfill his obligation. It wasn't a long wait: Herb was out of the building and headed toward the railroad yard within five minutes of my departure. He must have heard about the chain gangs too.

I didn't want to leave El Paso at that time. The weather there was warm, but the weather to the north was cold. I didn't know of another place where there were jobs and not hundreds of hobos, except Mr. Hensen's sheep station. A job was waiting there, if I wanted to travel hundreds of cold and dangerous miles, but I didn't want to take that risk.

El Paso was as good a place as any to be in the middle of that winter. I figured the sheer size of the city would help me blend in and stay out of the way of my recent landlord. I walked to the park and slept on a bench for the rest of the night.

The next morning I continued my search for work. I had covered a good portion of the city and was crossing an intersection when I looked up and saw my landlord, the last person I wanted to see, talking with a police officer. He turned, saw me and pointed.

I ran in the opposite direction with the officer in hot pursuit. But he was no match for my youthful speed and energy. I lost him in the distance of two blocks. It was not fun being a wanted man. While I felt the charge of not paying rent was groundless, the fact that a ball and chain, with my name on them, were waiting for me at the county jail made me realize I was in danger.

Peeking around street corners and over my back became routine, and so did keeping a low profile. Checking the people on the other side of the street before crossing became a fact of life. And though our paths crossed from time to time during the few months I stayed in El Paso, each time I encountered that officer, the results were the same.

43

Fort Bliss is Home for a Little While

Looking for work and scrounging for food continued to be my routine in El Paso. The only difference, now that I no longer had the room, was that I had to sleep in the park. If I was lucky, I found a park bench before they were all taken by other hobos. Otherwise, I slept on the grass.

Finding food was a bit harder in El Paso than in most cities I had visited. The mission was not as friendly either, and I avoided going there until my hunger pains relayed the message that food was necessary or my health would suffer. I

begged most of my food, and I considered that an honorable way for a hobo to eat, if the hobo offered to do some work first.

Every so often luck shined on me: Like the time I was walking down an alley at the same time a restaurant worker was dumping a bowl of food that had been scraped from the plates of paying patrons. I waited until the worker was back inside the building, then I opened the can and looked at the makings of a feast. There were clumps of fried potatoes, parts of five eggs and three pieces of partially-eaten link sausage. I put the sausage in my pocket; I could eat that later. The eggs and potatoes were too messy to go into a pocket; they had to be eaten right then and there. I shoved as much food from that garbage can into my mouth as I could, and gulped it down. Eating out of a garbage can doesn't allow much time for chewing, just gulping.

Without warning the restaurant door opened.

"Hey, get out of there!" yelled a man dressed like a cook.

I grabbed one last handful of potatoes, turned and ran up the alley.

"If ya want to eat our food, come in and pay for it!" he yelled after me. He wasn't chasing me, so I stopped about 20 yards away and looked at him as I shoved the last of the potatoes into my mouth. The worker who had scraped the food into the can appeared at the door and deflected the cook's anger from me.

"I've told ya before: throw dirt on the food after putting it in the garbage, like this," he said using a small piece of wood to scrape up a bit of dirt.

"Now not even a tramp like that will eat what's in there," the cook said, pointing his finger at me.

"I'm not a tramp! I'll work for my food. Do you have any work?"

"Not today, sonny. Next time ya ask for work knock on this door, and stay out of my garbage cans."

I turned and walked back to the park. It was amazing to me that so much food was wasted in this town when so many people were starving.

At the park there were a couple of men wearing Army uniforms putting up a tent. Then they set out signs inviting men to join the Army. I didn't go near the tent on the first day, or the second. There were lots of hobos checking out their options, and the Army men seemed too busy to just visit with a kid.

On the third day I made my usual trip around the city looking for work: There was none. When I arrived back at the park the crowd around the tent had thinned, and I walked over for a visit. I found out that the recruiters, who were friendly, were from Fort Bliss and there were lots of hobos signing up for a tour of duty.

"Why don't you enlist, Monrad?"

"How old do ya have to be?"

"Eighteen."

"Oh, I'm much younger than that."

"Then you'll need your parent's permission to join."

"But I don't want my father to know where I am, and I'm not sure I want to join up anyway."

"Look, Monrad, I've got an idea. You're having a hard time findin' enough to eat right?"

"Yes."

"And I've noticed you've been sleepin' here in the park right?"

"Yes."

"Well, why don't ya let me sign you up, and you can go to Fort Bliss. It'll take at least two weeks for the Army office there to hear from your father, with the mail the way it is. In the meantime you'll be able to eat all ya want and sleep in a bed in the barracks."

"But I'll be in the Army, and I'm not sure I wanna join up."

"No, ya won't be officially in the Army until they swear ya in, and that'll happen only after they get word from your father. Before the swearin' in ceremony you can just take off, unless, that is, ya decide to join up."

So I joined the Army, but not really. I was taken by truck to Fort Bliss. The Army people assigned me a bunk, and they fed me three meals a day. I was allowed to eat all I wanted, and the food was good. What's more, I didn't have to work one lick because, not being officially in the Army, they couldn't tell me to do anything. They didn't issue me any Army clothes for the same reason, but I did get a chance to wash and repair the clothes I owned. I spent the time between meals listening to the radio and visiting with the other soldiers. In the evening, some of the soldiers would go to the movie theater, and I was allowed to go twice.

After seven days at Fort Bliss, I got nervous and began to think about what might happen if I stayed much longer or if the Army wanted money for putting me up and feeding me when I didn't join. Would I then be sentenced to a chain gang because I didn't have any money? What if my father agreed and said it was all right with him if I joined the Army when I really didn't want to? What if I was called to headquarters and found my father waiting for me, ready to take me home?

The next morning I went to the mess hall just before it was scheduled to close. It was a risk showing up that late, because they might be low on food. But luck was with me: The breakfast included ham, and there was plenty left. I asked for an extra helping, and my request was granted. I was a little embarrassed as I sat down at an empty table, my food tray was piled high with thick slices of ham.

"A little hungry this morning, are we little soldier?" the head cook asked as he sat down beside me.

I looked at the stack of ham, then at the cook. I wasn't fooling him and there was no use in trying.

"Yeah, well, I've gotta get goin', and this extra ham'll be important to me tomorrow."

I started to wrap the ham in a napkin, but the cook stopped me.

"We can't have ya doing that, now can we?"

For a moment I thought I was going to have to make a run for it.

"Here, let me fix you up."

And he was up and walking into the kitchen. Five minutes later he brought out some wrapping paper and a large sack.

"I'm wrappin' this ham in meal-size portions. You'll need to eat the ham up first, then ya can eat the fried chicken I've packed for ya. There are also five apples in here. Don't eat those till all the meat is gone."

"I'm sure grateful," I said, trying to fight back tears.

"It's got to be tough for ya out there. It makes me feel good that I'm able to help out a nice kid like you. Just don't tell anyone else that I'm givin' ya all this food."

I thanked him again and we shook hands. Then I got up and walked out the mess hall door. The Army didn't know it, but that great military machine allowed me to take a breather in my hobo life. They allowed me to get back on my feet at full strength.

44

El Paso Friends
Juarez Jail

I returned to El Paso and the same routine as before; only I didn't have to look for food during the first three days, thanks to the cook at Fort Bliss.

The Army tent was still there, in the park. It took four days before I was able to muster the nerve to talk to the recruiter. I explained to him that a life in the military was not for me, but I also told him how much I appreciated the stay at Fort Bliss.

"I'll bet ya you'll be in the Army some day, now that you've had a taste of military life with the good food and a bed every night."

"Maybe, but I doubt it. See ya tomorrow?"

"No we're headin' out tonight. We'll travel to another town and try to get more hobos to join up."

I watched as the tent was taken down and loaded into their truck. We exchanged waves as they pulled out of the park. I turned and headed across the park, intent on making an extra effort to find work.

I passed a group of hobos standing next to a tree, then turned right and literally bumped into Sam. He was wearing my missing sweater!

"How ya doin' Sam?"

He wouldn't look me in the eye.

"Ah, I'm OK, a little sick with a cold, but otherwise OK."

"Are ya warm enough?" I asked him with a sly grin.

He glanced up at me, then down again.

"Look, Sam, you may need it more than I do, so you just keep it."

He was around me and gone from my sight in an instant. The incident was a demonstration of what a man is like when he has lost his self respect and why character is so important. But I couldn't let what Sam lacked in character and self respect slow me down: I was going to find a job.

I walked to the alley door of the restaurant, where I had picked food out of the trash a few weeks before, hesitated for a moment, then knocked with confidence.

"Yeah, what da ya want?"

"You said the next time I needed work, I should knock on this door."

The cook looked at me, then let out a deep belly laugh.

"You're the kid who ..." and he laughed again. "Yeah, I've got work for ya. Get in here and start peelin' those spuds."

As luck would have it, the cook's regular helper was sick, so I was hired to do his work until he returned. The job lasted eight days and not only provided a little money for my pocket, but I was given one meal a day. If the cook was watching me dump the leftovers in the garbage can, I sprinkled dirt on them as instructed. But I hated to do that. On the third day, I asked him if I could take all of the extra food with me when I left for the day. He had a hard time understanding why, but finally let me have my way.

My stomach wouldn't hold it all, so I walked to the park with the leftovers and gave them to whatever hobo I felt needed it the most. I left that job with enough money to rent a room for two weeks, though it was several blocks away from my first room in El Paso and my problem with the landlord there. With spring right around the corner, I felt that I would be able to head north again soon without fear of freezing to death.

In the meantime, I made lots of friends, but knew most of them only by their first names or nicknames. Making friends was easy for those hobos who were open to sharing conversation. Continuing a friendship beyond a day or two became a more difficult task. In El Paso, I made friends with many hobos. Some of those friendships lasted a few hours; others lasted days, months and years.

I became friends with an old man who was living in the same rooming house as me. We shared many wonderful conversations while seated on the front porch of the house. One day I was there alone when the largest and nicest limousine I had ever seen pulled up and stopped. The driver got out of the vehicle and walked up to me.

"Is Mr. Florsheim here?" he asked.

"What's he look like?"

The driver described my friend, the elderly man.

"I'll go see if he's here."

I climbed the stairs to my friend's room and knocked on the door.

"There's someone here in a fancy car to see ya," I said when he answered the door.

He grunted, then turned and walked to the window, looked at the car and grunted again.

"Mooney, you go down there and tell that man Mr. Florsheim is not in."

I didn't like to lie, unless my life or someone else's was in danger, but I did as my friend asked.

The driver talked briefly to a man in the back seat, then he got in the front seat and drove away. When the limousine was out of sight my friend stepped onto the porch and took a seat.

"That was my brother, Mooney," the old man said. "That Mr. Florsheim owns the Florsheim Shoe Company and I never want to see him again."

"What happ ...?"

My friend raised his hand, stopping the question. I didn't ask again, but felt it was sad that two brothers wouldn't even talk to one another — no matter what the reason. It was obvious that his brother wanted to help him, but even though he needed the help, my friend would not take it.

During this time I also met a World War I veteran who had gotten his bonus not long before he met me. He had invested his money in the stock market and was doing surprisingly well. At least it was a surprise to me. Al was a real nice man and seemed to like me.

"Mooney, let's go to the exchange," he would say, and we would walk to the local securities office.

"Where's your money?" I asked the first day we were there.

"It's there, in the market," he said, gesturing with both hands toward the ticker tape.

"Didn't it crash?"

"Yes, but it's doin' better now."

"But what do you live on?"

"Oh, I sell a little stock, now and then, but if I sell it all, my money won't be working for me."

He took me there several times but I couldn't get a grip on what was happening. Having money in the stock market wasn't always a good thing. Somedays, Al would be happy because his stock was up. On other days, his stock was down and he wasn't so happy.

One day, after a good market session, Al walked out of the securities office to where I was sitting and soaking up the sun.

"It's been a good day, Mooney. Let's go to

Juarez and see the bullfights. What do you say?"

"Sure, let's go."

We walked across the bo rder to Juarez and up to the window at the arena. Al bought two tickets. We sat at the lower level, near the action. There is a lot of colorful pageantry and a lot of ceremony in a bullfight, but it didn't make any more sense to me than the stock market. Everyone in the stadium seemed to be cheering for the bull, but the animal always lost.

After the last bull had been killed, the crowd filed out of the stadium and dispersed throughout the town. Al and I headed down a side-street which led to the border. Then he turned into an alley, saying it was a shortcut. We were halfway through the alley, near the door of a bar, when three men appeared at the end of the alley and started running at us.

"Let's get out of here," Al said as he turned, reaching top speed in a few steps. I followed. As we neared the beginning of the alley, two police officers grabbed us.

"Why are you men running?" one asked.

"To get away from those other men," I said, pointing down the alley. The men chasing us stopped, turned to the left and entered the bar.

"We have a place for men who run for no reason," the other officer said, and Al and I were handcuffed and taken to the Juarez jail.

We were placed in a small holding cell on the outside of the main building. That left us exposed to the people who were walking by. It must have been a local sport to traumatize the prisoners because some people who passed by picked up rocks and threw them at us. Others stopped and spat at us. After 30 minutes, a small crowd, made up mostly of children, gathered to torment us. The number of kids grew steadily, with older ones, whose aim was more accurate, joining the others. Al and I dodged rocks and spittle for the better part of two hours before three police officers chased them off, opened the cell door and ushered us into the main jail.

The jailers strip-searched us but they

wouldn't touch us or our clothing — we were covered with so much spit. They made us turn our pockets inside out to make sure we weren't hiding anything, then we were allowed to get dressed. Al was savvy enough to bring just enough money with him to pay for admission to the bullfight, so the jailers found nothing of value. One policeman closely examined my shoes, but they were so worn that he threw them at me and told me to put them on.

A husky officer, the one who appeared to be in charge, stood in front of us.

"You are free to go," he said.

As we walked out the door, the officer kicked me in the rear, sending me sprawling into Al. We both fell to the dirt and lay there for a moment as the police officers laughed. We awkwardly struggled to our feet, turned slowly and started toward the border.

"You two better get out of Juarez," one policeman yelled after us.

"Unless you like our hospitality," the officer in charge added; then they all laughed again.

Al and I didn't run, but we continued to the border at a fast walk. As tough as life was for me in the United States, I was sure glad to be back. Al and I continued to be friends, spending a few hours visiting from time to time, but we never went to Juarez again.

It seemed like more and more hobos were arriving in El Paso every day. That made it harder to find work and food. One day I was in a park and spotted a well-dressed man who looked to be in his fifties walking in my direction. I was getting desperate to find food so I approached the man.

"Sir, I'm real hungry and would be happy to work for my food, but seein' that you don't have any work, could you help me out anyway with some food money?"

The man cursed at me and walked off. Now I really felt bad as well as hungry. An old Mexican woman, who happened to be sitting nearby, heard the exchange. She got up, walked over to me and held out her hand.

"You take," she said, then she dropped a dime into my hand.

It was obvious that this woman was poor and really couldn't afford to give me the dime.

"Ma'am, you can't ... I can't accept this."

"You take!" she insisted, shooing me away with her hands.

I thanked her and set about studying the best way to stretch that dime into as much food as possible. A nearby grocery store provided several possibilities. Fresh fruit and meat would have tasted good, but my need right then was to buy something that would last a week or more, instead of just one or two meals. I circled the inside of the store twice before the manager approached me.

"What are ya lookin' for, kid?"

He was keeping an eye on me, thinking I might grab something and run.

"I've got money, sir, but I need to make it go as far as possible."

"How much ya got?"

"Just a dime."

"Let's see here, if I was trying to make a dime stretch, I'd buy this here box of Quaker Oats," he said pulling a box off the shelf.

His recommendation was a good one. I couldn't afford milk or anything else to put on the oatmeal, so I just washed it down with water. That box lasted me a week and, although I con-

tinued to make an unsuccessful search for work, it took one worry from me: looking for food. I protected that box of Quaker Oats like my life depended on it, and it did. When it was gone, I continued my search for more work and food.

A steady stream of hobos made it harder by the day to find something to eat and a place to sleep, even in the park. I was still a wanted man because Herb hadn't paid the two weeks' rent when it was due, and I continued to stumble into the one police officer who thought I was responsible for that debt. What's more, he pointed me out to a few other officers, and I was running foot races with one or more of them on a daily basis. It was obvious that my luck was running out in El Paso; it was time to leave.

I mentioned heading north and going on the range again to another young man.

"Ain't it lonely out there?" he asked.

"Yeah, but ya have a full belly."

"Sounds mighty appetizin' right now; name's George," he said, extending his hand.

He was from Minnesota and was raised on a farm. George agreed to travel with me to Montana. I went to see Al and let him know I was heading north.

"Gee Mooney, I hate to see ya go."

"I'm not gettin' anywhere here, Al, and I don't want to spend time on a chain gang. It's time to move on."

Al walked us to the rail yard to see us off. As we were waiting for the outbound to start its roll, Al pulled me aside, away from George.

"It's been nice knowin' you, Mooney. Here, I want you to have these," he said extending his hand.

He dropped two silver dollars in my hand. I started to protest, but he would have none of it.

"She's rollin', Mooney!" George yelled at me.

"Get goin', and good luck," Al said.

"Thanks, God bless you," I said as I shook his hand, then I ran for the freight.

It had been an interesting stay in El Paso.

45

Walking to Santa Fe and Denver

George and I kept watch for a bull on the freight train from El Paso to Las Cruces, New Mexico, but we didn't have a bit of trouble. Many bulls were mean and some sadistic, but others were lazy. That didn't break my heart any, but a hobo didn't know what kind of bull was watching the train he was riding.

We headed for the hobo jungle in Las Cruces. The place was packed with men and a few women. Groups of up to 15 were huddled around cooking fires, anticipating the next meal. We walked from camp to camp looking for someone we might know, but not one face was familiar. There was one thing about hobos at that time: They had all been in the same fix that George and I were in right then; we were hungry, but we didn't know anyone.

"Join us," a man from one small group said as we walked by.

We did and shared a sparse, but welcome meal.

After the meal was finished, I offered to wash the cooking pot and bowls. As I was walking back to the group, a man dressed like a rancher was talking to them.

"Here comes Mooney; he's a sheepherder," George said as I rejoined the group.

"I've got a flock that needs lookin' after," he said. "Now, I can't pay ya nothin', but if you take care of my 20 acres of beans, in addition to the sheep, I'll give ya 10 percent of what I make off the beans."

I knew it was hard to raise beans in that country and that looking after the sheep would take most of the day. What this man wanted was a slave to take care of the flock for free while taking a gamble on making some money on the beans.

It was obvious to me that this was a losing proposition. A herder could put in six months with this rancher and end up with just a few dollars — or nothing at all. I felt it would be better for me to continue looking for a paying job rather than speculate on a crop of beans.

"Sir, I appreciate you offerin' me an opportunity to be a partner, but I can't take a chance like that."

"You hobos are all alike: Ya don't want to work."

"I do want to work, and so do most of the others here," I told him. "But I won't work for nothin'."

"I'm offerin' ya 10 percent!"

"Will you guarantee the amount I'll be paid at harvest?"

"There's no way to know what beans 'll be bringin' to market."

"So if ya lose money on the beans, the herder gets nothin'. And you've had a herder lookin' after your sheep for free."

The rancher turned and walked away. "You hobos are all alike: Ya don't want to work!" he yelled over his shoulder. When he was 30 yards away, he stopped, turned and pointed a finger at me.

"I'm goin' to tell the cops you're no good. They'll take care of ya. Maybe a few months on a chain gang 'll teach ya what work is."

When he was out of sight, George and I grabbed our bedrolls.

"Thanks for sharin' your food with us, I told our group of new friends, standing around the fire. "Sorry for any trouble we might have caused ya. Just tell the cops we're headed for El Paso."

George and I ran to the rail yard and saw a freight train starting to roll.

"Where's it headin'?" I asked a nearby hobo.

"Albuquerque."

Let's go, George." And we made it into an open boxcar.

It's always best to look over a freight before climbing aboard, but we didn't have a chance in this case. We had to get out of town in a hurry. I was still a wanted man in El Paso. It wasn't clear how far the police there would go to find me, and I didn't want to find out either. The freight we were on was heading west, away from Las Cruces and El Paso.

The boxcar was occupied by four other hobos. They were all considerably older than George and me. We talked with them briefly, then settled into an unoccupied corner. Even though the other men seemed harmless, George and I took turns sleeping.

"Wake up, Mooney; Albuquerque is just ahead."

I wiped the sleep from my eyes, and the other men in the car were starting to stir also. It was 2 a.m. when the freight began to slow down. It had almost stopped when a figure darkened the doorway.

"Mornin' boys."

"Bull!" one of the other men yelled.

"Crack!"

I felt the lick of the whip on my shoulder, but I was out the door before the bull could hit me again. George was one step ahead of me. The

quickness of youth allowed us to escape the car. The older men weren't so lucky, and I could hear the whip connect with flesh again and again as the bull unleashed his fury on the men, now trapped in one corner of the car.

"Damn bull," I said. "If I could just get my hands on him in a fair fight ..."

"Will I do?" The voice from behind caught me off guard. It was another bull.

I turned, ready to do battle, then got a good look at him.

"He's got a whip!" I yelled, and George and I were running again with the bull close behind. We ran along the tracks, then turned 90 degrees and ran into the brush. We realized then the bull knew what he was doing: It was a brier patch. Thorns went through our clothes and tore at us. We could hear the bull laughing from the side of the track.

"Damn bull," I said again.

Ten minutes later the train started to roll.

"Mooney, let's make a run for it and try to get back on."

We ran parallel to the track for about 30

yards, then made a run for an open boxcar.

"Crack!"

"I've been waitin' for you boys."

The train picked up speed, and we continued to run along the tracks for another 200 yards, until the caboose light disappeared into the darkness.

"Boy, am I winded," George said, slowing to a stop. I stopped with him.

"Crack!"

"Good," the bull said. "Then you'll be wantin' a little of this."

"Crack!"

It's interesting how a body can do more than a person thinks possible. We were instantly off and running down the track again like we had been resting for an hour.

At the end of the yard, the bull stopped.

"Don't come back, unless you're ridin' inside a passenger car," he called after us.

We continued to run for another five minutes.

"How far's Santa Fe?" George asked when we slowed to a stop.

"About 60 miles, I think."

So George and I started for Santa Fe, one step at a time. Not long after we left the rail yard, a road began to parallel the rails. It was easier to walk on the road, and we thought someone might stop and give us a ride. We had no such luck. We hiked that night and all the next day. When the sun set the next night we were tired, hungry and thirsty. There was nothing we could do about the hunger and thirst, but we could rest for awhile. A dry culvert served as our bed for the night.

The next morning we were rested, but still hungry. We continued our journey and walked into Santa Fe that evening. We were able to beg a little food, and I taught George how to raid garbage cans, and we found a few that had not been dusted with dirt. Our bellies were full when we went to sleep in the city park. We spent the following day and night in that town, but it was clear we weren't welcome. The townspeople weren't friendly, but I suspect that was mainly because there were so many hobos asking for handouts.

George and I headed for the rail yard, but turned away when we saw three bulls patrolling the grounds. There would be a slim chance of catching a freight and a better chance of getting hurt or killed in that rail yard.

"Let's hitchhike to Denver," George suggested.

We weren't two miles out of town when a priest stopped his sedan beside us.

"Need a ride?"

We visited with that man for the next 40 miles, then his destination took him in a different direction than ours. It took us another three days to get to Denver, with very little of that time spent in a vehicle.

Instead of enjoying spring weather, like the rest of the country, Denver was still locked in winter. Snow fell as we crossed the city limits. George and I went from business to business asking for snow-shovelling jobs. We earned 25 cents each. Near the post office, a sign in the window of a little cafe advertised meals for 5 cents and coffee 2 cents. We went in and ate two meals each.

That left us with about 10 cents. I convinced George to save that money and eat in the bread line.

"Havin' a dime in your pocket might come in handy, George."

We stayed a couple of more days in Denver. No more snow fell so we couldn't find any more work. Although we got in the bread line to eat most of the time, the dime in our pockets made eating in the little cafe tempting, and we spent the money on two more meals each.

Most of our time was spent checking the rail yard. Sitting in the depot, we could overhear conversations between the railroad workers. By the end of the second day, we knew the names of the bulls and when they were on duty. This enabled us to catch the freight heading for Cheyenne when the bulls were chewing the fat between shifts. We also knew there was no bull on our train.

It was good to be ridin' the rails again instead of walking. I relaxed and let the rhythm of train wheels on track lull me to sleep.

46

It's the Same Story in Cheyenne, Wheatland and Casper

Cheyenne was another hungry town. There were lots of hobos looking for the same things George and I were: work, food and a place to sleep. The mission there was great, and we were able to get a belly full of food once a day, after listening to some preaching, of course. We slept in the jungle, with seven other hobos, in a tight circle around a slow-burning fire. After three days it became clear that this city was not a place for a hobo to settle down. It was time to leave.

The rail yard was patrolled regularly by three bulls on each shift. We had slipped through their defenses when we arrived, but word in the jungle indicated we were lucky to do so. I convinced George that we would be better off to walk to the next town and catch a freight where there would be few, if any, bulls.

George and I walked to Wheatland, a small Wyoming town. The door of the jail was open when we walked by and we could see a small bed, a little stove, a supply of wood and a stash of groceries. The place looked inviting to a couple of cold and hungry hobos, but we knew better than to go in without permission. We walked around the town until we found the policeman.

"Sir, we noticed your jail as we came into town and were wonderin' if it was all right if we spent the night there?" I asked him.

"Sure," he said. "Make yourselves at home."

So we went back to the small concrete build-

ing. While George lay down on the cot, I started a fire, filled a pot with water and gathered a few of the vegetables stored near a wall.

"I've never seen a town so accommodatin' to hobos, have you?" George asked.

"Never, Wheatland sure takes the cake. I'll have us a stew goin' in no time."

"What are you guys doin' in here?"

I wheeled around, surprised by the voice from behind. My knife was in my hand and it must have looked like I was ready to use it in self-defense.

"Whoa there mister, I ain't gonna hurt ya or nothin', but this here stuff belongs to me," said an old man.

"The cop said we could sleep here," George said.

"Sleep here? That's fine with me, but the cot's mine and so's the food."

"Look, we don't mean any harm," I said. "But we were told to make ourselves at home and that's what we were doin'."

"Well, you're welcome to sleep here on the floor, but the cot's mine, and I can't spare any of the food either."

There were three boxes of vegetables stacked in one corner of the small building and five boxes of canned fruit, vegetables and meat in another. It wasn't like a hobo not to offer what he had, and I couldn't understand why this man wouldn't share any of the food he had, so I asked him.

"The county took my farm two months ago for the taxes I owed, and they let me live here till I can get on my feet again. This here food was canned by my wife, but she died last year. Now I'm countin' on it lastin' me for the next year or so."

The man's situation was now clear to me. He wasn't a hobo at all, but just an old farmer who had lost his farm and who wasn't accustomed to the giving ways of a hobo.

"Did your crops fail?" George asked him.

"I had two years of the best crops ever," the man said. "But good crops don't do no good if it costs more to grow 'em than ya can get at market."

It was the same story I was hearing around the country, and it was another indication of what a terrible time our country was suffering. With the fire going strong and the three of us in the 12-foot-square building it was warm. I spread out my bed roll and lay down. I said a prayer thanking the Lord for taking care of me, and I asked Him to watch over this old farmer too, that he might once again know peace in his life. Then I was fast asleep.

Early the next morning George and I caught a freight and enjoyed an uneventful ride to Casper inside a boxcar with three other men. When the train slowed, we all jumped from the car and headed for the local jungle. On the way, George and I begged at a grocery store. The manager gave us what he could, which didn't amount to much, but we were thankful for all we got. At the jungle we found a cooking pot and started a hobo stew going. A couple of other hobos contributed what they were able to scrounge, and, when it was ready to eat, three others joined us. Seven hobos ate what was in the pot, and it didn't matter who contributed and who didn't.

It was cold enough that sleeping around a fire in the jungle wasn't a smart way to spend the night. The group of seven hobos split up to try to find a place to sleep. George and I headed for the jail. The idea worked in Wheatland; why not in Casper?

"Hell no!" the policeman said. "The last hobos I let sleep in the jail left a mess that I had to pay someone to clean up. Those guys ruined it for ya; sorry."

"But we'll be real quiet and make sure it's clean in the mornin'," I said.

"If ya don't leave right now, you'll be spendin' the next 30 days in my jail, not just the night."

George and I left. We walked to the railroad depot and laid down on one of the benches, but the ticket agent kicked us out of there, too. My next idea was to find a boxcar that was not going anywhere for the night, so we walked down the tracks for a few hundred yards. Along the way we met up with four of the hobos who shared our stew a few hours before.

At the end of the yard, sitting off to the side, we discovered an old caboose that had not been used for many years. This was evident because of all the dust that had accumulated inside. But it looked like a luxury hotel to us, with all of its glass in place and even a wood stove. There was no wood to be found in the caboose and finding wood on the ground was impossible because of several inches of snow.

"Look, there's a lumber yard," one man said, pointing off to the north.

So the six of us walked to the lumber yard but, because it was Sunday, it was closed. We borrowed a few pieces of the shortest lumber we could find: 6-foot-long two-by-sixes. Our next problem came when we tried to build a fire: We didn't have any way to make shorter pieces out of the long ones, so we let the wood stick out of the top of the stove. It's a miracle we didn't burn down the caboose because the fire became quite large and the inside of that car was full of smoke. No one complained. The six of us slept warm and dry on a cold and snowy night.

47

A Close Call
On to Great Falls, then Malta

It was clear that Casper was not a good town for hobos, so George and I thought it best to continue our journey by catching the next freight headed north. I found some old gunny sacks and put a couple around my feet and another around my head.

"Come on George, you should do the same."

I must have looked like an idiot because my traveling companion looked at me, smiled and shook his head.

"No thanks, I'll be warm enough."

"You think so now, but when that freight gets to movin' you'll be cold to the bone. Now wrap these around your feet," I said, throwing two sacks at him.

He refused my offer again, so we walked to a spot just outside the yard where we planned to catch the northbound in the early morning darkness.

"I know you've been on freights before, George, but headin' into the north country is different from down south. Don't grab a car unless you can get inside. Just hangin' onto the ladder or ridin' on top'll kill ya; you'll freeze to death."

"I'll be all right, Mooney, but what'll I do if I don't get on?"

"If we get split up, I'll meet ya at the Great Northern depot in Great Falls. Here it comes ..."

We both ran along the tracks trying to keep up with the train. It was picking up speed real fast, but I spotted an open boxcar and made that

my target. I planted my right foot and jumped for the opening, but my foot slipped and suddenly I was laying down with my feet over the track.

Startled for a split second, I was brought back to my senses by the train whistle. During periods of excitement or danger, time seems to slow down to the point where an event that uses up only three seconds seems to take much longer. Such was the case as I concentrated on moving my left leg until it was clear, then my right. I pulled and pulled, but the right leg wouldn't come clear of the rail.

I yanked with all my might as the wheel got closer and closer. I looked, and my right heel was

on the rail with my toes pointing up. The wheel was five feet away and closing fast. The thought of me limping around for the rest of my life on one foot flashed through my mind. Suddenly I realized that the gunny sack wrapped around my foot had snagged on the inside of the track. My only course of action was clear: I rolled to the left, to unwrap the burlap a little from around my foot. Then I pulled as hard as I could and covered my eyes with my hands, waiting for the pain that I was sure would come. But there was no pain. Three more cars passed and suddenly my leg pulled free with such force that I did a backward somersault.

I jumped up, looked at my right foot and was relieved to see it was still there, trailing four inches of burlap. I looked at the train and saw George catching the ladder of another boxcar. It was exactly what I had told him not to do. He was in for a cold ride. I watched until the train disappeared in the distance, tucked the extra burlap into my boot and walked back to the caboose.

The fire we started the night before was reduced to coals, but the stove was still hot. I sat down in the spot I had left an hour before and tried to sleep, but couldn't. I kept looking at my right foot and thinking how close I came to losing it. The eastern sky began to glow, and I watched as dawn transformed darkness into a new day. Then I once again slipped from the caboose and began my journey to Casper, this time I was walking. All the while, I was thinking about being on the range and herding sheep and stuffing my belly with all the food I wanted to eat.

Several vehicles passed me on the road, but finally a salesman stopped.

"Where ya headin'?"

"I'm tryin' to get to Great Falls."

"I can take ya part way."

It appeared my luck was changing. I opened the door and settled into the passenger seat.

"Thanks, mister," I said after the door was shut. "I appreciate ..."

My sentence was cut short when he pulled out a pistol and pointed it at me.

"Now don't you try anything," he said.

"I won't hurt ya, sir. I'm just lookin' to get to Great Falls and meet up with my friend, George; then we're goin' to Malta where we'll herd sheep for Mr. Hensen and ..."

"Look kid," he said, cutting short my nervous chatter. "You looked cold and I felt sorry for ya, but ya have to understand; a few weeks ago, a friend of mine picked up another hitchhiker along this stretch of the road and got murdered. I don't want that to happen to me."

We continued to chat and we both relaxed a little. Our route took us through several small towns, including Kaycee, Wyoming. As the car was picking up speed while heading out of town, the road made a sharp left turn that made it impossible to see more than 50 feet in front. Without warning, a large bull appeared. He was walking across the road and just happened to be in the middle. The bull stopped and looked at us as the salesman applied the brakes. There was one long screech — the sound of rubber on pavement — followed by a dull thump as the car hit the 1,000-pound bull.

"You OK?" the salesman asked.

"Yeah, I'm all right."

Steam was venting from the front of the car and the animal was laying on its side. The force of the collision had broken the bull's hind legs and torn open the belly, causing its intestines to spill onto the road. The bull, still alive but unable to get to its feet, was bellowing mournfully.

I was thankful then that the salesman had the pistol and suggested he use it to dispatch the bull, which he did. Some of the townspeople showed up and started butchering the bull. I could see that the car wouldn't be traveling any farther either, so I shook the salesman's hand and thanked him for giving me a ride, then once again started toward Great Falls, one step at a time.

It took me three more days of walking and hitchhiking to reach my destination. I slept in a couple of town jails along the way and spent one night hidden in a barn. When I walked into the Great Northern depot, there sat George with his back to me.

"George, how ya doin'? I've been worried about ..."

He turned, but I could hardly recognize him. Parts of the left side of his face were black.

"Yeah, well, I should've listened to ya, Mooney. I nearly froze to death, just like ya said. But I'm sure glad to see ya; now we can head to Malta and herd sheep like you were tellin' me."

I put my arm around his shoulder, and he started to cry.

"Let's find the mission and get ya some help," I said.

"Oh, I know where it is, Mooney. They've been helpin' me already. There's nice people here in Great Falls."

He stopped and turned to me, making me look in his face.

"Mooney, this was worse yesterday, and it'll be better tomorrow. The people at the mission told me so."

His face had a mottled appearance, with some areas as red as a severe sunburn and others scabbed over with a black crust.

"You look great, George," I said, lying. "It could be worse, ya know."

Together we went to the local mission and had a meal. George was awash with nervous talk about anything that came to mind. He was certainly glad to see me. I knew he was frightened about what had happened to him, along with what might have happened. He talked a mile a minute, and it was hard for me to get a word in edgewise: "... and, Mooney, when we're settled on the range, we'll get together and visit and talk about our sheep and laugh about ridin' the rails and how I froze my face and almost lost my nose, and how you almost lost your right foot and ..."

I let George talk all he wanted, to let him get it out of his system, because that's what I knew he needed to do. I didn't mind. Almost losing my right foot scared me plenty and I wasn't afraid to admit it. After two days in Great Falls, I felt George was ready to head north again. I checked with the people at the mission, and they agreed. We were on the next freight headed for Malta.

48

Time in Malta

Checking into the Great Northern Hotel in Malta was routine for me now. I introduced George to Joe, the hotel clerk, and once again I asked for the room that was less expensive. George shared my room, so we could split the cost, but we didn't cut corners on the food.

"This here sheepherdin' is quite a life, Mooney," George said after eating two meals at the hotel restaurant. "I like bein' able to eat all I want and not havin' to pay for it."

"Oh, you'll be payin' for it, George, but there's nothin' says we can't enjoy it now."

Mr. Hensen arrived the next evening. He walked into the restaurant as we were finishing our supper.

"How ya doin', Mooney?" he said, extending his hand.

"Hi, Mr. Hensen, do ya have a band of sheep I can care for?"

"I've always got a band of sheep for you. I told ya that before. We'll head for the ranch day after tomorrow, I've got some business in town and have to stay over."

"That's fine with me. Say, this here's George. Do ya have somethin' he can do?"

"I'm sure we can find somethin' for him. Nice to meet ya, George," he said shaking George's hand. "Oh, Tom and Blackie are in the truck."

I was up and out the door in an instant. When they saw me the two hounds barked, jumped from the truck bed and ran to me. I went to my knees

and they licked my face as we renewed our friendship. After a few seconds, Blackie backed up a few steps, threw his head to the sky and let go with a howl, and he kept it up for another two minutes. Until that time, I thought the howl of a dog or coyote was a sad and mournful sound, but Blackie's bay was happy and heart warming.

People stepped from the hotel and other buildings to see what the ruckus was all about. Finally I told the dogs to quiet down and ordered them to their place in the back of the truck.

"They're great dogs; I keep 'em with me all the time," Mr. Hensen said. "But like we agreed, they're yours for as long as you're workin' for

157

me."

Mr. Hensen, George and I went back to the restaurant and had some coffee. George learned about the ranch operation and what to expect when we got there.

"You've never been a sheepherder, George, so I'm gonna keep ya near the main ranch to help with the cattle and horses."

"Will I get to eat my fill there, like Mooney said?"

"You bet ya will; that is, if you're fast enough to eat your fill before the others eat your share," Mr. Hensen said, and we all laughed.

The three of us talked for two more hours before Mr. Hensen went to his room. George and I did the same an hour later, but before I took off my boots, I slipped out the back door of the hotel and brought Tom and Blackie back to the room.

"Are you sure it's all right to have these two in here?" George asked.

"I'm sure it's not, but they're stayin' anyway."

George didn't question me anymore, and I directed the dogs to lie on the floor at the end of my bed.

We were up early the next morning, and I took the dogs back to the truck before anyone noticed. Mr. Hensen was in the restaurant having breakfast when we got there. I asked if we could help him during the day and he said no; that we were to enjoy our last day in town. And that's what we did.

I picked out several dime novels, a deck of cards, a copy of the "Old Farmers' Almanac" and a few other books and charged everything to my account at the hotel.

"Don't ya think you're takin' more than's necessary, Mooney?" George asked with a chuckle.

"Wish I could manage to buy more. I'll most likely read each of these three times before I get back here to town for more."

That impressed George, so he bought a couple of books too. Then we went to the train depot and watched the 2:03 leave 10 minutes late.

"See that, George," I said pointing as two hobos grabbed the ladder of a boxcar just past the depot. "That could be us headin' for who knows where, not knowin' where our next meal's comin' from, sleepin' in a jungle, on a park bench or in a stinkin' jail."

Then I turned and made him look me in the eye.

"You remember that when you're workin' for Mr. Hensen," I said. "No matter how bad ya think your life is right then, it could always be worse; unless you're dead, of course.

"But there will come a time when ya get restless and think ridin' the rails is better than workin' at the ranch, and that's just fine with everyone. But remember, if ya do a good job at the ranch, you'll be welcomed back, even if ya leave for a spell. But if you ..."

I stopped abruptly, realizing that I was sounding like my father preaching a sermon.

"I understand, Mooney; I'll do my best."

We walked back to the hotel and sat in the chairs in the front lobby. As was the custom at the hotel, we tipped back our chairs and put our feet on the window sill. It was a picture of everyday life in a western town. I tried to record in my mind everything that happened on the street in front of me that afternoon. Women entered the general store to buy household goods.

It reminded me of the time I worked in a store like that. It was a fun place to work, where the customers were like friends, and I could help them find the flour, coffee, salt and beans they needed to feed a family. But helping them also meant providing the dreams people need to make life worth living instead of just sustaining life.

One woman might buy several yards of cloth to make a new dress that would make her happy and add color to her life. A man might shop for a hat to give to a loved one on a special occasion, and the youngsters entering the general store reminded me of the times my brothers, friends and

I would spend time looking at the jars containing hard candy; dreaming of the time when we could eat them.

The bank was another popular building. Men walked into it and out again; some stayed a few minutes but others were in there up to an hour. It was hard to tell by the expression on their faces whether their time in the building was successful. I remembered seeing my father in the line outside the First National Bank of Rapelje when it failed, and I was sad for a few minutes.

A cowboy's yell of joy brought me out of my melancholy state. I saw a group of five men riding hard into town and reining their mounts to a hard stop in front of the saloon. Nothing was going to stop them from having a good time; their cocky dismounts and arrogant swaggers were proof of that. The cowboy yells could be heard as the sun set and dusk became darkness.

"You two ready to eat?" Mr. Hensen asked as he appeared in front of us.

"I am," George said, rising to his feet.

I didn't say anything, but got up and started walking toward the restaurant.

George ordered the roast beef, as did Mr. Hensen. I ate a bowl of stew and saved the bread. Then, I asked for some roast beef to make a sandwich to eat while traveling to the Hensen ranch. I started to tell George about my idea of saving food for the road when Mr. Hensen stopped me.

"No need for ya to do that anymore, Mooney," he said. "The cook now makes me five big sandwiches, so I'll have somethin' to eat on the way to the ranch. I'll have him make a batch for the two of you. It sure beats eatin' only jerky to chase the hunger pains away."

I agreed and was pleased by the realization that Mr. Hensen had learned something from me.

We were on the road to the ranch by 4 the next morning. When we arrived, George and I headed to the bunkhouse to claim our bunks. It was just before supper when I opened the door and the other ranch hands were getting ready to head for the ranch house.

"Well, lookie here; it's Mooney, back to herd sheep again; you know what that means?"

"Yeah, he'll be a sheepherder all his life. Did ya know that, Mooney?"

"I don't plan on herdin' sheep all my life. This is just to fill my belly for a while."

"Well Mooney, I never seen a hand come back to the range as many times as you do and not stay a herder all his life."

"Me neither."

"That goes for me, too. Let's go eat." And they were out the door.

I stood there as if frozen to the spot, thinking about what the men had said. Staying on the range for the rest of my life would be a living, but the thought bothered me. There were other things to do in the world and I wanted to do them.

"Mooney, let's go eat," George said, bringing me out of my trance.

I threw my gear on an empty bunk and headed out the door.

49

Enjoying Nature

I went to the range again the next day, in the early spring of that year, and was given another band of 3,000 sheep to tend with the same sheepherder's wagon I had used the other times I had worked for Mr. Hensen in Montana. Watching over the sheep with me were my three old friends, Tom, Blackie and the Winchester .33.

We quickly resumed the routine we had developed before, but this time I was better prepared for a period without human contact and made the most of the time alone. My days were planned to fully enjoy the land and all the creatures living within the boundaries of my little world. The more I studied my surroundings, the more I enjoyed what was happening around me; even the little, routine things in life.

I found myself wanting to be up before the sun so I could watch the clouds turn color and signal the beginning of a new day. The lesson learned was that a sunrise could be as beautiful as a sunset, and to miss one was like missing a chance to watch a painting develop, as if fashioned by God's own hand. They were all different, but they were all perfect.

My meals were planned and cooked with great anticipation and precision. I planned my menu three days in advance in the belief that there is more to eating than just shoving meat and bread down one's throat. I also learned patience and that anticipation makes a meal special. Combining those two ingredients made cooking fun.

During the day I was able to work on my interaction with nature. Tom, Blackie and I became so close that I thought they could read my mind. A command yelled to a dog 100 yards away might be heard, but if it was windy, the command could go unheard. On my other trips to the range, we developed hand signals, and the dogs always obeyed. But our communications developed to the point Tom and Blackie reacted without me giving a command, and they always made the correct decision.

My flock was divided between ewes and lambs. There were a few more lambs in this band because some ewes gave birth to twins. The youngsters were fun to watch when they played. I was amused time and again as they gamboled from one small knoll to another, as most animals like to do.

It was hard for me to kill a ewe for the dogs and a lamb for myself after watching the lambs frolic and play hour after hour, but it was necessary. Still, the cry of the lambs I slaughtered will be with me forever.

But when I watched Tom and Blackie charge a coyote that was trying to kill one of the critters under our care, my faith was once again renewed. God's plan for those in the herd and the ones charged with watching over them was even more clear to me, and my place in the hierarchy of living things became evident as time passed and I observed more.

160

The inanimate parts of nature were also a part of my education on the range. I tried to finish my evening meal in time to circle the herd one more time before the sun dropped past the western horizon. The sunset would begin with many shades of colors, painting the sky a brilliant red or purple or one of a million other colors. Then the stars would push the sunset out of sight and put on a spectacular light show of their own: Twinkling points of light shimmered from horizon to horizon, with shooting stars making streaks of light across the sky like the light of a

locomotive going 1,000 miles per hour.

This show was my nightly entertainment, and I didn't want to miss a minute of it, but finally sleep would surpass my ability to keep my eyes open. If I woke up during the night, I would head for the wagon and crawl in bed, but many nights, my eyes would open just before sunrise, and I would still be outside with the dogs beside me. Then I would watch as another glorious day unfolded.

I learned to appreciate the bad weather that God sent my way, too. I already knew that thunderstorms could be deadly when a sheepherder was caught in the open. When clouds and winds signaled the possibility of violent storms, I stayed close to the wagon, if there was enough feed nearby for the sheep, or, when away from the wagon, I found a low spot in the landscape and stayed there until the storm passed.

But there was no guarantee that lightning wouldn't strike near me, no matter where I was. The jagged streaks of light that flashed around the countryside were dazzling and rugged, yet elegant too. If it was my fate to be injured or killed during a powerful and extreme Montana thunderstorm, then there was nothing I could do to keep that from happening, so I just relaxed and enjoyed the show.

When clouds blocked the stars and prevented a nighttime show, I would light my kerosene lamp and read a chapter from one of the books I brought to the range. I could have read all of the books during the first two weeks I was out there, but decided to read only a chapter at a time, and I imposed restrictions on when that would happen. The books were another way for me to exercise restraint and learn self-control.

Reading only one chapter at a time also allowed me to exercise my mind. I spent hours thinking about the story I was reading and what might happen during the next chapter. I was seldom correct, but I learned that there are many ways to tell the same story, and, sometimes — especially when reading the dime novels — I felt I could have written it better. The books also reminded me that there was life beyond sheepherding and the range.

I was content and enjoyed myself during the first three months on the range this time, but way back in my mind, and in my heart, I felt there was something missing; an emptiness that ached with an unbearable pain if I lost control and allowed it to creep into my mind. At first, I fought the feeling and was capable of pushing it out of my mind whenever it raised its ugly head, but the feeling was persistent, and I finally realized fighting it was useless. One evening, as I watched a brilliant sunset followed by a spectacular star-filled sky, I suddenly realized that the feeling I was fighting was in fact God's way of letting me know there was hope for the future; that there was a life for me after the range. I was overjoyed, and a warm feeling came over me. I enjoyed my time on the range even more and I tried hard to keep those good feelings from fading.

I also allowed myself to think about the things I saw during that last night while looking out the hotel window in Malta: The woman who left the general store with cloth and plans for a dress; the man who bought a hat for a loved one; the men who entered and exited the bank, with plans for breaking ground to start a ranch or buying a herd of sheep or cattle; and the cowboys who headed for the saloon to whoop it up for the night.

These things, which I put out of my mind until this time, reinforced my resolve to make something more of myself than just being the best sheepherder in Montana.

50

Explaining Life to George

The camp tender visited each sheepherder at four- to six-week intervals. When the tender made his second visit to my camp, he had a visitor with him. George jumped from the wagon when it was still 30 yards away and ran to me, extending his hand as he got close.

"Gee Mooney, it's sure nice to see ya," he said, pumping my hand enthusiastically.

"You too, George. What are ya doin' out here?"

"Well ... I ...," he stammered as he nervously looked at the tender.

The tender's wagon was now next to mine, so I turned my attention to him.

"I'm about out of water, hope ya can top me off."

"Yeah, as I always do."

"You're out awful late in the day; won't it make ya late back to the house?" I asked.

I knew the tender planned his resupply trips so he could visit two or three herders, then get back to the ranch house in time for the evening meal rather than spend the night on the range.

"Yeah, well, Mr. Hensen wants me to visit more herders on this trip because it's so dry out. I've got to spend three nights out here, then I'll be back this way to get George."

That was fine with me. I would have company for most of four days and three nights, and after almost four months on the range, I was ready for some company. We were unloading my sup-plies when I noticed an inside portion of the wagon that was covered with canvas, the edges being held down with rocks. I reached for the edge of the canvas when the tender grabbed my arm.

"That doesn't concern you, kid."

I grabbed another sack of flour and forgot about what might be under the canvas. We unloaded the rest of my supplies and topped off my water barrel, then I turned to the tender.

"Want to spend the night here?"

"Nope, I'll make it to the next camp."

And he got back on the wagon and headed down the trail.

I took George on a walk around the herd as the sheep were bedding down. My meat supply was getting low, so I killed a lamb for George and I, and an old ewe for the dogs.

"How can ya stand to listen to them blat like that?" George asked after I cut the lamb's throat.

"Ya know, George, it always bothers me, but it's a part of life, and if I want to eat, I have to kill something."

"I know, but ..."

"It's the best way, George," I said, raising my voice a bit. He didn't pursue the subject further, but he watched as I dressed the sheep, and helped me drag them back to the wagon. We feasted on a meal of fresh sourdough bread and leg of lamb. After supper we stretched out on the ground beside the wagon and watched the sun set and the stars put on their nightly light show.

"I never knew stars could be so pretty," George said.

"Have you ever really looked at 'em?"

"Ya know, Mooney," George said, taking the time to consider the question. "I guess I haven't."

"There's other things in this world that are worth lookin' at too, if ya just take the time."

"Like what?"

"Well, you've just seen how pretty a sunset can be, and the stars too ..." And, I went on to explain how a sunrise can also lift a person's spirits; how clouds that pass overhead during the day can be fun to watch as they take on different shapes; how the blowing wind can cause the grasses to make interesting patterns in the sur-

now beside me, one on each side — until I fell asleep.

My eyes opened when Blackie stretched and got to his feet. I sat up and noticed the eastern sky begin to herald a new day.

"George, wake up," I said. "You don't want to miss this."

My friend rubbed his eyes and focused on the sky. We sat there for 30 minutes, watching a beautiful sunrise.

After I cooked breakfast, we followed the sheep to their grazing grounds. While they were feeding, George and I sat down and watched from a knoll.

"I'm goin' home, Mooney," George said. "And I'm never leavin' again."

rounding dirt; how a pond of perfectly still water can reflect a sky full of clouds; and how watching the late-spring frost melt as the sun hits a blade of grass are special things.

I talked for a long time and stopped only when I realized George was asleep. I retrieved two blankets from the wagon and covered my friend with one. The stars continued to sparkle above me and I petted the dogs — who where

I didn't say anything, knowing that he would explain if he wanted to. "I'm just not cut out to work on a big ranch like this."

"Will your folks take ya back in?"

"Oh yeah, it was me who left in a huff. My mother begged me not to go, and my father, even if he didn't say it, didn't want me to go either."

"You're lucky, George. You've got a place to go home to and people who want you there.

But you've sure had an adventure, haven't ya?"

We laughed and relived our time together, talking for three days and two nights. I showed George around my sheepherding world, pointing out the interesting things to see, and showed him more about nature than he had ever noticed before.

"But don't ya get lonely out here, Mooney?"

"Sure do, but a person has to make the best of every situation, and that's what I'm doin' here. Look at it this way, at least I've got a full belly, right?"

"Say, remember when we spent that night in a culvert ...?" he asked.

"When we were walking to Santa Fe and we didn't eat for three days?" I replied.

"Yeah, my stomach aches whenever I think about it."

"Mine too. You see, George, those're the things that are on my mind when I get lonely. I try to remember why I'm here and two things come to mind: I have a full belly and I'm makin' money. I know this won't be my life forever, but for now, I'll stay here."

We watched every sunset and sunrise, and we ate our fill of lamb and sourdough bread, then let the stars lull us to sleep each night.

I was sad to see George leave; it had been fun to have another person around for a few days, but I shook his hand and wished him luck as he climbed aboard the tender's wagon. I watched the wagon as it lumbered down the trail toward the Hensen ranch. Just before it disappeared from sight, George stood up, leaned around the canvas covering and waved; I waved back.

"Camp tenders were a different bunch. Some of them were honest, but most of them would take some of the supplies that were supposed to be given to the sheepherders and sell them to cowboys, ranchers, general stores, and anyone else who would buy them. Most herders didn't know that some of the supplies, most likely the best food supplies like canned goods, that was to go to them really were sold by the tenders."

Diane Smith, author and historian

51

A Tough Winter

After George left, I suffered a terrible bout of loneliness. It had been easy to explain to my friend why I was there, and the feelings of being alone hadn't bothered me much during the four months before he visited me, but now I was hard pressed to justify the situation in my mind.

My belly had been full the whole time, so hunger wasn't a good reason to be on the range, but saving money was. The more I had stitched into my belt when I stopped looking after sheep, the better off I would be while trying to find another job.

It was another six weeks before I was again able to keep my emotions in check and settle back into a routine where a sunrise was beautiful. Until then, a sunrise was just a reminder that families all across Montana were sitting down to breakfast where they would not only enjoy a good home-cooked meal, but each other's company as well. When my mind drifted in that direction and my mood started to become melancholy, I tried to concentrate on life after the range, of someday having a family of my own. Those thoughts, along with the help of a friendly lick from Tom or Blackie, helped put my life back in perspective. I would again remember that the Lord had a plan for me and that I must be patient and allow that plan to unfold.

I stayed a long time out herding this time: all summer, fall and winter. The fall was pleasant and I once again enjoyed the books I had

bought for these lonely times. The tender continued to make his rounds every six weeks or so and the clothing salesman visited me once in early December.

I spent the winter in the old cabin that I had used before. It was a severe winter, even by Montana standards, and I learned to use old sheep dung for fuel to supplement the little wood I had. The sheep droppings would burn slowly and I maintained a fire at all times, but the fire didn't completely chase the cold out of the cabin. I spent most of my time huddled close to that stove, and at night I had Tom and Blackie sleep on my feet, which they didn't seem to mind.

Ice was so thick on the nearby spring that it was impossible to break through. Without the spring water, I had to melt snow to water the dogs and for my own use. I kept a large bucket on the stove and added snow to it several times a day.

I ventured outside four times a day to check on the sheep and to feed them. They ate snow to get the water they needed, but I could tell that the winter was hard on them too. They got the nourishment they needed, but every time I butchered a lamb or ewe as the winter progressed, I could see there was less fat on the animals. Many times I took one or more sheep into the cabin with me when I thought they were freezing to death, and that did keep some of them alive; still, several died from the cold. Then the weather worsened. It was so bad that the tender hadn't stopped by to resupply me for eight weeks and I was low on food for myself, food for the sheep and hope for the future.

Enduring the cold of that Montana winter was nothing less than a lesson in how to stay alive. I found no pleasure in playing solitaire or re-reading the books I had brought with me, so I did neither. The cold was with me always, and my actions to take care of the flock, the dogs and myself became more mechanical.

When I had nearly reached the end of my rope, and was in the depths of depression, thinking that Mr. Hensen and the rest of the world had forgotten about me, the first hint of spring hit me like a slap in the face. After feeding the sheep one afternoon, I followed the path in the snow to the corner of the cabin and had turned toward the door when a drop of water hit my cheek. I jumped and looked at the cabin roof. I watched as another water droplet fell from a short icicle attached to the corner log. I looked up and saw a bright sun shining in a blue sky. The sun was warm on my face and I stretched my arms out and felt the warmth on my arms and chest and legs.

"Whoopee!" I yelled, and, although I've never been one for dancing, I danced a jig right there, in the path. I stopped and held my arms

out again, this time with my back to the sun. A slight breeze chased the warmth from my back and brought me out of my trance. I entered the cabin smiling and whistling, for I knew the worst of the weather was over and spring was not far away.

A week later the tender arrived at the cabin in the late afternoon with two other men. They were surprised to see me alive; in fact, one of the men had been sent by Mr. Hensen to be my replacement in case I had starved to death. They spent the night, realizing that the trip back to the ranch would take another day's travel. It was nice to have human company, but none of the others were happy. As pleased as I was to spend the night in the company of three other men, they were just as displeased that they had to spend the night on the range.

They were up early and preparing to leave before the sun had cleared the horizon. The tender started to climb to the teamster's seat when I grabbed his arm and pulled, making him stumble back to the ground. He regained his footing and turned toward me, clearly annoyed at my actions.

"You tell Mr. Hensen that I want off this here range, and soon," I said softly, but through clenched teeth.

"Yeah, yeah, kid," the tender said, then he started to climb onto the wagon again.

I grabbed his arm and pulled him off the wagon again. This time he was ready to fight me, but he thought better of the idea when he realized he would most likely lose.

"Look, kid, what do ya want me to do?"

"I want off this range!" I yelled, then I settled down, surprised at the way I was acting. "You tell Mr. Hensen two more weeks, three at the most."

The tender nodded. "Anything else?" he asked.

"No."

"Can I go now?"

"Yeah, get outta here."

He was on the wagon in an instant and heading down the road.

Two weeks later, Mr. Hensen arrived at the cabin in the early afternoon with another herder and two other sheep dogs. He apologized for not getting to me during the dead of winter, but, even though I accepted his apology, I didn't really believe him. I had been on the range taking care of his sheep for many months, and it was apparent I was expendable, like one of those sheep. He hadn't been there 10 minutes when he started fidgeting.

"OK, Mooney, let's hurry," he said. "We can get back to the ranch before supper's over and get you some of that good ranch food."

I started to collect my gear, then stopped and looked at the other herder, a young man who, I guessed, was several years older than me; in his early 20s. As bad as I wanted to leave right then, I knew one more night out there wouldn't hurt me and it might benefit him.

"Your first time on the range?"

"Yeah," he said softly.

"We need to spend the night, Mr. Hensen."

"What d'ya mean?"

I faced him and looked him straight in the eye, "I mean, we're gonna spend the night here."

Mr. Hensen shrugged his shoulders in defeat and walked to the truck to get his bedroll. I spent the afternoon showing the new herder around the place, and I made sure Mr. Hensen was with us every step of the way. I took them to the spring and it was still frozen, so I explained what the pail on the stove was for.

We counted the sheep and found that 50 had died during the winter. I felt bad about that, but Mr. Hensen said other herds had lost up to 200. I explained my cooking system to the new man. I killed a ewe for the dogs and a lamb for us.

"I don't like ya killin' a lamb for us to eat," Mr. Hensen said.

I didn't answer, but dressed the animals and got them ready for the evening meal. I cooked all of the ewe, except for one slab of backstrap, and fed the four dogs first, letting them have the

bones for dessert. The lamb was prepared the same as the ewe and I cooked the remaining backstrap of the older sheep. When I served the meat, along with a hunk of sourdough bread for each of us, I made sure Mr. Hensen got the ewe. He took a big bite and chewed for awhile. Then he went to the door and spit it out and threw the rest of it to the dogs.

"Got any more of that lamb?" he asked.

After supper, I banked the fire and noticed Mr. Hensen getting ready to sleep on the bed.

"Mr. Hensen, that's his place," I said, pointing to the new herder. "We'll sleep here, next to the stove." And we did.

We all slept until the sun's rays were streaking across the countryside, but Mr. Hensen was on his feet first.

"Mooney, if we get an early start ...," Mr. Hensen stopped and looked at me as I lay on the floor, looking at the ceiling.

"What time we leavin', Mooney?" he asked.

"Around noon; there's more I've got to show you two."

I showed the new herder hand signals that Tom, Blackie and I used to communicate. His dogs were already trained to recognize some of them and I felt the three of them would make a good team. We shot a box of shells through the Winchester so that he could hit where he aimed. I gave him the books I had brought with me and the cards, then I explained that to fight loneliness on the range, I looked at the stars and the sunsets and other things from Mother Nature.

At noon, I put my gear in the truck and shook hands with the new herder.

"You'll do just fine," I told him, then climbed into the truck. We headed down the road with Tom and Blackie standing in the back, barking at the wind.

We were at the Hensen ranch before supper. I had time to heat water and take a bath, my first in several months. I was ravenous as I sat down for the evening meal and I showed the other ranch hands how much a young sheepherder can eat. Mr. Hensen tried to talk me into staying at the bunkhouse for the spring and summer, but I'd had my fill of working on a ranch.

The next morning he took me to Malta and we settled up. After deductions, my wages didn't amount to much. I had two extra shirts and pants, bought from the clothing man from Minneapolis, and felt that was a good way to spend my hard-earned money. I said good-bye to Tom and Blackie and watched them disappear from sight as the truck headed out of town. My hair was long and unsightly, so I headed for the barber shop.

"How's sheepherdin', sonny?" the barber asked as I sat down.

The question shocked me, and I didn't answer. It scared me that someone could just look at me and know I had been on the range for months with a flock of sheep. My stay in Malta lasted only a few hours this time. I was on the next freight headed for Chicago.

"In Montana they say you can smell a sheepherder a mile away before he takes a bath, and a block away after. That is not a derogatory remark – it's a fact."

Diane Smith, author and historian

52

The Dust Bowl
I See My Father

When I walked the streets of Chicago this time, it wasn't hard to see that our country was in worse shape than before I went to the range. There were three times as many hobos looking for work and standing in bread lines than when I was in the Windy City before.

The only option available to a young hobo like me was to leave Chicago and travel around the country until I found an employer who was willing to hire me permanently; at least that's the way I saw it. Working short-term jobs was a short-term solution that enabled me to earn a little money from time to time, but I needed long-term employment to get established and to build a solid foundation.

It didn't matter to me where I worked as long as I could earn a fair wage. Joining and becoming a respected member of a community was but a dream, but I believed the Lord had a plan and it would unfold before me as my life progressed.

From Chicago, I traveled by rail to New Orleans, Dallas, Atlanta and many other southern and eastern cities. The story was the same everywhere: lots of people looking for work and the next meal, with most finding neither. I had never been to California, but I was curious about the possibilities of work there after hearing the state mentioned many times, so I headed west.

The trip took me through Oklahoma, and I saw the dust bowl conditions firsthand. Dirt from farm fields was piled high along fence lines, and when even a slight breeze would blow, particles of fine dust would take to the air, making it hard to see and breathe. Before the train I was riding cleared the area, I had the misfortune of experiencing a bad storm.

"Look, there she comes," one of the seven men sharing the boxcar with me said.

Coming at us was a wall of dirt that looked as high as a mountain. There was no way the train was going to outrun it, so, five minutes before the storm reached us, the train simply stopped. I had never before seen a train stop like ours did.

When I asked about it, one of the men said, "You'll understand when the storm hits; now let's close this door."

"Cover your face with anything ya got, and breathe slow," another said as he took off his shirt and held it in place over his face.

I took one of my extra pants and put the waist band over my head until my head was going down one of the legs, then I folded the remaining leg over my face and held an extra shirt to my face also. The wind slammed into the boxcar and it rocked back and forth as the fine dust filtered into the car. I breathed slowly, but still the dust made it's way to my lungs causing me to cough, as did everyone else in the car. The storm lasted four hours, and I thought I was going to die before it was over. The engineer would have the same trouble breathing, and it would be impossible for him to see his instruments, not to mention the track — he had no choice but to stop.

When the train started to move again, I uncovered my head and was greeted by a different world. Everything left exposed during the storm was covered with dust; it resembled a landscape after a blizzard, but instead of being white, everything was the color of dust.

An inch of dust had accumulated on the floor of the boxcar, with drifts up to 6 inches deep angling from the downwind wall. We must have presented a comical sight as the eight of us sat there looking around the car. Our heads were relatively clean, but, from the shoulders down, we were also thoroughly covered in dust. One man started to laugh, and the rest of us joined in. We started to get to our feet and soon found that to be a bad idea; moving only caused the dust to once again become airborne.

"Let's open the door," someone said, but when we did, it turned out to be another bad idea.

As the train gained speed, the dust on the cars in front of ours and on the tracks was swept back to us, until it was again as bad as when we were in the storm. We quickly closed the door and covered our heads like we did before. It took another hour before the dust began to subside and we could uncover again. Dust was still blowing from the tracks, but it remained low and, two hours later, it had diminished considerably. We rode that freight into the night and, by the next morning, there wasn't a hint of the dust storm

we had experienced the day before. However, the accumulation of blowing dust from storm after storm became apparent when the tracks ran parallel to Highway 66 for several miles.

A steady stream of cars and trucks were traveling west, away from the devastation. Dust had drifted higher than fences and sometimes higher than houses. Each vehicle had the possessions of a family piled high and tied down with rope. Adults and children were also in the vehicles, some in the front seats and others perched on top of the bundles of possessions.

We passed vehicle after vehicle snaking their way along the road, and while several seemed to be part of an organized group, others were obviously alone. Not all of the vehicles were moving: Many were stopped beside the road with their hoods up and the families standing or sitting nearby.

The broken- down cars and trucks reminded me of the time my family was moving from Clarkston to Rapelje and we had many flat tires along the way. But back then, there was a festive air to our journey, even with the flat tires. We would wave to people in cars and trucks that passed ours, and most of them would stop to see if we needed assistance. The people in the exodus from the dust bowl area were a defeated bunch and every bit as broken as the vehicles along the road. I didn't see one smile on either adult or child; instead, they looked tired and disappointed. I said a prayer for them and thanked the Lord that I only had myself to look after, which was a full-time job in itself.

I rode freights through the Texas panhandle, across New Mexico and through Arizona on the way to California. I was soon to find out that California was different than the rest of the country during the Depression: They didn't want poor people visiting their state. The freight I was on stopped at the Arizona-California border near Blythe, and all of the hobos were kicked off. If a person didn't have money, he wasn't welcome. I was lucky because I had 25 cents in my pocket, so I walked to the nearest bus station and bought a ticket to Indio. If that money hadn't been in my pocket, I wouldn't have been allowed to cross the border into California. But once in the state, it was hard to find someone who was willing to share a little food; even if I asked for work first. Everyone called me an Okie, but I didn't even know what that meant, so I asked the next time it came up.

"Ma'am, do ya have some work I can do for a bit of food?" I asked one woman who answered the door of a house.

"No! And I'm tired of you damn Okies askin'."

"What's an Okie?"

"Where you from?"

"Montana."

"Did you go through Oklahoma to get here?"

"Yes."

"Then you're a damn Okie as far as I'm concerned."

I still didn't fully understand the term, but I didn't want to press the subject. It seemed like everyone in California had the same attitude. My only choice, if I didn't want to starve to death, was to leave the state.

So once again I circled the country, hopping freight after freight, chasing that elusive dream of finding a steady job and settling down. All I found was a lot of other people chasing the same dream. A day or two of work, once or twice a month, was all I found, and I was thankful for it, but it took a lot of begging to stay alive. I resisted stopping in the big cities because I knew conditions for hobos would be intolerable there and I didn't want to spend any more time in a bread line.

As the summer began to fade, I found myself passing through the state of North Dakota. I was sitting in the door of an open boxcar near the front of the train with four others when the train approached a road that crossed the track. I was in a position to see the road well before the train got there, and noticed a car stopped at the crossing. The driver could have crossed before the train arrived, but he didn't. Instead he just sat there, waiting for the train to pass.

The car didn't look familiar, but as the train approached, the driver got out of the car and stood by the door. We were fast approaching the crossing, and I looked at the man again: It was my father! My feelings were mixed; they ran the gamut, from excited and happy to ashamed and sad, in a matter of a few seconds. I sat there in tattered clothes, with a five-day growth of beard, and I didn't want him to see me like that. I tilted my head down a little, so he couldn't look directly into my face, but I watched him as we passed. He tried to look at every person riding the freight, but besides the five of us in the boxcar door, there were 10 others riding on the top, and there were 30 cars in the train, some of them carrying more hobos than ours.

When he was out of sight, I got up and walked to a dark corner, pulled my knees up tight to my body and cried softly. My thoughts turned to my mother and the fun we had as a family when I was young. I entered the worst state of melancholy ever experienced by a member of the human race. I stayed there until the afternoon turned to evening, then night. I don't know when I fell asleep, but I awoke when rays from the rising sun hit my face.

172

53

The Nelsons

When I was fully awake, I asked the others where we were, and I was told that we were nearly out of the Dakotas and about to enter Montana. The temptation to head for Malta and link up with Mr. Henson was strong, but I resisted it. While the time I spent on the range had been beneficial to me, once or twice to the point of actually saving my life, there just had to be something more than being a sheepherder in my future. So I stayed put as the train headed west, through Montana, Idaho and into Washington.

I jumped from the freight as it slowed to a stop in the wheat-country town of Tekoa. I walked to the jungle and found 25 other hobos there working on a stew.

"Join us, young man," one said, and I was instantly a member of the group.

The next morning I walked into town to check

the place out. I wanted to pull my own weight and contribute to the stew that the other hobos were planning that night, so I went to the grocery store and asked the owner if he had some work I could do for something to eat. He found me a job, then gave me some groceries; more than I deserved for the work I had done.

Over the period of five days, I visited the grocery store three times, and each time there was work for me. Another young man was working in the store, too, so it was obvious the store owner was being nice and finding extra work for a young hobo. Once, I went to his house, mowed his lawn and split some wood and again he gave me more groceries than I deserved for the work I had done. I shared my groceries with the other hobos in the jungle and, after combining all the food we could scrounge, our hobo stews were quite substantial.

As sweet as it was, the situation was a stagnant one. I wasn't getting ahead nor was I pursuing my dream of finding a permanent job. I shared my feelings with the store owner, and he seemed to take a liking to me, telling me he would help me find a job. I had been in Tekoa for another week when the young store helper came running to the jungle on a Friday afternoon.

"Mooney, if you want to work, there's someone at the store waitin' for ya," he said.

I certainly wanted to work, so I went to the store and found the owner talking with another man.

"Oh, here he is now," the store owner said as I joined them. "Mooney, this here's Ted Nelson. He has a wheat ranch near here."

"Nice to meet ya, Mr. Nelson," I said, extending my hand.

He shook my hand, then stood back and looked me over like he was buying a work horse or some other farm animal.

"I'll vouch for him, Ted," the store owner said. "I know he's a good worker."

"Yeah, but that's not farm work," Mr. Nelson said. "Look young man, I have a days work for ya and I'll pay ya a dollar for it, what da ya say?"

"Yes, sir, I'm ready to go." I said, and I thanked the store owner for his help before climbing into an old truck with Mr. Nelson.

We headed east for about two miles and stopped at the Nelson ranch which was just inside the Idaho border. The hired man and I ate supper with the family and then I threw my bedroll in the hay loft for the night. The next morning I was treated to a great breakfast before we went to work. The farmer had gone around the

edge of a wheat field with a binder, which put the green wheat in bundles for hay. This was to be the winter feed for the cattle and horses.

Mr. Nelson drove the truck, I pitched the bundles to the hired man, who was riding on the truck, and he stacked the bundles. The truck was equipped with racks, so the bundles could be stacked high. When the truck was loaded, it was driven to the barn and I pitched the bundles to the hay loft where they would be stored until needed. We hauled nine truck loads that Saturday and when the last bundle was put in place,

Mr. Nelson walked over to me.

"You're a good worker for such a young man. I'll take you back to Tekoa, if you want, but here's somethin' to think about: You're welcome to stay here tomorrow and milk the cows, take care of the horses and do some other chores that needs to be done. Now, I can't pay you for the Sunday chores, but I'll feed ya. On Monday we start the wheat harvest and I'll pay ya $1.25 a day, if you've a mind to stay."

"Yes, sir, I'll stay," I said shaking Mr. Nelson's hand. Naturally, I was going to accept an offer that paid good wages, but Mr. Nelson didn't know they were the highest wages I had ever been offered.

Monday was a big day as the horses, all 24 of them, were hitched to the combine. After the wheat was cut and threshed, it went into sacks and a person, called a sack sewer, would sew the sacks shut, then put them in a chute that led to the ground.

My job was to pick the wheat sacks off the ground and throw them to the hired hand who would stack them in the bed of the truck that Mr. Nelson was driving. After throwing a few sacks, the hired man taught me how to use my knee to boost the sack up. When we had a full load on the truck, we drove to the grain elevator, located about seven miles away, where we would unload the sacks. Then we would go back for another load.

Mr. Nelson turned out to be a real good man to work for. He expected me to produce a good days work, but I didn't mind working hard, especially when I was earning fair wages. Mrs. Nelson was nice to me, too. She was a good cook and I enjoyed sitting at the table with them and eating my fill. The couple had three sons, ages 3 to 10 – to young too work on the farm. The Nelsons hired a couple of young women to help with the cooking and other chores during harvest. It was a good time for me; I was getting the respect I deserved, and it was a good feeling.

One evening, after supper, I excused myself and started to head for the hay loft and go to bed, when Mrs. Nelson stopped me.

"Mooney, I've got something to show you," she said as she led me to a small room just off the kitchen. Inside was a bed and a chest of drawers.

"You're welcome to sleep here as long as you're workin' for us."

The gesture was unexpected and it caught me by surprise. I almost cried right there, but caught myself.

"Thank you, ma'am," I stammered. "I'll get my bedroll." And I turned and walked to the barn.

It took several deep breaths before my self control returned. I grabbed my bedroll, went to the room and started to close the door.

"Goodnight, Mooney," Mr. Nelson said.

"Yes sir, goodnight."

I settled into the fresh sheets of the bed and thought about my good fortune. My employer and his wife were nice people who respected me, my wages were good, and my quarters were as nice as a room in a fancy hotel.

My thoughts turned to the times when my mother made sure her children were well fed and as comfortable as she could allow. The Nelsons made me feel like I was a part of their family, a heart-warming gesture on their part and I felt good.

"My grandparents, Ted and Emma Nelson, arrived in the Tekoa area in 1933 from Moscow, Idaho. They were respected wheat farmers and would help anyone who was down and out.

"Wheat harvest was a big time in our family, with as many as 20 or more people hired to help. Two women were hired to help in the house with the cooking and other chores.

"Breakfast was cooked in the house and served on tables in the yard. A hot noon meal was delivered each day to the workers in the field.

"I now have an easel set up in the room where Monte stayed when he worked for my Grandparents."

Patricia (Patty) Nelson Leonard, Granddaughter of Ted and Emma Nelson

54

Saturday Night In Tekoa

Even during the harvest season no one worked on Sunday, and that made Saturday nights special. It provided a chance for the folks in Tekoa to get together, do a little shopping and visit. The Nelsons always invited me to go with them.

Mr. Nelson liked cars. He owned a 1935 or 1936 Oldsmobile and I thought it was the most beautiful car I had ever seen. His entire family would get all gussied up, climb in the car and head for town after Saturday night supper. It was great fun just riding in the Olds and so was our time in Tekoa.

There were maybe six stores in the town and they were all open. After Mr. Nelson parked the car, his wife and the hired women, would head for the general store where most of the ladies would gather.

Most of the men would visit the barber shop first. It was a busy place and packed with customers for the first two hours we were in town. We took our place in line, Mr Nelson, his three sons and I, and visited with the others until it was our time to sit in the chair. I was always first and, while Mr. Nelson and his sons were getting their hair cut, I had time to walk the short distance to the local hobo jungle for a few minutes and see if anyone I knew was there. Seldom did I find an old friend. Maybe it was because the harvest was in full swing, because only the hobos who couldn't or didn't want to work were not employed, and most everyone I knew wanted

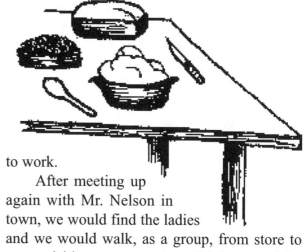

to work.

After meeting up again with Mr. Nelson in town, we would find the ladies and we would walk, as a group, from store to store, visiting as we went, as did the rest of the people in town. The Nelsons introduced me to their friends as Mooney, with no other title attached, such as harvest worker or hired man, and that made me feel even more like a member of their family. Everyone in the town of Tekoa was friendly, and I thought the weekly event was a wonderful way to spend a night off.

After four or five hours in town, we would climb into the Oldsmobile and head back to the ranch and another week of wheat harvest.

One afternoon, Mr. Nelson ask me if I wanted to go with him to St. Maries. A popular senator was going to speak, and he wanted some company during the hour-long ride. I was more interested in the car ride than meeting a senator, but I did listen to Senator William Borah speak, and when he was finished, Mr. Nelson introduced me to him. Then we headed back to the ranch

and the wheat harvest.

Bringing in the wheat was hard work, but I was earning a respectable wage during the five weeks it lasted. My feelings were mixed as we headed back to the ranch after unloading the last sack of grain at the elevator. We passed the stubble fields where golden grain had stood just a couple of weeks before and a feeling of accomplishment swelled inside of me. I had helped harvest that grain, and now it would be used to make bread and other foods that would feed people in all parts of the country. But just as the delivery of the last sack of wheat at the elevator signaled the end of the harvest, I also knew my reason for staying with the Nelsons was coming to an end.

After he parked the truck and we started walking to the house for supper, Mr. Nelson stopped and turned to me.

"Mooney, you've been a good worker, and I don't want to lose ya, but I'm in a pickle. If you would consider stayin' on for the winter, helpin' me feed and take care of the livestock, I'll pay ya in room and board, but I can't afford to pay ya any wages."

Now it was me who was in a pickle. The Nelsons had embraced me like a member of their family. I could easily have stayed with them for the rest of my life, and the feeling would have gotten stronger. But even though the country was in the Depression, and leaving the Nelsons would surely mean that I would be hungry again at some point, I just couldn't bring myself to work and not be paid a wage.

Deep down inside me there was a feeling that something bigger was in my future and I couldn't ignore it. With great reluctance I thanked Mr. Nelson, but explained that I would be in the same financial shape in the spring as in the fall.

"Maybe in that time I'll be able to find the job that keeps digging' at me."

Then I tried to tell him about the special job that I somehow knew was out there, somewhere, waiting for me to catch up to it, but I don't think I did a good job of explaining it.

"I don't understand completely, but I've got to respect your feelings, Mooney," he said. "There is another job not far away that you might consider. Art Crab lives south of Tensed and needs someone to help him with his plowin' this year. Says he'll pay a dollar a day, plus room and board."

"Oh, I'd like that."

My last supper with the Nelsons was fun. Instead of being a somber occasion with long, sad faces, we relived the many funny things that happened during the harvest, and laughter filled the house during and after supper, until we said goodnight and headed to our rooms. The next morning we picked up where we left off, and the humor continued as we enjoyed our last breakfast together.

"Mooney, why don't you help me with the chores, then I'll drive you to Art's ranch?"

So, I helped with the morning chores. When it was time to leave, Mrs. Nelson came out of the house with a picnic lunch and the Nelsons, their daughters and I climbed into the Oldsmobile for the trip to Tensed.

We drove through the Idaho countryside and visited; we stopped for a picnic lunch; and then we were at the Art Crab ranch. Mrs. Nelson and her daughters immediately headed to the house to visit with Mrs. Crab. Mr. Nelson introduced me to Mr. Crab, then the three of us drove around the ranch so I could see the fields that needed to be plowed. We got out of the truck a couple times, and it was clear that Mr. Crab was rather sickly and couldn't do much work. He had trouble breathing and couldn't walk far without resting.

When we returned to the ranch house, Mrs. Nelson and the girls came out of the house and we said our good-byes before they climbed into the Oldsmobile and headed down the road with waves from everyone.

"Come on in the house, Mooney," Mrs. Crab said. "Supper's about ready."

And I felt like I had been handed from one nice family to another.

"Saturday nights in Tekoa were always a big time – it was a great weekly social occasion. Thestreets were full of people and the stores were open until at least 9 p. m..The people would circulate from store to store and visit along the way. My father, Kenneth Nelson, was the oldest of the three sons.

"My granfather always favored Oldsmobile cars and he was proud to drive them."

Patricia (Patty) Nelson Leonard, Granddaughter of Ted and Emma Nelson

55

Working The Crab Ranch

Working for the Crabs was like working for the Nelsons, except they didn't have any children. I had a room in the house, and Mrs. Crab was as good a cook as Mrs. Nelson was.

Every morning I would hook the six horses to the plow and guide them around the field. At noon I would feed and water the horses, have lunch with the Crabs and then head back to the fields and plow until dusk. The work was enjoyable, and I relished the feeling of pride that came over me when looking back at the even rows left in the earth by the horses and me.

Plowing with horses was slow, and it took me five weeks to complete the fall plowing. Once again, I was sad when the last bit of earth had been overturned, for that meant my time with the Crabs was coming to an end. But Mr. Crab had another idea.

"Mooney, there's a portable sawmill set up about four miles from here," he told me. "Last spring I had 'em cut up some logs. Would ya consider gettin' that lumber to here for me? I'll pay ya the same as for the plowin'."

"Sure, Mr. Crab," I said.

For the next four days, I hitched the horses to a wagon in the morning and drove them to the lumber pile. There I would load each board by hand until the wagon was full and return to the ranch. After lunch, I would make another trip. I suppose an experienced teamster could have made three trips a day, but two was about

my limit and that's all Mr. Crab expected of me and his horses. Besides, driving through the backwoods near Tensed was wonderful in the early fall.

The only stop I made between the Crab ranch and the sawmill was to open and close a gate about a half mile from the lumber pile. Cattle were roaming free inside the fence surrounding the sawmill, so opening and closing the gate was annoying, but necessary.

On the second trip of the fourth day, I was loading the boards when I had a spooky feeling that someone was watching me. I shrugged it off because I knew no one lived within three miles. I finished topping off the load, climbed into the teamster's seat and headed for the gate. About 30 feet from the road was a large stump that I had to pass before stopping to open the gate. I had passed that stump seven times before, and I didn't pay any attention to it. I wouldn't have given it a second thought on this trip either, but a slight movement caught my eye. Then I noticed something sticking out of the brush behind the stump. It was a shotgun

barrel, and it was pointed at me!

I caught my breath and said a fast prayer, but didn't let on that I had seen it. I hadn't been in the sights of a firearm since a farmer shot at me for "borrowing" a couple of his chickens, and I was just as scared now as I was then. I watched the barrel out of the corner of my eye, and it followed me as the wagon passed. I opened the gate, guided the team through and closed the gate, but didn't look back once for fear I would be shot.

My heart didn't stop beating hard until I was back at the ranch. I told Mr. Crab what had happened, but he didn't seem overly concerned.

"There's a family lives back in the hills, some distance from the mill, that are not quite right," he said. "Must have been one of them."

"You've still got a few more loads of lumber at the mill, but I don't want to go back there without someone else with me," I said.

"You've done good to get this much wood here. The rest can wait till spring. But there's something else I want to talk to ya about, Mooney. I've got lung problems and we're goin' to New Plymouth, Idaho, for the winter. The air's dryer down there and I can get my breath better. Would ya help us drive there? I would help ya find a job around New Plymouth for the winter; then you could come back here with us in the spring and work the farm with me."

The unexpected proposal caught me off guard. In less than two months I had received a second invitation to work a job that could last a lifetime. The thought of having two nice, friendly families offer me so much after five years on the road, with hunger pains gnawing at my insides most of that time, was almost too much for me.

"I ... I don't know ...," I stammered, then excused myself to do the evening chores.

I thought about my options as I went about feeding the livestock. My head was spinning with the excitement of settling down and living a normal life, but, still, there was a feeling down deep inside me that other possibilities were waiting for me out there.

I had finished the chores and was standing just inside the barn when I heard the dinner bell. It was hard to sit down at the supper table that evening.

"Well, Mooney, are ya goin' to come to New Plymouth with us?" Mrs. Crab asked.

As I had done with Mr. Nelson, I tried to explain what was going on inside of me; that something bigger was in my future and I couldn't ignore it; that there was a special job waiting for me, and I had to keep going until the Lord let me know more about that job. Once again, I don't think I did a good job of explaining it. The mood at the table was gloomy, and I felt bad at having to leave.

"We'll sure miss ya, Mooney," Mrs. Crab said.

"Yes, we will," Mr. Crab said.

"You two have been like family to me, and I appreciate the chance to work for ya," I told them. "Say, let's plan it this way: I'll stop by next spring to help ya with the farmin', unless I've found that special job I'm looking for."

And with that statement, the dark mood changed to a happy one, and we had fun that evening talking about our time together until well into the night.

The next morning we ate breakfast; then Mr. Crab drove me to the nearest railroad station. He thought I was going to buy a ticket on a passenger train bound for Tacoma, but I had another idea.

I waved to Mr. Crab as he drove out of sight; then I walked to the edge of the yard and waited to jump on the next freight headed for western Washington.

"In 1934, my father developed lung problems after he and another man were treating wheat seed with a fungicide or other chemical in a closed building. The other man died from the exposure and my father was affected the rest of his life and couldn't do the amount of work he was used to doing.

"In 1935, my parents moved to New Plymouth, Idaho, because the weather is dryer down there and it was easier on my father's damaged lungs."

Ross Crab, son of Art Crab

56

Christmas At The Tacoma Depot

Once again I was riding the rails, but I felt good about myself and life in general. The freight I was on headed south through Colfax and Pullman; then it headed west through the flat country of Washington's Columbia Basin. At Othello, they switched the engines to electric locomotives for the long pull over the Cascade Mountains.

It was late November, and a blanket of snow covered the mountains. I was riding inside a boxcar and was expecting a long period of freezing weather, but the Cascades aren't like the Rocky Mountains. The freight made it across in just a short time, compared to the long haul it takes to cross the Rockies.

It was cool, sure, but the sun was shining during the climb up the east slope, and the snow-covered trees and mountains made for beautiful scenery. Clouds hovered at the summit, and it was snowing there. The snow turned to rain as we descended the western slope, and the increase in humidity chilled me. I hopped off the freight when it pulled into the Tacoma rail yard with a renewed sense of excitement about my life. This was the farthest point west I had ever traveled and, for some reason, there was a certain magic in the air. I could feel it, but I couldn't explain it.

At this point I had a few dollars in my pocket, so I headed to the skid road part of town looking for a room to rent. In my eyes, it was well worth the money to sleep in a room rather than in the parks or hobo jungle for two reasons: It was safer for me to have a room of my own, at least during the first couple of weeks I was in a new city, until I got my bearings and knew the lay of the land there. Also, my health was a concern after what had happened in the past, and a room would keep me out of the cool damp weather for a while — maybe forever, if I could find a good job.

That dream, however, was short lived. I looked hard for that permanent job, but it remained elusive. There were at least 10 men applying for each job, and the jobs were few. I ate at the local mission, and I was thankful for every bite that entered my mouth.

In between my work-searching excursions around the city, I would hang around the pool halls. The owners didn't mind a lot of people just sitting around watching others play. They knew most of the people there couldn't afford to play, but having

181

lots of people in the place made it look busy. However, anyone who fell asleep was asked to leave. The other hobos, like myself, sought information, companionship and protection from the weather. Pool halls provided all three, and I took advantage of the opportunity.

After two weeks, I was on the street again and penniless. I spent one night huddled around the fire at a hobo jungle and knew by the next morning that the Tacoma weather was not favorable for my continued good health. I walked the streets for most of the next day, trying to find a solution to the problem of sleeping outside. As the day turned to dusk, I found myself walking near the rail yard trying to figure out what to do next.

As I watched a freight begin to roll, my first thought was to head south, toward California and warmer weather. However, I knew that state was overrun with people who weren't wanted, and I didn't want to go through that experience again. I felt the same about Texas, Arizona and New Mexico. When I was about three blocks from the Northern Pacific Railroad depot, I stopped, and for the first time looked at it. It was a beautiful building with a high dome on the top.

I went to the front door and walked inside. It resembled other depots because there were lots of benches for waiting passengers to use, but the dome is what set it apart from the others. I walked to a point where I could look up and see it all.

"It's a beauty, isn't it?"

I jumped at the unexpected question and turned around to see the night watchman also looking up.

"Yes," was all that I could say.

"Where ya headed, young man?"

And that question started a short but respectful friendship. I explained my situation and the watchman, an older man who introduced himself as Steve, talked about his life. I went with him as he made his rounds; then he invited me to share his lunch of two sandwiches and an apple. I lost track of the time and just happened to look up as the big clock on the wall approached 10 p.m.

"Oh, it's late," I said. "I should get to the jungle and get a spot around the fire."

"You're out in this weather?" Steve asked. "Why don't ya just throw your bedroll back here in the furnace room? I can't let ya stay in here all day, but you're welcome to sleep here while I'm on duty."

So, thanks to Steve, I spent the next 10 nights sleeping in the furnace room. We had many good conversations about life in general and the condition of our country. Steve was encouraging and positive, and that's what I needed right then. It was warm and dry, and I was thankful for the company of a friend, as well as the chance to get a good night's rest.

On the fourth day I was there, Steve told me that he wouldn't be working the following two nights.

"Tomorrow's Christmas Eve, ya know," he said.

I had lost all track of time and was surprised at the date.

"But I've told Allan, who's on duty when I'm not, you'll be sleeping here."

"Thanks, Steve."

The next evening I visited with Allan for a little bit, but he wasn't as friendly as Steve. Then I curled up and fell asleep in the furnace room.

I was up early the next morning, Christmas Day, and set about finding any job I could with a renewed determination to earn enough money so I wouldn't have to eat another Christmas dinner in a mission. I walked several miles looking, but even the lowest paying jobs were taken. I surrendered to the inevitable and spent three hours in the soup line waiting for my turn to eat at the mission on Pacific Avenue. I was grateful for the meal, but with each bite, I was reminded of the Christmas dinners my family enjoyed when I was a young boy in Montana. My mother and sisters would make a delicious dinner, and there would be joy and fun throughout the house during the entire day. I concentrated on those meals of the past with every bit of food I placed in my mouth, but I couldn't make myself get into the mood of the day. I just felt sad and lonesome.

Allan waved to me as I walked through the front door of the depot, and I waved back. It was early, but I didn't feel much like visiting, so I went to bed early. I said a prayer before closing my eyes and relaxed as sleep overtook me. Then I had a wonderful dream.

I relived an entire Christmas day as a young boy — from the time I woke up in the morning until my father and mother tucked me and my brothers and sisters into bed at night. In between, there were presents, games and a wonderful Christmas dinner. When the dream was ending, I felt the presence of my mother. She told me that everything would be all right and to trust in the Lord. And I awoke feeling good, knowing that my life was still headed in the direction God intended me to take.

57

The Edmonds Jail

The day after Christmas, I renewed my search for work, but the few job openings I found were also discovered by at least 10 other men, and the boss never picked me.

Steve returned to work that evening, and I enjoyed our talks even more. When I explained the dream, he was even more encouraging and talked about all sorts of good things that I could find in my future.

"It's out there, Mooney," he would say. "Your future is just beyond the next curve or over the next hill. Don't you give up, no matter what."

My talks with Steve inspired me, so when Ted, an older hobo I had met at a pool hall, started talking about jobs up north, I listened.

"And I heard they're hirin' men to work the section gangs on the loggin' railroads in the Everett area," he said with a passion that would convince even the most skeptical job seeker — even me.

It was hard to leave the comfort of a warm, dry place to sleep each night, but I was once again stagnant. It was time to go looking for that special job that awaited me just over the next hill or around the next bend.

"Then let's go to Everett and get a job," I said.

"How we goin' to get there?" Ted asked.

"Well, it's not like we're goin' from California to Montana ya know. All we have to do is put one foot in front of the other until we get there. We'll start first thing in the mornin'."

It was too late in the day to get a good start anyway, and I wanted to spend one more night talking to Steve, and thank him for all his help. He was excited for me, and his excitement encouraged me even more. I said good-bye to him and gave him a final wave as Ted and I walked away from the depot on New Year's Day.

We made it to the outskirts of Sumner that evening and found a hobo jungle under the highway and railroad bridges near town on the road from Puyallup. No one else was there, but the usual fire rings and cooking pots were evidence that the place was used on a regular basis. Ted

184

and I were ready to cook, but we had no food. I spotted a small grocery store just across the bridge and went there to ask the owner if he had some work for me to do in exchange for food. He didn't have any, but gave me enough food for Ted and I to have a respectable New Year's Day dinner.

It was cold and damp, even with a good-sized fire going, so I told Ted we had to find a better place to sleep.

"But, Mooney, where we goin' to find a place around here?"

"Let's go check at the jail."

"It's all right with me," the city policeman said in reply to our request. He locked us in for the night.

We were the only ones there, and it was warm, but the place was a bit dirty. In the morning the policeman unlocked the cell door and pointed to a couple of mops and a bucket.

"Now ya have to mop all the floors for your night's lodging," he said.

"Do we get breakfast?" I asked.

"Nope. Now get busy," he said before stepping into the front office.

Normally I wouldn't mind doing some work after someone had been nice to me, but mopping the dirty floors wasn't part of the deal we had made with him the night before. It was obvious he was taking advantage of us because the floors hadn't been mopped in a couple weeks. I would have mopped every inch of the floor on my knees for breakfast, but cleaning up the entire jail was asking more than I was willing to do.

"We better get out of here while the gettin's good," I told Ted. "That guy might keep us here for a week doin' stuff he wouldn't ask others to do."

We simply opened the back door, left the jail building and started walking toward Seattle on our way to Everett. I checked the hobo markings at a big house along the way and found that nice people lived there. As always, I asked for work in exchange for some food for Ted and me,

but she didn't have any work. Instead she gave us enough food to chase the hunger pains away.

Ted and I walked through Auburn, Renton, and that evening, we entered south Seattle. We were hungry again and noticed a line of hobos leading to a mission. We got in line and, after a church service, were served an ample supper.

While we were eating, I asked another hobo seated nearby about a place to sleep for the night. He told me to check at Hooverville, "It's down by the waterfront and the rail yard." So we headed in that direction. I soon learned that Hooverville was a term named after President Hoover, who was blamed for the Great Depression. Many Washington cities and towns had one.

Seattle was full of hobos and, as in other big cities during this time, most of them were looking for a job. Instead of just sleeping in a jungle, some of them had started making small shacks out of old lumber, cardboard and anything else they could find. Hooverville resembled a small city of makeshift shelters with at least 1,000 people living there. Many of the people shared cooking fires, and, just like hobos in a friendly jungle, most welcomed new hobos and shared their meager food supplies. They were also willing to share sleeping space.

Ted and I stayed at the small village within a city for a couple of days, just to see what was going on in the area. We found out that some of the little shacks were for sale for as little as $10, but the person selling really didn't own the shack or property it was on. Still people had been there for years, and it was a permanent home as far as they were concerned.

We walked out of south Seattle after spending three days in the city. We made it to Ballard where, we had heard, there was a Salvation Army Mission that was especially nice to hobos. The rumor was true: After listening to a church service, we ate a large meal. Ted and I accepted their offer of a bed for the night, and I had a good night's sleep.

After a breakfast of oatmeal, milk and cof-

fee, we headed north again, toward Edmonds, on our way to Everett. We passed a small construction job a few miles north of Ballard. Ted had some training as a brick mason, so he asked the foreman for a job and was offered a couple of days' work.

"This is the best offer I've had in two months, Mooney," Ted said as we shook hands and said good-bye. "Where should we meet up when I'm finished here?"

"I'll be lookin' for ya at the Northern Pacific Depot in Everett in a couple days," I said, and I turned and continued my walk north.

I entered Edmonds late that afternoon. Throughout the hobo jungles of the United States it was known that if a hobo ever got to Edmonds, Washington, there was a hardware store owner who would give 25 cents to anyone who asked for work in exchange for something to eat. The first place I went was to the hardware store to ask for work. Sure enough, the kind man gave me the money. I thanked him, went to a nearby cafe and ate 15 cents worth of food. I placed the remaining dime deep into my pocket. It felt good to have it there because an hour before I had been flat broke.

When I walked out of the cafe I noticed a policeman standing on the next corner. I approached him and asked politely if I could sleep in his jail.

"Sure, ya can, young man," he said. "Come with me."

He took me in the direction of a building that was obviously the library, and at first I was confused. Why were we headed that way? The policeman explained that his jail was in the basement. When we got there, he didn't immediately take me to the jail. Instead he had me sit at a library table, and we talked for over an hour. At first he asked the usual policeman-type questions: Who was I, where was I from, what was I doing in Edmonds, etc. But he was a nice man and, after a few minutes, I felt like I had made a friend because he shared information about his life and family, too. Then he said he had to get home and led me to the basement.

The boiler for the building was also in the basement, so the jail was warm. After the cell door was closed and locked, I laid down on the cot and slept well.

The policeman came down to let me out of the cell early the next morning.

"Are ya hungry, Mooney?" he asked. Then he laughed, realizing the question was silly. "Come on, let's go get ya somethin' to eat."

I was treated to a large stack of pancakes smothered in butter and syrup. It was a great breakfast, and the policeman and I talked during the 30 minutes it took me to eat them all.

After I was finished and had let the food settle for a few minutes, the policeman walked me to the city limits, continuing our talk as we went.

"Thanks for breakfast and the warm bed, sir," I said at last, extending my hand.

"You take care, kid, and good luck to ya."

I turned and continued my walk north to Everett.

58

In Everett
There Are Many Helping Hands

The cold, wet weather of western Washington chilled me as I walked north to Everett. I passed through a small town called Lynwood, but didn't stop. The only businesses there were a blacksmith shop and a farm that sold eggs.

I crossed the Everett city limits at around 5 p.m. Although there had been a large amount of traffic on the roads, I had walked all the way from Tacoma without being offered a ride. Besides me, there were lots of other men walking from town to town, but the drivers couldn't stop for everyone, so most of the time they stopped for no one.

The work situation was really tough in Everett. There was a longshoreman's strike, and the sawmills were having a tough time of it, too. That meant there were even more men than usual out of work. There were three hobo jungles in this city, and I visited each of them looking for a familiar face, but didn't find one. Like most jungles, the majority of the men were friendly; some even offered to share their food and fire for the night.

I asked about jobs on the logging railroad section gangs, but no one had heard about such jobs.

"If there were jobs like that, do ya think we'd be eatin' and sleepin' here, young man?" one hobo asked.

My hopes of finding a good job were dashed, and I realized Everett was the same as the rest of the country. Lots of hobos were chasing rumors about the elusive dream of a permanent job; some traveling from one coast of the United States to another, and when they arrived at their destination, that elusive dream was still just out of reach.

Then my situation got worse: The temperature dropped, and it snowed. Sleeping in the jungles wasn't good for my health, so I knew I had to do something or I would get sick. Ted was supposed to meet me at the Northern Pacific depot on Riverside, so I went there and ended up spending the night.

The next day I waited for Ted for a bit, but then thought maybe he got mixed up and headed for the Great Northern depot on Bayside. I walked the two miles between the depots and looked for work along the way. I went back and forth for about a week, but never found my friend.

The watchmen at the depots weren't as friendly as the one in Tacoma. I tried to strike up a conversation with different ones from time to time, but that was useless. Because I was only in one or the other depot every other day, they let me sleep there most of the time. But some nights the place would be crowded with hobos trying to get out of the cold, and the watchmen would kick us all out an hour before a train was due to depart, and passengers were beginning to arrive.

Instead of heading for the nearest jungle and disturbing the others already sleeping by the fires, I would end up spending the rest of the night huddled in a doorway.

I started begging for food at restaurants, always asking for work first, and most of them were generous, but that didn't last long, for a person wears out his welcome begging the same place time after time. Then I turned to begging at grocery stores and houses, while raiding garbage cans when necessary.

I stepped into Werner's Grocery one day and asked the man there if he had some work in exchange for food.

"I have no work, but I'll give ya some food," the man said.

I thanked him and started to leave, but he stopped me.

"If ya need more food, come back," he said. "Say, what is your name?"

"My name's Monrad, but my friends call me Mooney."

"I'm goin' to call ya Mon," he said.

I waited two days before going back to Werner's Grocery because I didn't want to wear out my welcome.

Mr. Werner gave me more food and a suggestion:

"Young man, if you really want to get a job, ya need to get a haircut."

"I know I need one, but I have no money."

He gave me a note and sent me to a nearby barber shop. When I returned Mr. Werner smiled.

"That really helped," he said. "Now, the next time you need food, stop by and I'll have some work for ya to do."

He had me do a few odd jobs for him in exchange for food the next time I stopped by, and I was thankful that he knew I would feel better working for what was given to me.

During my first three months in Everett, the city

seemed much like every other I had visited. Then something strange happened; I started liking the place. It started to feel like home even though I was on the street. I decided to stay in Everett, to put down roots.

One day, I passed a junk yard and noticed a man taking an armload of brass and copper inside, so I started doing the same. As I walked the streets and alleys of the city, not one piece of scrap metal escaped me.

As winter gave way to spring, I was offered a few odd jobs. I worked in the yards of several

I did as he asked and he took out a piece of paper, signed it and handed it to me. It was the title to a 1929 Chevrolet Coupe.

"But ...," I stammered, but he stopped me.

"I don't want to discuss it," he said. "It's done and I'm glad ya have it. Now go take a look at her — take her for a spin."

"Thank you, Mr. Bannon."

"You're welcome, Mooney. Now get goin', go on," and he shooed me out the door with his hands.

The car was a beauty, and it was my first.

homeowners and split a great deal of wood. Finally, I had enough money to get off the street. It cost me $1.25 a week to rent a room at an old hotel that had a bed and a wood stove. The place was not the height of luxury, but it was warm and comfortable. The rooms were rented by people like me and a few elderly men. The family who owned the hotel offered room and board for $5, but I couldn't afford that, and had to hustle my food on the street every day.

One of the elderly men staying there was a Mr. Bannon. He was sick and couldn't take care of himself very well. His relatives lived out of the state, so he couldn't get any assistance from them. I took a liking to him and helped him shave, get dressed and sometimes would bring his meals to his room.

One day, after I finished shaving him, he asked me to sit down for a minute.

"Mooney, I know I won't live much longer, and you are the only one who has been nice to me," he said. "I want you to have the only thing I own. Now bring me that wallet there, and the pencil too."

Shortly after it was in my possession, Mr. Bannon was taken to the hospital. I visited him every day for the next two weeks, and I thought he was getting better, but one day the nurse stopped me before I reached his room to tell me he passed away early that morning. I was the only person at his funeral.

Mr. Bannon's gift opened up a whole new world to me. I could range farther to look for jobs and scrap metal. I could haul larger pieces of scrap, too. But that didn't mean there were more jobs or better jobs.

I stopped back at Werner's Grocery and told him about my good fortune.

"That's great, Mon," Mr. Werner said. "Sounds like things are lookin' up for ya. Tell ya what; I'm goin' to let ya charge the food you need."

I was shocked. No one had ever trusted me to that extent before. I charged groceries for about six weeks, but during that time I never earned enough money to pay my grocery bill. I could hardly pay for my room and a little gas for the car. I stopped going to the store because I was ashamed of not being able to make a payment.

Jobs were still scarce, but I kept looking. I heard of a job unloading sulfur from a ship and, with the strike over, asked why the longshoremen weren't offered the job.

"They refused to do it," the man offering the job told me.

I was glad to get the work and didn't ask why others didn't want to do it. I joined eleven other men in a two-level hold of a ship. The usual equipment used to unload the cargo was broken, and they had us shoveling the sulfur from one area to another. A big crane with a clam bucket attachment could reach the second hold and move the sulfur to the dock.

It was hard, dusty work, but it was work, and I was getting paid to do it. We had been working for about four hours when the clam bucket hit the side of the hatch as it went into the ship. A spark ignited the sulfur dust and the smoke and fire engulfed the second hold. We started up the ladder, our only way out, as the fire grew more intense, but one man panicked and climbed right over the top of me, nearly knocking me off. We all made it out safely, though. That was my one and only experience working on a ship. After that, I would hear about a job on the waterfront from time to time, but I figured if the longshoremen didn't want to do a job, there must be a reason.

I continued to make enough money to rent the room, put gas in the car and buy a meal once in a while, but that was all. If I did happen to get an extra penny or two, which wasn't often, I would put it aside in a hiding place.

The hotel owner's daughter asked if I would teach her how to drive. Her nickname was Putts, and she was about my age. I liked her and agreed to be her instructor when I wasn't looking for work. However, I was a bit disappointed when her mother went along with us during each lesson. It was obvious the mother didn't want her daughter to be alone with a hobo.

After six months of odd jobs and carefully watching my money, I returned to Werner's Grocery.

"Mornin' Mr. Werner," I said. "I've come to pay my bill."

He looked surprised.

"You know, of all the hobos I've helped, you're the only one to come back and pay his bill. I don't know how much you owe me; I never saved the slips, because I never expected you to return."

"I know just how much I owe you, Mr. Werner," I said, and placed $10.80 in his hand.

I walked out of the store feeling good. Although I didn't have a permanent job, I felt like I was living in my home town. I owned a car; a way to get around besides my feet and a man trusted me enough to let me charge groceries. I was able to meet the obligation and pay the tab, and I was eating regular meals and sleeping inside. My life was changing, and I liked the way it was headed.

59

The Riverside Junk Company

One of the other men renting a room in the hotel where I was staying told me about a job near the town of North Bend, 40 miles south and east of Everett.

"They're putting a pipeline across a canyon to get water to the Seattle area and they need men," he told me. "They're paying 90 cents an hour."

That was a fantastic wage for the time, and I was excited about the possibility of a good paying job, but I was cautious because it was a rumor.

"Let's go up there and see if it's true," I said.

At least this time I had a car, and we could get to the job site and back in the same day if the rumor didn't pan out. But it did turn out

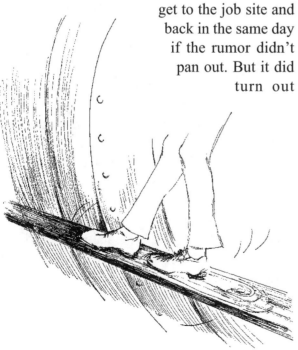

to be true, and we were hired. We rented a room at the old Thompson Hotel in North Bend and ate in the hotel restaurant. An old truck took us to and from the job site near Cedar Falls each day.

The pipe was big — 8 feet in diameter. It was being laid on a trestle that was 200 feet above the canyon floor. Each 12-foot section of pipe was carried into position using a steam donkey, cables and pulleys. Once in the proper spot, the new section was attached to the one already in place. My job was to put steel tapered pins in the connecting holes on the end of the pipes so a riveter could finish the connection.

The only way to put the pins in the holes was from the outside. The only place for me to stand was on a walkway just 8 inches wide. There were no rails, nets or safety harnesses in those days. If a worker slipped, he would fall to certain death.

The weather turned nasty on the second day and snow fell, making the walkway slippery and dangerous. I wanted to work, so I went out every day, but only for one week. The job was so dangerous that I went to the boss on Friday and told him I was quitting. He paid me $36, which was more than I had ever made in a week before. The man who was with me stayed another week, but the contractor went broke, and none of the other workers received any pay.

I went back to the same hotel in Everett

where I was staying before. Three other hobos in the same hotel were taking scrap iron out of the Clark Nickerson Sawmill on the waterfront. They would load the scrap on a truck that was owned by the Riverside Junk Company, and estimated their earnings to be about a dollar a day each because they were getting a dollar a ton.

"Want to join us, Mooney?" one asked.

"Sure," I said.

We placed the scrap on old lumber carts, then pushed the carts to the truck and made the transfer. The only tools we had were a few wrenches and sledge hammers. With these we would disassemble the pieces of scrap, or reduce them in size so we could handle them. It was hard work, but I was young and it was good to be working.

I had been working with this crew for about a week when I asked the others when we would get paid. They said they didn't know.

"Let's go to the junkyard and find out," I said.

It was owned by Mrs. Michelson and her three sons, Moe, Leo and Jarome. When I asked her about getting paid for the scrap we had taken out, she said the man who hired the other hobos had the payroll, but he hadn't been around for a couple of days. It was then that we realized that the guy skipped town without paying us.

"Ma'am, could we take the rest of the stuff out of the mill for ya?" I asked.

"You bet, young man," she said. "I pay a dollar a ton."

The four of us went back and started working again, this time for ourselves. A couple of weeks later, two of the men quit. They were getting itchy feet and wanted to get back on the road. A week later, the other one quit for the same reason, leaving me alone. I needed at least one other person to help me; two would be even better. The solution was simple: I hired my own crew and paid them 90 cents a ton. It took a few more weeks to get all the scrap out.

On the final trip to the junk yard with the last of the scrap, I asked Mrs. Michelson if I could clean the bricks I noticed piled in a corner of the saw mill.

"You bet," she said. "I'll pay ya a penny a brick if ya clean them and load them on the truck."

I continued to hire hobos and pay them 90 percent of what I was getting paid. Hiring men to help me take out the scrap iron and clean the bricks was my first experience as a boss. It was also my start in the junk business, and I liked the work.

When all of the bricks were cleaned, I asked Mrs. Michelson to take a walk with me to a pile of pipes in her junkyard. There were 30 pieces of 1-inch pipe, each 8 feet long, in each coil. Each pipe was attached to an ell with another pipe of the same length coming back out again. We stood before the mountain of pipes discussing a deal.

I offered to take the pile apart with pipe wrenches, then she could sell the used pipe. We agreed on a price of 3 cents per pipe and I would have to load them on the truck. I hired a man to help, and we used two 36-inch long wrenches with a 4-foot cheater attached to get the pipes to turn. But it was slow going because the pipes had been used to carry steam through a dry kiln at a sawmill. We would have to hit the joints with hammers for several minutes before the pipe would budge. Every night, Mrs. Michelson would come out to the pipe pile, we would both count them and she would pay me. I would pay my hired man every day, too. I was making about $5 a day, which I thought was good money. My only expense was the price of pipe wrenches, and we wore out 10 of them.

The total was 21,000 pipes, but I wish there would have been a million so I could have continued to work. But that's the nature of the junk business: The trick is to have the next job ready to start as the current one is ending.

I wasn't complaining — I felt more at home in Everett every day as my life continued to improve.

60

Tin Clothes

As Mrs. Michelson handed me the final pay for the pipe job, her son Moe spoke up.

"Mooney, we've bought the old sawmill at Verlot; you know, up by Silverton," he said.

"Oh yeah, I know the place."

"Well, we'd like to know if you'd scrap it out for us on contract."

"You bet I would," I said. "What do ya have in mind?"

The Michelsons were nice people and always paid me a fair price for my work. After a little discussion, we signed a contract for the job.

"I'm gonna let ya know right now, Mooney," Moe said, "there's no motels at Verlot. You'll have ta camp out up there."

"Doesn't bother me none," I said. "I've slept in tents before, but I've never owned one."

"We've got an old tent in the shed that ya can use," Mrs. Michelson said. "My husband used it on several jobs when he had to stay away from home. It's got a stove that goes with it too."

Moe and I dug the tent out and set it up. It was a large wall tent and was in good shape. I hired a man who was staying at the same hotel as I was, and we drove my '29 Chevy to the sawmill.

Verlot is in the Cascade mountains of western Washington. We arrived about midday and made camp. The stove was similar to one in a sheepherder's wagon, but there wasn't an oven. Finding the wood for the stove wasn't hard, since we were camped next to a sawmill, but all of it was wet from recent rains. Having the ability to make a fire was essential to our well-being; not only did we use it for cooking, but also for warmth and to dry our clothing.

Clouds forming over the Pacific Ocean regularly drift east and hit the Cascade mountains, dropping most of their moisture on the western slopes. I don't mind working in the rain, because I don't chill when I'm active, but when day turns to night and I have to stop working, I need to stay warm.

I was able to get a small fire going by using some dry tinder I found near the base of a tree with low hanging branches. I placed some of the smaller pieces of wet wood near the stove to dry out. We spent the rest of the afternoon drying a two-day wood supply.

The next morning I had a chance to look around. The tree-covered hills were beautiful. The first chore of the day was to gather more wood, then we started scrapping the mill. By the end of the first week, the Michelson truck arrived and we loaded it with the scrap we had collected.

After the truck disappeared down the road, my hired hand and I jumped in the Chevy and headed for Granite Falls, the next town down the road, to get supplies. The first stop was the gas station to top off the Chevy's tank. The station owner looked me over and asked what I was doing in the area. When I told him, he started asking questions.

"Don't ya get cold up there?"

"Yes, but we've got a stove in the tent."

"Don't ya get wet when you're out in the rain?"

"Yes, but I'm able to dry my clothes by the stove at night."

"Don't ya go through lots of coats and pants on a job like that?"

I looked at my coat and pants, and was a bit surprised that they were so tattered. Then, thinking this man was trying to put me down, I got mad.

"Look, mister," I said, trying to keep my composure. "Takin' out scrap is hard work and the metal tears my pants and coat."

"Whoa there," he said. "I'm not lookin' down on ya. I'm just tryin' to help ya."

"What do ya mean?" I asked.

"This here's loggin' country and the men around here spend lots of their time in the woods takin' out timber," he told me. "They wear tin clothes to stay dry."

"Tin clothes?" I asked. "What do ya mean, tin clothes?"

"I'm talkin' about Filson — lookie there," he said, pointing to three men walking past. "They're wearin' tin clothes."

"Where do I get these tin clothes?"

The man directed me to the general store and, once there, I asked to see "the best clothes for workin' in the woods."

"That's these over here," the woman said as she walked me to a clothing rack.

I picked up one of the coats and examined it closely: It was heavy for a coat and the outside was covered with wax.

"No wonder it's waterproof," I mumbled to myself.

"That's right," the woman said, "It's soaked in wax."

"But why do they call them tin clothes?" I asked.

"Because they wear tough, like tin," she said.

I asked the price, and found out the coat was very expensive.

"Oh, that's too much for me," I said, even though there was plenty of money in my pocket to buy it. I started to put the coat back on the rack.

"Looks like ya better think about that again," came a voice from behind me.

I whirled and found myself face to face with a large man.

"Look mister, it's just that if I can do without right now, I'll be money ahead," I said.

"You'll be spendin' more on clothes if ya keep buyin' coats and pants like those," he said, pointing at my tattered clothing. "Don't ya get wet and cold?"

"Yeah, but ..."

"I've been logging these hills for 25 years, and I've always worn Filson," the big man said as he reached around me and grabbed a large coat.

"If they're so good, why are you gettin' a new one?"

"Well, the one I gots has been mine for about 15 years. I gots an old hound dog that's about the same age, but I just didn't have the heart to put her down yet," the logger said. "That dog's gotten to where she pulls my tin coat over by the stove and sleeps on it. Last night she got it too close and burned a hole in the back before I noticed. When I pulls that smokin' coat away from the stove, that hound looks up at me with the most sorrowful eyes."

I watched as this seemingly tough and hardened man of the woods let his guard down and dissolved into a sensitive and caring person. Only others who have watched a dog that was considered a close friend and companion deteriorate with old age would understand. He continued the story in such a soft tone that I could hardly hear him.

"She knows she done wrong, but she's so stove up she can hardly raise her head. So I makes sure there's no fire and place that hound again on the coat by the stove. I sits with her and strokes her head and neck, and her breathin' gets easier, and I can see she's relaxin' the best she can. When the sun hits the top of the mountains across the sound, she breathes her last. I buttons the tin coat around her and carries her up the draw behind my place. And there I puts her and the tin coat in the ground together near the big cedar where we would sit, me in the tin coat and the hound beside me, and watch the sun go down in the Pacific."

I was looking into a sad face, and knew from my youth as a preacher's son that a tear or two was close to forming in this man's eyes. Crying wasn't a bad thing in my opinion, but this was logging country and loggers didn't cry; at least in public. The logger caught himself, turned away from me and cleared his throat a couple of times.

As I watched the big man's back, he unsnapped a scabbard that was strapped to his belt, pulled out a knife and turned quickly. I was startled and stepped back, but he had no intention of doing me harm.

"Ya see," he said, holding the coat in his left hand and the knife in his right. "This here coat is tough. I could take a knife and put a hole in the back of it, then pull and open a big cut, right here, and here, and here."

The logger simulated cutting the coat to pieces, then he put the knife away and looked me in the eye.

"But I could cut a sheet of tin the same way. There isn't a logger in this part of the country that doesn't own tin clothes."

I got the picture: While the clothing wasn't indestructible, it had a reputation for being extremely durable and waterproof. I bought a coat and pants, and my hired man did the same.

"Where you men workin'?" the woman asked as I handed her my money.

I explained where we were staying and what we were doing.

"That's up on the Hartford Eastern Railroad," she said. "My grandfather helped put it in way back in 1892. It was built by Rockefeller ya know. He put it in to take gold out of the Monte Cristo area. Grandpa used to tell a story about Horseshoe Curve, where they had put in a tunnel but hadn't cribbed it up yet. It caved in on a dozen workers, and they're still up there. Grandpa wanted to dig them out, but the boss said no, so they put the track around the mountain."

I knew exactly what she was talking about. As I had learned on the pipe-laying job, labor

195

was cheap and the bosses didn't think about the safety of their men.

My hired man and I headed back to our Verlot camp, where it took us four more weeks to junk the sawmill. During that time, the tin clothes proved worthy of their reputation. I also had time to explore most of the Hartford Eastern. The rails had been taken out a couple of years before, but the rail bed made for good walking. It had been built in rugged country with many tunnels punched through solid rock mountains. I even found the Horseshoe Curve tunnel where a dozen men were still buried. I paused and said a prayer for them.

The Michelsons had another proposition for me when I dropped off the last pound of scrap from the Verlot job. This time they wanted me to go to Oso, which is between Arlington and Darrington, to take out another sawmill. There was no hotel there either, so they let me use the tent again. The same hired man and I finished the job in five weeks. After that I was once again unemployed and without a contract. I paid my hired hand one last time and drove him to the rail yard, where he was planning to hop a freight heading east.

I shook his hand and wished him luck, then went back to the old hotel and rented a room. I had enough money saved to pay for the room-and-board package, which meant I didn't have to beg and scrounge for my food. Having the extra money and the security it provided was a new and pleasant experience for me. I could have lived that way for six months without working one lick, but sitting and doing nothing was not for me.

Once again, looking for work became my full-time job, but there was still little available. I kept in touch with the Michelsons, in case another job came up, while I searched for scrap metal throughout the City of Everett.

"The C. C. Filson Company has been outfitting workers and outdoorsmen in our durable Tin Cloth since the company was founded in 1897. The cloth had the reputation of being extremely tough and soon earned the moniker 'Tin' cloth as it was said to be as tough as tin."

Stan Kohls, owner, C. C. Filson Company

61

The Buggie Packing Plant
I meet Ruth

The Everett waterfront is a big part of the city's economic structure. The longshoremen load and unload the cargo ships, so there is no chance of getting that kind of work, unless, as I had learned earlier, it was such a dangerous job that the longshoremen didn't want it. But the waterfront was also a natural place to find a salmon or clam cannery.

At least once a week, when the canneries were in operation, I would stop by each one and ask if they had any work. The usual answer was one I had heard time and again for the past six years: ten men were waiting for each job.

My preference was to contract jobs where I could junk scrap metal, but there was no such work around. I figured my best chance to find work was to keep going back to the canneries and asking. I thought the odds would gradually swing in my favor that way, with the possibility that I would show up at the instant another worker was needed.

My persistence paid off when I walked into the Buggie Packing Plant one morning and asked for a job.

"I could use ya for a little while," the foreman said. "The pay's 27 cents an hour; take it or leave it."

I took it and was working in the clam-packing business. The clams were steamed and shucked, then placed in cans. The cans were sealed and then cooked again in the canning process.

I soon found out that I would make a poor clam cannery owner. I had never eaten a clam before but found them to be delicious. It was easy for me to eat a few each time a batch came out of the steamer.

The Buggie Packing Plant was a friendly place to work, and it reminded me of Rapelje when I was a youngster, and of Saturday night in the town of Tekoa. There weren't handshakes and slaps on the back, but mostly a nod of the head and a simple greeting: "Mornin'." However, I did hear some workers call others by name, and I knew they were closer friends.

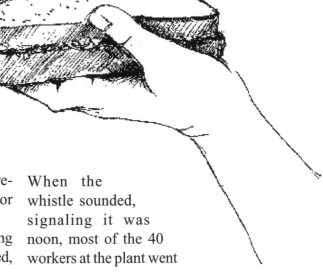

When the whistle sounded, signaling it was noon, most of the 40 workers at the plant went to a large room filled with tables to eat their home-made lunches. I didn't have a lunch, so I just sat and talked with the others.

As the lunch period was ending on my first day at the plant, and everyone was heading back to their workstations, I caught sight of a young woman who was close to my age walking ahead of me in the crowd. I watched as she climbed the stairs to the plant office; then I went back to cooking clams.

The next morning I went to the plant a few minutes early, so I could watch the woman as she arrived. I caught up to her as she neared the time clock.

"Mornin'" I said.

"Good morning," she said with a smile; then she turned and headed up the stairs to the offices.

At noon, I looked for her and sat at a table nearby. Although I was friendly with the others at my table, my focus was the young woman seated at the next table. I watched as she visited with the other workers. Her mannerisms were upbeat, energetic and dynamic. It was clear she was well liked and respected by the others. I liked the way she smiled, and she smiled and laughed a lot.

The following morning, I waited for her again and was rewarded with another greeting. At lunch I made sure I was seated at her table. She was as friendly with me as she was with everyone else.

"What's your name?" the man on my right asked.

"My given name is Monrad, but my friends call me Mooney," I replied.

The others introduced themselves, one after the other, but my attention was on the young woman and I watched her mouth when it was her turn.

"My name's Ruth Gulbrandson," she said. I immediately stuck out my hand, and she automatically did the same, and for the first time, I held her hand in mine. After a brief handshake,

she pulled her hand back.

"Where's your lunch?" Ruth asked.

"Oh, I don't have one," I explained. "I was gettin' room and board at the hotel where I'm stayin', but I can't afford that anymore, now that I'm not scrappin' junk anymore, and ..."

I rattled off half of my life experiences before I realized that I was hogging the conversation. The whistle blew, signaling that it was time to return to work, and I was embarrassed at my actions.

"I'm sorry ...," I said as we walked together to the door.

"That's all right," she said, and she touched me on the shoulder. Then she was gone; headed up the stairs to the office.

That evening my embarrassment grew as I pondered my noontime actions. In my mind, I acted like a fool for talking so much. I was sure in Ruth's eyes I was a bumbling idiot and not fit to socialize with a young woman like her.

I didn't go to the plant early the next morning; instead I was almost late in an effort to avoid Ruth. At noon, I walked into the lunchroom after everyone else had found a place to sit. I found a table near the back, which was occupied by just one other man. I had been sitting and chatting with the man for a few minutes when I felt a tap on my shoulder. I turned and found Ruth standing near me.

"Hi there," she said. "I brought this for you."

And she handed me a peanut butter and jelly sandwich.

This time, I was at a loss for words, but motioned for her to join us at the table.

"Thanks, but I'm sittin' with friends over there," she said, then walked away.

"Thank you," I managed to say.

Ruth turned and smiled at me.

I felt wonderful, and not at all embarrassed anymore. I didn't turn and stare or watch Ruth. Instead I sat there and ate the best peanut butter and jelly sandwich ever made.

62

A Name Change
Dinner With The Gulbrandsons

I continued to arrive at work a few minutes before starting time so I could see Ruth and greet her each morning. Then, I would head inside the plant to help cook, shuck and can clams.

This was a better job than most of the others I had been able to scrounge over the past six years. I was able to make enough money to pay my hotel bill, but not enough to pay for the room-and-board package. My food consisted mainly of the clams I was able to sneak into my mouth during the canning process, and the peanut butter and jelly sandwich Ruth handed me at noon each day. This kept me from having to beg for food at houses or to raid garbage cans.

From the beginning, Ruth made it clear that we were just friends: Sometimes she would sit at the same table as I did during lunch, and sometimes she would sit with other friends.

During one lunch period, Ruth and I were sitting with four others. Near the end of the hour, she got up, so I stood up too. She started walking toward the door, and it was clear she wanted me to go with her.

"I sure don't like the name Mooney that you use," she said, when no one else could hear us.

"I've been called Mooney ever since I can remember, but I have no idea why," I said. "If you don't like my name, why don't you give me a new name, and I'll use it."

Ruth stopped and thought for a minute, then turned and looked me in the eye.

"I'll call you Monte from now on, except if you get out of hand," she said, "then, I'll have lots of other names to call you."

Just then the whistle blew, and she headed up the stairs to the office. I felt like a million bucks as I entered the plant to resume work.

A couple of weeks later on a Friday, Ruth got up from the table again before the whistle sounded, and I knew right away that she wanted to talk to me alone.

"Monte, I would like you to come to my house for dinner Sunday evening," she said. "Mother and I will fix fried chicken. Do you like fried chicken?"

"Oh yes," I said.

Ruth wrote down the address and told me to be there promptly at 6 p.m.

When Sunday rolled around, I was a bit nervous. I was sweet on Ruth and wanted to make a good impression on her parents. I dug out every item of clothing I owned — three pair of pants and two shirts that were all work clothes. Still, that's all I had, and I had to make the best of the situation. I dressed as best I could and drove to the house on Rockefeller Avenue.

I turned on to her street, but I drove right past her house when I saw it. I turned the car around and stopped at the corner a block away. I knew that house. There were hobo markings on the back fence that let hobos know that the people who lived in the house were good people and would feed them. I had begged food at the back door of Ruth's house just two years before when I first arrived in Everett.

"Boy, am I in a pickle," I thought as I sat in my car, looking at the house a block away. I worried that Ruth's parents might recognize me. Surely, they would not want their daughter to have anything to do with a hobo who once begged food at their back door.

I sat there for a few minutes, agonizing over my options: drive away and never see Ruth again or walk in the front door with the hope that I wouldn't be recognized. The thought of never seeing Ruth again was not really an option. She was already special to me, and it would take more than being looked down upon for being a hobo to keep me away. I drove to the front of her house, walked boldly to the door and knocked. The door opened and a man stood before me.

"Hello there, young man," he said, opening the door. "Come in."

"Good evening sir," I said, then I stepped inside the house.

Ruth joined us in an instant and smiled at me, then looked at the man.

"Pop, this is my friend, Monte," Ruth said, introducing me to her father.

"It's nice to meet you, Monte," Mr. Gulbrandson said.

"You too, sir," I said.

"So your name's Monte?" he asked.

"Yes sir," I said nervously. "Well, my given name's Monrad; some of my friends call me Mooney, but Ruth likes to call me Monte," I said nervously.

"Well young man, do ya mind if I call ya Mon?"

"No sir, that's fine with me," I said, then I chuckled to myself as I wondered if every member of this family was going to give me a different name.

Ruth ushered me to the other room, where I was introduced to her mother, her sister Helene and brother Ronald. The whole family was friendly and considerate, and they made me feel

at home. I sat with Mr. Gulbrandson and Ruth in the parlor, and we chatted about working at the cannery until supper was on the table.

Once seated, everyone held hands and Ruth's father asked the Lord to bless the food. Then, everyone took a helping of fried chicken, mashed potatoes, gravy and peas. Also on the table were pickles, put up by Ruth and her mother during the last canning season.

While we were eating we talked, and it reminded me of when my family would sit around the dinner table in Rapelje. A sadness overtook me for a moment, but then quickly disappeared. I was sitting at the dinner table with a close family, and the love flooded the room when a member of the family would talk or joke with another member. I felt comfortable and at home, but I had no right to feel that way, for this wasn't my family.

"Monte, where are you from?" Ruth's mother asked.

"I was born in Clarkston, Washington, but I was raised mainly in Rapelje, Montana, ma'am," I said.

"What does your father do for a living?" she asked.

"He's a Lutheran Minister, ma'am," I said.

"So you're a preacher's son," Mr. Gulbrandson said.

"Yes, sir."

"How did you get to be in Everett?" he asked.

My head snapped to my left, to Ruth who was seated beside me. I didn't know how to answer. I had told her all about my life as a hobo and a sheepherder, but I did not want to tell her parents about all that during my first visit to their home.

"Pop, Monte's been through some hard times," she said.

"Well, he's here now, and that's what matters to us," Ruth's mother said.

"That's right," Mr. Gulbrandson said; then he turned to me and looked me straight in the

eye, "Mon, do you like dessert?"

"Yes sir," I said.

"Good, bring on the canned clams,"
he said; then he and everyone else at the table
laughed. I laughed so hard my side hurt.

The cherry pie was delicious, and Ruth's
family stayed at the table long after the last bite,
talking and having fun, joshing each other about
the most trivial things. Finally it was time for
me to leave.

"Thank you for havin' me to dinner," I told
Ruth's mother, as I got up from the table.

"You're welcome, young man," she said.
"You come back again."

Ruth and her father walked me to the front
door.

"I'll see you tomorrow, Monte," Ruth said,
standing beside her father.

"It was a pleasure having you here tonight,"
Mr. Gulbrandson said. "These women gang up
on me and Ronald sometimes," he said, and then
laughed.

"Oh, Pop," Ruth said.

Mr. Gulbrandson stuck
out his hand, and I shook hands with him, but he
didn't let go after a normal handshake. Instead
he squeezed my hand hard and looked me in the
eye.

"Mon, you're welcome in this house anytime," he said. "Do you understand?"

"Yes, sir," I told him. "Thank you." And I
knew he was a friend.

I heard the door close behind me as I walked
to my car. If the Gulbrandsons knew I once
begged for a handout at their back door, they
never let on. I felt good, and during the drive
back to my hotel the world seemed just a bit
brighter. My new friends, the Gulbrandson family, and the special feelings I held for Ruth, reinforced my belief that the Lord had led me to
Everett for a reason: to stop my wandering and
settle down.

63

Living in Silverton

The clamming season came to an end a few weeks after my first visit to Ruth's house, and the Buggie Packing Plant closed. By that time, Ruth and I had developed a solid friendship. The difference was that I wouldn't see her every day. Instead, I was out looking for work again, and I was looking hard because I didn't want to get to the point where I had to beg for my food or raid garbage cans. I had the most success finding and selling scrap metal to put money in my pocket.

I had an open invitation to stop by the Gulbrandson house for a meal or a visit at any time, but I didn't want to wear out my welcome. I would stop by and visit Ruth once a week, but my search for work was too serious for me to spend more time there. The only time I relaxed was on Sundays. Even prospective employers regarded Sundays as a day of rest.

Ruth and I used that day to take a drive in the Everett area. Our time together gave us a chance to visit and to enjoy each other's company. If I had the money, we would stop for a meal at a roadside diner. If I was low on money, Ruth would pack a picnic lunch, or we would return to her house in time to eat dinner with her family. It really didn't matter to me, and Ruth didn't seem to mind either. We were having fun, even though I was unemployed, and the future seemed bright. Whether I was with Ruth alone, or with the entire Gulbrandson family, I was as happy as when I was living with my family in

Rapelje and my mother was alive.

One Tuesday morning, I stopped by the Coyle Construction office, as I did the offices of many other employers each day, and asked about work.

"We got work for ya," a man inside told me. "The pay's 90 cents an hour, but ya gotta join the union first."

I joined the union and was told I would be helping to pave a road. I drove to the job site, near Scenic, Washington, which is close to the summit of Stevens Pass. The contractor had rented the base camp used by the workers who had built the seven-mile-long Great Northern Railroad tunnel through the Cascade Mountains a few years before. The camp had several sleeping quarters, a kitchen and a mess hall. Room and board were not part of the wages on this job, and they charged plenty to eat and sleep. Still, it was a job, and I wanted to keep working.

After a couple of weeks working there, I understood why I got the job. The foreman was a hard man to work for, and the turnover of workers was high. I ignored the pettiness of some of his orders and did what he said. Other workers got fed up and walked off the job.

It was not practical for me to drive to Everett, even once a week, to visit Ruth, so I would write her a letter every Sunday. It was wonderful to get her letters, and it was the first time I had ever corresponded by mail.

Another contractor, who was non-union, was paving a section of the same road west of ours. The union I belonged to was trying to organize the workers there without much luck. One evening the union organizer got all of us union workers together and told us that we were going to go on a raid to the other camp and beat up the non-union men. Most of the men in my camp grabbed pick handles, or other clubs, and started walking to the other camp. After my experience with the Minneapolis riot, I wanted no part in this type of escapade, so I hid until the men left.

Two hours later the men returned, but they were in sad shape. The people in the other camp got wind of the raid, and they ambushed the union men. As far as I know, no one was killed, but several were driven to the hospital with broken bones. I was fired for not participating, but I knew the Lord was again watching over me and guiding my behavior. However, it was a mixed blessing: I was again looking for work, but Ruth and I could be together every Sunday.

The main way I earned money, when I was not employed as an hourly worker, was to pick up scrap and sell it to the Michelsons' at the Riverside Junk Company. I had a knack for spotting scrap and would stop and pick up a piece of metal that other people would pass by. It provided enough money for me to pay for my room and board, but just barely. At least I was not reduced again to begging for food and raiding garbage cans.

A few months later, I found another job working on a road crew near Silverton, which was an old gold mining town about 40 miles northeast of Everett. The mines had given up all the precious metals they were going to, and the town was just a ghost town when I arrived. I could not find a room to rent in Silverton and I was directed to the Big Four Inn at the end of the road.

Before the rails had been removed, the inn was a luxury hotel only accessible by rail. Now, the only road in was the old railroad bed. The inn also had about 30 cabins and a golf course. My first impression was that I could not afford to stay at such a beautiful spot, but times were tough, and I was able to rent one of the cabins at a reasonable rate. I cooked many of my meals in the cabin but, when I got lonely, I would splurge a little and have a meal at the inn, just so I could visit with other people. The highlight of my week was when a letter arrived from Ruth and I sent her a reply.

Even though I enjoyed staying at the Big Four Inn, I would save money if I found a

place close to my work on the road construction crew. My persistent questioning paid off when a man quit the crew and moved back to Everett. He referred me to his landlord and I rented an old log cabin in Silverton.

The little town consisted of an old vacant hotel, that had fallen into disrepair, and a gas station. I had to walk up a hill from the gas station, past the old hotel, and then another fifty yards to reach my cabin. The station was owned by two old bachelor brothers, Eric and Albert Shedin. I spent many evenings visiting with them, and they seemed to welcome my company. It gave them a chance to tell stories of their prospecting days in Alaska.

"You remember when we climbed Chilkoot Pass in '98, Eric?" Albert asked.

"Sure do," Eric replied. "Tricky goin' all the way up with a full load. Then we'd slide back down on a shovel to get another load."

And they would both laugh with boyish glee. It was obvious that this was an adventurous and fun time in their lives.

"How many trips did ya make?" I asked.

"Five each," Albert said.

"That's not right, and you know it, Albert," Eric said. "I stepped off the trail when I was halfway up on the last trip and fell to the bottom, so I made five and a half trips. Nearly killed myself."

"It's that tin coat that saved ya, Eric," Albert said. "It was a coat just like the one yer wearin', Monte. Where'd ya get it?"

"I bought this a couple years ago in Granite Falls."

"Well, back when we was headin' for Skagway, there was only one place to get tin clothes," Eric said.

"That's right," Albert said. "From old Mr. Filson himself. He staked us for a piece of our claim, if we hit gold: all our supplies, tin clothes, mackinaws, blankets ... ."

"He even let us put our food on account," Eric said. "Ya know, I really think he was wantin'

to go with us."

"If it wasn't for his wool mackinaws, we'd have froze for sure," Albert said, and Eric agreed.

They talked into the night about the hardships they endured on their way to Whitehorse, and the time they spent there. They asked me about my past and seemed genuinely intrigued by my life riding the rails and on the range.

Sundays in Silverton were lonely. I missed visiting with Ruth and her family. I would write her a letter, but that didn't take all day. I started exploring the deserted mines in the area and collecting what junk I could find. There were no roads to most of the mines, so I would hike in and spend the day poking around. Seeing the old metal at the mines made me wish I could junk it all out, but one mine, the 45 Mine, was six miles from a road and another, the Bonanza Queen Mine, was in a few miles too. It was unrealistic to get any of that junk to sell, except for what I could carry out, and on each trip I carried out a handful.

I was happy with my life. I was working six days a week, sleeping inside, eating regular meals and I was able to save some money. Yet something was missing. Ruth's next letter arrived on a Tuesday and it helped me understand the situation. On the second page she wrote, "Monte, do you realize we have known each other for nearly two years now?"

Time had slipped by and I wasn't going to waste any more of it. I sent her a reply the next day, asking if she wanted to go for a drive on Sunday, and told her I would pick her up at 1 p.m.

"During the Alaska Klondike Gold Rush, company founder C. C. Filson was said to have helped some prospectors by staking part of their equipment and then saying, 'Pay me when you can – when you get back to Seattle.'"

Stan Kohls, owner, C. C. Filson Company

64

I Propose

Ruth was ready when I pulled up in front of the Gulbrandson house that next Sunday. I knocked on the door and her father opened it, but I only spent five minutes visiting with the rest of the family. Ruth had a picnic basket packed and it was obvious she was ready to start our drive.

I drove and drove and we talked and talked, until I spotted a park and stopped the car. We spread a blanket and enjoyed the meal that Ruth had prepared. The afternoon slipped by and, all too soon, it was time to leave. We gathered our things and headed to the car. I placed the basket in the back seat and turned to Ruth before she got into the car. I looked into her eyes and started to speak but hesitated.

"Yes, Monte?" she asked. "What is it?"

"Ruth, I love you and I want to know if you'll marry me."

"I love you too, Monte," she said, and she kissed me. "The answer is yes."

Then I kissed her. I was happy and felt like the luckiest man in the world.

We drove back to her house and she suggested I talk to her father alone before we make an announcement to the rest of her family. They were still seated at the table, having just finished dinner.

"There's still plenty of food for you two," Ruth's mother said.

"No thank you," I said. "I'm full for right now."

"Mon, full?!" Mr. Gulbrandson said; then everyone laughed.

"Sir, I'd like to talk to you," I said.

"Sure, what's on your mind?" he said, not budging from his chair.

"Well, ah, if ya don't mind, sir ..."

"Oh, you want to talk to me alone?"

"Yes, sir."

Mr. Gulbrandson led me into the backyard. He stopped by a big tree, looked me in the eye and waited for me to begin.

"Well, Mr. Gulbrandson," I said, nervously, "I love your daughter and I've asked her to marry me."

"What'd she say?" he asked.

"She said yes."

"Hurray!" he yelled, causing the rest of the family to spill into the backyard.

"What's happening out here; something wrong?" Mrs. Gulbrandson asked.

"Nothing's wrong, they're gonna get married."

And there were hugs and handshakes all around. Back inside the house, we talked about dates and selected June 22, 1939, just five months away, for the special event. The wedding was to take place at 8 p.m., with dinner scheduled first at Ruth's house at 6:30.

Those were the only plans that I needed to be concerned about, so I left and drove back to

Silverton before it got too late. I had asked Harold Weiss, a fellow worker at the cannery who had become a close friend of both mine and Ruth's, to be best man. On June 19, he hitchhiked to my cabin to spend a few days with me.

It was like a three-day bachelor party, except there wasn't much of a party. I still had to work each day on the road crew, but after work Harold and I would visit during dinner in my cabin before heading down to the gas station for an evening of listening to Eric and Albert spin yarns. As dull and mundane as that may seem to some, I considered those three days to be great fun and a great way to spend my final days as a bachelor.

I had to work on June 22, too, so Harold and I were not able to leave Silverton for Ruth's house until 5 p.m. Rain during the preceding two days complicated matters by making the roads muddy and nearly impassable in some areas. It reminded me of traveling between Malta and the hog ranch in Montana when I was working on the range. The mud built up on the tires and my boots just like the Montana gumbo did. What's more, just like in Montana, we got stuck several times, requiring either Harold or me to get out and push. We were over an hour late by the time we got to the outskirts of Everett and better roads.

"I think you're about to find out how understandin' a woman Ruth is," Harold said as we neared the Gulbrandson house. I knew what he meant, but for some reason I wasn't worried.

Ruth opened the door when we neared the front porch.

"You all right, Monte?" she asked.

"Sorry we're late, Ruth," I said. "The roads were just awful, and we got stuck."

"I'm just glad you're here, safe and sound."

Then she stepped back as we walked up the steps. As we entered the glow of the porch light, Ruth got a good look at Harold and me, and our clothes, and she laughed.

I laughed too, because we were soaked and covered in mud.

"I've brought a change of clothes," I told Ruth.

Then her father was at the door and he let out a deep belly laugh when he saw us.

"Come on in, Mon; you too, Harold," he said. "You two can change up here. And he led the way upstairs, where we cleaned up a bit and changed clothes.

We headed downstairs and enjoyed a great dinner with the entire Gulbrandson family. When we finished, Ruth's sister Helene, her brother Harold, Ruth and I walked three blocks to the church, where we met the minister and he performed the wedding ceremony. It was that simple. In those days, people didn't feel they had to attend the actual wedding ceremony. The fact that a couple got married and planned a life together was thrilling enough.

When the four of us returned to Ruth's house 30 minutes later, there were hugs and handshakes for all, and lots of best wishes too.

"Welcome to the family, Mon," Mr. Gulbrandson said, shaking my hand.

Mrs. Gulbrandson gave me a hug and said, "I'm glad to have you as a son, Monte."

Ruth brought two suitcases from her room, and I loaded them into the backseat of the Chevy next to mine. I opened the car door for Ruth and she took her seat. The rest of the Gulbrandson family, along with Harold, stood by the street and waved as we drove off.

We spent our first night as a married couple at the President Hotel in Mount Vernon. When we checked out the next morning, I placed the key to the room in my suitcase as a memento.

Ruth and I honeymooned in Vancouver, British Columbia, Canada. Although Canada is a lot like the United States, there were differences like some of the customs and the way the people talked — which I found exciting and interesting. Of course, my focus was mainly on Ruth. I was proud to have her by my side as we visited the quaint shops, walked along the waterfront or ate dinner at a restaurant.

As we were eating breakfast on our third day

in Vancouver, Ruth saw me looking at the money in my wallet.

"What's the matter, Monte?"

"Oh, nothing, what would you like to do today?"

"I would like to go home; our home."

"But ... ," I tried to protest.

"Look, Monte," she said. "This has been a great time, but wouldn't it be better to save the money we have left? After all, we have to buy groceries and pay next month's rent on the cabin."

I smiled and marveled that I had found a woman with such insight. I paid our breakfast bill, then we checked out of the hotel and headed back to Silverton. We only made one stop, to buy a week's worth of groceries.

I parked the Chevy in the usual parking spot next to the gas station. Eric and Albert were out the door in an instant.

"Congratulations, you two!" Eric said.

"Welcome to Silverton, Mrs. Holm," Albert said, and both of the men laughed in their boyish way.

"Thank you," Ruth said.

With the help of Albert and Eric, we were able to pack our food supplies and suitcases from the car to the cabin in one trip.

"Well, we'd better be going," Albert said as the four of us stood outside the front door.

"But, Albert, what if they wants to visit a bit?" Eric said.

"Come on now, it's time we left these newlyweds alone," Albert said as he grabbed Eric by the arm and led him down the trail. Then both of them laughed again.

"Wait a minute," Ruth called after them, which caused them to pause in their tracks and turn around. "Would you boys be interested in having dinner with us in, say, three days? That'll give me time to figure this stove out."

"We'd sure like that," Eric said. Then the brothers turned and continued down the trail.

Ruth and I took our supplies and suitcases inside the 14-foot-square cabin, our first home together, and put them away. Ruth made a pot of coffee and poured us each a cup. I opened the cabin door and we stepped outside. We stood on the porch overlooking the forested valley and I put my arm around my bride's waist. She took a step in my direction and snuggled closer.

My thoughts turned to my life a few years before, when I was on the road alone and hungry. Then I said a fast prayer, thanking the Lord for guiding me to Ruth and a life I had dreamed of. I knew we were a strong team and would overcome any obstacle.

65

Married Life
We Have A Daughter

When the road job came to an end, Ruth and I moved back to Everett. For $15 a month, we rented a small house at 2121 33rd Street that wasn't much more than a cabin.

I was now an unemployed married man with more responsibilities than the hobo I was before. My daily search for work was intensified by that fact, but there were still more men looking than jobs available.

Early on the morning of the third day, I headed for the Riverside Junk Company to talk to the Michelsons. They were glad to see me, and before I could ask, they offered me a job taking out the Old Railroad Interurban that ran from Seattle to Everett carrying logs and lumber between the two cities. I got $7 to completely dismantle each railway car and load all of the scrap iron on the old Dodge truck.

The wheels were on what was called Arch Bar trucks, and they were put together with 1 1/4-inch bolts, six on each side, with the nuts located on the bottom on the trucks. What's worse, the nuts and bolts that held the trucks together had been bent, and the threads were damaged from so much use. It was very difficult to remove them.

Once again I bought a couple of 4-foot-long pipe wrenches and used a 5-foot-long pipe, which I slipped over the wrench handle as a "cheater". That gave me close to seven feet of leverage and still the bolts gave up the nuts reluctantly. Working 12 to 14 hours per day, and with the help of a hired man, I was able to average one rail car per day.

About this time, cutting torches were coming into use. The Michelsons offered me a contract to cut up the Monroe Logging Company's engine number 3, a Shay locomotive which weighed 70 tons.

The contract required that it be cut into 2- by 5-foot pieces and loaded on the old Dodge truck. I took the contract for $129, and I had to furnish the torch, oxygen and gas. The locomotive was cut up and the scrap loaded in nine long days. I would have done it in less time, but I had never used a torch before and there was no one to show me how. I didn't make any money on that job, considering the time it took and the cost of the torch. I did gain a wealth of experience, however, and when the job was finished, I considered myself skilled with a cutting torch.

Scrap iron was in demand, and I liked the work and was proud to be called a junk man. What's more, I was my own boss, and I paid fair wages to those who worked for me.

The Michelsons offered me job after job, and I was able to get top dollar from them because I produced the scrap on time and in the size required. Other salvage dealers offered work too, and I took those jobs when the Michelsons didn't have work for me. The scrapping contracts allowed Ruth and me to save a little money, which came in handy when Ruth's father offered us a deal.

He was a building contractor and had just finished a two-bedroom house on 75th Street, just off Broadway. It was the first house built on that street. We bought it for $2,500, with a $200 down payment, and the contract called for a $20 monthly payment.

When we moved in, it looked empty because all the furniture we had consisted of Ruth's bedroom set and a piano. I found an old pot belly stove in a pile of junk and set it on bricks in the living room. We used apple boxes for chairs. Mrs. Michelson sold us an old wood-burning cook stove for $10.

I built a chicken coop behind the house, and we raised a couple of hundred chickens a year. We ate those chickens, and they supplied our eggs too. Having the chickens helped us save money, and we kept a vegetable garden for the same reason.

One day, I took a load of junk to the Riverside Junk Company that included a couple of electric motors. Mrs. Michelson stopped me before I unloaded them.

"Mooney, if ya take the copper off these motors, I'll pay ya 5 cents a pound for it," She told me.

It was a great opportunity and a way to make extra money. I built a shed next to the chicken coop, so I could work on old car generators, starters and electric motors. In the evenings, after supper, Ruth and I would go to the shed and spend several hours unwinding or otherwise removing the copper wiring from those generators, starters and electric motors. The empty housings were sold as scrap, and the copper was sold separately at a higher price.

Together we could make a dollar in that shed in an evening. What surprised me was that some of our neighbors would laugh at us and make fun of us for spending so much time in the shed for a dollar here and a dollar there. But hard work was all I knew, and I was proud that Ruth was by my side. Many times I would find my bride in the shed when I arrived home after a day on the job.

"What ya doin' out here?" I would ask her.

"Just thought I'd finish up that motor we started last night before I fixed dinner," she would reply, and we would finish the motor together; then we both would fix dinner.

After a few months of working in the shed, we had an extra hundred dollars saved, so Ruth and I went to Goldberg's Furniture to look at a couch and chair he had on sale. The price was $140.

"Mr. Goldberg, we've worked hard for this money, but all we have for this furniture is $100," I told him.

"That's all right," he said. "You can charge the other $40."

"No, if you won't sell them to us for $100, we'll leave," I said, and we started for the door when he shook his head. But he called us back and we talked some more. We started for the door three times and, in the end, the furniture was ours for the price we offered. I never did like owing

209

people money, except for the house, and even that bothered me.

Ruth and I scrimped for a couple of more years, then asked for a meeting with the company that held the mortgage on our house. We still owed $1,800 on it when we walked into the mortgage office.

"Would you be willin' to settle our mortgage for $1,500?" I asked.

They were a bit surprised by the offer, but said yes. I immediately took out the money and placed it on the desk. Ruth and I owned our house when we walked out of the building.

Two fundamental principles of dealing with people and money were working for me when I was dealing with Mr. Goldberg and the mortgage company. From a young age, my mother and father had taught me that it was best not to be obliged to another person, but if you have to be, pay them what is due as soon as possible.

Mrs. Michelson taught me the second principle.

"Mooney, you work hard for your money, so I want to give ya a tip to make it go further," she said. "If ya want something, make the owner an offer for it, but when ya make that offer, have the money in your pocket so ya can give it to 'em before they change their minds — and don't forget to get a receipt at the time ya hand over the money."

Ruth and I continued to unwind motors in the shed and save our money, and more salvage jobs continued to come my way. The trouble was, many of the jobs required me to camp or live near the job site. I hated to be away from Ruth. I felt as lonely when I couldn't spend at least part of the day with her as I was when I had been on the range herding sheep. To finish the jobs faster, I worked longer hours. At the same time, I knew Ruth was spending several hours a day taking copper from motors, generators and starters.

I scrapped out junk for timber companies like Ozette, Sound, Sauk River, Lyman, Warnick, Eagle and many more. My contract stated that I would cut up and haul out the equipment used by these companies, which might be steam locomotives, donkeys, cars and even the rails.

Some of the jobs were dangerous just by the nature of using a cutting torch and working in mountainous terrain, and once I came close to making Ruth a widow because of a stupid mistake.

I contracted to take out all of the scrap metal at the M & B Logging Company near Aberdeen, and I was using the locomotive to haul the rails from way back in the mountains — there were about 22 miles of track — to the siding, which was the headquarters for the operation. My men and I would load the rails on two cars attached to the front of the engine, then the engineer would back it to the siding where they would be loaded on a truck. On one trip, the engineer was in the cab and I noticed the water was getting low in the boiler, and I told him so. He said there would be enough to travel the five miles to the siding, where we could take on more water.

His estimate may have panned out if we were traveling on a level track, but as we broke over a small hill, the water in the boiler spilled and the boiler blew up. The locomotive was raised into the air at least 10 feet and the engineer, sitting in the open window of the cab, was blown clear of the engine. Fortunately, he landed in soft dirt, unhurt.

One of my men and I were sitting on a car in front of the engine when she blew. The explosion hurled the smoke box door, which is 3-feet in diameter and weighs 200 pounds, several hundred feet. It missed my head by six inches. Hot bricks and metal started several fires that we had to rush to put out. Soot and dust hung in the air for a good 30 minutes. The only redeeming factor was that the engine was the cleanest locomotive I've ever cut up, because the soot had been removed by the explosion. After that, I made sure every locomotive I was riding on had plenty of water.

I was scrapping out some railroad material at the Eatonville Lumber Company the day Pearl

Harbor was attacked. I didn't like to see the war begin because Ruth and I had many relatives and friends who would have to go fight. Four of my brothers and one sister were already in the service; Gary, Oscar and Gertrude Ann were in the Navy, Paul was in the National Guard and Norman was in the Army Air Force.

Gary was serving on the battleship California, which was sunk during the Pearl Harbor attack. Initially we received word that he had been killed, but a letter a few days later confirmed that he was alive.

As the need to build more ships, tanks and other weapons of war grew, so did my significance as a junk man. I was sought after to take contract after contract to scrap out sawmills and railroads.

I stayed busy, working more hours than ever before, and the weeks, months and years rolled by. Everyone in the country participated in the war effort, and Ruth and I did our part. We used our ration books properly and tried to save resources that could be used by our fighting men and women.

In all of the saving and scrimping during this time of national and world crisis, Ruth and I experienced the highlight of our lives on March 25, 1943, when our daughter Karen was born. I was about the proudest father there ever was. Ruth was in the hospital with Karen for about 10 days after the birth. There was nothing wrong, but in those days, that was the normal hospital stay. I visited the hospital every day and gave each of the nurses a silver dollar to keep Karen in the front row of the nursery. I would stand and admire her and show everyone our daughter.

I paid the hospital bill the day I took Ruth and Karen home. It came to $82.75. The doctor was Elmer Van Buskirk, and he charged $50 for his services. I handed him a fifty dollar bill and he looked at it, then at me.

"You know, Monte, that's the first fifty dollar bill I've ever seen," he said.

"That's the first one I've seen, too," I said. Then I took my wife and our daughter home, beaming all the while as a proud father does.

66

I'm in the Army Now

With the world at war, everyone in the United States was sacrificing and doing without items that many thought were essential a few years before. Doing without was a way of life for Ruth and me, and the transition was not as difficult for us as it was for many. We helped others start victory gardens, and we shared our food with those who couldn't. We raised more chickens and gave some of those away, too.

I considered myself to be lucky. I was able to be home most of the time in the evenings, which meant I was able to be with my wife and daughter, and that made all of the extra hard work worthwhile.

I was still in demand as a junk man, and contracts continued to come my way. I considered working extra hard at my job to be my part of the war effort, because I knew the scrap I was collecting was used to make ships, artillery shells and bombs to help fight the enemy. So, it was a surprise when I received a letter from my local draft board advising me to report for active duty in the United States Army.

As I sat in my house with my wife and daughter, thinking about the three contracts left to be completed and all of my experiences to date, I considered it ironic that my Uncle Sam and the good Lord thought that I needed another experience in life. But I was proud to be an American and to serve my country in any way that they

deemed necessary.

In February of 1945, I boarded a bus and waved goodbye to Ruth, who was holding Karen, and began my second and only official stint in the U. S. Army. I reported to Fort Lewis, where I underwent a battery of written tests and one physical examination. The written tests took several hours, but my time with the doctor was over in a matter of seconds. There were so many men reporting for duty that the doctor couldn't conduct a proper physical. In fact, the only requirement to pass seemed to be that a recruit be slightly warm. As I raised my right hand with a roomful of other men and was sworn in, I looked around and realized I was a good five years older than most of the others.

The group was herded into another building, where we were given our first issue of army clothing and boots. For some reason, I was selected for KP immediately. Peeling potatoes and doing dishes for several hundred men takes a fair amount of work, and hard work never bothered me, but the military likes to make people do unnecessary things to the point that they become comical.

On my second day in the army, the group of us assigned to KP finished the dishes, so we mopped the floor and put away the mops. Then we sat down and started talking about our families.

212

"What are you men doing sitting down?" the sergeant in charge said when he came into the room. "Mop the floor," he said before anyone could answer.

"We just did," I said.

"Look, soldier, if I tell you to mop the floor, you mop the floor," he yelled, standing 6 inches from my face. Out came the mops and the clean floor was mopped again.

The next day, as two other men and I were doing dishes, I reached into the soap barrel without looking, dipped a gallon of soap out and threw it into the dishwater. About 30 seconds later, it became evident that the stuff I threw into the vat wasn't soap, but powdered eggs. I turned and looked behind me; the 50-gallon barrel of soap was sitting right beside the 50-gallon barrel of powdered eggs. I never admitted that it was my mistake, but I can attest to the fact that powdered eggs stick to everything they come in contact with and, once attached, are hard to remove.

After a few days, my new Army-issue boots were hurting my feet, and one of the other recruits said I should go on sick call. After waiting 90 minutes in a room filled with other men, it was my turn to see the doctor.

"What's wrong, soldier?" he said.

"My feet are killing me," I told him.

He had me take my boots off and noticed how flat my feet were.

"How did you get them so flat?"

"I guess it was from following sheep all over Montana and running to hop freights," I said.

"What doctor examined you when you came into the Army?"

"You did," I replied.

"Why didn't you say something?" he asked. "I wouldn't have taken you in with those feet."

"You never gave me a chance to tell you, but I'd be willing to leave right now, if it's all right with you."

The doctor never even acknowledged my offer. You see, that would have saved the Army and me time and money, and that would never

do. No, once you have been sworn into the military, you become government property and must serve until discharged.

When I told the doctor that I was to go to Sheppard Field, Texas, for basic training, he suggested I go on sick call as soon as I arrived there and the doctors would fix me up with proper-fitting boots. It was that easy for him to get rid of his mistake.

The next day, 19 others and I boarded a bus to Tacoma, which stopped at the beautiful train terminal there. I asked the security man about Steve, the night watchman, and found out he still worked there, but was not working until that evening. I left him a note telling him how much I appreciated his advice a few years before and how it had paid off for me. Two hours later, we boarded a passenger train.

"At least this is not a step backwards," I thought as the train started to move. But I said a prayer for the hobos riding the rods a few inches beneath my feet and those on the roof over my head.

My group was wearing wool uniforms when we left Fort Lewis, and their warmth was appreciated there, but when we arrived in Texas the weather was scorching. The first time I set foot on Sheppard Field, which is near Wichita Falls, a man told me the temperature was 100 degrees. I suffered for three days in that wool uniform, until my duffel bag containing my other uniforms arrived.

I had been to Texas when I was riding the rails, but that was always during the winter months, when the weather was cooler. Now it was almost as hot at night as it was during the day, and 100 degrees was not uncommon. The base was crowded with recruits and the barracks were full, so I was assigned a cot in a tent, which only intensified the heat.

Four days after I arrived, there were enough of us to form a training company, and we started hiking in formation. On the third day, we went on a 10-mile hike. That didn't sound bad to me because walking was a normal mode of transportation in those days. However, the Army started the hike five miles from my tent, which made the hike a total of 20 miles.

My boots still didn't fit properly, so the day after the hike, I went on sick call as the doctor in Fort Lewis told me to do. I entered a room full of soldiers, then a sergeant came in and told us to expose where we ached, so I took off my boots and waited with the bottoms of my feet pressed together.

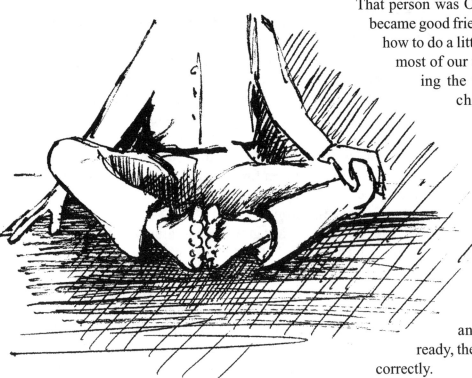

A doctor entered the room and went from man to man telling the sergeant what treatment was needed for each. He stopped in front of me, but only for a few seconds. He didn't once look at my face, just my feet.

"Soldier, if you have to crawl, you've got to do it," was all he said, then he stepped to the next man.

Two days later, my training company was given another battery of written tests. I tried hard to do well, because I figured there might be an Army job that didn't require so much marching.

Lo and behold, after studying the test scores, the Army said I would make a good specialist in their finance department. I could hardly believe my good fortune, and wondered if the Army read the test scores correctly. The only hitch was that there were no openings in the finance field, so the Army said I would make a good mechanic until a position opened up.

I only had a basic knowledge of what a vehicle mechanic does, so I figured my talent would be best utilized if I assisted a real mechanic. That person was Oscar Johnson, and we became good friends. Oscar showed me how to do a little mechanic work, but most of our time was spent checking the trucks that other mechanics fixed to make sure the work had been done properly. That meant we had to take lots of test drives, and we figured that a proper test drive was a long test drive. Our sergeant didn't complain, because he knew when Oscar and I said a truck was ready, the repairs had been done correctly.

A few weeks later, I was ordered to report to Roswell, New Mexico. The motor pool sergeant was furious and protested to headquarters.

"When I get a good man down here, you take him away from me," I heard him tell the company commander. But orders are orders, and neither the sergeant nor I could change them. Oscar took me to the station, on a test drive, and I boarded a troop train bound for New Mexico.

The base at Roswell was a discharge center for U.S. Army officers and a POW camp for Italian prisoners of war. Those two facts had a bitter-sweet affect on my time there. The Italian prisoners worked in the mess hall, which meant I didn't have to pull KP.

The officers out-numbered the enlisted men at Roswell, which was unusual for any Army base. I was in charge of officer's travel pay, and each of those officers had to see me before they could get that pay. Most of them were younger than me, and it was hard for me to put up with their rude and demanding ways. Several of them went out of their way to give me a bad time. Since they out-ranked me, I could not tell them what I thought of them without getting in trouble, so I kept my mouth shut and did my job.

The food was terrible at the mess hall, so another soldier and I would hitchhike to the town of Roswell and eat at a restaurant two or three nights a week. Meals were cheap then, and I felt it was worth it. One night a man in civilian clothes stopped and picked us up.

"Why don't you eat in the mess hall?" he asked, when we told him where we were going.

"I wouldn't feed that slop to pigs," I told him.

The man's neck and face got red, and he stopped the car, yelling at me, "I'm the colonel in charge of the mess hall and the food is good. What's your name soldier?"

"Monte Holm," I told him, then I got out of the car and saluted him as he drove off.

The Enola Gay, the B-29 that dropped the first atomic bomb, was stationed at Roswell for a while after it returned from the pacific. I met the crew and was allowed to take pictures and go on the plane while it was there. I made arrangements for them to get their travel pay, too. Then they were assigned to another base.

Orders were issued in January 1946 for several of us stationed at Roswell to go to McLellan Army Air Base in Sacramento, California, to be discharged. I was excited, and paid for a telephone call to Ruth instead of just writing to her about the good news. She was as excited as I was. We had not seen each other in 12 months.

The colonel in charge of the finance office, who was one of the few officers I respected,

called me into his office shortly after the discharge orders arrived.

"Holm, you've done good work for me here, and I'd like you to stay," he said. "If you reenlist, I'll make sure you get a promotion."

"Colonel, if you gave me a general's rank, I wouldn't stay," I replied. "With all respect sir, I've got a wife and daughter to look after, and a business to get going again."

"I understand," he said. "Good luck to you, Holm."

Three days before I caught the train bound for Sacramento, a young officer stopped in front of my desk and demanded that I take care of his travel pay right away. I explained that first I needed a copy of his orders. From that piece of paper, I could figure out how much he had coming and then complete the paperwork that authorized his travel pay. I saw about 100 officers a day, and it seemed all of them were demanding and wanted to throw their weight around. Only a few of the officers I dealt with those last three days were nice to me.

One of the reasons may have been that there was a travel-pay backlog of several days because of the overwhelming number of officers being discharged. If the orders became lost, the officer would have to get another copy of the orders from another officer who came from the same place.

My mother and father taught me that there was no place in life for retaliation or revenge, but I betrayed those teachings on my last full day in the army. I had about 400 orders ready for processing in front of me on the day before I was due to leave Roswell. I said a prayer, asking the Lord to forgive me, then I went through the orders and picked out 25 belonging to officers who had given me an especially bad time.

Then the thought occurred to me that I really didn't like any of the officers, but I remembered the few who had been nice to me. I pulled their orders, about 17 in all, and placed them in the top desk drawer where they would easily be found. The rest, about 383, ended up in the trash

The driver asked me to take the wheel and to wake him when we got to Portland. In Portland I bought a bus ticket to Everett, from which I took a cab to the house. I walked in the front door of my home about midnight and into the open arms of Ruth and Karen, and I felt good and whole again.

The next morning, Ruth handed me a letter from a friend of mine at the Roswell finance office.

"You ought to see all of these officers running around wanting to know what happened to their orders and trying to find other copies so they can get paid," he wrote. "No one can find the orders. Do you know where they are?"

I wrote back and told him that I had no idea. It wasn't a complete lie, for I did not know where those ashes were by that time. Sometimes it is interesting and fitting when rude and arrogant people get a little of their own medicine. I said another prayer asking the Lord to forgive me; then I put the incident out of my mind. It was time to get back to being a junk man.

bin, just before it was emptied into a furnace.

My train left early the next morning, and I was in Sacramento on January 18. I received my honorable discharge on January 21 and caught a ride out of Sacramento that evening. Before we left, I called Ruth and told her I would be home in the next day or two.

67

Expanding The Junk Business
Karen And The Trumans

I spent the day after I got home working around the house, but there really wasn't much for me to do because Ruth had everything under control. Being January, it was too early to plant the garden for this year. However, the pantry was full of vegetables that had been grown, harvested and preserved in jars the previous fall. What's more, Ruth had been busy butchering and canning the chickens she raised.

"I kept Mom supplied and I gave lots of chickens to other people," she told me. "But I wanted to make sure we had some stored away, in case you couldn't find a job."

With all of the military people coming home, jobs were scarce. I had been thinking about it for weeks, but didn't let on in my letters home. It was a testimony to our relationship that Ruth should be thinking the same way without our discussing it. Some of my hobo ways must have rubbed off on Ruth, too, for hobos always hoard food.

"I'd better get us some motors so we can start salvagin' copper again," I told Ruth as we neared the shed I had built for that purpose. "At least it would give us a little money comin' in, just in case I can't find anything else."

Ruth just smiled and opened the shed door. Inside was a pile of motors, generators and starters with the copper removed. In the corner of the shed was a large mound of copper wire, ready to be taken to the junk yard.

"But ... How'd you find the time?"

"Well, I was so lonely after you left that I tried to stay busy, so the time would go by faster," she said. "But takin' care of the garden took only a couple of hours a day, and the same with the chickens."

"But what about takin' care of Karen?"

"Look Monte, she may only be 4-years-old, but she helped me with the garden and the chickens," Ruth said. "I called Mrs. Michelson after the first week and told her what I had in mind. At the beginning of every month since then, one of her men has dropped off a bunch of starters, generators and motors. When we had time, Karen and I would come here and salvage copper."

"Wow," was all I could say as I stood looking at several hundred dollars' worth of copper wire.

"The men hauled away the empty casings each month, but I wouldn't let them take the wire. I wanted you to take care of that." I gave Ruth a hug, picked up Karen and we walked to the house.

Mrs. Michelson sounded excited that I was home when I called to arrange for a truck to pick up the copper.

"Is there any work around for a junk man?" I asked her.

"Mooney, you follow that truck back here tomorrow," she said. "We'll settle up with the copper, then we'll talk about work, and you better be prepared to sign a few contracts."

The next morning, Ruth, Karen and I were right behind the old Dodge truck when it arrived at the Riverside Junk Company. The whole Michelson clan was at my door when I opened it and there were handshakes all around.

Mrs. Michelson was going to hand me the money for the copper, but I pointed to Ruth, who proudly put it in her pocket.

She talked me through a plan of having three crews working at the same time, on different jobs, in different places. I signed three contracts, shook her hand and turned to leave when Ruth stopped me.

"What about some more starters, generators and motors?" she asked.

"But Ruth, I'm goin' to be so busy ...," I protested.

"That's right; you'll be working 16 hours a

"You ready to go to work, Mooney?"

"I'd heard jobs were hard to find," I said. "Why do ya have so much work?"

"The war's over and the military has lots of things to scrap," she told me as she placed a list of 15 big salvage jobs on the table in front of me. "Which ones do ya want?"

"I want 'em all, but just one at a time."

Mrs. Michelson let out a big laugh and said, "Mooney, you can have 'em all, but I think you can do three at a time."

day and the garden will just take a couple hours of work a day for Karen and me, and the chickens too," Ruth countered.

Mrs. Michelson let out another laugh. "I'll have the men deliver some more to ya in the mornin'," she said.

"Thank you," Ruth said with a smile.

I was both amazed and proud as we drove home. After only a couple of days off, I was again a junkman with good contracts in my pocket.

The next morning I set about gathering up a

crew to begin the first job. When that one was progressing nicely, I rounded up a second crew and started the second job, and finally a third crew. The crews kept me busy every one of those 16 hours each day that Ruth had talked about, but I wasn't afraid of hard work, and the men seemed happy to be working at a time when others were unemployed.

One day, while a crew and I were cutting up a large naval vessel, a couple of men in suits approached the crew.

"Who's in charge here?" one asked.

I stepped forward and introduced myself and asked what the problem was.

"There's no problem," the man said. "President Truman will be making a speech from his train tomorrow and you'll have to stop your work while the president is here."

I thought President Truman was the best president we ever had, and this was a chance for Karen to see her first president.

"Can you tell me exactly where the train will stop?" I asked, and explained why I wanted to know.

Ruth didn't want to go. She was just as excited as I was about President Truman coming to town, but she wanted to avoid fighting the crowds.

Karen and I arrived at the designated spot early to assure we would be in the front row. Other people started drifting in as time passed, and after nearly two hours, there were hundreds of people surrounding us. The train arrived on time and it stopped with the rear platform of the presidential car just 15 feet away from our position.

President Truman, his wife Bess and daughter Margaret stepped onto the platform and a great cheer went up from the crowd.

"That's the president," I leaned down and whispered to Karen. She smiled, then frowned. "Papa, I have to go to the bathroom," she whispered to me. "Will you stand in front of me while I go?"

There wasn't anything else I could do for her. The nearest restroom was several hundred yards away and I doubted she could hold it if we tried to walk that far, so I told her to go ahead. She bared her little bottom to the president, his wife and daughter, then squatted and did what she had to do.

I was watching the Trumans and they saw everything. They smiled, then chuckled. The president and his family understood what was happening, and I knew they thought it was all right. When Karen finished, she pulled up her pants, then motioned for me to bend down, so she could whisper to me.

"If you have to go, Papa, I'll stand in front of you," she said.

I assured her that I was fine, then I picked her up as we listened to the president deliver his speech. We clapped when he finished and waved as the train pulled away. All three of the Trumans looked at Karen and I and waved back.

68

The Wedding
We Move To Moses Lake

In 1952 my sister Ann called me from her home in Billings, Montana.

"Monte, Cecil Ann is getting married and I wanted to call and personally invite you and your family to the wedding," she said. "I want to see if father will come too and this will be a chance for all of us to visit."

I told her we would be there.

Ruth, Karen and I arrived at the church during the wedding rehearsal. At first my father didn't recognize me because it had been over 20 years since he had last seen me and that visit wasn't a pleasant one.

Once he saw that it was me, he shook my hand and gave me a hug, then I was proud to introduce him to my wife and daughter. After the rehearsal there was a dinner and he wanted us to sit with him so we could visit. I didn't tell him about the bad times in my life, but how I was doing then in the junk business. My Father seemed proud that I was making a living and that I had a family. The next day Ruth, Karen and I attended the wedding, but we were only able to visit with my father for a few brief moments.

Our meeting in Billings was very short, but my Father was able to meet my wife and daughter for the first and last time. For that I am grateful.

Back in Everett, the contracts kept rolling in and I was busier than I ever imagined. What's more, my family life was great. Ruth, Karen and I made the most of the time we had together, which sometimes wasn't much because of the long hours I worked. But I wasn't complaining. My life was just about as perfect as I ever thought it could be.

Then I started having health problems. I had double pneumonia several times and bronchial trouble.

"It's the damp weather here in Everett that's the problem," my doctor told me after my fourth bout with pneumonia. "If you want to become an old man, you better move to a place with a drier climate."

Ruth and I discussed our options and decided on either Arizona or eastern Washington. I flew to Arizona and had a look around, but couldn't find anything to suit the needs of a man trying to start a small junkyard.

Because of my connections on the Washington coast, I concentrated on eastern Washington. I first tried to buy property in Wenatchee, but the owners were proud of their land and didn't want to part with it unless I paid handsomely. Several of my friends suggested I check out Moses Lake.

"There's no junkyard there, yet," one said.

"The irrigation from Grand Coulee Dam is sure to make the town grow, don't ya think?" another asked.

I had been to Moses Lake a few times. The

first was in 1937, which was well before the irrigation water arrived. The town claimed a population of 350, and that may have included all of the dogs, too. It was not an inviting place at that time.

Years later, after the war, I traveled to the Ephrata and Moses Lake air bases to take part in surplus sales.

During those later visits, I could see that Moses Lake was growing and the people were excited about the development of the area for agriculture. That alone was sure to increase the population of the area, but I was worried that it might not be enough to support even a small junkyard. Then I read an article about the Moses Lake Air Base reopening. The expected growth might be enough to support me and my family.

I drove over to the Columbia Basin in 1953 and started looking for property to buy where I could establish my business. On the surface that task seemed simple, but it is not an easy thing to do because some people don't want a junkyard located near them. I was becoming disheartened about settling in Moses Lake when fate once again led me to the one person who could solve my problem. I met and confided in a young man in the real estate business named David Jones.

"Let's go for a ride, Monte," he said.

He took me to Commerce Street, which is about two blocks long. The east side of the street had just been zoned for industrial use and the west side was zoned for residential use.

"The industrial side is for sale," David told me.

While the street was at one edge of the prop-

erty, the Milwaukee Railroad tracks were at the other edge, and I had to have railroad access to ship my scrap iron. It was an ideal place for a junkyard. David told me who owned the property, and I visited the person that afternoon. He wanted $1,500 a lot, and there were 16 lots, each about 100 feet wide. That was a bunch of money for each lot, but I could see that the man was not going to come down in price.

"I have other people interested in that property, so if you want it, you better make up your mind," he said.

I bought lots 6, 7 and 8, figuring that would be enough land for the business, but soon I had to buy more. I purchased different lots at different times, at one time owning all 16, and each time they cost me more. The last one was $5,000.

Having tracks running alongside my property was good, but I had to have a small line of tracks running into my junk yard in order to load scrap into the cars. I called the Milwaukee Railroad, which sent a man by the name of Danny Sullivan to see me.

"I'm lookin' for the railroad to put a spur into the yard for me," I told him.

"Sure, we'll do it, but you'll have to pay for it," he replied.

"Listen, Mr. Sullivan, if you lay the spur, I will guarantee that I will ship at least 50 railroad cars a year, beginning the second year."

Mr. Sullivan laughed. "Monte, in the entire history of Moses Lake there has been only two railroad cars of scrap iron shipped out by rail, and you tell me you can ship 50 cars a year," he said. "You must think this country is full of scrap iron."

The railroad charged me $2,500 to bring

the spur into my yard, and the second year I shipped 52 railroad cars of scrap iron to the steel mill. Mr. Sullivan was man enough to come down and apologize to me.

"How about the railroad giving me back the $2,500?" I asked, but he just laughed.

For a short time, while I was getting the junkyard started and before we were able to sell our house in Everett, I was staying in Moses Lake alone. I rented a room at the Basin Motel, which was located near Five Corners. After the house in Everett sold, Ruth and Karen joined me to look for a house in Moses Lake.

We noticed one that was in the construction phase on Hill Street and stopped to look at it. The contractor, Floyd Swenson, was working on it at the time, and we started asking him questions. I could tell that it was a well-built house. We bought it and moved in as soon as it was finished.

A few weeks later, I went to see Floyd again about another project. I told him about the new junkyard and my need for a large building for my shop. I awarded him the contract because I liked his work, and that was his first commercial job. After building my shop, Floyd became a large commercial builder in the Columbia Basin.

I was proud to be the owner of my own junkyard, with its own railroad spur and shop. I named it

Moses Lake Iron & Metal. Now all I needed were customers. It was slow going in the beginning, and there were times when the money I made selling scrap was hardly enough to meet payroll. I put ads in the Columbia Basin Herald, which serves Moses Lake and environs, and in the other small-town newspapers around the Basin.

My approach to owning my own business was to always give a customer a little more money for their scrap than they had coming, but attracting new customers was only part of the reason.

People in the junk business are looked down upon as a lower form of humanity because they collect what others throw away. During my life in the junk business, I have tried to give people a different image, because disposing of what others throw away is one of the most essential businesses on this earth. If it were not for junkmen, our countryside would be overrun with refuse.

The strategy of being a junkman, who was fair to deal, with paid off as word got around the Basin. Soon ordinary people started bringing their copper, brass and aluminum to me, and farmers started bringing their old machinery and scrap iron, giving my business a boost.

The newly reopened Larson Air Force Base, formerly the Moses Lake Air Base, brought me a constant flow of scrap from the construction that was taking place there. Also, the local Public Utility District built two dams, Wanapum and Priest Rapids, on the Columbia River, and any scrap from those projects ended up in my junkyard.

The Columbia Basin was booming and it was my job to collect the scrap metal that no one else wanted and dispose of it at a profit. It was hard work, but I was never afraid of hard work. The effort allowed me to make a decent living and pro-

vide others with jobs.

Ruth was always ready to help in any way she could. As soon as Karen went to school each morning, Ruth would head to our business and spend the day working as the Moses Lake Iron & Metal bookkeeper. She would return to our house just before Karen was due to arrive home. By doing so, she saved us the need to hire another bookkeeper, which allowed the business to expand at a greater rate than would have been possible otherwise.

As happy as I was to take in scrap metal, local contractors began requesting new steel. The demand increased to the point where I started carrying it, which not only proved to be a smart move, but was also natural. At one end of the operation I was selling new pipe, bolts and almost anything else in the steel line, while at the other end, I was taking in the scrap iron that had served its purpose and was no longer needed.

It was the type of operation that makes a junkman smile as he drives home every evening. For example, I once sold a contractor 100 10-foot pipes on a Wednesday morning. Six of those pipes were damaged Wednesday afternoon as the workers tried to install them. Thursday morning, the damaged pipes, along with other scrap metal, were loaded onto a truck and hauled back to Moses Lake Iron & Metal as scrap. I sold the pipes as new steel, and made a reasonable profit, then bought the pipes back as scrap, and made a reasonable profit.

I supplied the new steel that was essential to the construction of various Columbia Basin projects and I helped clean up those sites by buying back the scrap.

And I smiled a lot as I drove home each evening to Ruth and Karen.

Epilogue

Perhaps history will record my life as meanigful and worthy; time will tell. The fact is,I beleive that I have been successful as a businessman, husband, father, and politician. It took a lot of hard work, but I have never been afraid of hard work. However, if you ask me if I now feel secure or if I have made it, as some people put it, I will say no, because you never know what will happen tomorrow. Perhaps the bottom will drop out of the junk business and I will have to revert back to my hobo ways.

Granted, at this point such a scenario is remote, but I like to keep it in the back of my mind where it can be brought forward once in a while. The possiblity, be it remote, keeps me from getting soft. Just because Moses Lake Iron & Metal has become a going concern, doesn't signal the end of the story.

It may be unusual for an Epilogue to have multiple chapters, but my life has been anything but usual. A man's life does not end with the last period on the last page of his autobiography, and much more has happened in my life since I became established. I would feel bad if I didn't share some of it with you.

Epilogue, Part 1

Karen and Wayne Get Married

While trying to make Moses Lake Iron & Metal a profitable business was a rewarding experience, it was only part of my life. Ruth and Karen were my reasons for working so hard. It was a pleasure to help Ruth raise Karen, and we were close as a family.

We were proud parents as she marched into the auditorium in 1961 as part of the graduation ceremony at Moses Lake High School. That fall, we drove her to Pullman, Washington, the home of Washington State University. Karen was excited to start her college career, and we were happy for her, but it was a heart-wrenching experience for Ruth and me to leave that afternoon. We knew that our daughter had a life of her own to live, and that gave Ruth and me food for discussion as we drove back to Moses Lake that evening. Still, the house on Hill Street was empty without her.

Three weeks later, Karen called and asked if we would like to travel to Pullman for a visit. We sure did, and left after I finished work at the shop at noon on Saturday. The three of us had so much fun that weekend, traveling to Pullman became a common occurrence.

Ruth and I would get two rooms at a motel, then pick up Karen and her friends, Marilyn Thorneycroft Shoemaker, Cathy Yancey Olson and Barbara Bowen Freer. We would go to dinner as a group Saturday evening and continue our visit into the night. The next morning, we'd treat the group to breakfast, then we would take the girls back to Scott Hall on the WSU campus.

One Saturday afternoon, Karen brought along a young man to meet us.

"Father, this is Wayne Rimple," she said, introducing us.

He seemed like a nice young man, but I could see he was a bit nervous and afraid we might not approve of him. He did turn out to be a fine young man, and on December 14, 1963, I was proud to walk Karen down the aisle to become his bride.

Wayne went to work for me in the junkyard. I am sure it was hard for him to work for his father-in-law, but we got along just fine and I could see he had a lot of good qualities.

Epilogue, part 2

The House of Poverty Museum

An old hobo who is also a junkman tends to collect things, and sometimes they are good things. I'm no exception, but it wasn't long before the area in my junkyard became so congested that my men were tripping over my treasures while doing their work. It was obvious that I needed to build another structure and call it a museum. So that's what I did. I call it The House of Poverty because all of my treasures came from that one dime I had in my pocket when I walked into Everett.

This is what my friend, Kathy Kiefer, wrote about my museum a few years ago:

"This museum in Moses Lake is by far the most unusual museum I have ever been in. It is not a typical museum with specially-designed display cases and roped-off areas. The House of Poverty is the result of one man's vision. Although he doesn't readily admit it, the museum was established to preserve his own memories of the golden years in American history. Monte Holm, 'curator and former hobo,' had a dream of owning his own railroad. The dream has come true, and the proof is in the front yard of the museum.

"Monte Holm is a walking, talking, billiard-ball bald and blessed person who is his museum's most notable artifact. While pressing a piece of Werther's candy into your hand, he smiles and says, 'The only thing that doesn't work in this museum is me.'

"The museum contains a veritable array of antiques spread willy-nilly throughout a huge one-room warehouse. Few items are labeled. Monte maintains a running dialogue with explicit details on each item. It is hard not to be dazzled by the 1917 Model T, one-ton truck, or the 1921 Oldsmobile Roadster, or the 1927 Model T Roadster or the 1932 Packard, or the 1956 Thunderbird, all in mint condition.

"Some of the rare items include a hundred-year-old butter churn, an elaborate cast iron coal stove, one of the first portable washing machines, a 125-year-old Singer sewing machine owned by the Jessie James family, a whistle from the first steamship on the Pacific coast, a large collection of original cast iron trivets, a Harley Davidson motorcycle with one of only 12 side cars made for them, several rare hot air engines, a chastity belt, a 1919 Stutz fire engine, a 1914 Evinrude outboard motor and many, many more historic items.

"The train cars in his yard were purchased to make good a promise he made to people who used to kick him off their trains when he was a hobo. He told them that some day he would own his own railroad. He is one of the few remaining registered owners of a private rail line. His collection includes a presidential dining car once used by President Wilson and later President Truman, the last steam engine operated in Alaska and several cabooses.

"The House of Poverty museum provides a view of the past and a peek into the heart of an exceptional human being."

Kathy said some mighty nice things about me, and I must give her a big thank you for that, but the fact is she only had room in her article to list some of the items in the museum. However, she did tell about a few, including steam engine Number 557.

I bought the engine, then had it put on a ship and brought to Seattle. From there it was towed, by rail, to Moses Lake. But before its arrival, I had to get a rail for it. The Milwaukee Railroad owned a 100-foot right of way, and I bought a strip that measured 25-feet wide and 400-feet long that was next to my junkyard and the museum. I paid $10,000 for that strip of land, but it was necessary.

The next obstacle was to acquire and lay track for the engine. I bought about 22 miles of track that ran from Adrian to Coulee City and took it out for junk. This was the route used to haul most of the material that was used in the construction of Grand Coulee Dam.

The rails were first put down by the Northern Pacific Railroad when it came west in the late 1880s. When the Northern Pacific updated their rails, they moved the old rails to branch lines like the one between Adrian and Coulee City around 1903. These are the rails under Number 557. The presidential car was added to my collection a few years later.

Old 557, with the presidential car attached, followed by an old caboose, makes a fine railroad for this old hobo. I sponsored a name-the-train contest in 1965 and chose Mon-Road Railroad to have painted on her side.

I enjoy showing people through the House of Poverty, but I will not charge admission or allow donations.

Epilogue, part 3

Our life is further enriched

On May 24, 1968, Karen and Wayne added to Ruth and my already full life; Larry Rimple, our first grandson, was born. I called the hospital and had the nurses open the window of Karen's room. Then I steamed up old 557 and started sounding the whistle. After 10 minutes, two city policemen arrived and climbed the steps to where I was sitting in the engineer's seat.

"What's goin' on Monte?" one asked.

"My first grandson was just born," I told him.

"Don't ya think you've sounded that whistle enough?"

"Not on your life," I told them. "I'm goin' to keep pullin' on this cord for an hour."

"I'd hate to have to throw you in jail for disturbin' the peace," the other policeman said.

"After this hour is up, I'll go with ya if you want, but right now I suggest you go call your commander and tell him what's goin' on," I told them.

They started to leave and I stopped them.

"Tell your boss that he should be happy that my grandson was born during the day, because I was prepared to do this at night, too."

The policemen walked away from the engine and back to their car. I was watching them as they used their radio to call headquarters, then one shook his head and they both waved, climbed into their car and drove away.

April 17, 1972, was another big day for Ruth and I; Steven Rimple, our second grandson, was born. I would have fired up old 557 again, and blown the whistle for two hours this time, but the police department, knowing that Karen was about to give birth and remembering what had happened the first time, asked me to resist my urge to show my pride in that way. When people ask in a nice way, it's hard to do otherwise, even though this old hobo wanted to blow that whistle in the worst way.

I said a prayer and thanked the Lord for giving me another healthy grandson, then returned to work for the rest of the day.

Our family has grown and been blessed three times since then. Steven married Shari Johnson on August 14, 1993. They have given Ruth and I our first great grandsons: Jacob Monrad Rimple was born on July 19, 1994, and Kyle Steven Rimple was born on July 1, 1998.

Epilogue, Part 4

A new business

In the early 1970s, the new steel part of Moses Lake Iron & Metal was growing at such a rate that we needed a new location just to run that part of the operation. Wayne and his college buddy Larry Buckley both worked for me at the time. They asked for a meeting with me one day and suggested that we lease the old Colfax Machine Company from Harold Mast, with an option to buy. I thought it was a grand idea and agreed.

We moved the new steel to the new location and named it Moses Lake Steel. After two years, we bought the property and Wayne built the business into a large operation. He was proud, and so was I, when he handed me a check a few years later to buy me out of that part of the business.

Wayne continued to succeed as a businessman, and his leadership ability did not go unnoticed. He served as the Mayor of Moses Lake from January 1988 through December 1995 and has continued to serve the citizens of the city as a councilman.

Epilogue, Part 5

Stories

Interaction with other people has been an enjoyable part of my life. Once Moses Lake Iron & Metal was established, I was able to relax a little and enjoy the daily contact with family, business associates and friends. Here are some stories, written by some of those people.

From Cathy Kersey

The Easter Egg - In 1969, my son Donnie Kersey attended kindergarten at Midway school in Moses Lake, which required a 6-block walk to school for him and his friends. They soon found a shortcut that took them past Moses Lake Iron & Metal.

One day Donnie told my husband Paul and me about the poor man who lived in the junkyard. When we asked him why he thought the man was poor, he said, "Because the man has holes in his sweater."

We knew the junkyard man was Monte Holm. I went to school with Monte's daughter Karen, and Paul and I have had business dealings with him.

When Easter came around that spring and we were coloring Easter eggs, Donnie insisted on coloring a special egg for the poor man in the junkyard. He delivered the egg the next day, and that was the beginning of a long-term friendship.

Later on that same year, Donnie had his tonsils out and he developed complications from what is usually a simple and routine operation. One day, while Donnie was lying on the living room couch recovering, there was a knock on our front door. When we opened it, there stood Donnie's junkyard-friend Monte with a sack of goodies.

Monte also presented Donnie with some coins he had collected, asking that Donnie save them for his college fund. Donnie still has the coins and plans to keep them for his own children's education.

The story served as a reminder to all young people that kindness is the greatest gift of all. Monte Holm is a special man who has the ability to sense the needs that many of us overlook. His caring ways and a generous spirit serve as an inspiration to all who know him. He always finds beauty in this precious life we live.

Jackie - On a trip to Albuquerque, New Mexico, in 1989, Monte decided to get his shoes shined. The shoeshine lady's 8-year-old daughter, Jackie, was there at the hotel while her mom was working. Monte took a real liking to this young girl and she to him.

They corresponded often during the next year, and Monte sent Jackie cards and candy. The Holm family, Monte, Ruth and Karen, planned another trip to Albuquerque and invited me to join them. Before we left, Monte contacted Jackie's mother and told her that he was returning for a visit, and that he had a surprise for Jackie.

At the appointed time, we picked up Jackie in a white stretch limousine and treated her to eight hours of Queen-For-A-Day treatment. We went to Santa Fe, where we shopped and had a grand time. Jackie was excited about all of the attention; she had never had such royal treatment before. I think Monte felt sorry for Jackie, and he wanted to give her a day she would never forget.

When we returned to Jackie's house, her family was waiting and dinner was prepared for us.

Monte rarely goes to other people's homes for a meal, but this family was so unique, and Jackie was such a special little girl, that Monte couldn't say no to the invitation.

Monte and Jackie are still in contact.

From John Munson

Christmas Champagne - Twenty five years ago, or close to that time, I was visiting with Monte and when I asked him how he was doing, he gave his standard answer, "I've never had a bad day in my life."

He went on to tell me, "Really I'm the luckiest man in the world. I have a warm comfortable home, plenty to eat, a good wife, a beautiful daughter, a good son-in-law and two healthy, good-looking grandsons. What more could a man possibly want?"

Then after a short hesitation, he added, "Except maybe a bottle of champagne."

Well, that Christmas Eve I took Monte a bottle of champagne, reminded him of what he had said, and a tradition was born with Monte commenting, "Now it is Christmas!" He, of course, always had a gift for me, too.

One year, I was quite a bit late in getting the bottle of champagne to him, and when I did arrive he remarked, "Boy, finally it is Christmas; I was a little afraid it wasn't going to be complete."

Our tradition continues.

From Ruth Findlay

Three barrels for the kids -My family hadn't lived in Moses Lake very long when my children, Darrell, Ron, Ken and Diane, wanted to try barrel racing — a timed event where a horse and rider circle three 55-gallon barrels. I knew Monte had a bunch of those barrels, so I paid him a visit.

He told me they were 50 cents each, which was $1.50 total. We didn't have much money in those days and $1.50 would buy a lot of groceries, so I told Monte that I would hold off buying the barrels. Monte asked me what the barrels were to be used for, and I told him.

He sent a worker out to load the barrels in my truck and didn't charge me one penny for them.

Harry Luchi

A helping hand - Being a bit of an inventor, I had been working on a new propeller idea for boat motors and needed the new propeller tested. I'm getting up in years and have a little trouble getting around, so I went to Monte to see how I could arrange the testing.

He provided two men, a forklift and an elevated tank so I could conduct the initial testing — then he wouldn't take any money for helping me.

From Ron Baker

Opening the safe - Monte had a safe that came from a branch office of a bank that was located on Larson Air Force Base. Trouble was, he couldn't open it; didn't have the combination. I had a cousin, Jerry Fleming, who wanted to buy the safe. Monte's asking price was $500, which was accepted by Jerry, but I made a counter offer.

I asked Monte if he would give us back $250 if we were able to open the safe within 30 days. He accepted. I called Monte four hours later and told him the safe was open. Another cousin, Lois Jean Flemming, worked at a sawmill years before, and they had a safe just like the one purchased from Monte. She tried the old combination and it worked.

Either it was the same safe, or all of the safes had the same combination when they left the factory. The new owner was expected to change the combination, but apparently some didn't.

When I called Monte and told him that we had the safe open, he asked two questions: "What was in the safe, and how do I know you really opened it?" The safe contained only a paper clip and a nickel.

To prove the safe was open, I gave Monte a picture of the open safe with Lois standing by the open door. That picture still hangs in Monte's office to this day.

Monte was as good as his word, as always, and he gave us the $250 like he said he would.

From Jerry Lester

Monte is Mr. Whisper - Sometime in the early 1960s, a local radio station sponsored a contest called Mister Whisper. The station would randomly select a number from the telephone book, then call that number. The person who answered was asked to identify the person who was whispering a recorded message that was played over the air. If the individual could name the person whispering the message, they would get a prize.

One morning our phone rang and my mother, Francis Lester, answered it. The disc jockey spent half of his youth digging through the junk at Moses Lake Iron & Metal looking for workable motors.

Mom told the DJ the whispering voice was that of Monte, and with that correct answer, she won the first color television set our family owned.

From Steve Hill

The rock bar - I needed a rock bar, a long steel bar used to pry rocks loose when digging post holes. Everyone knows the best place to get one is Moses Lake Iron & Metal, so I paid Monte a visit.

He sent one of his workers to get an old axle and then cut one end to a point. When that was done, Monte weighed the bar and told me the bill was $3.75. I didn't have any cash with me, so I pulled out my checkbook and started to write a check.

"What are ya doin'?" Monte asked. I explained my lack of cash and that my check was as good as cash. Monte said that wasn't the problem, "I just don't want to deal with such a small check; make it out to Boy Scout Troop number so and so."

"But Monte," I said, "You aren't making any money on this sale."

"That's why I call this The House of Poverty," Monte said.

From Susan Alsted:

Easter and the hobo - In the spring of 1971, I was a cashier at Boyle's Plaza, a grocery store in Moses Lake. A very kind man came in each day and counted out his pennies to buy veggies and a little meat. He told me the items were used in his hobo stew. I never asked his name, but looked forward to his kind words, and I felt bad for him just barely being able to buy $2 or $3 worth of food with mostly small coins.

A couple of days before Easter that spring, the man came in and asked me to help him pick out the nicest Easter lily from the bunch we had on display. I showed him the one I thought was best, and he asked how much it was. Then he said, "Well for a poor hobo, like I am, I can buy this plant, but I won't have my hobo stew."

He bought the plant, and my heart felt so bad, but I felt even worse when he handed me the plant and said, "Here, Susan, this is for you; happy Easter!" I knew this kind man had spent his last dime on that plant, so I told him I couldn't accept it. But he insisted and left, again wishing me a happy Easter.

I took the plant home with much guilt, knowing he may be going hungry. I told my husband Dave about the plant and how this hobo gave it to me. Dave asked me to describe the hobo. I did, and Dave just laughed and said that I shouldn't worry about that hobo going hungry.

Every year since 1971, Monte, Moses Lake's favorite hobo, has sent me an Easter lily. In the accompanying card this year, he wrote, "To one of the nicest young ladies this old hobo ever met. I am too poor to afford it, but when I saw this beautiful Easter lily I thought of you. Have a good Easter. With love, a poor old hobo."

Every Easter he sends a different card with a different note, but it is always signed, "a poor old hobo," and there is always a bag of his special candy attached to the plant.

From Dennis L. Clay

Rich and I salvage scrap - After my high school buddy Rich Soden and I were old enough to drive, we were faced with the reality of buying gas for our vehicles. This was made worse by the fact that we also needed money to take girls out for Saturday night dates.

One day, we were sitting in my living room discussing ways of getting money when my father overheard us.

"Why don't you two go pick up some old scrap and sell it to Monte?" he asked.

We drove to a couple of old dumps and salvaged as much scrap metal as my 1951 Buick would hold. Monte weighed the scrap, then asked what we were going to use the money for. When we told him we planned to take our dates to a movie and to get hamburgers (they were five for a dollar in those days), he handed us a five-dollar bill. The payment was about 10 times what the scrap metal was worth.

"Now I can't do that for you every week, but you two have a good time tonight," he said.

Monte has always given more to his customers than was expected of him, but the idea of two boys scrounging scrap metal to make a buck must have touched a soft spot in his heart.

Knife-making material - My friend Ray Groff, who lives in Davenport, Washington, was showing an interest in making knives. He needed old files or saw blades to use as stock to make the knife blades, so I visited Monte. He sent me out into the junkyard with one of his workers. We found two large saw blades and headed back to the office.

Monte looked them over and said, "That'll be $20, or we could flip for double or nothing." Monte's luck is legendary in the Columbia Basin and I didn't have $40 to spare in case I lost the bet, so I declined his offer and paid him the $20.

I gave Ray the saw blades, so he could pursue his hobby. That December, Ray gave me a skinning knife with an antler handle and a wooden scabbard for Christmas. Now I have a knife made by my friend Ray that came from the scrap salvaged from Monte's junkyard. That makes it a one-of-a-kind knife and extra special to me.

From Anne Peterson Dieham

The tip of the spark plug - I believe it was in 1959 that my husband and I were going to Washington State University on a very tight budget. Monte made us a deal when we returned to Moses Lake for the Christmas break. If we would sort through these enormous barrels of airplane spark plugs and clip off the platinum tips, we could keep those tips and sell the platinum.

To get the job done my brother Ben, my husband and I hung our frozen bodies over the sides of the oil drums and clipped the tip off of every spark plug. My father melted down the platinum to the pure form and contacted a metals buyer for us. That money paid for the rest of our school year at WSU; books, tuition, and our apartment. Monte could have assigned one of his men to do that work, then the money from selling the platinum would have been his. But when someone is willing to work, Monte can usually find a way to help them out and I think he has a soft spot for people going to school. Monte, obviously, is tops as far as I'm concerned. He really saved the school year for us.

From Bobbie Campbell

Payback time - One summer, I was on my annual trip back home to Ritzville, Washington, from Arizona, where I live now, when I met Monte. I always stay with my friend, Normadine Kulm. A couple of years ago, Normadine showed me an article that mentioned my father's creamery and the man who bought all of the equipment after my father passed away. That man was Monte Holm.

We went to visit Monte, and when I told him that my father owned the creamery, he told me the story about how my father helped him with some food and bought him a meal when he was a hobo.

Normadine and I had stopped by just before noon, and after visiting for a few minutes, Monte told us that he couldn't leave the office. But he handed me $20 and told us to go have lunch. I said I couldn't take his money, but he told me it was payback time for when my father bought him a meal.

From Monte

A trip with Steven - Ruth and I enjoyed taking our grandsons, Larry and Steven, on trips when they were youngsters. We did this many times with the length of the trips lasting from a few hours to several days. When my grandson Steven was about 6 years old, he called me one day and asked if just he and I could take a trip. I told him we sure could and that I would pick him up after I got off work at noon on Saturday.

He was ready and waiting with his suitcase when I pulled in his driveway. Ruth and I had taken Steven to Wenatchee, about 70 miles from Moses Lake, many times, and I thought this is where he might be thinking about going. I told him that we would go anywhere he wanted to and that he was to tell me when he wanted to stop.

I pointed the car toward Wenatchee, and when we were about two miles from home, at the west edge of Moses Lake, Steven looked to the right and pointed to a large inn.

"Let's go there, Grandpa," he said.

We got a room, had supper and spent the night. In the morning, we ordered breakfast in bed, then headed home. Two weeks later, Steven called me again and said he wanted to go on a trip, just the two of us again, so we did. A trip doesn't have to be a long one to experience quality time with a family member.

Sometimes a junkman gets lucky - There came a time when the City of Moses Lake wanted to get rid of their old water tower and get a new one. I submitted a bid to take it out, as did several other people. My bid was lowest, so I got the contract that stipulated I was responsible for removing it.

As the bids were being considered, I got word that Coulee City, located about 30 miles north of Moses Lake, was in need of a water tower. When I learned that Moses Lake's water tower was mine, I called Coulee City and offered it to them at a reasonable, but profitable, price. I made sure the contract read that the new owner would be responsible for moving the water tower from its present location.

I was paid by Moses Lake for removing the water tower and I was paid by Coulee City when they took possession. All this and I didn't even touch it. The last I heard, Coulee City is still using that water tower.

It's deals like this that make a junkman smile.

The FBI visits the House of Poverty - When Larson Air Force Base, located near Moses Lake, was active, a B-52 crashed and burned on one of the runways. I bid on the contract to scrap what was left of the plane. I ended up losing about $3,000 on the deal because there was not as much salvageable metal as I thought there would be.

However, there was one part of the plane that was not damaged: a gun turret complete with machine guns, and I enjoyed showing it to people who visited me at Moses Lake Iron & Metal. I had the turret for about a year, maybe two, when two men in suits walked into my office and flashed identification badges at me. They were from the FBI.

"Do you have a B-52 gun turret?" one asked.

I told them that I did and showed them the contract papers which listed the turret and machine guns as part of the salvage operation.

They looked surprised and said it was a mistake that I had the turret and machine guns. I asked what they wanted me to do with it, and they said to scrap it. I told them that I would personally cut the turret and machine guns up with a cutting torch. They posted a guard by the turret for two days until I completed the job, and loaded all of the cut up turret and machine gun pieces onto a railroad car.

Paying a debt - About 50 years after I had been allowed to sleep in the Tacoma Railroad Depot for several nights, I read about an endeavor to fix up the old depot. The people behind the effort were looking for donations.

I wrote and told them I wanted to settle up my old obligation. I figured my debt consisted of $20 a night for 10 nights, so I sent them a $200 check. In return, they sent me a nice picture of the depot, which is now in The House of Poverty Museum.

The Tacoma Narrows Bridge - The State of Washington built the Tacoma Narrows Bridge to shorten the highway trip to the Olympic Peninsula. In 1941, strong winds caused the

bridge to collapse. There were two approaches to the bridge, one on each end which consisted of the area from the shore to a tower. After it gave way to the wind, those approaches were about all that remained, and they had to be dismantled. Other workers did the dismantling and brought the pieces to solid ground. I cut up the dismantled pieces for scrap.

Food mystery solved - In the 1960s, my friend Clark Jones, who was then the superintendent of the U & I Sugar plant in Moses Lake, and I made a trip to Montana to visit some of the places I traveled years before. When we were in Malta, I went to the barber shop where the barber had recognized me decades before as a sheepherder just because of the way I looked and smelled. As the old barber started cutting my hair, I asked him how long he had been there.

"Oh a long time," he said. "About 20 years."

"That's not long enough," I told him.

I was either going to thank him or give him hell if he was the same barber who cut my hair years before. After all, I didn't know if he did me a good turn or not. I might have been better off if I would have stayed a sheepherder. The barber told me the other barber had died.

On this same trip, Jones and I traveled to Zortman. We found a bar in town and made ourselves comfortable. In the same room was the bartender and another couple.

I told the bartender that I herded sheep out east of Zortman years before.

"Who did you herd for?" he asked.

"The Hensen brothers."

"Then you might know this lady sitting here; she used to be a cook at the Hensen ranch."

The lady and I started talking, and she said she worked for the Hensens in 1938. I told her that I was long gone before she arrived. Then I mentioned that the Hensens didn't take care of their herders very well. I told her that the camp tender would bring me sowbelly, beans, flour and just a few other items.

"They didn't bring me any canned goods, so I had to cook everything from the ground up," I told her. "And the tender would get the water he brought me from alkali ponds."

She said the Hensens thought the herders working for them were getting everything they wanted. After I had left, they found out that the tender was loading canned goods and other supplies to sell to his brother who had a cabin along the Missouri River. I also found out that instead of getting clean water from a well at the Hensen Ranch, like he should have done, the tender would pull his wagon into an alkali pond and fill the water barrels at the same time the horses were defecating and urinating.

Although I don't consider myself to be a violent person, I would have killed or at least done some bodily harm to the tender from the Hensen ranch if I could have gotten my hands on him right then. He would have deserved whatever I did to him for all of the alkali water and bum food I got over the years while herding sheep.

George (Cowboy) Pruitt - One day in 1954 a man walked into my office and introduced himself as George Pruitt. His nickname was Cowboy.

"I understand that you are an old hobo, Monte," he said.

I told him that I was at one time, for six years during the Depression. George said he was a hobo at the same time, so we compared notes to see if we were ever in the same place at the same time during our hobo days.

We couldn't think of a time when we might have met before, but because we were hobos during the same time we became friends — a friendship that lasted for thirty-five years, until George died.

I attended weekly meetings when I served on the City Council. After the meetings I would pick up George and we would go to a local restaurant and have a meal, usually a steak. Then we would compare that meal to the ones we had during our hobo days, and we were thankful for what we were eating.

Ruth and I invited George to our house every Christmas. He was like family to us and was known as Uncle George to our grandsons, Larry and Steven. They thought he was the greatest man in the world as he told stories of his youth, when he was a soldier in the Army and about his days as a hobo on the road. He was a positive influence on my grandsons and to this day, my family misses him very much.

Amtrak trips

Amtrak trips - When my grandsons were in grade school, I felt the need to show them some of the places I had been when I was a hobo. Well, there is only one way for an old hobo to travel and that is by rail. The difference between my hobo days and traveling by Amtrak is that I get to ride inside.

So twice a year Ruth and I, along with several of our family and friends, depending upon their schedule, board the train in Ephrata and travel. Making the trip with us have been our grandsons, Larry and Steven, friends Cathy Kersey, Lana Jackson, Marilyn Shoemaker and Pat Boushey (our niece).

We have traveled all over the United States, but now we only go to Minneapolis. I have a fondness for that great city, because of the time I spent there in the soup line. The women along on the trip like Minneapolis because they get to shop at the Mall of America. The Marriott Hotel has become our home away from home.

Notaras Lodge - Marina Romary owns the Notaras Lodge in Soap Lake, Washington. It is a beautiful place with a theme for each of the nine rooms. I was pleasantly surprised when Marina called and said she was building a few new rooms and that she wanted to name one of them after me. It is called the House of Poverty room.

When it was finished, Marina invited me and my family over to see it, and to spend the first night in the room. She did a great job and I'm proud of the room. I had no trouble finding it because there are railroad tracks in the sidewalk leading to the room. It is quite an honor for an old hobo.

You too can spend a night in The House of Poverty Room at the Notaras Lodge. Just call the lodge and make a reservation.

A reporter learns a lesson - When I returned home from work one evening in the early 1980s, Ruth handed me a newspaper article that appeared in the Spokesman-Review, a newspaper based in Spokane, Washington.

"I want you to read this, but you're not going to be happy," she said.

The gist of the article was that junkmen are on the lowest rung of the social ladder. My lovely wife was correct, I wasn't happy. In fact I was downright mad.

I called the paper's editor and explained that the writer had a lesson to learn and asked for his telephone number. When I had the writer on the phone, I invited him to visit me in Moses Lake. We had a great visit and he tagged along as a group of people toured The House of Poverty Museum.

In the end, the writer shook my hand and said, "Monte, I learned a great lesson today, thank you."

In a full-page article about the visit he wrote, "Holm is also a living refutation of old-fashioned notions that a junkdealer belongs at the bottom of the social order."

When I read that, I knew that this writer would pass along the lesson he had learned to others. I now have the article framed and hanging in the museum office, so I can read it once in a while. You can read it, too. Just look up page C11 of the August 26, 1981 issue of <u>The Spokesman-Review</u>.

Werther's - While spending a winter in the bread line in Minneapolis, I vowed to "make sure everyone I meet gets something from me, even if it's just a smile or a handshake."

After I became established in Moses Lake, I started buying bags of wrapped candy and giving a few pieces to the people I visited with during the day. One day a friend gave me three pieces of Werther's Original. I thanked him and continued on my way to the post office.

I popped a piece of the candy in my mouth and discovered it was the best candy I had ever eaten. I finished the three pieces, one after the other, then went to a grocery store and bought a bag of Werther's. I couldn't stop eating them and finished the entire bag in short order.

I knew eating so much of the candy wasn't food for me, so after finishing that batch, I decided not to eat another. But, because they are simply the best there is, I give a few pieces to everyone I visit with during the day. I buy so much Werther's Original candy that I now order direct from the distributor.

Dennis Clay once asked me how much money I spend each year on the delicious candy called Werther's.

"I don't want anyone to know." I told him.

"Is it more than $1,000?"

I just laughed.

"More than $5,000?"

Again I laughed

"More than $10,00?"

Well, it may be, but I just laughed again.

"I don't want anyone to know." I told him.

Running for City Council - In 1964, I decided to take a real interest in our fine town, so I ran for a position on the city council. Being a non-conformist, my campaign and campaign card were altogether different from anything that anyone had ever seen before.

On the front was a picture of me swiping wild rhubarb, but the picture was of my backside; I was bent over.

On the back of the card the copy reads: **Vote for *Real* Experience**
• Hobo and Sheepherder from age 13 to 19 years, which is **wonderful experience to learn the value of the dollar**. • Started in the junk business with ten cents, at the age of 19, and have made a success out of things people throw away. • I have a lot at stake in Moses Lake and want the opportunity to work for the betterment of our city. • I am past president of nothing – but have the distinction of being made the first Honorary Member of Theta Chi Fraternity since its origin in 1919, at Washington State University on Nov. 10, 1963. For an ex hobo and sheepherder this is indeed an honor.

Shortly before the election, my opponent was named Man of the Year, but when the ballots were counted, I beat him nearly two to one. He said that it's not so bad to lose an election, but to be beat by an old hobo is awful. My opponent was and continues to be a great servant of the people of Moses Lake and Grant County.

I served nearly six years on the Council and stopped running for the position. It seemed that every complaint there was came to my office. But it was a very educational time for me. People will complain about anything, and there is no way you can satisfy all of the people.

Some of them are just plain unreasonable, and I would tell that bunch to run for my position if they didn't like how I was serving them, but the complainers would rather complain than expend the energy to run for office.

However, I found most of the people to be understanding. If they gave me the chance to explain things to them, they understood the situation. I just tried to do the best job I could.

From Larry Peterson

It was me ... - I'm the person who ran against Monte during the 1964 general election for city council. He did indeed run an unusual kind of campaign. Monte has always been a popular person in Moses Lake, but his campaign really struck a cord with the voters. If I was going to lose, I don't know anyone I would rather lose to than Monte. He is a fine person and he was a good councilman.

I just filed for another term as Port of Moses Lake Commissioner, and I sure hope Monte doesn't toss his hat in that ring. Who knows what kind of campaign he would run this time. He is as well thought of today as he was in 1964.

Larry Peterson has a long history of serving the citizens of Moses Lake and Grant County. He was a member of the Moses Lake City Planning Commission, he was appointed by the mayor to be the first chairman of the Moses Lake Interracial Commission for Human Rights, he went on to become the manager of the Grant County PUD and has now served as a Port of Moses Lake Commissioner since 1987.

From Paul Sickler

Knowing Monte and considering him a friend, I couldn't resist putting pen to paper to the tune of "Shanty In Old Shanty Town"

He's just an ex-hobo,
Montana was home
But Moses Lake beckoned,
He'll no longer roam.
He has a big shack,
His own railroad in back.
It's an ex-hobo's dream,
And it costs lots of jack.

He doesn't want a palace,
Nor to be a king,
To be called a good fellow,
Is his everything.
There's a queen waiting there,
When at night he goes home.
I'm talking about no one,
But our Monte Holm.

Epilogue, Part 6

My Staff

Running a junkyard like Moses Lake Iron & Metal takes a bit of manpower as well as the use of some heavy-duty machinery. A lot of people have worked for me over the years and the workforce varies depending upon the amount of scrap coming in and leaving by rail. I have been blessed with a core staff of three loyal and hard-working men. The four of us have become a close-knit team. These three men are a vital element to the life and efficient running of Moses Lake Iron & Metal.

Norm Estoos

"I started working for Monte in the spring of 1959 when I was 17 years old and still in high school. Most of my time after school and on Saturdays was spent at the junkyard where I would poke around the piles of metal and visit with Monte. One day he asked me if I wanted a job. I've been here ever since. This is the only job I've had, except for a summer working on a farm with my father when I was 16.

"Monte has been like a second father to me. He took me under his wing and taught me about metals and heavy equipment."

David Fazende

"After a little time in the Air Force and working various other jobs, I answered an ad for a welder at Moses Lake Iron & Metal. That was in 1969 and I'm still here. Working at the junkyard has been more enjoyable than any of my other jobs. It must be or I wouldn't still be here after 30 years. Monte has been good to me — there's a closeness like family."

Tom Tenaglia

"In 1974, when I was 19 years old, I heard there was a job opening at Moses Lake Iron & Metal. After graduating from Moses Lake High School the year before and spending a year doing farm work, which I didn't like, I stopped by and applied for the job. I find the work interesting and enjoyable. I seem to be doing something different every day, not the same thing day-in and day-out, and a lot of interesting people stop by the shop to visit with Monte."

Epilogue, Part 7

The final word

When someone asks me, "How are ya, Monte?" I usually reply, "Never had a bad day in my life." There were times when I wouldn't have said that because things certainly weren't so great. Now I realize that every situation I experienced during my life, even the most fearful and horrifying ones, could have been worse.

It's for sure that being honest, working hard and being nice to people has paid off for me. I believe many other people could benefit by following that same simple philosophy. However, one person can't force even a simple philosophy on another and I wouldn't want to do that. It's true that some things in life must be learned and how each individual lives their life is up to them.

Some people have asked if I am bitter toward my father's new wife, my stepmother. I must admit that I did harbor a resentment for many years. Then one day I realized that if it wasn't for that woman, I wouldn't be where I am today. It truly was the Lord's will that I experience some bad times to help me understand the ups and downs of life.

Today I have as much as an old hobo could hope for and I live a comfortable life. I'm still the boss at Moses Lake Iron & Metal and work there Monday through Saturday. I operate the scales, weighing vehicles as they bring scrap metal in and again when they leave empty. I then write a check giving the person driving that vehicle their due, along with a few pieces of candy of course.

Part of my job requires me to go to the post office and the bank every day. Along the way I see old friends and meet new ones. They all get something from this old hobo, even if it's just a smile and a few pieces of candy. When a person likes what they are doing, going to work isn't something that's painful. I enjoy visiting with my old friends and meeting new ones that stop at my office. I'm productive and my time at work is good.

I spend every Sunday morning at my museum, The House of Poverty, where I write letters, read a book and listen to the radio. Sometimes I act as tour guide if a car stops and the people want to see inside the museum. Before departing, I always crank up the old Victrola and listen to a song titled "*The Dying Hobo.*" I consider the effort to be a tribute to all my hobo friends that have passed on before me. The song refers to an old hobo catching the west-bound train, meaning the hobo has died. I don't dwell on the song in an unhealthy way, but each week it helps me put my life in perspective. At noon, I go home to my lovely wife Ruth, and we go for a drive in the country.

Working at Moses Lake Iron & Metal and spending time at the museum is just one part of my life these days. I'm blessed with a wonderful wife, a great family and many close friends. There are times when we get together and share the attachment, fondness and camaraderie that family and friends offer. An example would be when Ruth and I recently spent Christmas Eve at Karen and Wayne's house. Our grandsons, Larry and Steve, were there along with Steve's wife Shari and my great grandsons Jacob and Kyle.

We shared an evening meal, then retired to the living room to visit when Garnet Wilson and Dennis Clay arrived. We talked and gifts were exchanged, then everyone went home. The feeling of love and friendship that was shared that night is a true treasure to me.

Some would call this the autumn of my life. If so, I hope it is a long season. It wouldn't hurt my feelings any to continue working and enjoying my family and friends for many years into the future. But even an old hobo knows that life doesn't go on forever.

However, until my time on this earth is complete, when I catch that west-bound train, I plan to continue living this lifestyle.

If you are ever in Moses Lake, come by and visit me at Moses Lake Iron and Metal or my museum; The House of Poverty. You are always welcome.

The Reverend N. J. Holm and his family. This was taken shortly after my mother died. Gary is on the left, with Anna behind and Norman in front of her. My father is seated in the middle with Paul on his knee. Signie is behind my father. That's me beside Paul and Oscar is behind me.

When I was 2 years old, I had hair and didn't wear any shoes.

My mother and father were married in 1908. This is their wedding picture.

The graves of my mother, right, and my aunt at the Rapelje cemetary.

This is my father with his congregation at the church he built in Rapelje. The picture was taken on June 3, 1925. I believe that's me, fourth from the right, in the front row.

Here I am in the new clothes bought from the Minneapolis Woolen Mills man. I believe this pricture was taken at the Hensen Ranch after I'd spent several months on the range. That's why I have the new clothes.

This is what it looked like on the range when I was herding sheep. I'm sitting on the step to my wagon and the right bumper of Mr. Hensen's truck is visible on the right side of the picture. There are 3,000 sheep in the background. Mr. Hensen took this photograph.

That's me with my in-laws, the Gulbrandsons. Ruth's mother and father are next to me. Her sister, Helene, is behind them and her brother, Ronald, is on the right.

These are the rugged mountains around Silverton where Ruth and I rented a cabin when we were frist married. Our cabin is in this picture, but it is hudden behind some trees in the middle of the photograph. All that is visible is the peak of the roof.

Relaxing on the front porch was a favorite way for Ruth and me to spend time at the cabin.

This is our first house in Everett. That's Ruth's
mother on the front step with an unidentified person.

Ruth and Karen standing in the front yard
of our house.

Here I am in my dress uniform.

Eric Johnson and I outside our barracks
at Sheppard Field, Withita Falls, Texas.

Eric Shedin and I posed for this picture when Ruth and I went to Silverton for a visit in 1940. Eric had a top hat in his store and he asked me to wear it for the photo. His brother, Albert, had passed away before this visit.

George (Cowboy) Pruitt and I were good friends. He was a hobo like me, and we enjoyed sharing memories of riding the rails. George spent every Christmas at my house for over 30 years. He and I went out to dinner together once a week for at least that long. My grandsons knew him as Uncle George.

Engine Number 557 on a run in Alaska. Here she is bound for Palmer and the first Alaska State Fair. The engine now sits in my yard as the main attraction of The House of Poverty Museum.

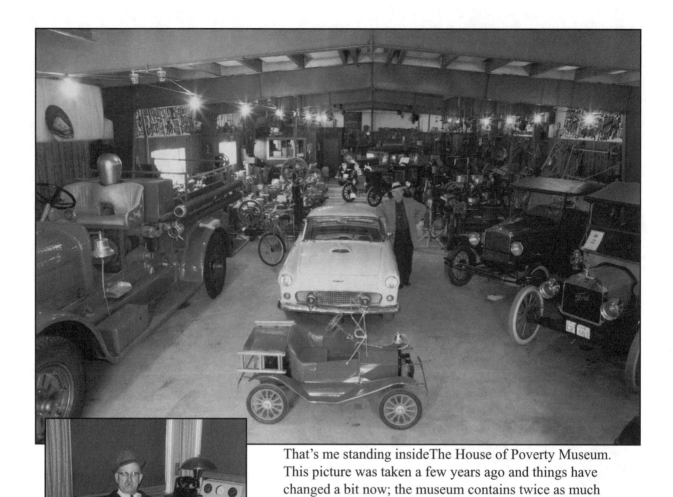

That's me standing insideThe House of Poverty Museum. This picture was taken a few years ago and things have changed a bit now; the museum contains twice as much stuff and the exhibits are closer together.

Sometimes I go to the Mon-Road Railroad Presidential car and relax for a while.

This small Hershal locomotive engine was used in the first World's Fair in New York.

Below are my great grandsons, Jacob and Kyle.

This is my family in front of The House of Poverty Room at the Notaras Lodge in Soap Lake. Left to right is Ruth, Karen, Wayne (behind Karen), Steven, Shari, me, and Larry.

This picture was taken in 1952 at the wedding. I'm on the left, then my father, brother Gary and brother Oscar on the right.

This is my great grandson Jacob riding the Great Northern mini train in front of The House of Poverty Museum.

Ruth is a good shot. When we lived in Silverton, target practicing served as our entertainment.

This is where I took out the Seattle-Everitt interurban in 1939.

I scrapped out a railroad on Vancouver Island near Victoria, British Columbia. That's The Empress Hotel in the background.

This is old 557 getting ready for a run near Moses Lake.

This is our house in Rapelje that my father built.

MON-ROAD RAILROAD

MONTE HOLM, President

JACK CRONKITE, Sec.-Treas.

BOX 1444
MOSES LAKE, WA 98837

Monte's Letters

Letters have become a form of communication that tickles my funny bone. I've made a lot of friends by writing letters and I expect to make a bunch more in the future.

The following letters are an example of some of the fun I've had over the years.

Once a Hobo . . . .

MON-ROAD RAILROAD

MONTE HOLM, President

JACK CRONKITE, Sec.-Treas.

BOX 1444
MOSES LAKE, WA 98837

E. Clark Jones, First Vice President
Joshua Green, Sr., Vice President and Financial
   Consultant, Seattle, Washington
E. C. Olander, V.P. in charge of Western Division
William N. Duncan, V.P. in charge of Eastern Division
Larem Severson, V.P. in charge of Northern Division
Alex Hood, V.P. in charge of Southern Division
John R. Lewis, Senior V.P.
R. E. Lewis, Executive V.P.
Norman Day, V.P. in charge of Traffic
Major General Howard S. McGee, Office of Adjutant
   General, Camp Murray, Washington, V.P. in charge
   of Operations
Brigadier General Lyle Buchanan, Camp Murray,
   Washington, V.P. in charge of Security
Charles J. Edwards, V.P. in charge of Sugar Production
Allen Sircin, V.P. in charge of Livestock Installation
Elmer Yoshino, V.P. in charge of Processing Plants
Roy Kaylor, V.P. in charge of Minerals
Ich Konishi, V.P. in charge of Entertainment
V. H. Noone, V.P. in charge of Communications
Jalmer Moe, V.P. in charge of Engineers
Carl Melcher, V.P. in charge of Wheat Production
C. E. Marchand, V.P. in charge of Production
George C. LaValley, V.P. in charge of Tariff
George Pruitt (Cowboy), V.P. in charge of Hog Production
Gus Tenaglia, V.P. in charge of Investments
Walter Franz, V.P. in charge of Agriculture Division
Nick Badovinis, V.P. in charge of Tunnels
Thomas G. Jones, Riverside, Washington, V.P. in charge
   of History
Duke Moore, V.P. in charge of Speed
Ben I. Peterson, Denver, Colorado, V.P. in charge of
   Prospectors
Howard Passein, V.P. in charge of Freight Rates
O. R. (Slim) Lovins, V.P. in charge of Potato Production
Mode Snead, V.P. in charge of Public Relations
Dick Penhallurick, V.P. in charge of Right-a-ways
Joe Cavender, Spokane, Washington, V.P. and Road
   Foreman of Engineers
John Barrier, Spokane, Washington, V.P. in charge of
   Foreign Relations
Clyde C. Andrews, V.P. in charge of Refrigeration
Fred Gulbrandson, Everett, Washington, V.P. in charge
   of Depot Construction
Earl Terwilleger, Warden, Washington, V.P. in charge
   of Irrigation
P. W. Davis, Seattle, Washington, V.P. in charge of
   Real Estate
R. D. Argue, Seattle, Washington, V.P. in charge of
   Industrial Engineering
Moe Mickelson, Everett, Washington, V.P. in charge
   of Salvage
Bob Bernard, V.P. in charge of Livestock
Chuck McInroy, V.P. in charge of Livestock Appraisal
J. O. English, V.P. in charge of Stocks and Bonds
Tim Bernard, V.P. in charge of Zortman Division
Howard Copenhaver, V.P. in charge of Loans
Eric Ryberg, Salt Lake City, Utah, V.P. in charge of
   Fire Protection
Wade B. Hall, Seattle, Washington, V.P. in charge
   of Lanterns
Brick McFadden, V.P. in charge of Labor Relations
The Rev. Paul Dickson, V.P. and Chaplain
Dr. C. W. Covey, V.P. in charge of Safety
Henry Munroe, V.P. in charge of Catering
Walt Thayer, Wenatchee, Washington, V.P. in charge
   of Photography
Al Anderson, V.P. in charge of Pullman Department
Herb Rademacker, Sunnyside, Washington, V.P. in
   charge of Bearing Maintenance
Fred Weber, Sumner, Washington, V.P. in charge of
   Complaints
Van Bustkern, Spokane, Washington, V.P. in charge
   of Youth Activities
Dr. Charles Stevenson, Spokane, Washington, V.P. in
   charge of Mergers
Woodrow D. Barber, Seattle, Washington, V.P. in
   charge of Organization
Manney Burman, Seattle, Washington, V.P. in charge
   of Purchasing
Andrew Yurkenin, Seattle, Washington, V.P. in charge
   of Dining Cars
Roger Bullas, V.P. in charge of Printed Matter
Dr. J. W. Young, V.P. in charge of the Health of the
   President and Vice Presidents

December 18, 1986

Leone Gacke
4528 Grand
Everett, Washington 98203

Dear Leone:

I read with deep sorrow the passing of my very dear friend and your uncle, Ed Werner. I had the highest respect for Ed that a person could have for another person. He helped me when I really was in need. He maybe has told you but I want to tell you the story and it will show you what a fine and thoughtful man your uncle was. But I am sure you already know that.

So here is the story. I will go back a ways first. My mother died when I was six years old. When I was about eight years old my father remarried and my stepmother and I never got along at all. So when I was 13 years old I left home and only went home once for three hours.

i was a hobo for six years. I walked from Tacoma to Everett 50 years ago about this time of the year. I had ten cents in my pocket and never knew a person in Everett and had never been there before. I had wanted to settle down and get a job - jobs were very very scarce.

Since I had no money, I had to beg for my food. I always asked for work and would work but one has to eat. I would first beg the restaurants and you soon wear out your welcome and Everett was small 50 years ago. Next I would beg the grocery stores and after I wore my welcome out there I would beg houses. So the stores is where your Uncle Ed comes in.

252

MON-ROAD RAILROAD

MONTE HOLM, President

JACK CRONKITE, Sec.-Treas.

BOX 1444
MOSES LAKE, WA 98837

E. Clark Jones, First Vice President
Joshua Green, Sr., Vice President and Financial Consultant, Seattle, Washington
E. C. Olander, V.P. in charge of Western Division
William N. Duncan, V.P. in charge of Eastern Division
Larem Severson, V.P. in charge of Northern Division
Alex Hood, V.P. in charge of Southern Division
John R. Lewis, Senior V.P.
R. E. Lewis, Executive V.P.
Norman Day, V.P. in charge of Traffic
Major General Howard S. McGee, Office of Adjutant General, Camp Murray, Washington, V.P. in charge of Operations
Brigadier General Lyle Buchanan, Camp Murray, Washington, V.P. in charge of Security
Charles J. Edwards, V.P. in charge of Sugar Production
Allen Sircin, V.P. in charge of Livestock Installation
Elmer Yoshino, V.P. in charge of Processing Plants
Roy Kayior, V.P. in charge of Minerals
Ich Konishi, V.P. in charge of Communications
V. H. Noone, V.P. in charge of Engineers
Jalmer Moe, V.P. in charge of Wheat Production
Carl Melcher, V.P. in charge of Production
C. E. Marchand, V.P. in charge of Production
George C. LaValley, V.P. in charge of Tariff
George Pruitt (Cowboy), V.P. in charge of Hog Production
Gus Tenaglia, V.P. in charge of Investments
Walter Franz, V.P. in charge of Agriculture Division
Nick Badovinis, V.P. in charge of Tunnels
Thomas G. Jones, Riverside, Washington, V.P. in charge of History
Duke Moore, V.P. in charge of Speed
Ben I. Peterson, Denver, Colorado, V.P. in charge of Prospectors
Howard Pessein, V.P. in charge of Freight Rates
O. R. (Slim) Lovins, V.P. in charge of Potato Production
Mode Snead, V.P. in charge of Public Relations
Dick Penhallurick, V.P. in charge of Right-a-ways
Joe Cavender, Spokane, Washington, V.P. and Road Foreman of Engineers
John Barrier, Spokane, Washington, V.P. in charge of Foreign Relations
Clyde C. Andrews, V.P. in charge of Refrigeration
Fred Gulbrandson, Everett, Washington, V.P. in charge of Depot Construction
Earl Terwilleger, Warden, Washington, V.P. in charge of Irrigation
P. W. Davis, Seattle, Washington, V.P. in charge of Real Estate
R. D. Argue, Seattle, Washington, V.P. in charge of Industrial Engineering
Moe Mickelson, Everett, Washington, V.P. in charge of Salvage
Bob Bernard, V.P. in charge of Livestock
Chuck McInroy, V.P. in charge of Livestock Appraisal
J. O. English, V.P. in charge of Stocks and Bonds
Tim Bernard, V.P. in charge of Zortman Division
Howard Copenhaver, V.P. in charge of Loans
Eric Ryberg, Salt Lake City, Utah, V.P. in charge of Fire Protection
Wade B. Hall, Seattle, Washington, V.P. in charge of Lanterns
Brick McFadden, V.P. in charge of Labor Relations
The Rev. Paul Dickson, V.P. and Chaplain
Dr. C. W. Covey, V.P. in charge of Safety
Henry Munroe, V.P. in charge of Catering
Walt Thayer, Wenatchee, Washington, V.P. in charge of Photography
Al Anderson, V.P. in charge of Pullman Department
Herb Rademacker, Sunnyside, Washington, V.P. in charge of Bearing Maintenance
Fred Weber, Sumner, Washington, V.P. in charge of Complaints
Van Bustkern, Spokane, Washington, V.P. in charge of Youth Activities
Dr. Charles Stevenson, Spokane, Washington, V.P. in charge of Mergers
Woodrow D. Barber, Seattle, Washington, V.P. in charge of Organization
Manney Burman, Seattle, Washington, V.P. in charge of Purchasing
Andrew Yurkenin, Seattle, Washington, V.P. in charge of Dining Cars
Roger Biallas, V.P. in charge of Printed Matter
Dr. J. W. Young, V.P. in charge of the Health of the President and Vice Presidents

I can remember it as if it were yesterday when I walked into Mr. Werner's store on Colby Ave. I never liked begging but I was forced into it. And survival is real dear. I asked Mr. Werner if he had some work I could do for something to eat. He said, "I have no work but I will give you something to eat", which he did. He must have kind of liked me because he said, "If you need more food stop in". I was polite and waited two days before I returned. He gave me some food and said, "Young fellow, if you are to get a job you should get a hair cut". I said, "I know I need it but I have no money". He said, "I will give you a note and you go down to that barber shop and come back here when you are through", which I did. When I returned he said "That really helped and I can find a little work for you the next time you need food". When I returned again he had me do some work he never needed done. But he knew I would feel better if I worked for my food. The next time I came to his store I told him I had gotten a little work and made enough to get a room on Bayside with a stove and bed in it for $1.25 a week. He thought that was real good and he said, "Mon (that is what he called me as my real name is Monrad) I am going to trust you and let you charge groceries". That was quite a shock as I had never been trusted by anyone before. So I charged groceries for about six weeks and never got enough work to pay Mr. Werner. I could only pay for my room. After six weeks I was ashamed to go in and charge more. It was at least six months before I got enough money to return and pay my bill. I was very proud when I walked into the store and went to Mr. Werner and told him I wished to pay my bill. He looked at me and said, "You know of all the hobos I have

-2-

Once a Hobo . . . .

MON-ROAD RAILROAD

MONTE HOLM, President

JACK CRONKITE, Sec.-Treas.

BOX 1444
MOSES LAKE, WA 98837

E. Clark Jones, First Vice President
Joshua Green, Sr., Vice President and Financial
   Consultant, Seattle, Washington
E. C. Olander, V.P. in charge of Western Division
William N. Duncan, V.P. in charge of Eastern Division
Larem Severson, V.P. in charge of Northern Division
Alex Hood, V.P. in charge of Southern Division
John R. Lewis, Senior V.P.
R. E. Lewis, Executive V.P.
Norman Day, V.P. in charge of Traffic
Major General Howard S. McGee, Office of Adjutant
   General, Camp Murray, Washington, V.P. in charge
   of Operations
Brigadier General Lyle Buchanan, Camp Murray,
   Washington, V.P. in charge of Security
Charles J. Edwards, V.P. in charge of Sugar Production
Allen Sircin, V.P. in charge of Livestock Installation
Elmer Yoshino, V.P. in charge of Processing Plants
Roy Kaylor, V.P. in charge of Minerals
Ich Konishi, V.P. in charge of Entertainment
V. H. Noone, V.P. in charge of Communications
Jalmer Moe, V.P. in charge of Engineers
Carl Melcher, V.P. in charge of Wheat Production
C. E. Marchand, V.P. in charge of Production
George C. LaValley, V.P. in charge of Tariff
George Pruitt (Cowboy), V.P. in charge of Hog Production
Gus Tenaglia, V.P. in charge of Investments
Walter Franz, V.P. in charge of Agriculture Division
Nick Badovinis, V.P. in charge of Tunnels
Thomas G. Jones, Riverside, Washington, V.P. in charge
   of History
Duke Moore, V.P. in charge of Speed
Ben I. Peterson, Denver, Colorado, V.P. in charge of
   Prospectors
Howard Pessein, V.P. in charge of Freight Rates
O. R. (Slim) Lovins, V.P. in charge of Potato Production
Mode Snead, V.P. in charge of Public Relations
Dick Penhallurick, V.P. in charge of Right-a-ways
Joe Cavender, Spokane, Washington, V.P. and Road
   Foreman of Engineers
John Barrier, Spokane, Washington, V.P. in charge of
   Foreign Relations
Clyde C. Andrews, V.P. in charge of Refrigeration
Fred Gulbrandson, Everett, Washington, V.P. in charge
   of Depot Construction
Earl Terwilleger, Warden, Washington, V.P. in charge
   of Irrigation
P. W. Davis, Seattle, Washington, V.P. in charge of
   Real Estate
R. D. Argue, Seattle, Washington, V.P. in charge of
   Industrial Engineering
Moe Mickelson, Everett, Washington, V.P. in charge
   of Salvage
Bob Bernard, V.P. in charge of Livestock
Chuck McInroy, V.P. in charge of Livestock Appraisal
J. O. English, V.P. in charge of Stocks and Bonds
Tim Bernard, V.P. in charge of Zortman Division
Howard Copenhaver, V.P. in charge of Loans
Eric Ryberg, Salt Lake City, Utah, V.P. in charge of
   Fire Protection
Wade B. Hall, Seattle, Washington, V.P. in charge
   of Lanterns
Brick McFadden, V.P. in charge of Labor Relations
The Rev. Paul Dickson, V.P. and Chaplain
Dr. C. W. Covey, V.P. in charge of Safety
Henry Munroe, V.P. in charge of Catering
Walt Thayer, Wenatchee, Washington, V.P. in charge
   of Photography
Al Anderson, V.P. in charge of Pullman Department
Herb Rademacker, Sunnyside, Washington, V.P. in
   charge of Bearing Maintenance
Fred Weber, Sumner, Washington, V.P. in charge of
   Complaints
Van Bustkern, Spokane, Washington, V.P. in charge
   of Youth Activities
Dr. Charles Stevenson, Spokane, Washington, V.P. in
   charge of Mergers
Woodrow D. Barber, Seattle, Washington, V.P. in
   charge of Organization
Manney Burman, Seattle, Washington, V.P. in charge
   of Purchasing
Andrew Yurkenin, Seattle, Washington, V.P. in charge
   of Dining Cars
Roger Biallas, V.P. in charge of Printed Matter
Dr. J. W. Young, V.P. in charge of the Health of the
   President and Vice Presidents

helped (and he helped many) you are the only hobo to return to pay his bill". Mr. Werner said "I don't know how much you owe me. I never saved the slips because I never expected you to return". I said, "Mr. Werner I know just how much I owe you and I am going to pay you. It is $10.80", which was a lot of money at that time. So we became very good friends. Without that trust, faith and help, there is a good chance I maybe would have stayed a hobo. In the condition I was in at the time, a good friend could make the difference.

I often think of the help Mr. Werner gave me and I never turn away a hungry person because you never know what food and a kind word means to one unless you have been there.

The first time I got a chance to buy some scrap iron I could see that I could make some money if I had $300.00. This was some time later. I went to Mr. Werner and told him. As I said before, I think he like me because he said, "Let's go to the bank and I am sure they will loan you $300.00". I still have the bank note and Mr. Werner co-signed it for me. With that kind trust you put all your efforts into being successful.

When we moved to Moses Lake in 1953, we had to sell our house in Everett. By that time Mr. Werner was in the real estate business. I had a party wanting to buy our house and I told him I wanted Mr. Werner to sell them our house so he could get his commission which he earned many years before.

Mr. Werner was one of my very very best friends and it would be so nice if the world had more people like him.

3

254

Monte Holm and Dennis L. Clay

MON-ROAD RAILROAD

MONTE HOLM, President

JACK CRONKITE, Sec.-Treas.

BOX 1444
MOSES LAKE, WA 98837

E. Clark Jones, First Vice President
Joshua Green, Sr., Vice President and Financial
  Consultant, Seattle, Washington
E. C. Olander, V.P. in charge of Western Division
William N. Duncan, V.P. in charge of Eastern Division
Larem Severson, V.P. in charge of Northern Division
Alex Hood, V.P. in charge of Southern Division
John R. Lewis, Senior V.P.
R. E. Lewis, Executive V.P.
Norman Day, V.P. in charge of Traffic
Major General Howard S. McGee, Office of Adjutant
  General, Camp Murray, Washington, V.P. in charge
  of Operations
Brigadier General Lyle Buchanan, Camp Murray,
  Washington, V.P. in charge of Security
Charles J. Edwards, V.P. in charge of Sugar Production
Allen Sircin, V.P. in charge of Livestock Installation
Elmer Yoshino, V.P. in charge of Processing Plants
Roy Kaylor, V.P. in charge of Minerals
Ich Konishi, V.P. in charge of Entertainment
V. H. Noone, V.P. in charge of Communications
Jalmer Moe, V.P. in charge of Engineers
Carl Melcher, V.P. in charge of Wheat Production
C. E. Marchand, V.P. in charge of Production
George C. LaValley, V.P. in charge of Tariff
George Pruitt (Cowboy), V.P. in charge of Hog Production
Gus Tenaglia, V.P. in charge of Investments
Walter Franz, V.P. in charge of Agriculture Division
Nick Badovinis, V.P. in charge of Tunnels
Thomas G. Jones, Riverside, Washington, V.P. in charge
  of History
Duke Moore, V.P. in charge of Speed
Ben I. Peterson, Denver, Colorado, V.P. in charge of
  Prospectors
Howard Pessein, V.P. in charge of Freight Rates
O. R. (Slim) Lovins, V.P. in charge of Potato Production
Mode Snead, V.P. in charge of Public Relations
Dick Penhallurick, V.P. in charge of Right-a-ways
Joe Cavender, Spokane, Washington, V.P. and Road
  Foreman of Engineers
John Barrier, Spokane, Washington, V.P. in charge of
  Foreign Relations
Clyde C. Andrews, V.P. in charge of Refrigeration
Fred Gulbrandson, Everett, Washington, V.P. in charge
  of Depot Construction
Earl Terwilleger, Warden, Washington, V.P. in charge
  of Irrigation
P. W. Davis, Seattle, Washington, V.P. in charge of
  Real Estate
R. D. Argue, Seattle, Washington, V.P. in charge of
  Industrial Engineering
Moe Mickelson, Everett, Washington, V.P. in charge
  of Salvage
Bob Bernard, V.P. in charge of Livestock
Chuck McInroy, V.P. in charge of Livestock Appraisal
J. O. English, V.P. in charge of Stocks and Bonds
Tim Bernard, V.P. in charge of Zortman Division
Howard Copenhaver, V.P. in charge of Loans
Eric Ryberg, Salt Lake City, Utah, V.P. in charge of
  Fire Protection
Wade B. Hall, Seattle, Washington, V.P. in charge
  of Lanterns
Brick McFadden, V.P. in charge of Labor Relations
The Rev. Paul Dickson, V.P. and Chaplain
Dr. C. W. Covey, V.P. in charge of Safety
Henry Munroe, V.P. in charge of Catering
Walt Thayer, Wenatchee, Washington, V.P. in charge
  of Photography
Al Anderson, V.P. in charge of Pullman Department
Herb Rademacker, Sunnyside, Washington, V.P. in
  charge of Bearing Maintenance
Fred Weber, Sumner, Washington, V.P. in charge of
  Complaints
Van Bustkern, Spokane, Washington, V.P. in charge
  of Youth Activities
Dr. Charles Stevenson, Spokane, Washington, V.P. in
  charge of Mergers
Woodrow D. Barber, Seattle, Washington, V.P. in
  charge of Organization
Manney Burman, Seattle, Washington, V.P. in charge
  of Purchasing
Andrew Yurkenin, Seattle, Washington, V.P. in charge
  of Dining Cars
Roger Biallas, V.P. in charge of Printed Matter
Dr. J. W. Young, V.P. in charge of the Health of the
  President and Vice Presidents

I wanted you to know the full story
of our meeting. I do hope you stop to
visit us when you are in Moses Lake. I
would like to show you our museum.

You had a wonderful uncle.

Sincerely,

Monte Holm

Monte Holm

4

Dear Mr Holm —

As you can see by the enclosed article —
Uncle Ed passed away — He had a stroke the first
of November and went into a nursing home and
was there a couple of weeks and suffered kidney failure
He always had one of your calendars in his kitchen
and told everyone about your personal life story —
You gave him many hours of happyness

Thank you for remembering him

Sincerely

Leone Gacke

(Eds' niece)

Edwin L. Werner

Edwin L. Werner, 92, died Nov. 29, 1986, in a local nursing home.

He was born Nov. 12, 1894, in Minneapolis, Minn. He came to Everett in 1902 with his family. As a young man, he worked in Alaska before entering the Navy during WWI. He spent many years in the grocery business and then opened his own real estate company where he trained many of Everett's present real estate people. He helped organize the Everett Boys Club and was an officer in the organization for many years. He taught swimming at the local YMCA. He was a life-time member of Everett Elks Lodge no. 479 and the American Legion, and held office in many of the local civic organizations.

He was preceded in death by his wife, Lilly; son, Roger; and granddaughter, Jennifer.

He leaves a sister, Minnette and her husband, Paul Strout, Sr. of Seattle; daughter-in-law, Marilyn Werner of Australia; three granddaughters, Gretchen and her husband, Mark Block of Aptos, Calif., Loree and husband, Richard George of Novato, Calif., and Joslyn Werner of Hawaii; three great-grandchildren; and many nieces and nephews.

At his request, no services will be held. Burial will be at Evergreen Cemetery, Everett.

Memorials may be made to the Everett Boys Club, the Providence Foundation or a charity of your choice.

Arrangements under the direction of Solie Funeral Home.

Monte Holm and Dennis L. Clay

MONTE HOLM, President

JACK CRONKITE, Sec.-Treas.

BOX 1444
MOSES LAKE, WA 98837

E. Clark Jones, First Vice President
Joshua Green, Sr., Vice President and Financial
 Consultant, Seattle, Washington
E. C. Olander, V.P. in charge of Western Division
William N. Duncan, V.P. in charge of Eastern Division
Larem Severson, V.P. in charge of Northern Division
Alex Hood, V.P. in charge of Southern Division
John R. Lewis, Senior V.P.
R. E. Lewis, Executive V.P.
Norman Day, V.P. in charge of Traffic
Major General Howard S. McGee, Office of Adjutant
 General, Camp Murray, Washington, V.P. in charge
 of Operations
Brigadier General Lyle Buchanan, Camp Murray,
 Washington, V.P. in charge of Security
Charles J. Edwards, V.P. in charge of Sugar Production
Allen Sircin, V.P. in charge of Livestock Installation
Elmer Yoshino, V.P. in charge of Processing Plants
Roy Kaylor, V.P. in charge of Minerals
Ich Konishi, V.P. in charge of Entertainment
V. H. Noone, V.P. in charge of Communications
Jalmer Moe, V.P. in charge of Engineers
Carl Melcher, V.P. in charge of Wheat Production
C. E. Marchand, V.P. in charge of Production
George C. LaValley, V.P. in charge of Tariff
George Pruitt (Cowboy), V.P. in charge of Hog Production
Gus Tenaglia, V.P. in charge of Investments
Walter Franz, V.P. in charge of Agriculture Division
Nick Badovinis, V.P. in charge of Tunnels
Thomas G. Jones, Riverside, Washington, V.P. in charge
 of History
Duke Moore, V.P. in charge of Speed
Ben I. Peterson, Denver, Colorado, V.P. in charge of
 Prospectors
Howard Pessein, V.P. in charge of Freight Rates
O. R. (Slim) Lovins, V.P. in charge of Potato Production
Mode Snead, V.P. in charge of Public Relations
Dick Penhallurick, V.P. in charge of Right-a-ways
Joe Cavender, Spokane, Washington, V.P. and Road
 Foreman of Engineers
John Barrier, Spokane, Washington, V.P. in charge of
 Foreign Relations
Clyde C. Andrews, V.P. in charge of Refrigeration
Fred Gulbrandson, Everett, Washington, V.P. in charge
 of Depot Construction
Earl Terwilleger, Warden, Washington, V.P. in charge
 of Irrigation
P. W. Davis, Seattle, Washington, V.P. in charge of
 Real Estate
R. D. Argue, Seattle, Washington, V.P. in charge of
 Industrial Engineering
Moe Mickelson, Everett, Washington, V.P. in charge
 of Salvage
Bob Bernard, V.P. in charge of Livestock
Chuck McInroy, V.P. in charge of Livestock Appraisal
J. O. English, V.P. in charge of Stocks and Bonds
Tim Bernard, V.P. in charge of Zortman Division
Howard Copenhaver, V.P. in charge of Loans
Eric Ryberg, Salt Lake City, Utah, V.P. in charge of
 Fire Protection
Wade B. Hall, Seattle, Washington, V.P. in charge
 of Lanterns
Brick McFadden V.P. in charge of Labor Relations
The Rev. Paul Dickson, V.P. and Chaplain
Dr. C. W. Covey, V.P. in charge of Safety
Henry Munroe, V.P. in charge of Catering
Walt Thayer, Wenatchee, Washington, V.P. in charge
 of Photography
Al Anderson, V.P. in charge of Pullman Department
Herb Rademacker, Sunnyside, Washington, V.P. in
 charge of Bearing Maintenance
Fred Weber, Sumner, Washington, V.P. in charge of
 Complaints
Van Bustkern, Spokane, Washington, V.P. in charge
 of Youth Activities
Dr. Charles Stevenson, Spokane, Washington, V.P. in
 charge of Mergers
Woodrow D. Barber, Seattle, Washington, V.P. in
 charge of Organization
Manney Burman, Seattle, Washington, V.P. in charge
 of Purchasing
Andrew Yurkenin, Seattle, Washington, V.P. in charge
 of Dining Cars
Roger Biallas, V.P. in charge of Printed Matter
Dr. J. W. Young, V.P. in charge of the Health of the
 President and Vice Presidents

January 6, 1998

Dear Ted,

You are one of the nicest men in the whole world. You have made this Christmas the best that two guitar-playin' young men (Larry and Steven, my two grandsons) and this old hobo, ever had. You should have seen their faces light up when they saw the autographed pictures of you, their hero, that our mutual friend, Dennis Clay, brought to our house on Christmas eve. That was so very nice of you to send them along, Ted.

I am just an old hobo from the late 1920s and 1930s that is blessed with the greatest family and friends that anyone could have. Dennis tells me you play "hard rock" music. Well, I have to tell you that I'm familiar with the term "hard rock," but it has nothing to do with music. When I was riding the rails as a hobo, the Railroad Bulls would dangle a coupling pin under the train cars from a rope, which would send rocks flying past me when I had to ride the rods under the car. Those rocks were nothing but hard.

I want to invite you and your family to come to Moses Lake and I would love to show you the museum (The House of Poverty) this old hobo put together, and to meet my family. It would be the greatest day in our grandson's lives. I will even cook hobo stew for you Ted and serve you in our private railroad car that hauled Presidents Wilson and Truman.

I'm sure a visit to Moses Lake and the House of Poverty is a trip you would never forget Ted. I know this old hobo and his family would cherish the memories forever.

Thanks Ted.

Your Friend,

Monte Holm

Monte Holm

Enclosed:
Pictures of me at The House of Poverty museum, at my office at Moses Lake Iron and Metal, several chapters from my autobiography that Dennis and I are working on, a calendar (with me, Larry, Steven and my great-grandson, Jacob, standing by my train), and Dennis' Little Bits & Pieces booklet that has a few stories about me in it.

Shortly after I wrote this letter to Ted, Dennis Clay visited with his Rock-Star friend in Las Vegas. Before their scheduled radio interview, Ted asked Dennis to relay to me his best wishes *to me.*

Ted said he had read the letter on his own radio show in Detroit and that he would contact me the next time he traveled out this way.

As always, Ted, you can stop by anytime: You are always welcome.

BNSF KENNETH CRANE   **Burlington Northern Santa Fe**

Director Business Continuity/Y2K   777 Main Street
Fort Worth, Texas 76102-5384

June 4, 1999   **Patron ID 4160**

MOSES LAKE IRON & METAL
PO BOX 448
MOSES LAKE, WA 988370068

Dear MOSES LAKE IRON & METAL

During our Year 2000 compliance project we identified your company as a critical Intermodal or Car Load trading partner. It is important that we develop a clear picture of what will happen the first few days, or even months, of the Year 2000. Consequently, we would like you to address specific questions related to your Accounts Payable process.

We understand that many of our trading partners utilize some combination of Electronic Commerce and manual transactions to conduct their daily business. For some applications Electronic Commerce may be the primary vehicle for notifications with manual transactions being used only in the event of an outage. Other applications may rely exclusively on manual transactions. Most companies fall somewhere in between, utilizing a combination of Electronic Commerce and Manual transactions. Three areas have been identified as critical to an Accounts Payable process:

1.) Transmission of the Bill of Lading document to the carrier (BNSF) in an accurate and timely fashion.
2.) Ability to receive a Freight Bill from the carrier (BNSF).
3.) Ability to process a Freight Bill through an accounts payable system.

Please use the attached questionnaire to identify you level of Y2K compliance. Return the completed questionnaire by June 15, 1999. You can contact me at (817) 333-5605, or Kelly Christian at (817) 333-1309, with your compliance questions concerning this request.

Sincerely,

Kenneth Crane
Director Business Continuity/Y2K

KHC/kjb

Enc.

Once a Hobo . . . .

BNSF

KENNETH CRANE

Director Business Continuity/Y2K

Burlington Northern Santa Fe

777 Main Street
Fort Worth, Texas 76102-5384

Patron ID **4160**

Accounts Payable Year 2000 Compliance Questionnaire

Company Contact: _____

Company Name: _____

Contact Title: _____

Company Address: _____

Circle One

1. Will your information systems and internal processes, used to support your   Yes No
Accounts Payable process, be Year 2000 compliant by January 1, 2000? Year 2000
Compliance is defined as being able to accurately process date data from, into
and between the twentieth and the twenty-first century including leap year calculations.
The system/process must continue to function accurately without interruption to normal
business processes.

2. Will you be able to transmit Bill of Lading documents to the carrier (BNSF) on January 1, 2000
to the same extent, as you are able to do so on December 31, 1999?

Electronic Commerce	EDI (404)	Yes No
Other transaction method i.e. fax	_____	Yes No

3. Will you be able to receive Freight Bills from the carrier (BNSF) on January 1, 2000
to the same extent, as you are able to do so on December 31, 1999?

Electronic Commerce	EDI (410)	Yes No
Other transaction method i.e. mail	_____	Yes No

4. Will you be able to generate an instrument of payment on January 1, 2000
to the same extent, as you are able to do so on December 31, 1999?

Electronic Commerce	EDI (820)	Yes No
Other transaction method i.e. check, wire, ACH	_____	Yes No

5. In answering the above questions, have you taken into account the Year 2000 compliance of your
suppliers, service providers, and other business relationships to the extent such compliance may impact
your ability to conduct business with BNSF in the Year 2000?

Yes   No

Signature *Monte Holm*   *If the Post office*

Title: *Boss*   *Runs I will Pay by Check*

Date: *6/11/99*   *if not by Corrior Pidgen*

Please return this questionnaire to Kelly Christian, Y2K Project Lead, 817-333-7147 (fax).. Any questions
concerning it may be addressed to Jim Streadwick at (995) 298-2151 or via e-mail to kelly.christian@bnsf.com.

So don't worry about Y K E Kenneth

MON-ROAD RAILROAD

MONTE HOLM, President

JACK CRONKITE, Sec.-Treas.

BOX 1444
MOSES LAKE, WA 98837

E. Clark Jones, First Vice President
Joshua Green, Sr., Vice President and Financial
  Consultant, Seattle, Washington
E. C. Olander, V.P. in charge of Western Division
William N. Duncan, V.P. in charge of Eastern Division
Larem Severson, V.P. in charge of Northern Division
Alex Hood, V.P. in charge of Southern Division
John R. Lewis, Senior V.P.
R. E. Lewis, Executive V.P.
Norman Day, V.P. in charge of Traffic
Major General Howard S. McGee, Office of Adjutant
  General, Camp Murray, Washington, V.P. in charge
  of Operations
Brigadier General Lyle Buchanan, Camp Murray,
  Washington, V.P. in charge of Security
Charles J. Edwards, V.P. in charge of Sugar Production
Allen Sircin, V.P. in charge of Livestock Installation
Elmer Yoshino, V.P. in charge of Processing Plants
Roy Kaylor, V.P. in charge of Minerals
Ich Konishi, V.P. in charge of Entertainment
V. H. Noone, V.P. in charge of Communications
Jalmer Moe, V.P. in charge of Engineers
Carl Melcher, V.P. in charge of Wheat Production
C. E. Marchand, V.P. in charge of Production
George C. LaValley, V.P. in charge of Tariff
George Pruitt (Cowboy), V.P. in charge of Hog Production
Gus Tenaglia, V.P. in charge of Investments
Walter Franz, V.P. in charge of Agriculture Division
Nick Badovinis, V.P. in charge of Tunnels
Thomas G. Jones, Riverside, Washington, V.P. in charge
  of History
Duke Moore, V.P. in charge of Speed
Ben I. Peterson, Denver, Colorado, V.P. in charge of
  Prospectors
Howard Pessein, V.P. in charge of Freight Rates
O. R. (Slim) Lovins, V.P. in charge of Potato Production
Mode Snead, V.P. in charge of Public Relations
Dick Penhallurick, V.P. in charge of Right-a-ways
Joe Cavender, Spokane, Washington, V.P. and Road
  Foreman of Engineers
John Barrier, Spokane, Washington, V.P. in charge of
  Foreign Relations
Clyde C. Andrews, V.P. in charge of Refrigeration
Fred Gulbrandson, Everett, Washington, V.P. in charge
  of Depot Construction
Earl Terwilleger, Warden, Washington, V.P. in charge
  of Irrigation
P. W. Davis, Seattle, Washington, V.P. in charge of
  Real Estate
R. D. Argue, Seattle, Washington, V.P. in charge of
  Industrial Engineering
Moe Mickelson, Everett, Washington, V.P. in charge
  of Salvage
Bob Bernard, V.P. in charge of Livestock
Chuck McInroy, V.P. in charge of Livestock Appraisal
J. O. English, V.P. in charge of Stocks and Bonds
Tim Bernard, V.P. in charge of Zortman Division
Howard Copenhaver, V.P. in charge of Loans
Eric Ryberg, Salt Lake City, Utah, V.P. in charge of
  Fire Protection
Wade B. Hall, Seattle, Washington, V.P. in charge
  of Lanterns
Brick McFadden V.P. in charge of Labor Relations
The Rev. Paul Dickson, V.P. and Chaplain
Dr. C. W. Covey, V.P. in charge of Safety
Henry Munroe, V.P. in charge of Catering
Walt Thayer, Wenatchee, Washington, V.P. in charge
  of Photography
Al Anderson, V.P. in charge of Pullman Department
Herb Rademacker, Sunnyside, Washington, V.P. in
  charge of Bearing Maintenance
Fred Weber, Sumner, Washington, V.P. in charge of
  Complaints
Van Bustkern, Spokane, Washington, V.P. in charge
  of Youth Activities
Dr. Charles Stevenson, Spokane, Washington, V.P. in
  charge of Mergers
Woodrow D. Barber, Seattle, Washington, V.P. in
  charge of Organization
Manney Burman, Seattle, Washington, V.P. in charge
  of Purchasing
Andrew Yurkenin, Seattle, Washington, V.P. in charge
  of Dining Cars
Roger Biallas, V.P. in charge of Printed Matter
Dr. J. W. Young, V.P. in charge of the Health of the
  President and Vice Presidents

Dear Mr Kenneth Crone- 6/10/99

I want to thank you for your letter about Y2K.

I first will tell you about my Railroad. It is not as long as yours but jest as wide.

I was a Hoboe during the late 20 and early thirties for 6 years and the Railroad Bulls kiked me off of so many trains I use to tell them that someday I will own my my own Railroad and you won't be able to kike me off.

So I bought the last steam Locomotive to run on the Alaska Railroad and a Private Railroad car that houled President Wilson and President truman and this Y2K buisness I know nothing about and I don't plane to learn about it.

I have a Junk yard and I ship My scrap iron on the BN.17. And you people give me good service and I pay my freight bills by check when I get them.

Once a Hobo . . . .

MON-ROAD RAILROAD

MONTE HOLM, President

JACK CRONKITE, Sec.-Treas.

BOX 1444
MOSES LAKE, WA 98837

E. Clark Jones, First Vice President
Joshua Green, Sr., Vice President and Financial
    Consultant, Seattle, Washington
E. C. Olander, V.P. in charge of Western Division
William N. Duncan, V.P. in charge of Eastern Division
Larem Severson, V.P. in charge of Northern Division
Alex Hood, V.P. in charge of Southern Division
John R. Lewis, Senior V.P.
R. E. Lewis, Executive V.P.
Norman Day, V.P. in charge of Traffic
Major General Howard S. McGee, Office of Adjutant
    General, Camp Murray, Washington, V.P. in charge
    of Operations
Brigadier General Lyle Buchanan, Camp Murray,
    Washington, V.P. in charge of Security
Charles J. Edwards, V.P. in charge of Sugar Production
Allen Sircin, V.P. in charge of Livestock Installation
Elmer Yoshino, V.P. in charge of Processing Plants
Roy Kaylor, V.P. in charge of Minerals
Ich Konishi, V.P. in charge of Entertainment
V. H. Noone, V.P. in charge of Communications
Jalmer Moe, V.P. in charge of Engineers
Carl Melcher, V.P. in charge of Wheat Production
C. E. Marchand, V.P. in charge of Production
George C. LaValley, V.P. in charge of Tariff
George Pruitt (Cowboy), V.P. in charge of Hog Production
Gus Tenaglia, V.P. in charge of Investments
Walter Franz, V.P. in charge of Agriculture Division
Nick Badovinis, V.P. in charge of Tunnels
Thomas G. Jones, Riverside, Washington, V.P. in charge
    of History
Duke Moore, V.P. in charge of Speed
Ben I. Peterson, Denver, Colorado, V.P. in charge of
    Prospectors
Howard Pessein, V.P. in charge of Freight Rates
O. R. (Slim) Lovins, V.P. in charge of Potato Production
Mode Snead, V.P. in charge of Public Relations
Dick Penhallurick, V.P. in charge of Right-a-ways
Joe Cavender, Spokane, Washington, V.P. and Road
    Foreman of Engineers
John Barrier, Spokane, Washington, V.P. in charge of
    Foreign Relations
Clyde C. Andrews, V.P. in charge of Refrigeration
Fred Gulbrandson, Everett, Washington, V.P. in charge
    of Depot Construction
Earl Terwilleger, Warden, Washington, V.P. in charge
    of Irrigation
P. W. Davis, Seattle, Washington, V.P. in charge of
    Real Estate
R. D. Argue, Seattle, Washington, V.P. in charge of
    Industrial Engineering
Moe Mickelson, Everett, Washington, V.P. in charge
    of Salvage
Bob Bernard, V.P. in charge of Livestock
Chuck McInroy, V.P. in charge of Livestock Appraisal
J. O. English, V.P. in charge of Stocks and Bonds
Tim Bernard, V.P. in charge of Zortman Division
Howard Copenhaver, V.P. in charge of Loans
Eric Ryberg, Salt Lake City, Utah, V.P. in charge of
    Fire Protection
Wade B. Hall, Seattle, Washington, V.P. in charge
    of Lanterns
Brick McFadden V.P. in charge of Labor Relations
The Rev. Paul Dickson, V.P. and Chaplain
Dr. C. W. Covey, V.P. in charge of Safety
Henry Munroe, V.P. in charge of Catering
Walt Thayer, Wenatchee, Washington, V.P. in charge
    of Photography
Al Anderson, V.P. in charge of Pullman Department
Herb Rademacker, Sunnyside, Washington, V.P. in
    charge of Bearing Maintenance
Fred Weber, Sumner, Washington, V.P. in charge of
    Complaints
Van Bustkern, Spokane, Washington, V.P. in charge
    of Youth Activities
Dr. Charles Stevenson, Spokane, Washington, V.P. in
    charge of Mergers
Woodrow D. Barber, Seattle, Washington, V.P. in
    charge of Organization
Manney Burman, Seattle, Washington, V.P. in charge
    of Purchasing
Andrew Yurkenin, Seattle, Washington, V.P. in charge
    of Dining Cars
Roger Biallas, V.P. in charge of Printed Matter
Dr. J. W. Young, V.P. in charge of the Health of the
    President and Vice Presidents

And if Y 2 K comes and being a Old Hoboe I will be prepaired for Y 2 K with plenty of food to make lot of Hoboe Stew.

And if things get to tough for you during Y 2 K Kenneth I will put on a little more Hoboe Stew for you and you might bring Jest Kelly along Not all of the B N S F. Employer because my Pot is not quit, that big.

I will enclose a colander with a picture of one of my train and my two grandsons and 2 great grandsons on the picture.

I also have the Burlington Northern Mini train a third scale locomotive caboose and gondola It is beautiful

And if you are Ever this way be sure to stop in you are always welcome at the House of Poverty and don't worry about Y 2 K Kenneth it wont be real bad.

Your Freind
Monte Holm

262

BNSF

KENNETH H. CRANE

Director Business Continuity/Y2K†

June 16, 1999

Monte Holm
President
Moses Lake Iron & Metal
P. O. Box 448
Moses Lake, WA 98837-0068

Dear Monte:

Thank you for your prompt response to our Y2K survery.

Your letter was truly a joy to read and really brightened up my day
with me and sharing it with my peers.

The photographs are delightful and I will certainly take you up on
through your area.

Please accept these trinkets as a token of my appreciation.

Sincerely,

Kenneth H. Crane
Director Business Continuity/Y2K

KHC/kjb

Enc.

Once a Hobo . . . .

MON-ROAD RAILROAD

MONTE HOLM, President

JACK CRONKITE, Sec.-Treas.

BOX 1444
MOSES LAKE, WA 98837

E. Clark Jones, First Vice President
Joshua Green, Sr., Vice President and Financial
    Consultant, Seattle, Washington
E. C. Olander, V.P. in charge of Western Division
William N. Duncan, V.P. in charge of Eastern Division
Larem Severson, V.P. in charge of Northern Division
Alex Hood, V.P. in charge of Southern Division
John R. Lewis, Senior V.P.
R. E. Lewis, Executive V.P.
Norman Day, V.P. in charge of Traffic
Major General Howard S. McGee, Office of Adjutant
    General, Camp Murray, Washington, V.P. in charge
    of Operations
Brigadier General Lyle Buchanan, Camp Murray,
    Washington, V.P. in charge of Security
Charles J. Edwards, V.P. in charge of Sugar Production
Allen Sircin, V.P. in charge of Livestock Installation
Elmer Yoshino, V.P. in charge of Processing Plants
Roy Kaylor, V.P. in charge of Minerals
Ich Konishi, V.P. in charge of Entertainment
V. H. Noone, V.P. in charge of Communications
Jalmer Moe, V.P. in charge of Engineers
Carl Melcher, V.P. in charge of Wheat Production
C. E. Marchand, V.P. in charge of Production
George C. LaValley, V.P. in charge of Tariff
George Pruitt (Cowboy), V.P. in charge of Hog Production
Gus Tenaglia, V.P. in charge of Investments
Walter Franz, V.P. in charge of Agriculture Division
Nick Badovinis, V.P. in charge of Tunnels
Thomas G. Jones, Riverside, Washington, V.P. in charge
    of History
Duke Moore, V.P. in charge of Speed
Ben I. Peterson, Denver, Colorado, V.P. in charge of
    Prospectors
Howard Pessein, V.P. in charge of Freight Rates
O. R. (Slim) Lovins, V.P. in charge of Potato Production
Mode Snead, V.P. in charge of Public Relations
Dick Penhallurick, V.P. in charge of Right-a-ways
Joe Cavender, Spokane, Washington, V.P. and Road
    Foreman of Engineers
John Barrier, Spokane, Washington, V.P. in charge of
    Foreign Relations
Clyde C. Andrews, V.P. in charge of Refrigeration
Fred Gulbrandson, Everett, Washington, V.P. in charge
    of Depot Construction
Earl Terwilleger, Warden, Washington, V.P. in charge
    of Irrigation
P. W. Davis, Seattle, Washington, V.P. in charge of
    Real Estate
R. D. Argue, Seattle, Washington, V.P. in charge of
    Industrial Engineering
Moe Mickelson, Everett, Washington, V.P. in charge
    of Salvage
Bob Bernard, V.P. in charge of Livestock
Chuck McInroy, V.P. in charge of Livestock Appraisal
J. O. English, V.P. in charge of Stocks and Bonds
Tim Bernard, V.P. in charge of Zortman Division
Howard Copenhaver, V.P. in charge of Loans
Eric Ryberg, Salt Lake City, Utah, V.P. in charge of
    Fire Protection
Wade B. Hall, Seattle, Washington, V.P. in charge
    of Lanterns
Brick McFadden V.P. in charge of Labor Relations
The Rev. Paul Dickson, V.P. and Chaplain
Dr. C. W. Covey, V.P. in charge of Safety
Henry Munroe, V.P. in charge of Catering
Walt Thayer, Wenatchee, Washington, V.P. in charge
    of Photography
Al Anderson, V.P. in charge of Pullman Department
Herb Rademacker, Sunnyside, Washington, V.P. in
    charge of Bearing Maintenance
Fred Weber, Sumner, Washington, V.P. in charge of
    Complaints
Van Bustkern, Spokane, Washington, V.P. in charge
    of Youth Activities
Dr. Charles Stevenson, Spokane, Washington, V.P. in
    charge of Mergers
Woodrow D. Barber, Seattle, Washington, V.P. in
    charge of Organization
Manney Burman, Seattle, Washington, V.P. in charge
    of Purchasing
Andrew Yurkenin, Seattle, Washington, V.P. in charge
    of Dining Cars
Roger Biallas, V.P. in charge of Printed Matter
Dr. J. W. Young, V.P. in charge of the Health of the
    President and Vice Presidents

Dear Kenneth

I want to thank You Kenneth for Your fast respond to my letter and I do hope my letter eased Your Worry about K Y E. But old Hoboer are no doubt some of the wisest people on earth. If they had not been they would not be alive today.

And I do want to thank You for the nice gifts You sent me the pen is a very nice one and I will use it when I send the B.N.S.F. there checks for houling my scrap iron.

And the nice cup that keeps drinks either warm or cold brought back memories of nearly 70 years ago of how I could of used it when I was riding in a Box car on a freight train on the Santa Fe going through the Dessert in Arizona.

264

MON-ROAD RAILROAD

MONTE HOLM, President

JACK CRONKITE, Sec.-Treas.

BOX 1444
MOSES LAKE, WA 98837

E. Clark Jones, First Vice President
Joshua Green, Sr., Vice President and Financial
    Consultant, Seattle, Washington
E. C. Olander, V.P. in charge of Western Division
William N. Duncan, V.P. in charge of Eastern Division
Larem Severson, V.P. in charge of Northern Division
Alex Hood, V.P. in charge of Southern Division
John R. Lewis, Senior V.P.
R. E. Lewis, Executive V.P.
Norman Day, V.P. in charge of Traffic
Major General Howard S. McGee, Office of Adjutant
    General, Camp Murray, Washington, V.P. in charge
    of Operations
Brigadier General Lyle Buchanan, Camp Murray,
    Washington, V.P. in charge of Security
Charles J. Edwards, V.P. in charge of Sugar Production
Allen Sircin, V.P. in charge of Livestock Installation
Elmer Yoshino, V.P. in charge of Processing Plants
Roy Kaylor, V.P. in charge of Minerals
Ich Konishi, V.P. in charge of Entertainment
V. H. Noone, V.P. in charge of Communications
Jalmer Moe, V.P. in charge of Engineers
Carl Melcher, V.P. in charge of Wheat Production
C. E. Marchand, V.P. in charge of Production
George C. LaValley, V.P. in charge of Tariff
George Pruitt (Cowboy), V.P. in charge of Hog Production
Gus Tenaglia, V.P. in charge of Investments
Walter Franz, V.P. in charge of Agriculture Division
Nick Badovinis, V.P. in charge of Tunnels
Thomas G. Jones, Riverside, Washington, V.P. in charge
    of History
Duke Moore, V.P. in charge of Speed
Ben I. Peterson, Denver, Colorado, V.P. in charge of
    Prospectors
Howard Pessein, V.P. in charge of Freight Rates
O. R. (Slim) Lovins, V.P. in charge of Potato Production
Mode Snead, V.P. in charge of Public Relations
Dick Penhallurick, V.P. in charge of Right-a-ways
Joe Cavender, Spokane, Washington, V.P. and Road
    Foreman of Engineers
John Barrier, Spokane, Washington, V.P. in charge of
    Foreign Relations
Clyde C. Andrews, V.P. in charge of Refrigeration
Fred Gulbrandson, Everett, Washington, V.P. in charge
    of Depot Construction
Earl Terwilleger, Warden, Washington, V.P. in charge
    of Irrigation
P. W. Davis, Seattle, Washington, V.P. in charge of
    Real Estate
R. D. Argue, Seattle, Washington, V.P. in charge of
    Industrial Engineering
Moe Mickelson, Everett, Washington, V.P. in charge
    of Salvage
Bob Bernard, V.P. in charge of Livestock
Chuck McInroy, V.P. in charge of Livestock Appraisal
J. O. English, V.P. in charge of Stocks and Bonds
Tim Bernard, V.P. in charge of Zortman Division
Howard Copenhaver, V.P. in charge of Loans
Eric Ryberg, Salt Lake City, Utah, V.P. in charge of
    Fire Protection
Wade B. Hall, Seattle, Washington, V.P. in charge
    of Lanterns
Brick McFadden V.P. in charge of Labor Relations
The Rev. Paul Dickson, V.P. in charge of Chaplain
Dr. C. W. Covey, V.P. in charge of Safety
Henry Munroe, V.P. in charge of Catering
Walt Thayer, Wenatchee, Washington, V.P. in charge
    of Photography
Al Anderson, V.P. in charge of Pullman Department
Herb Rademacker, Sunnyside, Washington, V.P. in
    charge of Bearing Maintenance
Fred Weber, Sumner, Washington, V.P. in charge of
    Complaints
Van Bustkern, Spokane, Washington, V.P. in charge
    of Youth Activities
Dr. Charles Stevenson, Spokane, Washington, V.P. in
    charge of Mergers
Woodrow D. Barber, Seattle, Washington, V.P. in
    charge of Organization
Manney Burman, Seattle, Washington, V.P. in charge
    of Purchasing
Andrew Yurkenin, Seattle, Washington, V.P. in charge
    of Dining Cars
Roger Biallas, V.P. in charge of Printed Matter
Dr. J. W. Young, V.P. in charge of the Health of the
    President and Vice Presidents

the train stoped and a Railroad Bull jumped into the Box Car I and another Hobo was in and with his whip that Railroad Bull at that time realy liked to use on Hoboes. He Ran us out of the Box Car and Yealed at us that its 15 Miles to water so you Hoboes better get walking. I was even dry when I got Kiked off of the train and after 15 Miles I would of loved to have had Ice Water in the nice cup You sent me, and I sure will keep the cup handy in case I get run out of Moses Lake. But it is comforting to know there are no Railroad Bulls in Moses Lake. But after being chased by Railroad Bulls for 6 Years I am on my guard at all times. But then I think I have

Once a Hobo . . . .

MON-ROAD RAILROAD

MONTE HOLM, President

JACK CRONKITE, Sec.-Treas.

BOX 1444
MOSES LAKE, WA 98837

no doubt outlined all of the
mean Railroad Bulls,
   I will send you a artical
that was in the paper
about 7 month ago that
You might like to read
And if you get this way
be sure to stop in,
   You are always Welcome
at the House of Poverty.
   And I do hope I have
eased your worry about K2Y
But I will have my New
Cup full of Ice Water sestin
Case,
   One should be Prepared
Kenneth.

                     Your Freind
                     Monte Holm

266

OFFICE OF GRANT COUNTY

PROSECUTING ATTORNEY

P.O. BOX 37 • EPHRATA, WASHINGTON 98823 • (509) 754-2011

PAUL KLASEN
Prosecuting Attorney
KENNETH L. JORGENSEN
Chief Criminal Deputy
LUCY WOLFORD
Administrative Assistant

June 6, 1986

Monte Holmes
Chairman of the Board
President & Chief Operating Officer
Mon Road Railroad
228 S. Commerce Way
P. O. Box 448
Moses Lake, WA 98837

Re: Application for Chief Legal Counsel for Mon Road
      Railroad

Dear Mr. Holmes:

Please accept and consider my application for the position
of Chief Legal Counsel for Mon Road Railroad.

This application is being submitted as the result of
extensive and exhaustive legal research into the perils of
the operation of railroads, particularly steam
locomotives. I am deeply concerned about the liability of
Mon Road whenever you start shoveling the coal. Claims
from four footed bovine and equine critters who are hell
bent for destruction because of suicidal tendencies need
to be properly defended. Not to be overlooked, of course,
are possibilites of your switchman being seduced by the
enticements of beautiful ladies of questionable motives
and lustful desires.

Please examine closely the enclosed examples of the perils
above mentioned; they are the product of my research into
the matter, and, hopefully, will convince you of the need
for my services.

Deputies
JERALD R. HAMLEY
MARY ANN BRADY
BRUCE LEMON
STEPHEN HALLSTROM
PETER G. WALES
Ephrata, Washington

Monte Holmes
May 12, 1986
Page -2-

Regarding remuneration, my first thought is a yearly pass good on the Mon Road Railways for myself, my family, grandchildren, and all inlaws and outlaws. It is, of course, understood that Mon Road passes are honored on all Trunk, Main, Branch, Baggage, and Hobo lines in the U.S. on a reciprocal basis. I am inclined to believe that Am Trak will refuse to honor Mon Rail Passes which is not surprising since it seems the only thing the Feds will accept is payment to Internal Revenue.

Oh yes, there is one last item and that is since I am the Grant County Prosecuting Attorney, and by law prohibited from doing private legal matters, if Mon Road gets a claim or is sued you will have to walk the track or catch the next (FFF) first fast freight out of town by yourself.

Your prompt reply will be appreciated.

Very truly yours,

PAUL KLASEN
Prosecuting Attorney

PK:lw
enclosures

P.S. The enclosed research papers are actual case histories which are supposed to be based on fact, at least to the extent of truthfulness of the Hobos that referred them to my attention.

P.P.S.
I would appreciate further discussion of the matter over your next Hobo Stew, and I will bring my own empty tin can, at least it will not be full of rust and stagnant rain water.

Monte Holm and Dennis L. Clay

The Dockery Answer

© *Jerry Buchmeyer, 1981*

My personal favorite as *the* outstanding piece of inspired and humorous legal writing is the legendary First Amended Answer in *The Dockery Case.* The Plaintiff, one Hattie Beatty, sued for $10,000 damages because of personal injuries sustained when "her bare knee did touch an open electric switch upon the wall" of the defendant-railroad's signal tower, throwing her to the floor and causing severe injury to her back and spinal column." The Dockery Answer begins:

". . . in truth and in fact the plaintiff, Mrs. Hattie Beatty, for several nights prior to the occasion of which she now complains had strolled by the signal tower in question and on each occasion persistently propositioned this defendant's employee at said tower, one Dockery (a man of over sixty winters, with snow in his hair but with summer in his heart), to engage with her in an ancient and popular pastime.

". . . the faint odor of Hoyt's perfume touched his delicate nostrils and the full red painted lips of this modern young Aphrodite brought back youthful dreams to his aging head. Although the season was Fall time the sap began to rise in his erotic soul as in romantic Springtime of yore. It was on the unlucky night of Friday the 13th of September, A.D. 1934, that the said Dockery finally succumbed to plaintiff's feminine allurements, the price being one dollar paid in advance."

Then, the traditional personal injury defenses of uninvited guest, contributory negligence, and assumption of risk were asserted — but in very non-traditional language and with novel supporting facts:

"That in all truthfulness the only mechanical contrivance or unique lever about the said tower in which the plaintiff expressed interest whatsoever was that which hung on the person of the said Dockery. [But] that this defendant Railroad Company had not equipped its said signal tower for such passionate purpose and had, in fact, instructed its said employee to admit no visitors there, but that unbeknown to this defendant the said Dockery permitted the plaintiff to come into the crowded quarters of said tower to indulge with him in an indoor session of Spanish athletics. . .

[handwritten note: Monte — I have verified That the papers in the KATY Ry Rw Case also known as the Dockery (defendant "name") actually do exist as stated herein — Paul]

"That the said Dockery urged the plaintiff to remove herself from the cushioned chair to the floor of the tower in order that his engagement might be fulfilled in the good old American way, but that the plaintiff proclaimed her proficiency and maintained her ability to handle the entire situation from her position in the chair and that she remained in said chair contrary to Dockery's urgent solicitations and entreaties and received the electric shock as a direct and proximate result of her insistence upon departing from well recognized precedent; that plaintiff was negligent in failing to pursue her activities horizontally from the floor in the time honored, accepted and orthodox style and that her failure to do so proximately contributed to cause her injuries if any.

" . . .

"That in any event, it is a matter of judicial knowledge that the business in which the plaintiff was engaged entails certain risks, one of the least of which is the risk of being shocked, and in this connection it is shown that the plaintiff held herself out as an expert in her art, while the said Dockery was to an observant eye a man fresh from the soil and reared to the manners of the pioneer countryside, a man entirely untrained to innovations of perpendicular postures and therefore completely unable to anticipate plaintiff's new-fangled hip and knee movements from a cushioned chair or to warn plaintiff of the probable consequences thereof, and that plaintiff assumed the risk of her injuries, if any."

The answer also pleads failure of consideration and — if "by some manner of judicial reasoning unknown to it this defendant should be held to have enjoyed vicariously the benefits anticipated by the said Dockery from his relations with the plaintiff" — counterclaims for the return of "one devalued dollar of United States Currency." Next, the core defense (hard or otherwise) was alleged:

"That as to this defendant, the transaction in question was *ultra vires* and completely outside the scope of employment of the said Dockery, and clearly without benefit to this defendant corporation' except for the publicity that might possibly attend this proof to the world of the exemplary manner in which the Katy Railroad cares for and preserves the virility of its aging employees."

The prayer concludes with the plea that the defendant railroad 'be further relieved of all possible insinuations against its chastity that may arise as the result of this lawsuit.'

'*Beatty v. MKT Railroad Co.*, Cause No. 18338, 54th Judicial District Court of McLennan County, Texas. Plaintiff's attorney: Leonard Cox. Defendant's attorney: Naman, Howell & Brooks.

The petition alleged that the plaintiff, Hattie Beatty, was about to eat her evening meal at the Post Office Cafe when one Ellis Dockery, the signal tower operator, "called to the plaintiff . . . and invited and persuaded her to approach and enter such signal tower, telling her that the apparatus contained in said signal tower, and the mechanical construction thereof, and the manner in which it was operated by lever and electric current were peculiar and unique" — and that she accepted Dockery's invitation only because of her interest in "the mechanical mechanism and operation of defendant's said signal tower."

'Here, defendant's counsel were guilty of modest poetic license. Dockery's deposition testimony:

"Q. Mr. Dockery, was she a pretty good looking woman?
A. Not so very good looking, no.
Q. But you thought it would be worth a dollar, though?
A. Yes, I thought I'd risk a dollar on it.
Q. And a dollar is all she wanted to make.
A. That is all she asked for."

'After the shock, either "from shocked surprise at the seemingly remarkable amative powers of the said Dockery for other reasons," the plaintiff Hattie Beatty "sank to the floor of said tower in an apparent swoon, leaving the said Dockery unrewarded and bewildered, with raiment disarranged, and struggling desperately to operate his signals for a fast train which he discovered at that moment approaching unexpectedly upon the defendant's tracks."

'". . . which is, as the Court has often heard plaintiff's counsel charge, a heartless and bloodless corporation, a poor creature of the statute without pride of ancestry or hope of posterity and physically incapable of becoming enraptured in the ethereal paroxysms of love. . ."

Monte Holm and Dennis L. Clay

The Process:

Demand Letters and Settlements

Demand letters are usually lacking (woefully, of course) in imagination. But they need not be so trite and uninspired — because demand letters offer a Fertile Field for imaginative legal writing. They can be *sipid*, indeed. For example:

. . . H. Allen Smith reported this gem by an Indian attorney: "Dear _____, If you do not pay the money you owe my client, I will take steps that will cause you the utmost damned astonishment. Yours very truly."[1]

. . . Cornelius Vanderbilt once wrote a "gentleman" who had acted dishonorably in a financial matter: "You have undertaken to cheat me. I will not sue you because the law takes too long. I will ruin you."[2]

And, a computerized form demand letter certainly would not have satisfied the needs of the client in *"The Old Stager and the Exchequer Suit on the Information of the Attorney-General Issuing Out of the Petty Bag."*[3] The Old Solicitor's clients were owed a lot of money by a Firm of High Standing. The clients needed the money immediately and/or forthwith since they were in a Wobbly Financial Condition — but the Firm of High Standing, although they had not a Leg to Stand Upon, could easily delay payment by putting up some Rotten Sort of Defense.

So what was the Old Solicitor to do? Well, being Replete with learning found in the third edition of "Bullen & Leake," he told the client it was clearly a case for an Exchequer Suit on the Information of the Attorney-General Issuing out of the Petty Bag — and began work, without delay, on the Draft of the Necessary Formal Document:

. . . It Began with the Observation, 'Oyez, Oyez, Oyez,' and Recited that the Right Honourable the Attorney-General had been Informed by his Trusty

and Well-beloved Thomas Binks and Thomas Bin the Younger (Trading as Binks & Company) that t Firm of High Standing Owed them the Sum 3,921*l.* 4*s.* 8*d.* It Proceeded to Warn the Firm of Hi Standing that by Declining to pay the said Mone they had Rendered themselves Liable to the Pai and Penalties Made and Provided by 1 & 2 Ric. II, 4, 18 Eliz. c. 14, and Divers Acts Amending t Same, the Provisions whereof were Preserved a: Maintained by and Incorporated in the Judicatu Acts of 1873 and 1875 (36 & 37 Vict. c. 66 and 38 39 Vict. c. 77). It then Summoned Each and Every the Members of the Firm of High Standing to Atte at Twelve O'Clock (Midday) on Monday (*Die L nae*) next after the Morrow of All Souls at the Bar the House of Lords and there Show Cause in Pers why they should not be Committed to the Cloc Tower of his Majesty's Palace of Westminster or his Majesty's Keep or Tower of London and there Imprisoned until Further Order. In a Few Closi Sentences it Pointed Out that if they Desired to Assoilzied, Purged, and Acquitted of the said De and Relieved from the Obligation of Attending at t said Bar of the said House of Lords, the Firm of Hi Standing must Cause the said Sum of 3,921*l.* 4*s.* £ to be Paid in Cash to the said Thomas Binks a Thomas Binks the Younger (Trading as Binks Company) within Twenty-four Hours. At the End the Draft the Old Solicitor Added the Devout As ration, 'God Save the King.'"

The Old Solicitor had this Imposing Document ¢ grossed on parchment and served upon the defenda: by a Mounted Policeman. The Firm of High Standi was so terrified that, without consulting their solicito they paid up at once. When the clients later asked wh the Old Solicitor had unearthed this Most Satisfacto Procedure, he modestly confessed . . . *that he had vented it.*

Settlement techniques — "this is my final offer," "I'd like to offer more, but my client just won't give me the authority," etc. — need not be so repetitious and routine, as they invariably are. Consider this example[4] of a truly imaginative and, no doubt, effective technique used in September of 1917 by William H. Peterman, an attorney in Alexandria, Louisiana.

The plaintiff's claim: $100.00 for the alleged value of a cow killed by defendant's train. The "final offer" by the plaintiff's attorney: $75.00. The $50.00 counteroffer by the defendant's attorney and the Truly Devastating Spiel:

"[I offer you $50.00], simply in the way of a compromise for the railroad company in making this offer does not acknowledge liability.

"I say to you, confidentially of course, that *the animal in question undoubtedly committed suicide.* The statements furnished me show that she hid behind a cattleguard fence, evidently by design and quietly awaited the approach of the train in order to leap in front of it and end her life. What her thoughts must have been as she thus calmly waited for death, we will not inquire. The subject is too painful.

"There must have been some powerful motive that actuated her taking this dreadful course. Possibly she was afflicted with some incurable disease and saw only a future of suffering. Possibly, again, she suffered from the pangs of unrequited love; or, it may be, she sacrificed her virtue to the blandishments of some scoundrelly young bull of the neighborhood and could not survive the disgrace of exposure.

"Now, if you will take $50.00, I will see to it that this secret of her suicide will be sacredly guarded. If you decline it and the case is aired in the Courts, her family will be dishonored and her memory stained, and for this, your client will be answerable."

The letter continues with a somewhat more traditional justification, and supposedly practical matter, which might appeal to the plaintiff "if he is not susceptible to the appeals of sentiment":

"It is this: If he will take $50.00 he will get it now. If he sues and obtains a judgment, say for double this amount, when and how will he obtain payment? He cannot issue execution, for the railroad is in the hands of receivers. *He must await action by a Federal Court. These courts move leisurely. You don't know the height and the depth and the length and the breadth of the word 'leisure,' unless you have had dealings with a Federal Court.*[5] If your Client insists on $100.00 his grandchildren may enjoy disbursing it. If he takes $50.00 now, there is no telling how much it will yield if judiciously invested in cotton futures. Or, if he is not of a speculative turn, let him buy a heifer or two and he will have a herd of milk cows before any judgment he may secure will be collectible.

"Think of these things, dear friend and let me hear from you."

---

1. Responses to demand letters can be equally imaginative. A creditor who sent a nasty demand to a British naval officer in the 19th Century received this reply:

   "I am in receipt of your 'Final Demand' for payment of my account. I have to inform you that my normal practice concerning the settlement of debts is to place all of my bills in a hat once a month, from which I draw out two or three for payment. I have followed this procedure with regard to your bill. However, if I receive another letter from you, Sir, the tone of which I consider to be rude, your bill will not be put in the hat at all."

2. Oscar Wilde is credited with *an idea* for an even more devastating response to a demand for payment: "Dear Sir: I am seated in the smallest room in the house. I have your letter before me. Soon it will be behind me."

3. *Fifty Forensic Fables* by "O" (the pen name of Theobald Mathew), published by Butterworth & Co. (London 1961).

4. Contributed by **Lee Simpson** (and passed down by his father, an attorney with the Missouri Pacific Railroad).

5. **Mr. Dooley**, of course, had the answer for judicial delay: "Ye see they're wurrukin' on time now. I wondher if they wudden't sthep livelier if they were paid by th' piece." Bander, *Mr. Dooley & Mr. Dunne* (The Michie Co. 1981).

MONTE HOLM, President

JACK CRONKITE, Sec.-Treas.

BOX 1444
MOSES LAKE, WA 98837

July 7, 1986

E. Clark Jones, First Vice President
Joshua Green, Sr., Vice President and Financial
  Consultant, Seattle, Washington
E. C. Olander, V.P. in charge of Western Division
William N. Duncan, V.P. in charge of Eastern Division
Larem Severson, V.P. in charge of Northern Division
Alex Hood, V.P. in charge of Southern Division
John R. Lewis, Senior V.P.
R. E. Lewis, Executive V.P.
Norman Day, V.P. in charge of Traffic
Major General Howard S. McGee, Office of Adjutant
  General, Camp Murray, Washington, V.P. in charge
  of Operations
Brigadier General Lyle Buchanan, Camp Murray,
  Washington, V.P. in charge of Security
Charles J. Edwards, V.P. in charge of Sugar Production
Allen Sircin, V.P. in charge of Livestock Installation
Elmer Yoshino, V.P. in charge of Processing Plants
Roy Kaylor, V.P. in charge of Minerals
Ich Konishi, V.P. in charge of Entertainment
V. H. Noone, V.P. in charge of Communications
Jalmer Moe, V.P. in charge of Engineers
Carl Melcher, V.P. in charge of Wheat Production
C. E. Marchand, V.P. in charge of Production
George C. LaValley, V.P. in charge of Tariff
George Pruitt (Cowboy), V.P. in charge of Hog Production
Gus Tenaglia, V.P. in charge of Investments
Walter Franz, V.P. in charge of Agriculture Division
Nick Badovinis, V.P. in charge of Tunnels
Thomas G. Jones, Riverside, Washington, V.P. in charge
  of History
Duke Moore, V.P. in charge of Speed
Ben I. Peterson, Denver, Colorado, V.P. in charge of
  Prospectors
Howard Pessein, V.P. in charge of Freight Rates
O. R. (Slim) Lovins, V.P. in charge of Potato Production
Mode Snead, V.P. in charge of Public Relations
Dick Penhallurick, V.P. in charge of Right-a-ways
Joe Cavender, Spokane, Washington, V.P. and Road
  Foreman of Engineers
John Barrier, Spokane, Washington, V.P. in charge of
  Foreign Relations
Clyde C. Andrews, V.P. in charge of Refrigeration
Fred Gulbrandson, Everett, Washington, V.P. in charge
  of Depot Construction
Earl Terwilleger, Warden, Washington, V.P. in charge
  of Irrigation
P. W. Davis, Seattle, Washington, V.P. in charge of
  Real Estate
R. D. Argue, Seattle, Washington, V.P. in charge of
  Industrial Engineering
Moe Mickelson, Everett, Washington, V.P. in charge
  of Salvage
Bob Bernard, V.P. in charge of Livestock
Chuck McInroy, V.P. in charge of Livestock Appraisal
J. O. English, V.P. in charge of Stocks and Bonds
Tim Bernard, V.P. in charge of Zortman Division
Howard Copenhaver, V.P. in charge of Loans
Eric Ryberg, Salt Lake City, Utah, V.P. in charge of
  Fire Protection
Wade B. Hall, Seattle, Washington, V.P. in charge of
  Lanterns
Brick McFadden V.P. in charge of Labor Relations
The Rev. Paul Dickson, V.P. and Chaplain
Dr. C. W. Covey, V.P. in charge of Safety
Henry Munroe, V.P. in charge of Catering
Walt Thayer, Wenatchee, Washington, V.P. in charge
  of Photography
Al Anderson, V.P. in charge of Pullman Department
Herb Rademacker, Sunnyside, Washington, V.P. in
  charge of Bearing Maintenance
Fred Weber, Sumner, Washington, V.P. in charge of
  Complaints
Van Bustkern, Spokane, Washington, V.P. in charge
  of Youth Activities
Dr. Charles Stevenson, Spokane, Washington, V.P. in
  charge of Mergers
Woodrow D. Barber, Seattle, Washington, V.P. in
  charge of Organization
Manney Burman, Seattle, Washington, V.P. in charge
  of Purchasing
Andrew Yurkenin, Seattle, Washington, V.P. in charge
  of Dining Cars
Roger Biallas, V.P. in charge of Printed Matter
Dr. J. W. Young, V.P. in charge of the Health of the
  President and Vice Presidents

Paul Klasen
Prosecuting Attorney
P. O. Box 37
Ephrata, Washington 98823

My Dear Friend Paul:

I have received your application for
Chief Legal Counsel for the Mon-Road
Railroad. I am sorry for the delay in
answering your application but I have
been reading the extensive and exhaustive
legal research and my first reaction is
Uff Da. And if you don't know what that
means, ask a Norwegian.

I do realize the tremendous liability
when you start shoveling the coal in the
boiler so we have had to switch to buffalo
chips which are much easier to get as
everyone figures I am full of it and it
shovels much nicer. But the bovines can
be a real liability. I am now talking
about the two legged ones - not the four
legged ones.

I have a procedure I go through when
I show off my private railroad car. I
always lock the car door after I get the
guests in the car, otherwise people just
walk in and don't wipe their feet and I
have to clean the car so I find this much
easier. One day a lovely woman wanted to
go through my museum. We got to the railroad car and, as usual, I locked the door.
As I was taking her through the car we
came to the nice bedroom that I call mine.
I said, "I want you to come and see my
bedroom and nice shower", which I show

everyone. She said, "No. You won't get me in your
bedroom", and she ran for the front door that she saw
me lock. She nearly went plumb through the door. As
she was about twice my size she could have just slugged
me if I got any ulterior motives. But you know, Paul,
the liability was surely there if she had gone right through
the door without opening it and the damage to the car
would have been tremendous. I was telling my good wife
about it that night and she said, "Well, Father, for
84 years old at least some think there is still life
in you yet!" After that when I take a female along
through the car I explain about the one woman and the
door. So my liability there has become nill.

In reading further it appears to me like some of the
material you sent me would make ideal fuel for the
locomotive. It does appear like a lot of buffalo chips.

In the Dockery Answer, Mr. Dockery was put in a much
tougher position than I was; at least my woman ran and
poor Mr. Dockery was put in a terrible position with Hattie
Beatty. My experience with the Katy Railroad was somewhat different. Now as to the Katy Railroad, my sympathies
are with Hattie Beatty as I have had some experience with
Katy employees although a little different. But I feel
sure all Katy employees are of the same caliber.

Another hobo and I got off a freight train on the
Katy line in Temple, Texas, and after having ridden for
many miles on the train we became very hungry. If you
ever rode a freight train over 50 years ago before welded
rails, you would understand how easy it was to get hungry.
We were both without funds. My partner who was older than I
and maybe wiser was sitting next to me by the railroad
tracks swatting flies which were plentiful. I noticed as
he killed a fly he would look at it and after about 50
flies he put the two largest ones in his shirt pocket.
I had found in my hobo days it is best not to ask too
many questions and you get along much better. My partner
said, "There is a nice restaurant in the railroad depot.
They call them Harvy Houses and I hear they feed real
good". I said, "What good is that to us as we are flat
broke?" He said, "You just let me take care of it and
order whatever you want". Being good and hungry and
having been taught to obey my elders, we entered the
restaurant and sat down at the counter. The nice waitress
asked us what we wanted and I said a hamburger steak. My
partner had the same. When our dinner came, I noticed my
partner ate real fast. I thought that because he was so

-2-

274

hungry and it was so good that he was eating so fast.
I did notice he was watching me real close. When I got
down to a small piece of meat left, my partner said,
"Lift your meat up a little with the fork", which I did.
There was a real large fly under it which I did not like
with my dinner. The waitress was quite close and I said
in a loud voice, "Look what is on my plate". She called
the boss over. Because the place was quite full and my
partner and I were quite upset, the boss said, "If you
fellows will be quiet and leave the restaurant right
away, we will not charge you". I then realized why my
partner was swatting flies on the track. I saw a big
man on the other side of the restaurant looking our way.
A Katy Railroad Bull. If you have never had any experience
with Railroad Bulls, Paul, you have really missed something.
Since we were not too well dressed I am sure someone told
him they saw the hobo tuck the fly under my meat.

Here is where the liability starts. The Bull is in
the same catagory as Mr. Dockery - both employed by the
Katy Railroad. At that time I had no counsel either. I
saw the Bull was moving rather fast around the counter and
having had many other encounters with Bulls and knowing
the tremendous liability if I did not move faster than the
Bull did and not having anyone handling my private legal
matters at that time either. I also thought, as you do,
the only difference instead of walking the track and
catching the next FFF out of town as you suggest, I thought
it was much better to run and catch the next FFF out of
town. The Railroad Bulls must do a lot of running because
he ran me clear past the next freight. He sure seemed to
want to get to know me better and nearly did. I ran so
fast I never saw my partner again. And I was not too upset
as I never thought he was a very good influence on me. I
did not go back to Temple, Texas, for 50 years. Then I went
on Amtrak. I just peeked out of the window as the train
stopped. I looked for the Bull hoping he would not see me
because I am sure he was still looking for me and wanting
to run another foot race.

My exposure for liability has been tremendous during
those years and my ability to run has slipped some so with
that I will appoint you Chief Legal Counsel for the Mon-
Road Railroad.

Your Friend,

Monte Holm
Monte Holm
President, Mon-Road Railroad

-3-

275

Once a Hobo . . . .

MOSES LAKE POLICE DEPARTMENT
401 S BALSAM, P.O. BOX 1579
MOSES LAKE, WASHINGTON 98837

June 21, 1993

TO: MOSES LAKE IRON & METAL

FR: Chief of Police

RE: **False Alarms**

1. The Moses Lake Police Department has responded to alarms on the following dates 04-29-93, 06-17-93, at your residence/business, and those alarms were determined to be false.

2. Within three working days after receiving this notice please make a written report to me on the attached form setting forth the cause of the false alarm, and the corrective action taken.

3. You are hereby notified that three or more alarms within a three month period will subject you to a monetary penalty of fifty ($50.00) dollars, for the third or subsequent false alarm received during this three month period. Additionally, if action is not taken to correct the malfunctions, you are subject to having your alarm disconnected until repairs are made.

4. Please review Moses Lake Municipal Code 8.24.240 on false alarms. A copy of this code section is enclosed with this letter.

5. For further information, contact the Moses Lake Police Department, 401 S. Balsam, or phone 766-9230.

Sincerely,

Fred Haynes
Chief of Police

by:

KELLER\FALSE.1

MOSES LAKE POLICE DEPARTMENT
401 S BALSAM, P. O. BOX 1579
MOSES LAKE, WASHINGTON 98837

TO: Police Chief

FR: MOSES LAKE IRON & METAL

RE: **False Alarm Ordinance**

1.   Circumstance surrounding false alarm situation.

    See attached letter.

2.   Corrective action taken.

    See attached letter.

Signature

KELLER\FALSE.2

Once a Hobo . . . .

MON-ROAD RAILROAD

MONTE HOLM, President

JACK CRONKITE, Sec.-Treas.

BOX 1444
MOSES LAKE, WA 98837

June 23, 1993

Fred Haynes
Chief of Police
P. O. Box 1579
Moses Lake, WA 98837

Dear Chief Haynes:

I want to really apologize for my false alarm going off in my museum. If you wish to fine me $50.00 for each time I would enjoy it much better than the 10 years I lost when the second false alarm went off.

My Grandson, Steven Rimple who has a key for the museum, had gone in and had pressed the wrong button by mistake and the next person to open the door would set off the alarm immediately. Well, I was the next person and I nearly went through the roof of the building. The 10 years I lost I cannot afford when one is already 84 years old!

As for the corrective action taken, I did not know what to do but say "Uff Da" and if you do not know what that means just ask a Norwegian.

As for the first false alarm, one of my employees, David Fazende, went to my museum to give a bus load of school children a tour of the museum and a train ride which all children like. He also pressed the wrong button so all I could say again was "Uff Da". I didn't loose another 10 years because I was a long way from the building.

I am sure, Chief, that "Uff Da" is not a very corrective action but the only person who never made a mistake was crucified. We are only humans and I am very sorry.

MON-ROAD RAILROAD

MONTE HOLM, President

JACK CRONKITE, Sec.-Treas.

BOX 1444
MOSES LAKE, WA 98837

E. Clark Jones, First Vice President
Joshua Green, Sr., Vice President and Financial Consultant, Seattle, Washington
E. C. Olander, V.P. in charge of Western Division
William N. Duncan, V.P. in charge of Eastern Division
Larem Severson, V.P. in charge of Northern Division
Alex Hood, V.P. in charge of Southern Division
John R. Lewis, Senior V.P.
R. E. Lewis, Executive V.P.
Norman Day, V.P. in charge of Traffic
Major General Howard S. McGee, Office of Adjutant General, Camp Murray, Washington, V.P. in charge of Operations
Brigadier General Lyle Buchanan, Camp Murray, Washington, V.P. in charge of Security
Charles J. Edwards, V.P. in charge of Sugar Production
Allen Sircin, V.P. in charge of Livestock Installation
Elmer Yoshino, V.P. in charge of Processing Plants
Roy Kaylor, V.P. in charge of Minerals
Ich Konishi, V.P. in charge of Entertainment
V. H. Noone, V.P. in charge of Communications
Jalmer Moe, V.P. in charge of Engineers
Carl Melcher, V.P. in charge of Wheat Production
C. E. Marchand, V.P. in charge of Production
George C. LaValley, V.P. in charge of Tariff
George Pruitt (Cowboy), V.P. in charge of Hog Production
Gus Tenaglia, V.P. in charge of Investments
Walter Franz, V.P. in charge of Agriculture Division
Nick Badovinis, V.P. in charge of Tunnels
Thomas G. Jones, Riverside, Washington, V.P. in charge of History
Duke Moore, V.P. in charge of Speed
Ben I. Peterson, Denver, Colorado, V.P. in charge of Prospectors
Howard Pessein, V.P. in charge of Freight Rates
O. R. (Slim) Lovins, V.P. in charge of Potato Production
Mode Snead, V.P. in charge of Public Relations
Dick Penhallurick, V.P. in charge of Right-a-ways
Joe Cavender, Spokane, Washington, V.P. and Road Foreman of Engineers
John Barrier, Spokane, Washington, V.P. in charge of Foreign Relations
Clyde C. Andrews, V.P. in charge of Refrigeration
Fred Gulbrandson, Everett, Washington, V.P. in charge of Depot Construction
Earl Terwilleger, Warden, Washington, V.P. in charge of Irrigation
P. W. Davis, Seattle, Washington, V.P. in charge of Real Estate
R. D. Argue, Seattle, Washington, V.P. in charge of Industrial Engineering
Moe Mickelson, Everett, Washington, V.P. in charge of Salvage
Bob Bernard, V.P. in charge of Livestock
Chuck McInroy, V.P. in charge of Livestock Appraisal
J. O. English, V.P. in charge of Stocks and Bonds
Tim Bernard, V.P. in charge of Zortman Division
Howard Copenhaver, V.P. in charge of Loans
Eric Ryberg, Salt Lake City, Utah, V.P. in charge of Fire Protection
Wade B. Hall, Seattle, Washington, V.P. in charge of Lanterns
Brick McFadden V.P. in charge of Labor Relations
The Rev. Paul Dickson, V.P. and Chaplain
Dr. C. W. Covey, V.P. in charge of Safety
Henry Munroe, V.P. in charge of Catering
Walt Thayer, Wenatchee, Washington, V.P. in charge of Photography
Al Anderson, V.P. in charge of Pullman Department
Herb Rademacker, Sunnyside, Washington, V.P. in charge of Bearing Maintenance
Fred Weber, Sumner, Washington, V.P. in charge of Complaints
Van Bustkern, Spokane, Washington, V.P. in charge of Youth Activities
Dr. Charles Stevenson, Spokane, Washington, V.P. in charge of Mergers
Woodrow D. Barber, Seattle, Washington, V.P. in charge of Organization
Manney Burman, Seattle, Washington, V.P. in charge of Purchasing
Andrew Yurkenin, Seattle, Washington, V.P. in charge of Dining Cars
Roger Biallas, V.P. in charge of Printed Matter
Dr. J. W. Young, V.P. in charge of the Health of the President and Vice Presidents

But Chief, you have the nicest officers there are. Very polite, very helpful and just real good people. But having a leader like you, they would have to be.

I sure do hope you do not have my alarm disconnected as I have a lot of nice things in my museum and people come from all over the world to view it. The small children all get train rides and you would disappoint a lot of people.

Do stop to see me anytime. You are always welcome at the House of Poverty.

Your Friend,

Monte Holm

Monte Holm
Moses Lake Iron & Metal

Enclosed in letter from the School group that was going through the Museum when the alarm went off one of the times

-2-

279

thanks!

June 19, 1993

Mr. Monty Holm
407 E. Hill
Moses Lake, WA. 98837

Dear Mr. Holm,

Thank you so much for letting our Almira-Hartline Second Graders visit your Train Park. They enjoyed every part of the visit. They liked ringing the bell in one of the trains. They liked seeing the train in which one of our American presidents stayed while campaigning. They liked seeing the many interesting items in your House of Poverty. They got a "kick" out of riding the little train around in a circle. They liked seeing all the "junk" in the scrap pile. They thought the Werther Originals were great.

We appreciate you taking the time to show us your business and the many fantastic things you have collected. We were impressed!

Sincerely,

Anita Sieg

Anita Sieg and the Almira-Hartline
Second Graders

5-27-98

Dear Monty Holm,
Thank you for letting
our Second Grade Class
visit your business. I loved your
collection. It was great. Thank
you for the Werther's
Originals.

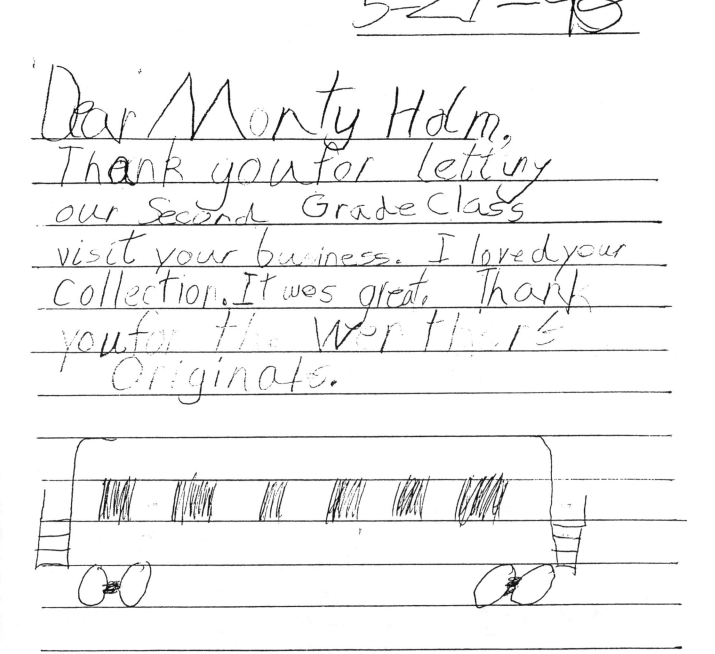

from

Seth

MONRAD HOLM
818 COMMERCE ST.
MOLESLAKE, WASH.

YOUR LIABILITY POLICY
OLD BLP 213138
NEW BLP 264142

SOME POTENTIAL QUESTIONS FOR YOUR LETTER.

1. DO YOUR EMPLOYEES HAVE PERSONAL USE OF YOUR TRUCKS?

2. HOW DO YOU SELECT YOUR DRIVERS?

3. WHAT HAS BEEN YOUR ACCIDENT EXPERIENCE THE PAST 3 YEARS?

4. WHAT ARE YOUR PLANS FOR YOUR STEAM LOCOMOTIVE?

5. HOW WOULD YOU DESCRIBE YOUR ACTUAL OPERATION/BUSINESS?

6. WHY DON'T YOU KEEP A GOOD INVENTORY ON YOUR STOCK OF JUNK & NEW EQUIPMENT?

If your answers are anywhere as delightfully humorous as the letters I read, you'll create quite a blast for our underwriters in Seattle. Your attention to the necessary inspections was greatly appreciated.

Best Personal Regards.
LEONARD PRICE
N1801 MONROE ST.
SPOKANE, WASH.

VL-11 5/62

                                        Moses Lake Iron & Metal
                                        Box 448
                                        Moses Lake, Washington
                                        12 February 1966

Safeco Insurance Group
N. 1801 Monroe
Spokane, Washington 99205

ATTN: Mr. Leonard Price

Dear Mr. Price:

      In regards to your questionnaire on my insurance, I will try to
answer all parts to the best of my ability. I will assure you all of my
replies shall be honest as that is, I am sure, what you want. In noticing
the name of your outfit, Safeco Insurance Group. It sounds like such a
nice friendly deal, and that you are just one big family. The Group on
it has such a nice effect on me and that I am protected by a Group. I
am sure that if anything happened I would be privileged to see the Group
also. But on second thought, this Group business can be rather bad, too.
I shall have to tell you, Mr. Price, of an experience I had with a Group
at one time. This was in the depression and, things not being too good,
I was in the bread line in Minneapolis, Minn., which is a bad place to
be in the middle of winter. So I would stand twelve hours a day as the
line was rather long. So you would hear lots of stories and being only
17 years old I always listened. So one day I heard that there was to be
a large group gather at the city hall to demand more food. Anytime I
heard the word food I was sure interested, as that had been something I
had not been too use to since I had left home at the age of 13. So I
thought I will go up and see this group and get there early, which I did.
I was very near the city hall, and I could see people coming up every
street. No cars just people because there were so many people there was
no room for cars. Me being at a street intersection, I found myself in
the very middle of the group, which was I found out a very bad place to
be as it was definitely not a friendly group, Mr. Price, and turned in
to be the worst riot this country ever had up to that time. There was
about ten thousand in this group. All of them very mad but me. I was
just hungry. So after nearly getting killed and being in this group
three hours because you cannot get out of this kind of group when you
are in the middle of it. So finally they got the fire department out with
hoses and at 20 below zero it sure did quiet this group down. The worst
part of it was I missed a meal at the bread line which it takes a long time
to get over, Mr. Price. If you ever were in a bread line, you would surely
understand. Since then when I see a group of three or more gather, I just
kind of walk away.

But with the word Safeco on your Group, there is a much better feeling of security as I want no more fire department at 20 degrees below zero.

I hope I don't bore you, Mr. Price, but having had a very limited education, I have a problem answering inquiries of your kind and want to do my best as I would definitely not want to be without your insurance the way people want to sue nowadays. I will hold my remarks down on this subject as I am sure you are more aware of it than I am.

As to how I select my employees, I will first have to tell you, if you have not already guessed, that I am an old hobo and am really partial to hobos. I will tell you how I got three employees last summer. I had been up town on a Tuesday and came back to my place of business about one P.M. and noticed a bunch of blankets and bags outside my office and knew at a glance that some of my old hobo pals were here. So as I walked in the office, I saw three hobos gathered there. So after greeting them, I asked them what brought them here. They said they were kicked out of the last town and were sitting along the highway when a large Cadillac came by and stopped. The man in the car said, "Where are you going?" The hobos said, "To Moses Lake." "We heard there is a junk man there and we have some copper to sell." The man in the Cadillac said, "Get in the car, I know just where to take you, one of your old hobo pals, Monte, and he is in the junk business, too." So after paying them for the copper, I asked them if they would like to go to work as I like nothing better than having hobos around because after being a hobo for six years one gets awful lonesome for his brother hobos. So after working the rest of the day, they came in my office and asked if they could jungle up in my yard. If you don't know what this means, Mr. Price, I shall tell you. It means cooking and sleeping in the yard. I said, "Sure you boys just make yourself at home." So one of the hobos said, "Will the cops bother us?" I said, "I am glad you brought that up because this is one old hobo that now has some influence in city hall being a City Councilman, so I will call the police department", which I did and told them that three of my old pals were going to jungle up in my junk yard and I did not want them bothered. They said, "Yes, sir, Councilman, we will even protect them for you." When I got off the phone one of the hobos said, "You know, Monte, I have been a hobo for thirty years and this is the first time someone called the cops and they never came down and picked me up." So you will see, Mr. Price, I am very particular when I pick my employees, which I am sure you people are very interested in.

2

Now as to my accident experience, I guess I am lucky. I credit my luck to being born on Friday the Thirteenth and being very careful what I let my men haul. Take for instance about three months ago. A customer of mine needed a piece of pipe that was 60 feet long and wanted to know if I would deliver it. Being poor and wanting to make the sale, I said yes. After telling one of my men where to deliver it, he said, "You know, Monte, the truck is only 20 feet long and the pipe will stick over 20 feet on each side." You will notice my men are very good with figures, Mr. Price. So he said, "What shall I do if the police stop me?" I said, "You just tell the cops that Monte said it was all right." About five minutes after he left, I had to go to town. It being near noon and I needed some baloney to cook for lunch. As I drove up the street, I could see two State Patrol and my truck driver talking. So not wanting to get in a group, I quickly turned up another street. When my driver arrived back to my shop, he said, "I was stopped by two State Patrol with that long pipe." I definitely acted surprised because I think one should in such cases. I said, "What happened?" He said, "The cop said don't you know better than hauling a pipe that is so long?" Well, he said, "Monte said it was all right." The cop said, "Who the hell is Monte?" I really don't think, Mr. Price, a cop should swear like that. "Did you get a ticket?" I asked. He said, "Oh no, they just walked off shaking their heads." Then last week this same truck was just sitting in the junk yard and the front wheels fell off. So you can see, you don't want to cut this Friday the Thirteenth very short, Brother Price, you don't mind me calling you brother, do you, as I think by now we should nearly be brothers.

So you can see, Brother Price, my accident experience other than being hard on the nerves is excellent. Which reminds me of another form of transportation I have now. A two hundred ton steam locomotive that I bought and shipped down from the Alaska Railroad. The traffic being what it is now, I am looking towards the future when it will take a machine like that to get through the traffic. It is a beauty and being an old hobo and kicked off of so many freight trains, I thought it would be nice to get one I won't get kicked off of, although it is very possible to get blown off of one of them so I am equipping it with seat belts as I know, Brother Price, you people will like to hear that. I have lots of plans for my railroad, Bother Price. I am listing it with the American Association of Railroads and me as President then I get a first class pass on every railroad in the United States as every President of a railroad does. Then if need be, I can go back on the bum in style. And with taxes and everything going like it is, this is not as remote as some people think. So I am preparing for my old age as you can see, Brother Price.

3

Also in about a month, I will make application to the Interstate Commerce Commission to put in a railroad from Moses Lake to George, Wash., to Royal City, Wash., Walluke Slope, Wash., and come out at Mesa, Wash. The Northern Pacific and Milwaukee Railroads are now fighting over the territory and with my luck I think I shall get the permit. If I do, as I have no money, I believe I can get on Johnson's Poverty Program to put in the railroad as there will be no question on the poverty part. If not, I shall merge with one of the railroads and then we can start splitting stocks, which I have heard are good deals.

Actually, the actual operation of my business is in a terrible mess. What I think I really need is one of those efficiency experts. I have junk scattered over a quarter of a mile of yard. If that isn't bad enough, last week I went and bought an Atlas Missile Base. That is something I would just love to see an efficiency expert try even to inventory let alone do any efficiency on. But I find in my operation you get inquiries for everything. So now I am waiting for some wise guy to come to my junk yard and ask me if I have any Missile Bases for sale. This, Brother Price, is the only reason I can think of for buying it. Also, it is a good place to look and see where ones tax dollars go.

I have tried, Brother Price, many times to take inventory so have decided in the last few years, as me feet are very flat and I get tired easily, so I now take inventory mentally while I lay in bed. I find it much easier on my flat feet and go to sleep with such nice pleasant thoughts because I am sure this way you do skip some stuff, Brother Price, and I am hoping the tax man has flat feet like I have, too, which most of them look like they have.

I hope, Brother Price, the Safeco Insurance Group can sleep as good as I can now after explaining to you what a nice smooth operation I have here, and the satisfaction I have of being protected by such a nice Group.

If there are any more questions you might have, I will be glad to answer them and will keep my replies short and to the point, as I have done here, because I know you are a busy man and want short and to the point replies, Brother Price.

In Brotherly Love,

Monte Holm

Monte Holm

MOSES LAKE IRON & METAL

Surplus • **Salvage** • **Scrap** • **Iron** • **Metals**

818 COMMERCE STREET   P. O. BOX 1448   PHONE RO 5-6342

MOSES LAKE, WASHINGTON

The reason for writing this letter to Mr. Gray is because he sent
me a nice letter from the bank telling me my credit is good and that
I can borrow money for such nice deals as an Education Plan, new or
used car, medical and dental bills, modernize the home, or a vacation
under the low cost Seattle First Installment Plan.

As he was a new man in the bank that i never knew, and as it is where I
bank, I thought such a generous man should have a reply. And when you
apply for a loan you have to explain everything down to the finest
detail, which I tried doing.

I sent my reply on scratch paper in long hand so he would not think
me a spend thrift and sent it in a plain envelope Special Delivery -
the Post Office being just across the street from the bank.

My request for a loan follows and then his reply to my request.

                    Monte Holm

MOSES LAKE IRON & METAL

Surplus • **Salvage** • **Scrap** • **Iron** • **Metals**

818 COMMERCE STREET   P. O. BOX 1448   PHONE RO 5-6342

MOSES LAKE, WASHINGTON

Dear Mr. Gray,

I have read your letter and you sound like such a generous
man that some day I would like to meet you; but I would be awful
careful about loaning money to me. You might not know it, but I
am an old hobo and they are very poor risks. But as you sure as
hell should admit, I need the Education Plan.

A car I need, Mr. Gray, but there is one problem. I live
next door to the infernal revenue man and what would he say when
the poor old hobo shows up with a new car? You see, I have problems.
I am trying to help you out so you can loan that money out, but one
has to be awful careful, Mr. Gray.

Now we get to the Medical and Dental bills, Mr. Gray. I will
have to go into a little detail here, Mr. Gray; as you will see, I
am trying to make it possible for you to loan money and no one needs
it worse than I. You will notice I need the education. But I will
tell you of my trying experience with the medical line.

Before I came to Moses Lake, I was in Canada for a year. The
doctor I had in Everett told me "you have two hernias and they are
the strangling type", which you will have to admit, Mr. Gray, does
not sound good. So he says, "Monte, if you get a pain down below
you should get to a doctor." So one Saturday I got a pain down below.
By Sunday morning I had an awful pain down below. You will notice I
am not swearing, Mr. Gray, but I sure feel like it. So I get in my
car and went to Everett. I got there about 8 p.m. I called the
doctor and said I have an awful pain down below. It is hard not to
swear now but will try to control myself, Mr. Gray. Because I had
an awful pain the doctor said, "you better come to the hospital,
Monte, and we will look," which I did. This strangling business
does scare one, Mr. Gray, even though I don't know how down below
can strangle one. But without your Education Plan anything is
possible. The doctor said, "get on this table," which I did as I have
been taught to be obedient. He said, "Monte, you have hemeroids,"
I said, "can you fix them now?" He said, "sure". I said go ahead as
I was on the table anyway. It is wonderful that one only goes through
these deals once. He said afterwords, "these hernias are bothering
you, Monte, aren't they?" I says yes, Doc. So he says "why don't we
fix them," which sounded simple, Mr. Gray. So I says, "yes, let's
fix them." So he says "tomorrow night you come in then the next
morning we will operate," but he says tonight you better sit in warm
water in the bathtub which was a very good idea. You do that, Mr.
Gray, if you ever have hemeroids. So the next night I went to the
hospital for the two hernias which the doctor assured me would be
nothing. You know, Mr. Gray, what the first thing they met me with

288

Monte Holm and Dennis L. Clay

MOSES LAKE IRON & METAL

Surplus • **Salvage** • **Scrap** • **Iron** • **Metals**

818 COMMERCE STREET   P. O. BOX 1448   PHONE RO 5-6342

MOSES LAKE, WASHINGTON

at the hospital? A enema! So, Mr. Gray, as far as the Hospital Plan is concerned, I don't feel up to no more hospitals.

Now the Dental Plan. I hope I don't bore you, Mr. Gray, but I feel that one so generous as you I should explain. I am sure by now I don't have to explain the Education Program no more - I am sure by now you know I am beyond an education.

Now, the Dental part. The last time I went to a dentist I was a hobo. I stopped in the town and I have an awful tooth ache and no money. So I see a sign that says Painless Dentist. I goes in about 10 minutes to 12. I says Doc, I have a terrible tooth ache. It is so hard not to swear, Mr. Gray. And I says, Doc, I have no money and maybe never will (I did not know of your plan then), but I have an awful aching tooth. He says sit in that chair, so I did. He says which one is it. I say, that one. He pulls it out without anything for the pain. I never even thanked him. So as you can see, Mr. Gray, I don't have any use for the Medical or Dental Plan.

So we get to the Home Modernizing (which I can't even spell).

You will have to pardon the delay, Mr. Gray, but I got tired and had to go to bed. When you get my age, Mr. Gray, you will go to bed too after such a strenuous day.

Getting back to the repair or modernizing of the house, Brother Gray. (You don't mind me calling you brother Gray, do you? By now we should be nearly brothers.) This we need bad, but we run into the same trouble as the new car. The infernal revenue man still lives next door and what would he think? He will say the old hobo is making too much money. So let's forget that, Brother Gray.

Now we get to the vacation, which I really need. I will tell you of my last vacation, and if you see fit maybe you will let me have enough money for it. It will cost somewhat more than the last one. The last one I took I had $5.00 to spend. I was in Montana and I heard about the World's Fair in Chicago. So I got a freight train that was going to Chicago. I got a loaf of bread, can of beans, and a hunk of baloney. I got to Chicago three days later, still with the five bucks, and some baloney left. I spent $4.80 at the fair and kept 20¢ to get a street car to the freight yards, which is an awful way out of Chicago. I hope, Brother Gray, you have 20¢ if you ever have to catch a freight out of Chicago. Also, you will have one more problem, Brother Gray, because at Cicero, which is near the freight yards, Al Capone had a bread line which I ate in, but I understand he does not have that anymore. He also lived near the infernal revenue, you see. So you should

-2-

289

Once a Hobo . . . .

MOSES LAKE IRON & METAL

Surplus • **Salvage** • **Scrap** • **Iron** • **Metals**

818 COMMERCE STREET   P. O. BOX 1448   PHONE RO 5-6342

MOSES LAKE, WASHINGTON

take along an extra hunk of baloney. So now I figure there is a
Fair going on in New York City which I would love to see. But it
will take more baloney and beans - as you can see it is much farther
than Chicato. And I don't know about the bread lines no more. So
if you can spare it, I know the freight train charges is no more but
baloney is much higher, Brother Gray. But the freight yards are much
closer. So I can maybe save the 20¢ and walk. I know the bank wants
one to be conservative. So I think if you can see your way clear and
loan me $10.90 because of the high cost of baloney, I can get my
vacation which I sure as hell deserve. I cannot pay over 10% interest
and would like say 4 years and 2 months to repay. I would like this
on the low cost Seafirst Installment Plan.

I wish to thank you, Brother Gray, for this offer as I have lived
here now ten years and this is the first offer I have yet to have from
your bank to loan the old hobo money. I can't take too many shocks like
that, Brother Gray.

In Brotherly Love,

Monte Holm

Monte Holm

P.S. I will keep my fingers crossed till I hear from you on this loan.

-3-

290

SEAFIRST BANK
SEATTLE, WASHINGTON

JOSEF E. GRAY
PRESIDENT

July 2, 1993

Dear Brother Holm,

Thank you for the nice letter, but it appears that I should be congratulating you. When we last corresponded in 1964, you were in the junk yard business and now I see you are a museum curator and railroad president.

I appreciate the invitation and will visit your museum. When things settle down a bit, I'll call you and let you know when I will be in Moses Lake.

Thanks for the copies of our old letters. I thought I had saved them but haven't been able to locate them of late so appreciate the opportunity to try again.

Sincerely,

Josef E. Gray

Mr. Monte Holm
President
Mon-Road Railroad
Box 1444
Moses Lake, WA 98837

Once a Hobo . . . .

MON-ROAD RAILROAD

MONTE HOLM, President

JACK CRONKITE, Sec.-Treas.

BOX 1444
MOSES LAKE, WA 98837

E. Clark Jones, First Vice President
Joshua Green, Sr., Vice President and Financial
    Consultant, Seattle, Washington
E. C. Olander, V.P. in charge of Western Division
William N. Duncan, V.P. in charge of Eastern Division
Larem Severson, V.P. in charge of Northern Division
Alex Hood, V.P. in charge of Southern Division
John R. Lewis, Senior V.P.
R. E. Lewis, Executive V.P.
Norman Day, V.P. in charge of Traffic
Major General Howard S. McGee, Office of Adjutant
    General, Camp Murray, Washington, V.P. in charge
    of Operations
Brigadier General Lyle Buchanan, Camp Murray,
    Washington, V.P. in charge of Security
Charles J. Edwards, V.P. in charge of Sugar Production
Allen Sircin, V.P. in charge of Livestock Installation
Elmer Yoshino, V.P. in charge of Processing Plants
Roy Kaylor, V.P. in charge of Minerals
Ich Konishi, V.P. in charge of Entertainment
V. H. Noone, V.P. in charge of Communications
Jalmer Moe, V.P. in charge of Engineers
Carl Melcher, V.P. in charge of Wheat Production
C. E. Marchand, V.P. in charge of Production
George C. LaValley, V.P. in charge of Tariff
George Pruitt (Cowboy), V.P. in charge of Hog Production
Gus Tenaglia, V.P. in charge of Investments
Walter Franz, V.P. in charge of Agriculture Division
Nick Badovinis, V.P. in charge of Tunnels
Thomas G. Jones, Riverside, Washington, V.P. in charge
    of History
Duke Moore, V.P. in charge of Speed
Ben I. Peterson, Denver, Colorado, V.P. in charge of
    Prospectors
Howard Pessein, V.P. in charge of Freight Rates
O. R. (Slim) Lovins, V.P. in charge of Potato Production
Mode Snead, V.P. in charge of Public Relations
Dick Penhallurick, V.P. in charge of Right-a-ways
Joe Cavender, Spokane, Washington, V.P. and Road
    Foreman of Engineers
John Barrier, Spokane, Washington, V.P. in charge of
    Foreign Relations
Clyde C. Andrews, V.P. in charge of Refrigeration
Fred Gulbrandson, Everett, Washington, V.P. in charge
    of Depot Construction
Earl Terwilleger, Warden, Washington, V.P. in charge
    of Irrigation
P. W. Davis, Seattle, Washington, V.P. in charge of
    Real Estate
R. D. Argue, Seattle, Washington, V.P. in charge of
    Industrial Engineering
Moe Mickelson, Everett, Washington, V.P. in charge
    of Salvage
Bob Bernard, V.P. in charge of Livestock
Chuck McInroy, V.P. in charge of Livestock Appraisal
J. O. English, V.P. in charge of Stocks and Bonds
Tim Bernard, V.P. in charge of Zortman Division
Howard Copenhaver, V.P. in charge of Loans
Eric Ryberg, Salt Lake City, Utah, V.P. in charge of
    Fire Protection
Wade B. Hall, Seattle, Washington, V.P. in charge
    of Lanterns
Brick McFadden V.P. in charge of Labor Relations
The Rev. Paul Dickson, V.P. and Chaplain
Dr. C. W. Covey, V.P. in charge of Safety
Henry Munroe, V.P. in charge of Catering
Walt Thayer, Wenatchee, Washington, V.P. in charge
    of Photography
Al Anderson, V.P. in charge of Pullman Department
Herb Rademacker, Sunnyside, Washington, V.P. in
    charge of Bearing Maintenance
Fred Weber, Sumner, Washington, V.P. in charge of
    Complaints
Van Bustkern, Spokane, Washington, V.P. in charge
    of Youth Activities
Dr. Charles Stevenson, Spokane, Washington, V.P. in
    charge of Mergers
Woodrow D. Barber, Seattle, Washington, V.P. in
    charge of Organization
Manney Burman, Seattle, Washington, V.P. in charge
    of Purchasing
Andrew Yurkenin, Seattle, Washington, V.P. in charge
    of Dining Cars
Roger Biallas, V.P. in charge of Printed Matter
Dr. J. W. Young, V.P. in charge of the Health of the
    President and Vice Presidents

May 4, 1993

Dear Brother Gray:

I read with great interest the article in the Seattle Post-Intelligencer on Wednesday, April 28, 1993, about your climb up the ladder in the Seafirst Bank. You know, it never surprised me in the least. I knew that you would go far after our meeting and correspondence back in 1964. If you have forgotten, I am enclosing copies of our correspondence to refresh your memory.

I am just an old junk dealer and ex-hobo but I do keep everything just in case someone I have had contact with amounts to someone important as you have, Mr. Gray, and I can enlighten them on how far they came up the ladder.

From having to deal with old hoboes to the head of one of the largest corporations in the State of Washington, I want to sincerely congratulate you, Mr. Gray. It could not have happened to a nicer person.

I do want to give you a personal invitation to come to Moses Lake and visit my museum which I did not have when you were here. I have the last steam locomotive to run on the Alaska Railroad and a private railroad car that hauled President Truman and President Wilson. I also have a building full of old cars and antiques. You will make an old hobo real happy if I could meet you again. I will try to have Hobo Stew for you.

ONCE A HOBO

P.O. Box 448
Moses Lake, WA 98837
(509) 765-6342

NAME	Cash		
ADDRESS			
SOLD BY	DATE 7/27/??	PH. NO.	

			ACCT. FORWARD	
1 Book			25	00
			1	90
			26	90
paid				

No. 001669 **TOTAL**

ALL CLAIMS & RETURNED GOODS MUST BE ACCOMPANIED BY THIS BILL.

GP-152-2   PRINTED IN U.S.A.   Thank You

MON-ROAD RAILROAD

MONTE HOLM, President

JACK CRONKITE, Sec.-Treas.

BOX 1444
MOSES LAKE, WA 98837

E. Clark Jones, First Vice President
Joshua Green, Sr., Vice President and Financial
  Consultant, Seattle, Washington
E. C. Olander, V.P. in charge of Western Division
William N. Duncan, V.P. in charge of Eastern Division
Larem Severson, V.P. in charge of Northern Division
Alex Hood, V.P. in charge of Southern Division
John R. Lewis, Senior V.P.
R. E. Lewis, Executive V.P.
Norman Day, V.P. in charge of Traffic
Major General Howard S. McGee, Office of Adjutant
  General, Camp Murray, Washington, V.P. in charge
  of Operations
Brigadier General Lyle Buchanan, Camp Murray,
  Washington, V.P. in charge of Security
Charles J. Edwards, V.P. in charge of Sugar Production
Allen Sircin, V.P. in charge of Livestock Installation
Elmer Yoshino, V.P. in charge of Processing Plants
Roy Kaylor, V.P. in charge of Minerals
Ich Konishi, V.P. in charge of Entertainment
V. H. Noone, V.P. in charge of Communications
Jalmer Moe, V.P. in charge of Engineers
Carl Melcher, V.P. in charge of Wheat Production
C. E. Marchand, V.P. in charge of Production
George C. LaValley, V.P. in charge of Tariff
George Pruitt (Cowboy), V.P. in charge of Hog Production
Gus Tenaglia, V.P. in charge of Investments
Walter Franz, V.P. in charge of Agriculture Division
Nick Badovinis, V.P. in charge of Tunnels
Thomas G. Jones, Riverside, Washington, V.P. in charge
  of History
Duke Moore, V.P. in charge of Speed
Ben I. Peterson, Denver, Colorado, V.P. in charge of
  Prospectors
Howard Pessein, V.P. in charge of Freight Rates
O. R. (Slim) Lovins, V.P. in charge of Potato Production
Mode Snead, V.P. in charge of Public Relations
Dick Penhallurick, V.P. in charge of Right-a-ways
Joe Cavender, Spokane, Washington, V.P. and Road
  Foreman of Engineers
John Barrier, Spokane, Washington, V.P. in charge of
  Foreign Relations
Clyde C. Andrews, V.P. in charge of Refrigeration
Fred Gulbrandson, Everett, Washington, V.P. in charge
  of Depot Construction
Earl Terwilleger, Warden, Washington, V.P. in charge
  of Irrigation
P. W. Davis, Seattle, Washington, V.P. in charge of
  Real Estate
R. D. Argue, Seattle, Washington, V.P. in charge of
  Industrial Engineering
Moe Mickelson, Everett, Washington, V.P. in charge
  of Salvage
Bob Bernard, V.P. in charge of Livestock
Chuck McInroy, V.P. in charge of Livestock Appraisal
J. O. English, V.P. in charge of Stocks and Bonds
Tim Bernard, V.P. in charge of Zortman Division
Howard Copenhaver, V.P. in charge of Loans
Eric Ryberg, Salt Lake City, Utah, V.P. in charge of
  Fire Protection
Wade B. Hall, Seattle, Washington, V.P. in charge
  of Lanterns
Brick McFadden V.P. in charge of Labor Relations
The Rev. Paul Dickson, V.P. and Chaplain
Dr. C. W. Covey, V.P. in charge of Safety
Henry Munroe, V.P. in charge of Catering
Walt Thayer, Wenatchee, Washington, V.P. in charge
  of Photography
Al Anderson, V.P. in charge of Pullman Department
Herb Rademacker, Sunnyside, Washington, V.P. in
  charge of Bearing Maintenance
Fred Weber, Sumner, Washington, V.P. in charge of
  Complaints
Van Bustkern, Spokane, Washington, V.P. in charge
  of Youth Activities
Dr. Charles Stevenson, Spokane, Washington, V.P. in
  charge of Mergers
Woodrow D. Barber, Seattle, Washington, V.P. in
  charge of Organization
Manney Burman, Seattle, Washington, V.P. in charge
  of Purchasing
Andrew Yurkenin, Seattle, Washington, V.P. in charge
  of Dining Cars
Roger Biallas, V.P. in charge of Printed Matter
Dr. J. W. Young, V.P. in charge of the Health of the
  President and Vice Presidents

I am enclosing our correspondence and a 1993 calendar which you might like

Again, congratulations, Mr. Gray. You have earned your promotion.

Your Friend,

Monte Holm

Monte Holm

-2-

Once a Hobo . . . .

MOSES LAKE BRANCH
SEATTLE-FIRST NATIONAL BANK
ESTABLISHED 1870

▼ ▼ ▼

MOSES LAKE, WASHINGTON 98837
October 26, 1964

Monrad Holm
Box 1448
Moses Lake, Washington

Dear Brother Holm:

I have taken the liberty to address you as "brother" although my
feelings are somewhat hurt that you dont remember our meeting
several weeks back. I recall also that you were a member of the
Theta Chi Scholastic fraternity and undoubtedly are not in need of
an education loan.

Your prompt reply to our letter is greatly appreciated and I in turn
will try to show you the same consideration. We also appreciate the
fact that you did not swear for ours are delicate ears. Your medical
and dental experiences as you described would certainly have
produced cursing and swearing from almost any one but those few of
your gently and prudent nature.

I am trying to keep this reply short and too the point because I
realize as you stated you tire easily and that our answer should be
gently stated so as not to endanger your health with another shock.
The $10.90 is not unreasonable, in fact, I think maybe you should
borrow $21.80 and take your neighbor, the Internal Revenue agent,
with you. Anybody who works as hard as he does needs a vacation, too.

Before we say anthing about the 4 years, 2 months requested repayment
time let me explain that my authority here is very limited. The $21.80
or $10.90, I think they will let me approve but if you dont mind I
would refer you to Mr. Hardin our Manager regarding the 50 months
time.

Sincerely

Josef E. Gray
Manager LCD

JEG/er

294

                                        Box 448
                                        Moses Lake, Washington
                                        17 December 1965

The Boeing Company's Commercial Airplane Division
P.O. Box 707 - HIA
Renton, Washington 98055

ATTN: Mr. Robert Farrell

Dear Mr. Farrell:

     I was reading in the Moses Lake, Washington, paper where you are
in need of tool fabricators and mechanics at your Renton, Washington,
plant. I have never applied for many jobs in my life, Mr. Farrell, so
will do my best.

     I am definitely a U.S. citizen and am well over 18 years of age.

     I will tell you first of my draft status, as that should have some
bearing on the job. I checked with the draft board when I read your
job inquiry, and they told me, "Monte, we are now scraping the bottom
of the barrel, but we are not underneath it yet so you have nothing to
worry about that".

     Now my personal record I don't quite understand, Mr. Farrell. If
you wish, I shall give you some of my background, if that is what you
want. Some people will say it has been pretty dull. At 13 years of age,
I left home to conquer the world, which looked easy. But all there was
to do at that time was become a Hobo, which is a hard way, Mr. Farrell,
to conquer the world. It is even rough at times to get something to eat,
let alone do any conquering. But it gives one lots of time to think
and that is something that is lacking today. It looks to me that today
the Government wants to do most of the thinking for us now. I remember
the winter I was 17 years old. I stood in a bread line in Minneapolis
12 hours a day, 7 days a week, for 2 meals a day. The line had normally
7,000 people in it so you would get something to eat and get back in
line right away for the next meal.

     So I thought there must be something better in the world than bread
lines, so I went to Montana to heard sheep, which is another good place
to meditate. So I gets off of a freight train at Malta, Montana, and a
sheep man from 60 miles south of Malta needs a sheepherder. I was pretty
hungry so I says,"I am a sheepherder." So he says,"tomorrow morning we will
leave for the ranch at 4 a.m." I did not know why so early as it was only
60 miles. So at 4 a.m. we left Malta and after being stuck in gumbo and
breaking down, we arrived at the ranch at 10 p.m., which he thought was
good. So he says at 5 a.m. the next morning he would take me out to my

sheep as the last herder he had left in town drunk. So at 5 a.m.
we leave the ranch and drives another 20 miles to the sheep wagon.
All I could see was sheep, so I asked him "how many sheep do I have
to herd?" He says "there is only 3,000 of them at the last count."
So he left me with the sheep and two dogs. So I went in the sheep
wagon to look around. There was a sack of beans, potatoes, sugar,
and a big hunk of sowbelly, flour, and baking powder. No can opener
because there were no cans to open. He told me that the camp tender
would be buy in six weeks to give me more grub and water which you
had to keep in a 50 gal. barrel by the wagon. My first thought was,
"Was this better than the bread line?" I had never done much cooking
and I could see that I would have to if I was going to eat. But then
I thought of the wages I was to get, $30.00 a month, and that it was
steady, 7 days a week, and it was steady. I chased sheep over a good
part of Montana from daylight till dark, the dogs did not understand
me so well, and the sheep not knowing the difference between Sundays
and holidays and trying to boil beans and sowbelly after running all
day I was as trim as a coyote. So after two years of this and only
going to town twice, I began to wonder. So the third time I went to
town I had been out 8 months and was in need of a haircut. So I goes
to a barber and sat in the chair. I had never seen this barber before.
So when he started cutting my hair he says how is sheepherding and I
got scared. I thought if they can tell you are a sheepherder it is
time to quit, because it is a toss up between a hobo and sheepherder
so I quit. But you have to admit, Mr. Farrell, I do not quit easy,
which I am sure are the kind of men you want.

I am sure by now, Mr. Farrell, we have gone deep enough in my
personal record as I am sure you get more applications than just from
me. If not, you people are in awful shape and will make awful bad
airplanes. So I will try to keep my job application short so you can
read others.

Now as far as the education. I had an awful time in school. All I
would do was look out the window and wonder what was on the other side
of the hill. So in the 7th grade the teacher came to me and said, "Monte,
if you will promise not to go to the 8th grade, I will pass you through
the 7th". I thought this is a wonderful deal, so I took him up. I hope,
Mr. Farrell, you won't hold this against me as I have had a lot of
education since.

Now we will have to pass the vocational work as I don't know what
that means, Mr. Farrell. If it has anything to do with vacations, then
I surely would be interested, as I love to go to a little town in Nevada
for these vacations. Its name is Los Vegas. So if vocational has anything
to do with this I am all for it.

2

Wood I want nothing to do with. But metal is much different. That is something I know a lot about as I have a junk yard and you get lots of it there. I don't quite know what your requirements are as to metal, but I know what copper is and aluminum and even platinum . I have even had experience with you B-52 plane. I bought one that cracked up at Larson AFB about four years ago and learned all about it and that you can lose money on them, too, as I lost $3,000 on it, which is a wonderful way to learn metals.

I believe, Brother Farrell, you don't mind me calling you brother do you, as I think by now we should nearly be brothers, I think we should skip the machine and auto shop part and jump to the mathematics part, as that is where I have had lots of experience. I shall have to tell you of my mathematics part I played in the second World War. I hope I don't bore you, Brother Farrell, but not having much experience in applying for jobs, I want to explain my qualifications. So Uncle Sam says, "Monte, we want you". So being drafted, I says yes. What else could you say, he had me stumped. But I am sure he was sorry afterwards. So after the fun of basic training in the Texas desert in the middle of summer, I was put in the Finance Department, which you will have to admit, Brother Farrell, has lots to do with mathematics. If I was to tell you how I fouled up about 1,000 officers, Brother Farrell, with their travel pay, Uncle Sam might frown on it, so I better not. But if you were ever in the service as an enlisted man and had to just deal with officers, you would surely understand. All I hope is that you were not an officer and stationed at Roswell, New Mexico, when I was. If so, I am sure you would not give me this job, Brother Farrell.

But you will have to admit I have a very strong knowledge of shop mathematics and would not try to foul Boeings up as I did Uncle Sam, because as you will notice he has not as yet recovered from my mathematics.

But when I read the wages you wanted to pay me, I thought that this is a far better way to conquer the world than sheepherding at $30.00 a month. I actually read your wages over twice, Brother Farrell, and know that $2,365 per hour is lots of money, and you have to have lots in return. At this time, Brother Farrell, I am receiving 17 cents per hour with lots of hours. So this will mean a nice raise for me. I do not understand how you can pay such nice wages, but I understand with the turmoil and traffic at your plant, it is much more confusing than sheepherding or standing in bread lines where you have only one thing on your mind and should be worth lots more money. I know that Bill Allen is concerned too because he told me that now Boeings have 65 per cent white collar workers and 35 per cent blue collar workers, and even sheepherding I wore a white collar. He told me this at the Olympic Hotel, Sept 23, when my old hobo pal Joshua Green Sr. and O. D. Fisher (whom you might have heard of) had me to dinner with them, and by the way, Brother Farrell, there was no beans and sowbelly there either, which was good, because, Brother Farrell, I still get upset when I look beans and sowbelly in the face. But with these wages I shall have no problem there.

3

Now as far as the travel allowance is concerned, I will not have to burden you with that as I have my own railroad and would like nothing better than to run my own Steam Locomotive through, I mean to, your Boeing plant. I know at the wages you shall pay me I can only be out maybe five hours pay which I don't mind and I do think that all them cars over there will let me through. The locomotive weighing 200 ton which it would take to stop them will let me through. I would like, Brother Farrell, if you would give me maybe at least two days notice when you want me to come as it takes nearly that long to steam the locomotive up. Otherwise I might blow some flues in the boiler and I am sure, Brother Farrell, you would not want that. I will send you, Brother Farrell, a picture of my transportation so you can see I am serious and will assure you it is not cheap to go by locomotive as I found out in shipping it from Alaska to Moses Lake. You can see I am trying to save you people money on the transportation part of it. And for these wages I would even go back to beans and sowbelly if you payed the grub bill too. So you will notice I have you people in my mind at all times.

So I can see only one place, Brother Farrell, where I might not meet your qualification for this job and that is the education part. But will if necessary go back to school and get my B.S. Degree, which most people say I already have.

I wish to thank you, Brother Farrell, for this opportunity and will be waiting for your reply.

I will close now as I like to make my applications short because I am sure you are a busy man and after fighting that traffic this morning you want short and to the point applications.

I want to wish you a very Merry Christmas and am sorry I could not apply in person. But with the two days notice and if it don't get no colder here I can steam up the locomotive and come over.

Thank you very much, Brother Farrell, for this opportunity.

In Brotherly Love,

Monte Holm

Monte Holm

4

ARMY SERVICE FORCES
CAMP JOHN T. KNIGHT
OAKLAND 14, CALIFORNIA

OFFICE OF THE POST ENGINEER
1 FEBRUARY, 1966

Monty Holm
Hobo General, Moses Lake Area
Moses Lake Iron & Metals   Subject- Secret Order
228 South Commerce Wy   SO19476r. Office of The
Moses Lake, Wash   Secretary Of Defense

Sir:
 You are hereby ordered to <u>CEASE AND DESIST</u> in accordance with
Special Order, SO19476r, Office Of The Secretaer Of Defense,
of this date, your plan, generally accepted and sponsored by
Mr. Allen of The Boeing Aircraft Co.

Mr Allen has denied any knowlege of your attempeted activity
in planto place steam locomotive in service , Construction of
necessary trackage to provide transportation of hoboes. tramps
and Bumbs to Boeing Facilities, other Bums elected to Office of
the City Hall of Seattle, including Senator Magnuson and his
kind, to appropriate quarters along Skid Row of Seattle as
selected by a committee selected from the National Hobo, Tramp
and Bum association, Unlimited.

The Thirteenth Naval District Commander has been directed to
restore all utilities, Streets and Structures to their original
status, including the Mono-Rail System which was placed under-
ground to gain required alignment necessary for track construction

All expenses incurred in phasing out and other costs generated
by this Project will be assessed to you and all other credited
Tramps Hoboes and Bums in the Washington, Idaho and Oregon Area
Associations.

Attorneys John Lewis and Nat Washington will represent the
Defense Department in the Over all Settlement of subject
Project Temporary Fees for theirbservices has been set at
4,974,389.03.

You will be advised at a later date as to the planned use of the
Steam Locomotive presently in your possession at Moses Lake.

Very Littledone,
Very Littledone,
Commander.
General, U. S. Army

Had to type this myself- Secretary on Sick leave

299

Once a Hobo . . . .

ROBERT L. HANSON
CHIEF OF POLICE

THE CITY OF SEATTLE

DEPARTMENT OF

POLICE

SEATTLE WASHINGTON 98104

OUR NO._____

YOUR NO._____

December 13, 1974

President Monte Holm
Mon Road Railroad
P. O. Box 448
Moses Lake, Washington 98837

Dear Monte:

Thank you very much for your kindness in having Virginia and me aboard your private train and the guided tour of your enterprises. We were especially pleased with the gourmet meal you provided us on the day of our departure from Moses Lake.

Virginia wishes to thank you for the special gift although she says she will feel guilty each time she partakes of the delicacy.

Both Virginia and I were impressed with the success you have made of your life, having had such a miserable start. We know how difficult it must have been to rid yourself of the hanger-ons from your past as your vast enterprises developed and your stature in life changed from a hobo to the presidency of your city's largest and most successful precious metals exchange. Just think, one day many years ago, you had to surreptitiously board and ride the railroads -- now you have your own, complete with a private presidential suite and tracks leading right to your own backyard.

Virginia and I are very pleased to have you as a friend and we look forward to visiting you and your enterprises in the near future.

I know you have not applied; however before you do, I feel I should inform you we do not appoint Assistant Chiefs, or for that matter, even Sergeants, Lieutenants, Captains or Majors, if the applicant once led a destitute life of wandering and unemployment. We feel if a man gets his start in bread lines, there is very little chance he will be successful in the police field. Therefore, we have restricted applicants with backgrounds such as yours for any rank above starting Patrolman. Hence, it gives me great pleasure to appoint you an Honorary Patrolman on the Seattle Police Department.

President Monte Holm
December 13, 1974
Page Two

I had planned on applying to you for a vice-presidency or a position on the Board of Directors of your railroad. However, now I suppose I will have to be satisfied with the position of brakeman or maybe only porter. Oh well, prior to going to Moses Lake last week, I had never known or ever been introduced to a railroad president, so I am that much richer, anyway.

Until our tracks cross again, make only good arrests and I will not ride on any railroad but yours.

Sincerely,

R. L. HANSON
Chief of Police

RLH/rh

MON-ROAD RAILROAD

MONTE HOLM, President

JACK CRONKITE, Sec.-Treas.

BOX 448
MOSES LAKE, WASH. 98837

January 6, 1975

Mr. & Mrs. Robert Hanson
1606 N.E. 143rd
Seattle, Washington 98125

My Dear Chief Robert Hanson and Virginia:

It was indeed an honor and pleasure to be able to meet you and your lovely wife, Virginia. I was overwhelmed with the appointment you presented me. I never in my wildest dreams felt I deserved or would receive such an honor. I have had some dealings with police officers in my early life and if I could have just had an appointment like that at that time it would have saved me a lot of foot work. I am sure at that time you did not have the authority to make such an appointment.

I am glad you appointed me a police officer rather than a Sergeant, Lieutenant, Captain, Major or Assistant Chief because police officers seemed to be the ones I became acquainted with so often when I was a young boy on the road. In fact, I had some real close contacts with many police officers.

I would like to tell you of my first encounter with a police officer. At the ripe old age of 13 years, I told my father I thought I was old enough to leave home. And he, being a very agreeable man, said, "Son, if that is what you want that will be fine." And he assured me that I would surely, with my stubbornness, make a mark in this old world. So after a few very good fatherly suggestions, I left home thinking that this was going to be easy. I left town on a freight train with two dollars, which I thought was a lot of money, it being the good year of 1930. It was such a nice warm day and all the other passengers seemed so happy, I thought boy this is the life. Just as if warm weather was the thing

year round. So after about three hours of
riding and listening and feeling the wheels
of the box car going over the joints in the
railroad track, I got sleepy and with not a
care in the world went to sleep. After about
five hours of sleep, I awoke to find it night
and a bit cold. But being young I did not mind.
The train was stopped when I awoke so I decided
to go to town to get something to eat. I
believe one gets much hungrier riding a freight
train than in any other method of travel. So
I found a restaurant not far from the rail yards
and sat down to a meal of stew which was cheap.
As I was rather poor financially, I did not want
to spend all my money too soon. After I had
finished eating and feeling wonderful, I thought
my train was about ready to leave, so I got up
to pay the bill. I reached in my pocket and to
my surprise found no money. I am sure I slept
too hard in the last box car and one of the
other passengers wanted to eat also, which I
don't blame him as you get very hungry in one.
So he no doubt relieved me of my finances,
which left me in a bad shape. So I told the
man I had no money to pay and told him my story,
which never impressed him in the least. He
said, "All you bums are the same, and I am
getting tired of this." I could see a police
officer in the other end of the restaurant and
the manager going over to see the police officer.
I had the feeling he was not going over to
refill the police officer's coffee cup and me
being the type of person that loves freedom,
I left and ran for about a mile with the police
officer in hot pursuit. I have noticed then
and later that the pursued has much the
advantage and can normally out run the pursuer,
which I did. I really hated to beat the man
out of the stew as it was very good stew, but
felt I had no way out. I feel sure he
survived the loss of the stew. But it could
have been hard on the police officer as he was
much older than I and could have acquired some
heart trouble from the ordeal. All it did for
me was settle the stew and make me hungry.

2

I am sure he was a real fine police officer but, as you can see, I never really got to meet the man. The only conversation we had was some remarks I could hear behind me and being some distance apart, I could have heard wrong. And to be very honest, I had more on my mind than a conversation at that time. Although under normal conditions I love nothing better than a conversation.

I would like to tell you of another meeting with a police officer. In fact, I met this police officer several times. I had been on the road about two years and didn't particularly care for the cold winters up north. I kept listening to the old hoboes telling about going south in the winter and just laying around in the sunshine. They all said Phoenix, Arizona, was the best place for hoboes. So in late October a real blizzard came to let me know it was time to head south. Arriving in Phoenix in November, I was not lonesome as the town was full of hoboes for the winter, which makes it rather hard to find enough to eat. So I thought I should find a better wintering place. Another hobo I met said lets go to El Paso, Texas, because they are real good to hoboes. And not having been there before, it sounded like fun. Having found a little work on the way to El Paso, I arrived there with five dollars—the other hobo had none. On arriving and talking to some other hoboes, we found out that El Paso did not greet hoboes as well as we had heard. It just goes to show you that you cannot always believe everything you hear. In talking the situation over, we thought it best to rent a room as that way we would be legal residents. We found a room that looked nice for two dollars a week. So my partner said, "If you will pay the first two weeks, Monte, I will pay the next two weeks." I really did not know where he was to get the money, but I let him worry about that as I felt I had enough to worry about. So after

3

two weeks elapsed, I told my pal the two
weeks had passed and he would have to pay the
rent. He said, "My doesn't time go by fast?"
After one more week I said, "Did you pay the
rent?" He informed me he never got any money
and therefore could not pay. I would go down
and sit in the plaza during the day and watch
the alligators with the nice feeling that I was
a resident of El Paso. In a conversation I had
with another Knight of the Road, he said whatever you do in El Paso don't skip out of a rent
bill because if you do and are caught, they have
what they called road gangs that you would be
taken to to build county roads without pay for
90 to 180 days. I got thinking about this and
felt that I did not owe any rent--it was the
other hobo that did. But I have the feeling
that I was the only one that felt this way.
The next morning at 2 a.m. I woke up, which was
real unusual as I am a very sound sleeper. So
I got dressed and thought this would maybe be
a good time for me to move. I felt I could go
and the alligators would not mind me sleeping
on a bench in the plaza. My partner also woke
up and felt he should move too. I guess he
thought about the road gang also. The next day
I was walking across an intersection and when
I got in the middle of the street whom should I
see but my landlord--the last person I wanted to
see. Walking with him was a police officer.
The landlord pointed at me to the police officer
and I was quite sure of their conversation so I
quickly turned the other way and ran with the
police officer in hot pursuit. I was glad that
in those days most police officers did not use
cars as today or I would have been in serious
trouble. I could sure run a good foot race in
those days, Chief, and I had no trouble keeping
ahead of him. I heard the weather report up
north and it was not good so I wanted to stay
in El Paso a little longer. But every time I
saw this police officer, he seemed to want to
run a foot race with me. So after two weeks of
this I ran clear out of El Paso and hoped that
police officer would not get transferred to

4

Tucson, Arizona, where I thought I had better go to. He was no doubt the most determined police officer I ever encountered, and if I had just gotten his name I am sure that he finally must have become Chief of Police in El Paso—or else had a heart attack from his foot work. And I really never felt I owed the rent as I had paid the first two weeks, and the other hobo never paid on his bargin. It just goes to show that sometimes you cannot even trust a brother hobo.

So not having had too many personal contacts with police officers, you will have to admit that I have had a few very close contacts with them. There were many more contacts that I had with police officers but will not bore you with them. I would like to forget some of them. If I would have had my police badge 007 at that time and had time to get it out of my pocket and held it up in my hand, I maybe would not have had to do so much running in my younger days. But it is good I got it in my older days when I just could not run so fast.

I am so happy that you and Virginia enjoyed your visit over here. For me it was a real pleasure to be able to meet such fine people. If at any future time you folks are in Moses Lake and wish to stay in my "camper", you are very welcome to. You folks are the first people I have made this offer to so that puts you on the top of the list.

I will see that you will be appointed a Vice President on the Mon-Road Railroad when I publish new stationery. I have a lot of stationery on hand and will have to write long letters in the future instead of such short ones! I will in the meantime give some thought as to a fine position for you.

5

I want to wish you and Virginia the best of everything in 1975. I will make none but good arrests in 1975 and hope I won't have to run any foot races with old hoboes.

Your Friend and Brother Officer,

Monte Holm

Monte Holm

About this book
By Dennis L. Clay

When I was growing up, my grandparents, Ray and Golda Grimshaw, would visit Moses Lake at least twice a year that would last anywhere from a week to a month. It was a great time for my immediate family as well as aunts, uncles, and cousins who live nearby. Grandpa would visit patiently for one day, maybe two, but after that, he could be found at Moses Lake Iron & Metal visiting his old friend, Monte Holm. Monte would put him to work so Grandpa could put a few extra dollars in his pocket. The first time I met Monte was when Dad and I went to pick up Grandpa at the end of a work day in the late 1950's. Like everyone else Monte meets, we became friends.

Monte and I have had sporadic contact over the years, visiting when our paths would cross. Then Steve Hill, the publisher of the Columbia Basin Herald, asked me to write a column about local history. When the subject of a local grocery store was covered in the column, word reached me that Monte wanted to see me. He took me to see the hand-cranked meat slicer used in the store. It was the first meat slicer in Grant County.

When we were back in his office, Monte reached into a drawer and pulled out a large envelope.

"Dennis, I'd like you to take a look at this," he said, as he thrust the thick envelope into my hands.

Inside was the story of his life, 129 double-spaced pages in draft form. It began, "This being my first book, I no doubt will have some trouble writing it, but I would not like to pass on without leaving something for posterity, even if for no one other than my daughter, who would read it out of respect, if nothing else."

Those words had my attention.

During the next couple of weeks, I thumbed through the manuscript several times. The writing was full of tidbits of interesting facts. Most were only a paragraph long with some detailed information contained in a single sentence.

On a a subsequent visit to Monte's The House of Poverty Museum, I handed the manuscript back to him and said, "I get the feeling that you want me to help you with this."

"I do," he said.

And that was the beginning of a many-faceted adventure. In the beginning, Monte and I spent two or three hours every Sunday for several months just talking. I found out the manuscript was just the tip of the iceberg. His memory was full of adventures that expanded on the ones that were written.

"For several years, I relied on my memory to jot down notes about certain events in my life," he told me. "Then my daughter Karen typed a rough draft from my handwritten notes."

The draft became a guide to construct this autobiography.

The accuracy of Monte's memory is almost scary. He thought the Minneapolis riot took place in late March, when it actually occurred on April 6 – and I'm talking about 1933. When I mentioned how close he was to the actual date, Monte said, "That's not bad for an old hobo."

When I wanted to verify Monte's time in Tekoa, Washington, working for Ted Nelson, I found myself talking with Patty Nelson Leonard, Ted's granddaughter. It was a similar story when I tried to contact a relative of Art Crab and ended up visiting with Ross Crab, Art's son. And the stories continued to hit the mark or be close enough to amaze me that a 13- to 19-year-old hobo could remember them more than 60 years later.

However, there are segments of Monte's stories that are not right on the money. The reasons became clear after some research. In Minneapolis, Monte told me he stayed at the Annex, when the actual name was the Manx, which was one of the four hotels controlled by the Union City Mission to house homeless men during the Depression.

When Monte talks about the St. James Mission, the correct name was the Union City Mission and that organization owned the St. James Hotel. What about the coal truck and lumps of coal being thrown during the Minneapolis riot? Newspaper accounts of the riot say it happened.

Diane Smith was helpful in verifying the sheepherding facts. Her knowledge of historical facts about Matador Bill, The Hensen brothers and the Great Northern Hotel, concurred with Monte's version. And Bobbie Campbell's story of her father meeting a young hobo supports Monte's account of his stop in Ritzville.

Although Monte and I attempted to confirm all of the facts in this book, some might be just a bit off the mark. You can understand where a young boy might mistake Manx for Annex and the end of March might be confused with the correct date of April 6 after a boy stands in the soup line all winter.

I agree with Monte — that's not bad for an old hobo.

Dennis L. Clay

Dennis L. Clay was born and raised in the heart of Washington State's Columbia Basin.

Shortly after high school, he joined the Army as a private and was selected to attend Officer's Candidate School at Fort Sill, Oklahoma. Dennis then attended helicopter flight school. He served one year in Vietnam where he attained the rank of Captain and flew the UHI Iroquois (better known as the HUEY), the OH6A Cayause (also known as the LOH), and the U6A Beaver (a fixed wing airplane) and other aircraft for the 9th Aviation Battalion of the 9th Infantry Division in the Mekong Delta. During his Vietnam tour, he was awarded the Bronze Star medal, 17 Air Medals and others.

After his Army career, Dennis returned to live and work in his hometown of Moses Lake. He has been employed by the Washington State Employment Security Department for about 24 years. His writing career began when he submitted a story to the *Columbia Basin Herald* in 1982. It was published and his writing career has not slowed since.

Dennis is a freelance writer, photographer, columnist and broadcaster. His credits include stories published in *Alaska Outdoors*, *Wild Sheep Magazine*, *British Columbia Sports Fishing*, *Ted Nugent Adventure Outdoors*, *The Outdoor Press*, *Boy's Life*, *Fishing and Hunting News* and others.

He writes three weekly columns for the *Columbia Basin Herald* and he contributes photographs and stories for other features and articles that appear in the Moses Lake newspaper.

Dennis is the host and producer of *Columbia Basin Outdoors*, broadcast every Thursday and Friday on KBSN-AM 1470. He is co-host of *Columbia Basin Lifestyles*, a one-hour live talk show aired Saturday mornings, also on KBSN.

Dennis is an avid outdoorsman where he enjoys birding, big game and bird hunting, fly and spin fishing, camping and many other outdoor activities.

His writings and photographs have earned Dennis numerous awards. His first national award was for a short story, "The Time Has Come, and Will Again," published in *the Columbia Basin's Herald's 1991 Progress Edition*. It placed first in the *National Hunting & Fishing Day* contest that year.

Dennis has several awards from the *Society of Professional Journalists* of both the Inland Northwest and the Pacific Northwest chapters. Dennis and Rock n' Roll legend and hunter Ted Nugent teamed up to place third in one SPJ Sports Reporting contest about hunting ethics.

He is a member of the *Outdoor Writers' Association of America* and the *Northwest Outdoor Writers's Association*. He serves as an elected member of the NOWA Board of Directors.

Dennis is a graduate of the Washington State University Master Gardener program serving Grant and Adams Counties and the Master Composter program in Spokane, Washington.

<u>WARNING</u>

Hopping a freight train today is different than it was during the Depression. The risk of injury or death is extremely high.

<u>Be smart</u>!
Do not ride the rails or attempt to ride the rails.

Monte